1 ENOCH AND SIRACH
A Comparative Literary and Conceptual Analysis of the
Themes of Revelation, Creation and Judgment

SOCIETY OF BIBLICAL LITERATURE

EARLY JUDAISM AND ITS LITERATURE

Number 08

1 ENOCH AND SIRACH
A Comparative Literary and Conceptual Analysis of the
Themes of Revelation, Creation and Judgment

by
Randal A. Argall

1 ENOCH AND SIRACH

A Comparative Literary and Conceptual Analysis of the Themes of Revelation, Creation and Judgment

by
Randal A. Argall

Scholars Press
Atlanta, Georgia

1 ENOCH AND SIRACH

A Comparative Literary and Conceptual Analysis of the Themes of Revelation, Creation and Judgment

by
Randal A. Argall

© 1995
Society of Biblical Literature

Library of Congress Cataloging-in-Publication Data
Argall, Randal A.
    1 Enoch and Sirach : a comparative and conceptual analysis of the themes of
revelation, creation, and judgment / by Randal A. Argall.
        p.   cm. — (Early Judaism and its literature ; no. 08)
    Revisions of author's thesis (doctoral)—University of Iowa, 1992.
    Includes bibliographical references and indexes.
    ISBN 0-7885-0175-5 (cloth : alk. paper).— ISBN 0-7885-0176-3 (pbk. : alk.
paper)
    1. Ethiopic book of Enoch— Criticism, interpretation, etc.
    2. Revelation (Jewish theology)—History of doctrines. 3. Revelation—Biblical
teaching. 4. Creation—History of doctrines. 5. Creation—Biblical teaching.
6. Judgment of God— History of doctrines. 7. Judgment of God—Biblical teaching.
8. Judaism—Doctrines—History. [1. Bible. O.T. Apocrypha.
Ecclesiasticus—Criticism, interpretation, etc.] I. Title.   II. Series.
BS1830. E7A44   1995
229'.406—dc20   95-39110
                                                                CIP

Printed in the United States of America
on acid-free paper

To Ann and Sam

CONTENTS

LIST OF TABLES

PREFACE

This book is a slightly revised version of my doctoral dissertation accepted at the University of Iowa in 1992. I take full responsibility for the work presented in the book, including all of its shortcomings.

Several scholars have enhanced my ability to study the variety of ancient texts reflected in this book. I must begin by thanking my thesis advisor George W. E. Nickelsburg for numerous conversations about the Enochic materials. His insightful criticisms, suggestions, and proddings have contributed greatly to whatever is of value in the following pages. I also wish to thank Helen Goldstein whose lectures introduced me to ben Sira; Jonathan Goldstein who taught me much of the history of the Greco-Roman period; J. Kenneth Kuntz with whom I studied the wisdom literature of the Hebrew Bible; James McCue who was always willing to rethink religious movements without relying on accepted results; and Donald Jackson whose work in Greek paleography impressed upon me the need to ask whether an ancient text might not contain more than was commonly assumed.

I am grateful to the Memorial Foundation for Jewish Culture for extending me a Doctoral Scholarship Grant in 1989-90.

One of the first persons to read the dissertation when it became available was Ben Wright. Some of his suggestions have been incorporated in this revision. My editor, Bill Adler, was prompt with his correspondence and helpful with advice related to publication matters.

I would be remiss if I did not state my gratitude to my wife Ann and son Sam. For some unfathomable reason, they understood my personal drive to complete this project and gave me the necessary time and space. I thank them for their patience, trust, support and love.

INTRODUCTION

This book offers a comparative study of selected passages in *1 Enoch* and Sirach. There have been very few such studies to date in the scholarly corpus.[1] The reason for this may be that the way was blocked by a rigid categorization of the two texts.

1 Enoch is conventionally classified among the "apocalyptic literature." But this is a genre whose precise scope remains unclear. Certainly texts in this category share some basic literary characteristics, as well as *topoi*.[2] However, no ancient text uses the self-designation *apokalypsis* ("revelation") until the end of the first century CE.[3] In addition, most examples placed by modern

---

[1] Of course, there is an abundance of cross-referencing in recent commentaries on the two texts. See, for example, the indices in the works of Matthew Black, *The Book of Enoch or 1 Enoch: A New English Edition with Commentary and Textual Notes* (SVTP 7; Leiden: Brill, 1985) and P. W. Skehan and A. A. Di Lella, *The Wisdom of Ben Sira* (AB 39; New York: Doubleday, 1987). This cross-referencing itself invites a more sustained comparison. Recently, Gabriele Boccaccini has argued that ben Sira's instruction on a number of topics was directed against apocalyptic traditions like those present in *1 Enoch*. For bibliography, see his article "Jewish Apocalyptic Tradition: the Contribution of Italian Scholarship," *Mysteries and Revelations: Apocalyptic Studies since the Uppsala Colloquium* (ed. John J. Collins & James H. Charlesworth; JSPS 9; Sheffield: JSOT, 1991) 33-50, esp. 41, n. 3. From the side of *1 Enoch*, Robert A. Coughenour tried to demonstrate that Enochic authors and editors were influenced by wisdom forms and thought (*Enoch and Wisdom: A Study of the Wisdom Elements in the Book of Enoch* [Diss., Case Western Reserve University, Cleveland, Ohio, 1972]).

[2] See the essays by John J. Collins, "Introduction: Towards the Morphology of a Genre" and "The Jewish Apocalypses," *Semeia* 14 (1979) 1-20 and 21-59. Collins reflects on this earlier work in his more recent article "Genre, Ideology and Social Movements in Jewish Apocalypticism," *Mysteries and Revelations*, 11-32.

[3] See the excellent discussion in Morton Smith, "On the History of ΑΠΟΚΑΛΥΠΤΩ and ΑΠΟΚΑΛΥΨΙΣ," *Apocalypticism in the Mediterranean World and the Near East: Proceedings of the International Colloquium on Apocalypticism, Uppsala, August 12-17, 1979* (ed. David Hellholm; Tübingen: J.C.B. Mohr/Paul Siebeck, 1983) 9-20.

scholars under this rubric, including *1 Enoch,* are mixed compositions and utilize many different literary forms.[4]

Sirach is designated "wisdom literature." Roland E. Murphy acknowledges that this designation is "merely a term of convenience," but argues that it is useful because the texts in this grouping are concerned with *hokmâ* ("wisdom") and have certain literary forms and themes in common.[5] The scope of this literature too is a matter of ongoing debate, depending on whether a particular scholar works with a narrow or broad definition of what qualifies as a wisdom form or *topos*.[6] In short, the ancient texts have resisted our modern labels. Perhaps if such labels are laid aside, even temporarily, the way may be opened to discover new, intertextual relationships.

The present study will proceed on the assumption that there is much to be gained by moving beyond conventional labels of macrostructure. Despite the placement of *1 Enoch* in the genre apocalypse, for example, the text itself claims to be a compilation of books of wisdom. This immediately begs a comparison with other books of wisdom, including Sirach. Conversely, the wisdom book of Sirach gives place to "revelation" and thereby invites comparison with other revelatory texts such as apocalypses. A pursuit of the comparative enterprise leads to the discovery that *1 Enoch* and Sirach share significant themes and literary features.

THE COMPARATIVE METHOD

Common Themes

Three major themes are developed in both *1 Enoch* and Sirach. It appears that these themes were subjects of learned inquiry in the late-third and

---

[4] John J. Collins, *Daniel, with an Introduction to Apocalyptic Literature* (FOTL 20; Grand Rapids: Eerdmans, 1984) 2-5.

[5] Roland E. Murphy, *Wisdom Literature: Job, Proverbs, Ruth, Canticles, Ecclesiastes, and Esther* (FOTL 13; Grand Rapids: Eerdmans, 1981) 3.

[6] On a minimalist or conservative view, the wisdom literature includes, in addition to Sirach: Proverbs, Job, Qoheleth, Wisdom of Solomon, and a few Psalms. For the arguments that the latter group consists of Psalms 1, 32, 34, 37, 49, 112, 127, 128, and 133, see J. Kenneth Kuntz, "The Canonical Wisdom Psalms of Ancient Israel—Their Rhetorical, Thematic, and Formal Dimensions," *Rhetorical Criticism: Essays in Honor of James Muilenburg* (ed. Jared Jackson and Martin Kessler; Pittsburg: Pickwick, 1974) 186-222. Scholars working with a broad view of the wisdom literature include Genesis 1-11, the Joseph Narrative (Gen 37-50), the Succession Narrative (II Sam 9-20, I Kgs 1-2), Esther, and certain sections of Deuteronomy and the Prophets. Bibliography on the narrower and broader views can be found in James L. Crenshaw, "Prolegomenon," *Studies in Ancient Israelite Wisdom* (ed. James L. Crenshaw; New York: Ktav, 1976) 1-60.

early-second centuries BCE. They include: (1) the nature and function of revelation, (2) the physical structure of the cosmos and its relevance for ethics, and (3) the reality of future judgment and its implications for the present. Our study will focus on the various ways these themes are played out within the two texts. It might be helpful to begin by sketching the body of this study.

Part I will focus on the nature and function of revelation. Enoch tours the outer reaches of the cosmos and is commissioned from heaven to bring revelation to the earth (*1 En* 12-36). He imparts this heavenly wisdom as his testament to his son Methuselah (*1 En* 81-82, 91) and to the last generation (*1 En* 1:2; 92:1). Ben Sira maintains that wisdom comes through study of the Torah in his school (Sir 4:11-19; 6:18-37; 14:20-15:10; 39:1-11). He explicitly warns against the revelatory claims of those who study esoteric traditions or rely on visions and dreams (Sir 3:17-29; 34:1-8). Of course, this is precisely what the bearers of Enochic literature do. Still, for ben Sira the Torah itself contains hidden things that can be revealed only by personified Wisdom who has come from heaven. Ben Sira is the recipient of such revelations and he passes them on to the generations of eternity (Sir 24:33).

Part II centers on the ethical lesson that the authors of *1 Enoch* and ben Sira derive from the structure and elements of the cosmos. In both traditions, the regularity of meteorological and astronomical phenomena teaches the importance of obedience to God. The cosmic order that Enoch sees on his heavenly journeys testifies to God's control and guarantees the validity of his warnings to the wicked (*1 En* 2-5; 100-102). Ben Sira is also interested in cosmic order, though he limits himself to what can be learned by keeping his feet on the ground (Sir 42:15-43:33)! Like the authors of *1 Enoch*, ben Sira argues that the instruments necessary to bless the righteous and destroy the wicked are constitutive features of the cosmos (Sir 39:28-35; 40:8-10). The fact that the cosmos is prepared for judgment will lead into the topic of our final section.

In Part III, the themes of divine justice and future judgment are treated. Ben Sira's petition for judgment (Sir 35:18-36:17) resonates with various judgment contexts in *1 Enoch*. In addition, both traditions polemicize against individuals who act in disregard for the reality of the coming judgment. Ben Sira quotes those who deny divine justice with the formula "Do not say ..." He then appeals to his revealed understanding of the judgment and expounds the correct view (5:3-7; 7:9; 11:23-24; 15:11-20; 16:17-30; cf. 23:18-21). The same strategy of quoting and refuting sinners is found in *1 Enoch* 102-104.

Our investigation of the themes of revelation, creation and judgment will explore both the similarities and the differences in the way each theme is conceptualized and developed. This will require that in each of the three parts passages from *1 Enoch* and Sirach be grouped together. The order in which the two books are analyzed is not significant; *1 Enoch* is studied first and

Sirach second in Parts I-III merely for the sake of consistency. Nothing would be lost, or gained, if the order was reversed. It is important, however, that all of the passages on a given theme in one tradition are reviewed before moving to the second. A holistic comparison of major themes will avoid the piecemeal approach of jumping back and forth continually between *1 Enoch* and Sirach.

Common Literary Characteristics

The analysis of the above themes will seek to determine the extent and significance of shared literary features; mainly forms and vocabulary. Questions of a common oral or written source may emerge at times, but it is not our purpose to identify such sources. The comparison of literary traits is intended to shed light on how each tradition explicates the themes of revelation, creation and judgment, thereby helping in the identification of similarities and differences.

The literary compositions in *1 Enoch* and Sirach have utilized and adapted forms and vocabulary found in the Hebrew Bible: in the Prophets, the Wisdom books and the Psalms.

The major prophetic forms of the Hebrew Bible are the prophecy of disaster, prophecy of salvation, oracle of salvation, and proclamation of salvation.[7] The so-called secondary prophetic speech forms include the woe-oracle, trial speeches, covenant lawsuit, disputation speech, summons to repentance, drinking song, love song, dirge, call to battle, and retreat order.[8] In addition, the prophets employ forms typically associated with the Psalter (hymn, lament) and the Wisdom tradition. Finally there are biographical and/or autobiographical forms such as the vision report and the call narrative.

Here, then, is a wealth of literary forms which a later author may draw upon and show his inventiveness. Indeed, some of the later prophetic material itself shows evidence of the combination and alteration of earlier forms.[9] This process continued throughout the Hellenistic age. In a seminal essay, W.

---

[7] See the discussion of W. Eugene March, "Prophecy," *Old Testament Form Criticism* (ed. John H. Hayes; San Antonio: Trinity University, 1974) 141-77.

[8] They are called "secondary" because these forms are used less frequently and are likely borrowed from some sphere of Israel's life not usually connected with the prophets (March, "Prophecy," 164).

[9] Paul Hanson, *The Dawn of Apocalyptic* (rev. ed.; Philadelphia: Fortress, 1979) illustrates this phenomenon in Isaiah, Ezekiel, Haggai and Zechariah.

Baumgartner called attention to the use of prophetic forms in Sirach.[10] The presence of prophetic forms in *1 Enoch* has also been recognized.[11] The analysis of the various prophetic forms must be sensitive to how they are employed in each of the two books. Are some forms used in the same way? Do different adaptations of traditional forms reflect basic conceptual differences on a given theme?

The utilization of earlier literary forms by ben Sira and the authors of *1 Enoch* also includes forms found in the wisdom literature. Of course, such forms are predominant in the work of ben Sira. He employs such traditional wisdom forms as the proverb (*māšāl*, of which there are at least five types), riddle, fable and allegory, hymn and prayer, disputation, autobiographical narrative, lists (onomastica), and didactic poetry or narrative.[12] Some of the same wisdom forms have been identified in *1 Enoch*. Again, research into the use and alteration of wisdom forms will assist in the effort to compare and contrast the messages of the two traditions.

THE TWO TRADITIONS: PRELIMINARY REMARKS

Overlapping Dates

The activity of ben Sira and the authors of some parts of *1 Enoch* is contemporary. Ben Sira's dates are approximated on the basis of three factors: his grandson's preface to the book (the grandson translated the book sometime after going to Egypt in 132 BCE), ben Sira's own eyewitness description of the high priest Simeon II (219-196 BCE) in Sirach 50:1-21 and, finally, the lack of any reference to the persecutions of Antiochus IV Epiphanes (175-164 BCE).

---

[10] W. Baumgartner, "Die literarischen Gattungen in der Weisheit des Jesus Sirach," *ZAW* 34 (1914) 161-98. He identified the prophecy of judgment, woe-oracle, promise of salvation, prophetic exhortation and love song; and found allusions to the drinking song and dirge (ibid., 186-91). Baumgartner was using the nomenclature of early form-criticism and thus his categories differ slightly from those listed above.

[11] Some of the more apparent examples are the prophecy of disaster, oracle of salvation, vision report, call narrative, woe-oracle, prophetic exhortation and descriptions of the judgment. Such forms are discussed by E. Rau, *Kosmologie, Eschatologie und die Lehrautorität Henochs: Traditions- und formgeschichtliche Untersuchungen zum äth. Henochbuch und zu verwandten Schriften* (Diss., Universität Hamburg, 1974); and George W. E. Nickelsburg, "The Apocalyptic Message of *1 Enoch* 92-105," *CBQ* 39 (1977) 309-28; idem, "Enoch, Levi, and Peter: Recipients of Revelation in Upper Galilee," *JBL* 100 (1981) 575-600.

[12] James L. Crenshaw, "Wisdom," *Old Testament Form Criticism* (ed. John H. Hayes; San Antonio: Trinity University, 1974) 225-64.

Many scholars, using the indicators above, place ben Sira's activity "securely in the first quarter of the second century B.C."[13] However, it should be noted that this is a very cautious, perhaps overly cautious, circumscription of ben Sira's activity. He had a long career, one that originated in the third century BCE. It is impossible to determine how much of the last quarter of the third century his earlier career included because of the paucity of historical references in his book. Ben Sira does mention sitting at the feet of earlier teachers; thus, some of his own work involves passing on third century traditions. Still, in spite of the efforts of some modern scholars, it is virtually impossible to distinguish earlier from later material in his book.

The activity of the authors of *1 Enoch* ranges from the fourth century to perhaps as late as the first century BCE. The compositional history of *1 Enoch* is filled with uncertainties, but George W. E. Nickelsburg has offered a plausible reconstruction, based in part on the Qumrân evidence, that may serve as a working hypothesis.[14] Nickelsburg suggests that at an early stage, *1 Enoch* consisted of the Book of the Watchers (chaps 1-36) with a narrative bridge (chaps 81-82 and 91) to the Epistle (chaps 92-105). At this early stage, the book was conceived as a testament and may or may not have included the Book of Dreams (chaps 83-90). In any case, the Astronomical Book (chaps 72-80; a redaction of older [fourth century BCE] and more extensive material) and the Book of Parables (chaps 37-71) were inserted at some later point, as were also the appendages which supply an account of Noah's birth (chaps 106-107) and a final piece of Enochic tradition (chap 108).

On paleographical grounds, the oldest manuscripts of *1 Enoch* 1-36 and 72-80 have been dated to about 200 BCE. The manuscripts that preserve fragments of *1 Enoch* 92-105 date from the first century BCE. This disparity explains some of the scholarly disagreement over the *terminus a quo* of the Epistle. The earliest that some scholars are willing to place *1 Enoch* 92-105 is the end of the second century BCE. However, the Apocalypse of Weeks embedded within the Epistle (*1 En* 93:1-10; 91:11-17), a classic example of *vaticinia ex eventu*, makes no reference to the persecutions of Antiochus Epiphanes in 167 BCE. While some scholars regard the Apocalypse as an ear-

---

[13] Skehan and Di Lella, *The Wisdom of Ben Sira*, 10. The new Schürer is even more conservative: "it is reasonable to conclude that Jesus ben Sira flourished between *c.* 190-175 B.C." (E. Schürer, *The History of the Jewish People in the Age of Jesus Christ (175 B.C.-A.D. 135)* [vol. III.1; A New English Version rev. and ed. by G. Vermes, F. Millar and M. Goodman; Edinburgh: T. & T. Clark, 1986] 202). But is it "reasonable" to conclude that ben Sira "flourished" for only fifteen years?

[14] Nickelsburg, *Jewish Literature Between the Bible and the Mishnah* (Philadelphia: Fortress, 1981) 150-51.

lier, independent piece, it shares a number of traits with the Epistle and there is no evidence that it once existed independently. For these reasons, among others, it is plausible to date the whole of chapters 92-105 before 167 BCE.[15]

Self-designation and Outlook

In the course of this study, close attention will be paid to how ben Sira and the authors of *1 Enoch* understand themselves and their role in society. For example, authors in both traditions view themselves as sages (Sir 6:32, 34; 15:10; *1 En* 98:9; 99:10) and "scribes" (Sir 38:24; *1 En* 12:3, 4; 15:1; 92:1 [Eth]). This is not to suggest that the two terms are synonymous,[16] although there may be some overlap in meaning when the latter is used in a non-professional sense. The definitions of sage and scribe will emerge from research into specific passages. Are offices or distinct institutions involved?[17] To what extent has the vocabulary of prophets and seers transformed the role of the sage and/or scribe?

In the Hellenistic era, sages are certainly scripture scholars. Ben Sira and the authors of *1 Enoch* interpret, retell, and expand scripture to address con-

---

[15] For a discussion of the dating of chapters 92-105 see James C. VanderKam, *Enoch and the Growth of an Apocalyptic Tradition* (CBQMS 16; Washington, DC: CBA, 1984) 142-49. VanderKam, by identifying the "apostate generation" (*1 En* 93:9) of the author's own time with the avid hellenizers early in the reign of Antiochus, concludes that the Apocalypse of Weeks and the Epistle itself were written between 175-167 BCE. However, the possibility of an earlier date is present if we leave the issue of the "apostate generation" unresolved. Nickelsburg points to evidence that the Epistle may have been known to the author of *Jubilees* and, if so, was likely written early in the second century BCE (*Jewish Literature*, 149-50). F. G. Martinez summarizes all of the issues in dating the epistle and settles for a premaccabean date (*Qumran and Apocalyptic: Studies on the Aramaic Texts from Qumran* [STDJ 9; Leiden: E. J. Brill, 1992] 79-92).

[16] *Contra* Di Lella, who states that ben Sira "was, first and foremost, a professional scribe (Heb *sôpēr*, Gr *grammateus*, cf. 38:24), which at this time meant wise man (Heb *hākām*)" (*The Wisdom of Ben Sira*, 10). For a good discussion of the important distinction between scribe and sage, see Elias J. Bickerman, *The Jews in the Greek Age* (Cambridge, MA: Harvard University, 1988) 161-76.

[17] According to V. Tcherikover, the scribes emerged as a class distinct from the priesthood sometime early in the Hellenistic period (*Hellenistic Civilization and the Jews* [New York: Atheneum, 1959] 124-25). This is not to imply that priests were no longer engaged in scribal activity. The evidence of *Aramaic Testament of Levi* (third century BCE) points to circles in which the priest has attracted scribal and wisdom motifs (Michael E. Stone, "Ideal Figures and Social Context: Priest and Sage in the Early Second Temple Age," *Ancient Israelite Religion: Essays in Honor of Frank Moore Cross* [ed. Patrick D. Miller, Jr., Paul D. Hanson, and S. Dean McBride; Philadelphia: Fortress, 1987] 575-86). Whether the sages comprised an institution or merely an intellectual tradition among the upper classes is still debated by modern scholars (Crenshaw, "Prolegomenon," 16-22).

cerns of their time. However, such work is expended in the two traditions to advance outlooks on society that stand in diametrical opposition.

For ben Sira, one of the chief benefits of wisdom is that it provides the practical skills necessary for attaining a life of success and happiness. Ben Sira writes to instruct young men how to occupy responsible positions in society. His instruction is the revealed wisdom of Torah. While ben Sira is critical of abuses within society, he always counsels his students to make decisions and take actions that preserve the current political, social and religious institutions.

The authors of *1 Enoch* view wisdom as esoteric teaching that promises eternal life. The authors are writing for a minority group that regards itself as the oppressed members of society. They are extremely critical of those who occupy responsible positions in society because such persons abuse their authority and promulgate harmful policies. The revealed wisdom of this tradition warns of the imminent overturning of present institutions in the coming judgment and promises salvation to the wise. Success and happiness are reserved for the new world.

In simple terms, ben Sira may be described as an advocate for the *status quo*, while the authors of *1 Enoch* anticipate the collapse of the *status quo*. Still, this basic difference in outlook should not obscure the fundamental fact that the two perspectives are undergirded by the same kind of activity, viz., the scholarly interpretation of oral and written traditions to explicate the major themes of the period.

The possibility that the two traditions were formulated in opposition to one another should be left open. If this proves to be the case, the comparative study will shed additional light on the intellectual and social history of Israel in this period.

Awareness of Rival Jewish Traditions

There is evidence to suggest that ben Sira and the authors of *1 Enoch* were aware of one another and that their respective views were formulated, at least in part, over against one another. Of course, references to contemporary persons and events are hard to come by in either text. The problem here is similar to that faced by the historian V. Tcherikover, who asked whether ben Sira referred to the abusive practices of Jewish tax-farmers in the Ptolemaic period and, in particular, to Joseph the Tobiad.[18] Tcherikover reviewed the

---

[18] The ancient historian Josephus tells us the stories of the Jewish tax-farmers Joseph the Tobiad and his son Hyrcanus (*Ant.* XII, 154-236). Joseph collected taxes for twenty-two years in Syria-Palestine, and the best scholarly estimate is that this took place from 227-205 BCE; thus, his dates overlap with those of ben Sira. See Jonathan Goldstein, "The Tales of the Tobiads," *Christianity, Judaism and Other Greco-Roman Cults: Studies for Morton*

polemical passages in Sirach that deal with rich and poor and the "free spirit" of hellenism and concluded that "we are reminded of Joseph the Tobiad and his sons, the most characteristic representatives of the age."[19]

Our study will stimulate similar reminders. Some of ben Sira's polemic will call to mind the bearers of Enochic and other pre-Qumranic traditions and, conversely, the authors of *1 Enoch* write of matters that are applicable to ben Sira. However, given the nature of the texts involved, it is simply not possible to arrive at absolute certainty regarding mutual awareness.

The suggestion that ben Sira was aware of scholars and students of Enochic tradition should not come as a total surprise. Ben Sira explicitly refers to Enoch in his own text, and he does so in a way that shows his cognizance of extra-biblical traditions concerning Enoch. He calls attention to Enoch at two places within a unit known as the Hymn to the Fathers (Sir 44:16; 49:14).

There is a major textual problem with Sirach 44:16. The verse is not present in the Ben Sira scroll from Masada nor the Syriac version. Moreover, the Hebrew of ms B is obviously corrupt and must be restored by comparison with the Greek version. The result yields the following:[20]

Sir 44:16a	חנוך התהלך עם ייי וילקח
b	אות דעת לדור דור

Enoch walked with God and he was taken,
a sign of knowledge to all generations.

Smith at Sixty (ed. Jacob Neusner; Leiden: Brill, 1975) 85-123. Goldstein argues that Josephus used a pro-Ptolemaic, propagandistic source for the tales which can best be attributed to Onias IV in the period 131-129 BCE. This raises the intriguing possibility (assuming that ben Sira is critical of the abuses of the Ptolemies) that ben Sira's grandson translated his book (sometime after 132 BCE) for the express purpose of countering the propaganda of Onias IV.

[19] *Hellenistic Civilization and the Jews*, 149.

[20] The Hebrew of ms B reads: חנוך [נמ]צא תמים והתהלך עם ייי ו[י]לקח אות דעת לדור ודור. The Greek is: Ενωχ εὐηρέστησεν κυρίῳ καὶ μετετέθη ὑπόδειγμα μετανοίας ταῖς γενεαῖς. All commentators rightly regard the Hebrew phrase [נמ]צא תמים ("he was found complete") as a corruption from the following verse (44:17), where it applies to Noah. However, the suggestion of some scholars that ל[י]לקח/μετετέθη ("he was taken up") should be struck because it is present in 49:14 is unfounded (for details, see Y. Yadin, *The Ben Sira Scroll from Masada: with Introduction, Emendations and Commentary* [Jerusalem: Israel Exploration Society, 1965] 38; see also our discussion of 49:14 below). The translation offered above reads the Hebrew התהלך ("he walked") rather than the Greek εὐηρέστησεν ("he pleased", cf. LXX Gen 5:22, 24) and the Hebrew דעת ("knowledge") rather than the Greek μετανοίας ("repentance").

But is this verse original to Ben Sira? Many commentators are persuaded that it is not, although this opinion is by no means universal.[21] Yadin has proposed that while the verse is authentic, it has been moved from its original location between Sirach 49:14a and 49:14b. In the process, the cola of the displaced couplet were transposed and the verb לקח was added to what is now 44:16a. Yadin's reconstruction of the original is as follows:[22]

Sir 49:14a	מעט נוצר על הארץ כחנוך
44:16b	אות דעת לדור דור
44:16a	והתהלך עם אדני
49:14b	וגם הוא נלקח פנים

> Few have been created on the earth like Enoch,
>   a sign of knowledge to all generations.
> And he walked with God,
>   and he himself was taken to the heavenly sanctuary.

Such a rearrangement of the text, while ingenious, is ultimately unconvincing. In the first place, it makes Enoch's role as a revealer figure (44:16b) dependent on his creation (49:14a) rather than his ascension (44:16a). Secondly, there is no rationale for the displacement of the two cola. Yadin's assumption that there was a chronological motive for placing Enoch before Noah (44:17) would seem to also require the forward placement of later references to Shem, Seth, Enosh and Adam (Sir 49:16). The cola of Sirach 44:16 should not be repositioned and transposed.

Sirach 44:16a draws its two verbs (לקח, הלך) from Genesis 5:24. Indeed, this line ("Enoch walked with God and he was taken") is a condensa-

---

[21] The arguments against authenticity are stated by T. Middendorp, *Die Stellung Jesu ben Siras zwischen Judentum und Hellenismus* (Leiden: Brill, 1973) 53-54, 109, 112, 134. Skehan and Di Lella regard Sir 44:16 as an expansion on ben Sira's text, given Enoch's "popularity in the last centuries B.C. as the custodian of ancient lore" (*The Wisdom of Ben Sira*, 499). J. Marböck considers the verse authentic for two basic reasons: (1) the reference to Enoch combines with Sir 49:14 to form a large *inclusio* around Israel's ancestors, and (2) David is also mentioned in two places in the Hymn to the Fathers (Sir 45:25-26; 47:1-11). See J. Marböck, "Henoch—Adam—der Thronwagen: Zu frühjüdischen pseudepigraphischen Traditionen bei *Ben Sira*," *BZ* N.F. 25 (1981) 103-111, esp. 103-04. See also the treatment of Benjamin G. Wright, *No Small Difference: Sirach's Relationship to its Hebrew Parent Text* (SCS 26; Atlanta: Scholars, 1989) 155-56.

[22] Yadin, *The Ben Sira Scroll*, 38. The Masada Scroll ends with 44:17 and thus the complete restoration is based on ms B. The translation above is our own, since Yadin does not translate the complete restoration in the work cited.

tion of the verse in Genesis ("Enoch walked with God; and he was not, for God took him"). The syntax of Sirach 44:16b is awkward, but it seems clear that ben Sira does not read Genesis 5:24 as a reference to Enoch's final translation. Rather, the expression "a sign of knowledge for all generations" implies that Enoch has returned from heaven with revelation.

Two connections can be drawn between Sirach 44:16 and material in *1 Enoch*. First, *1 Enoch* 12:1-2 offers an identical interpretation of Genesis 5:24. While *1 Enoch* 12:1-2 represents an expansion, rather than a condensation, of the verse from Genesis, this expansion also reads the taking of Enoch in a penultimate sense. Enoch is taken and walks with the holy ones and is, thereby, in a position to be the mediator of revelation.[23]

Second, ben Sira's designation of Enochic revelation as "a sign of knowledge" is precisely the phrase used in the superscription to the Epistle of Enoch. The opening to the Epistle (*1 En* 92:1) reads "Written by Enoch the scribe—this complete sign of wisdom" (*za-taṣeḥfa 'em-ḥēnok ṣaḥafi ze-kʷello te'merta ṭebab*).[24] The Ethiopic expression "sign of wisdom" (*1 En* 92:1) is the linguistic equivalent of the Hebrew "sign of knowledge" (Sir 44:16). Both passages use the phrase, as common tradition, to designate the revelation Enoch brought from heaven to the earth.[25] The shared vocabulary is a preliminary indication that ben Sira had at least *some* appreciation for Enoch as a revealer figure, however heated his polemic against some purveyors of esoteric tradition.

---

[23] This interpretation would seem more logical for Gen 5:22 than 5:24, because the former refers to Enoch's "walk" with God (or the angels) during 300 years of his life. Still, it appears that in both Sir 44:16 and *1 En* 12:1-2, Gen 5:24 is being read into 5:22; that is, what became final in the last instance had been experienced by Enoch many times previously. See VanderKam, *Enoch and the Growth*, 130-31.

[24] The Aramaic is too fragmentary to read. VanderKam (ibid., 173, n. 99) states that *temherta* ("teaching") is better attested than *te'merta* ("sign"). The reading *temherta* does appear in Rylands Ethiopic Ms 23 and a number of manuscripts that Knibb collates with it; however, BM 491 and Tana 9 read *te'merta*, the reading we adopt (see Michael A. Knibb, *The Ethiopic Book of Enoch: A New Edition in the Light of the Aramaic Dead Sea Fragments* [2 vols.; Oxford: Clarendon, 1978] I.347).

[25] For a totally different understanding of Enoch as "sign" see *Jub* 4:24. The *Jubilees* passage relates the "sign" to Enoch's final translation, when he is placed in Eden to record the sins of humanity: "for he was established there as a sign to bear witness against all the sons of men and keep a record of all the deeds of every generation till the day of judgment."

The reference to Enoch in Sirach 49:14, like that in 44:16, shows an awareness of extra-biblical tradition:[26]

Sir 49:14a   Few have been created on the earth like Enoch,
        b   he himself was taken to the heavenly sanctuary.

It may seem logical to suggest that Enoch is being compared to Elijah, who was earlier said to have been "taken" (לקח) in a whirlwind (Sir 48:9).[27] The difference is that Elijah was taken "upward" (מעלה, 48:9a) and "to heaven" (מ[רום, 48:9b; cf. 2 Kgs 2:11), whereas Enoch was taken "within" (פנים, 49:14b),[28] or, as rendered above, "to the heavenly sanctuary." The terms פנים, לפנים, פנימה and פנימי are often used to refer to the "inside" of buildings, especially the temple (Lev 10:18; 1 Kgs 6:18; Ezek 40-46 *passim*). In Ezekiel 41:3-4, the פנימה is the most holy place of the heavenly temple. At this place, Ezekiel has a vision of the chariot-throne of God (Ezek 43:3-5).

Ben Sira praises Ezekiel for describing the faces of the chariot-throne (Sir 49:8). The reference is to the initial vision in Ezekiel 1:4-28. Still, the prophet later re-experienced this vision when he was brought to the holy of holies in the heavenly temple. It is this latter scene that seems to have influenced the description of Enoch in Sirach 49:14b.

Scholars have recognized that Enoch's temple tour and vision of the chariot-throne in *1 Enoch* 14 draws its imagery from the book of Ezekiel, particularly Ezekiel 1 and 40-48.[29] It would appear from Sirach 49:14 that ben Sira knows a piece of Enochic lore in which Enoch had an experience much like that of Ezekiel. Ben Sira's statement that Enoch was taken to the heavenly sanctuary is too general to support a claim of dependency on *1 Enoch* 14. He may simply know an oral tradition that adapts language from the book of Ezekiel to describe Enoch's journey to the innermost part of the heavenly temple.

---

[26] For the Hebrew, see above in connection with our discussion of Yadin's view. Burton L. Mack (*Wisdom and the Hebrew Epic: Ben Sira's Hymn in Praise of the Fathers* [Chicago: University of Chicago, 1985] Appendix C), excises every passage in Sirach that has esoteric or eschatological coloring, including Sir 49:14-16. However, there is no justification for eliminating Sir 49:14-16, since it is attested in all of the manuscripts (Hebrew, Greek, Syriac and Latin).

[27] Skehan and Di Lella, *The Wisdom of Ben Sira*, 545.

[28] This translation is found in Solomon Schechter & Charles Taylor, *The Wisdom of Ben Sira: Portions of the Book Ecclesiasticus* (Amsterdam: APA-Philo Press, 1979 reprint of 1896 and 1899) xlvi. The textual note suggests that פנים has the sense of לפנים or פנימה: taken "within (the heaven)" (ibid., 63).

[29] See below, p. 30, n. 69; and H. Ludin Jansen, *Die Henochgestalt* (Oslo: Dybwad, 1939) 114-17. Jansen also considers *1 En* 60 to be modeled on Ezek 1.

In sum, Sirach 44:16 and 49:14 show that ben Sira has some appreciation for traditions about Enoch. The extent to which his admiration for Enochic lore must be qualified will emerge in the course of our study.

It is also possible to approach the question of the awareness of rival Jewish tradition from the side of the authors of *1 Enoch*. A strong presumption exists that the bearers of Enochic tradition would have known such a prominent and reputable Jerusalem sage as ben Sira. Of course, there is no explicit reference to ben Sira in *1 Enoch*. Still, some of the polemics in *1 Enoch* will fit the activity of ben Sira and his support for the present establishment.

There are, then, intriguing indications that ben Sira and teachers of Enochic tradition are aware of one another. The comparative study of the themes of revelation, creation and judgment in Parts I-III will identify in more detail the ways the two traditions may be interacting. In the Conclusion, the evidence for a relationship between ben Sira and the authors of *1 Enoch* is summarized and assessed, and new questions are raised.

PART I

THE THEME OF REVELATION
IN *1 ENOCH* AND SIRACH

The plan of this first section is to group and analyze passages in *1 Enoch* and Sirach that explicitly treat the theme of revelation. The analysis takes its point of departure from the literary forms and motifs associated with revelation. Each book is considered separately to help preserve the integrity of its own perspective. However, throughout the investigation, the comparative goal is presupposed. Discrete passages are analyzed and concepts of revelation discussed insofar as they hold promise for the comparative aim. A synthesis and comparison of the results of the survey are presented in the closing section of chapter two.

1. THE ENOCHIC BOOKS OF WISDOM

In the Introduction, it was noted that the Enochic corpus views itself as wisdom material. In particular, it presents itself as the revealed wisdom Enoch offered as his testament. A testament is the farewell speech or last words from a great figure in the Hebrew Bible. Because the basis of Enoch's testament is a journey to heaven and its content is about heaven and the future judgment, it conforms closely to what A. B. Kolenkow termed a "blessing-revelation testament."[30] Our investigation will highlight the extent to which the Book of the Watchers, the narrative bridge to the Epistle, the Epistle itself, and even the Astronomical Book, employ motifs from the testament in the service of offering revealed wisdom from Enoch.

THE BOOK OF THE WATCHERS:
A BLESSING-REVELATION TESTAMENT

The Framework

Testaments have opening and closing passages that are similar in structure and vocabulary.[31] Variations of these elements in the Book of the Watchers illustrate its special concept of revealed wisdom.

---

[30] Among the blessing-revelation testaments, A. B. Kolenkow treats *1 Enoch* 91-94, *Life of Adam and Eve* 25-29 and the *Testament of Levi* ("The Genre Testament and Forecasts of the Future in the Hellenistic Jewish Milieu," *JSJ* 6 [1975] 57-71). The other type is the "ethical testament," found in the bulk of the *Testaments of the Twelve Patriarchs*. H. W. Hollander and M. de Jonge (*The Testaments of the Twelve Patriarchs: A Commentary* [SVTP 8; Leiden: Brill, 1985] 32-33, 41) do not adopt this designation but do argue that ethical sections form the center of the individual testaments.

[31] Hollander and de Jonge, *The Testaments: A Commentary*, 29.

Opening Passage (*1 Enoch* 1:1, 2-3b; cf. 5:8)

The opening passages of testaments begin with a superscription that reads "A copy of the testament (or: the words) of ...". The superscription adds that the patriarch spoke these things before his death and at a specific age. A description of the farewell scene follows: the children assemble around him, he kisses them and exhorts them to pay heed to what he is about to say.[32]

The Book of the Watchers opens with a superscription that signals the reader to interpret what follows as a testament. Here, however, the vocabulary recalls the testament of Moses in Deuteronomy ("The words of blessing with which Enoch blessed the righteous and chosen ones ...", *1 En* 1:1/"This is the blessing with which Moses the man of God blessed the children of Israel ...", Deut 33:1).[33] Indeed, even the structure of the two passages is similar, for there is no description of a farewell scene in Deuteronomy 33, rather the superscription moves directly to a recollection of the Sinai theophany (Deut 33:2). Likewise, the Enochic superscription is followed almost immediately by a description of a theophany on Sinai at the end-time (*1 En* 1:3c-9).[34] This description is an elaboration of what will happen on the day of judgment, a day referred to in the Enochic superscription ("... who will be present on the day of tribulation ...", *1 En* 1:1).[35]

The parallels to Deuteronomy 33 suggest from the start that the revealed wisdom imparted by Enoch stands on a par with its Mosaic counterpart. Enoch is a figure of Moses-like significance, who predates Moses! His blessing on the righteous and chosen presupposes that they are in possession of an Enochic Torah. In this, his final testament, the focus of Enoch's words is eschatological. Enoch reveals what will happen in the end-time.

An introductory address follows the superscription and summarizes the means by which Enoch received his knowledge of the day of tribulation:[36]

1 En 1:2   And he took up his parable and said,
           "Enoch, a righteous man whose eyes were opened by God,

---

[32] Ibid.

[33] Lars Hartman, *Asking for a Meaning: A Study of 1 Enoch 1-5* (ConBNT 12; Lund: Gleerup, 1979) 126.

[34] On this passage, see Chap. 5, pp. 169-72.

[35] Note the parallel to the superscription in the *Testament of Levi*: " ... according to all that they would do and that would befall them until the day of judgment" (*T. Levi* 1:1). For a discussion of "the day of tribulation," see Chap. 5, pp. 168-69.

[36] The translation here and elsewhere in *1 Enoch*, unless noted otherwise, is that of George W. E. Nickelsburg. His rendering of *1 En* 1:2-3b follows the Greek version.

> who had the vision of the Holy One and of heaven, which
>   he showed me.
> And from the words of the Watchers and Holy Ones I heard
>   everything;
>   and as I heard everything from them, I also understood what
>   I saw.
> And not for this generation do I expound,
>   but concerning one that is distant I speak.
> 3 And concerning the chosen ones I speak now,
>   and concerning them I take up my parable."

The language (eyes were opened, vision of the Holy One,[37] words ... heard, take up a parable) is drawn from the stories of the seer Balaam (Num 24:3-4, 15-16). However, the content of Balaam's "vision of the Almighty" (Num 24:4, 16) is not elaborated in the book of Numbers; the expression is merely formulaic. Enoch will give an extensive account of his vision of the Holy One (*1 En* 14-16). In addition, the content of Enoch's vision is expanded to include the places of heaven. This expansion illustrates that the heavenly journey traditions of *1 Enoch* 17-19, and possibly chapters 20-32 (+ 81:1-82:3) are in view.[38] For this reason, too, the introductory address emphasizes the indispensible role of the interpreting angels. Balaam heard the words of God, Enoch hears the words of the Watchers and holy ones. Thus, the opening address adapts the Balaam vocabulary to provide the reader with a summary outline of the Book of the Watchers.

As indicated, the expression "take up a parable" ($\dot{\alpha}\nu\alpha\lambda\alpha\beta\dot{\omega}\nu$ $\tau\dot{\eta}\nu$ $\pi\alpha\rho\alpha\beta o\lambda\dot{\eta}\nu$/'*awše'a mesla*), which frames this unit, is also drawn from the Balaam stories (נשא משל in Num 23:7, 18; 24:3, 15, 20, 21, 23).[39] The word "parable" is doubly appropriate for expressing the content of Enoch's revelation because not only was it used in the wisdom literature in the sense of a wise saying (proverb), but it also came to refer to obscure sayings, such as the

---

[37] Rau argues that the reference to a vision, among other factors, indicates that the opening of *1 Enoch* has been formed in analogy to prophetic books (*Kosmologie*, 39-40). However, the dependency on the Balaam stories tends to weaken this argument.

[38] Hartman (*Asking for a Meaning*, 138-45) shows that *1 En* 1-5 is the introduction to the entire Book of the Watchers. Noteworthy in his list of parallels between *1 En* 1-5 and 6-36 is the motif of judgment on human sinners (cf. 1:7, 9; 5:5-7 and 27:2-4).

[39] The Aramaic expression is נסב חנוך מתלה, "Enoch took up his parable" (*1 En* 93:3; 4QEn^g I iii 23).

oracles of Balaam.[40] In *1 Enoch*, both aspects are important. The notion of that which makes one wise is not surrendered, although here it involves eschatological instruction that will deliver one from the judgment. The point is especially clear from *1 Enoch* 5:8:[41]

1 En 5:8   Then *wisdom will be given* to all the chosen ones;
                  and they will all live,
                  and they will sin no more through godlessness or pride.
              But in the enlightened man there will be light,
                  and in the wise man, understanding,
                  and they will transgress no more,
                  nor will they sin all the days of their life.

The introductory chapters (*1 En* 1-5) conclude on the note that Enoch's testament contains the eschatological gift of revealed wisdom that will deliver the righteous in the judgment.[42] The phrase "to give wisdom" is a technical expression for Enoch's revelation. It serves as the corollary to the earlier phrase "to take up a parable" (*1 En* 1:2a, 3b).

Thus, the terms "parable" and "wisdom" refer to the heavenly mysteries that Enoch imparts to the righteous in the distant generation of the end-time. In the Book of the Watchers, these mysteries are conveyed through a number of different literary forms, but the dominant form is that of the vision.

---

[40] F. Hauck ("παραβολή," *TDNT* 5, 744-61, esp. 749-50) calls attention to the mysterious and enigmatic character of the משל in the book of Ezekiel and its further development along these lines in apocalyptic literature, such as 4 Ezra and *1 Enoch*. George M. Landes studied the appearance of משל throughout the Old Testament and concluded that it was not characterized by a fixed literary form, but did involve typical features based on the root meaning of the word ("likeness, comparison"). The features are: "the description of a representative case or object lesson, often focused in the experience of an individual and implemented by one or more comparisons from which those addressed are expected to make an analogy that will effect some reassessment in their thinking and conduct" (Landes, "Jonah: A *MĀŠĀL*?" *Israelite Wisdom: Theological and Literary Essays in Honor of Samuel Terrien* [ed. John G. Gammie, et al; Missoula, MT: Scholars, 1978] 145). As we will see, the Book of the Watchers does display these basic features. See also Timothy Polk, "Paradigms, Parables, and *Mĕšālim*: On Reading the *Māšāl* in Scripture," *CBQ* 45 (1983) 564-83.

[41] This verse occurs in a unit of alternating words of salvation and judgment (*1 En* 5:5-9). See Chap. 5, pp. 173-74.

[42] See George W. E. Nickelsburg, "Revealed Wisdom as a Criterion for Inclusion and Exclusion: From Jewish Sectarianism to Early Christianity," *"To See Ourselves as Others See Us": Christians, Jews, and "Others" in Late Antiquity* (ed. Jacob Neusner and Ernest S. Frerichs; Missoula, MT: Scholars, 1986) 73-91, esp. 77-78.

Closing Passage (*1 Enoch* 81:5-82:3)

In the closing passage typical of the genre testament, the farewell speech is said to come to an end, the dying figure instructs his children about his burial, the man dies and the children obey his instructions.[43] Obviously, these standard elements must undergo a radical alteration in the case of Enoch because he does not die and is not buried. But is there a closing scene that illustrates how the variation was carried out?

In the Excursus, the case is made that *1 Enoch* 81:1-4 is the seventh and final stop on the Second Journey of Enoch (chaps 20-32). It follows that *1 Enoch* 81:5-82:3 is the conclusion of this journey account. More than this, 81:5-82:3 provides a variation on the closing passage typical of the genre testament and, therefore, also serves to conclude the Book of the Watchers.

The variation takes its special character from the preceding cosmic journey (*1 En* 20-32 + 81:1-4) and the fact that Enoch does not die. "Those seven holy ones"[44] (cf. *1 En* 20) return Enoch to the earth, set him in front of the door of his house and commission him to impart his revelation to Methuselah and all his sons (81:5).[45] Enoch is informed that he will be left on the earth for a period of one year to complete the task; in the second year, he will be taken (81:6).

An exhortatory section follows in *1 Enoch* 81:7-9, spoken by the angels. It begins "Let your heart be strong ..." (81:7a). It is common in testaments for the patriarch to exhort his sons on the basis of some incident from his own life. However, as Himmelfarb has noted, it is not unusual for angels to issue exhortations to seers in the context of tours of hell.[46] In *1 Enoch*, this feature

---

[43] Hollander and de Jonge, *The Testaments: A Commentary*, 30.

[44] The Ethiopic manuscripts are divided along family lines between the readings "three holy ones" and "seven holy ones." According to Black, "either reading could be original" (*The Book of Enoch or 1 Enoch*, 253). Milik (*The Books of Enoch* [Oxford: Clarendon, 1976] 13-14) and VanderKam (*Enoch and the Growth*, 107) read "three holy ones" on the basis that this number was taken from the Book of Dreams (*1 En* 87:3-4; 90:31). But the number three could be a secondary reading necessitated by the dislocation of the passage.

[45] Rau sees the explicit mention of the "house" as a reference to the "house of instruction." In his view, the Book of Dreams (*1 En* 83-90) illustrates the beginning and ending stage of instruction in such a house and, in conjunction with other Jewish texts, yields an insight into the *Sitz im Leben* of Enochic tradition. For example, according to Rau, it was a common practice in the teaching house of Enoch for the student to sleep at night with the teacher who instructed him. By this means, the student "sees" the vision-reports he previously learned. Thus, authentic experience, on the one hand, and the conventional literary form of the vision report, on the other, coalesce in the house of Enoch (Rau, *Kosmologie*, 455-85, esp. 477). Needless to say, Rau's analysis is highly speculative.

[46] Martha Himmelfarb, *Tours of Hell: An Apocalyptic Form in Jewish and Christian Literature* (Philadelphia: University of Pennsylvania, 1983) 149.

occurs in the closing passage. Finally, the element of cessation of speech, typical of closing passages, is applied to the holy ones in *1 Enoch* 81:10. The testament has concluded, in essence, when the holy ones stop speaking with Enoch.

The content of the angelic exhortation stresses the important function of Enochic revelation:[47]

1 En 81:7a Let your heart be strong
        b   for the good to the good will make known righteousness,
        c   and the righteous with the righteous will rejoice,
        d   and they will greet one another.
        8a   But the sinner with the sinner will die,
        b   and the apostate with the apostate will sink.
        9a   And those who practice righteousness will die because of
                the works of men,
        b   and they will be gathered in because of the deeds of the
                impious.

The verb "make known" (*'ayde'a*) in 81:7b recalls the angelic commission from 81:5 ("*Make* everything *known* to your son Methuselah"). The content of this revelation, here called "righteousness," supplies the basis for encouragement. Although the righteous die at the hands of sinners, they can rejoice. Enoch's revelation brings salvation that transcends death.[48] This salvation is realized at the final judgment, which will also bring destruction to sinners.[49]

1 Enoch 82:1-3 is Enoch's announcement that he has fulfilled the angelic commission and, in effect, is ready to be taken from the earth. He informs his son Methuselah of what he has accomplished by introducing significant nuances to the earlier vocabulary of the commission:

Angelic Commission:

1 En 81:5 *Make known* (*'ayde'a*) everything to your son Methuselah
              and *show* (*'ar'i*) all your sons ...
        81:6 One year we leave you ...

---

[47] The translations given from the closing passage, *1 En* 81:5-82:3, are my own from the Ethiopic.

[48] John J. Collins, "Apocalyptic Eschatology as the Transcendence of Death," *CBQ* 36 (1974) 21-43.

[49] It is clear from *1 En* 81:5-10 that Enoch's revelation is related to (1) the death of the righteous at the hands of sinners and (2) the judgment that brings death to sinners (portrayed in flood language) and life to the righteous. These emphases follow naturally from the vision in 81:1-4. See the Excursus.

so that you may *teach* (*temharomu*) your sons,
and *write* (*teshaf*) for them,
and *testify* (*tāsamme'*) to all your sons.

Enoch's Fulfillment:

1 En 82:1a   And now, my son Methuselah,
       b   All these things I *recount* (*'enagger*) for you and
           write down (*wa-'esehhef*) for you,
       c   and everything I have *revealed* (*kašatku*) to you,
       d   and I have given you *books* (*masāheft*) about all these
           things.

The explicit verb "revealed" in *1 Enoch* 82:1c, along with the word
"blessed" from the opening passage (*1 En* 1:1), makes it appropriate to designate the Second Journey report a "blessing-revelation testament."   Enoch
returns from a trip to the outer reaches of the cosmos with revelation that he
passes on to Methuselah.   The accent of this fulfillment scene is on the fact
that Enoch has revealed everything in written form.   The commission to
"write" (*sahafa*) has been fulfilled and has resulted in the production of
"books" (*masāheft*).
The books, in turn, are identified with wisdom:[50]

1 En 82:1d   I have given you books about all these things
               (*wa-wahabkuka masāheftihomu la-'ellu kʷellomu*)

       82:2a   Wisdom I have given you
               (*tebaba wahabku laka*)

For the present, it is enough to make two points.   First, the phrase "to
give wisdom" takes the reader back to the opening chapters of the Book of the
Watchers.   This technical term was used in *1 Enoch* 5:8 for revelation that
brings deliverance at the time of the last judgment.   Here too, *1 Enoch* 82:3a
goes on to state the salvific benefit for those to whom wisdom is given: "And
they who understand it will not sleep" (82:3a).   The metaphor of not sleeping
alludes to the Remiel tradition and the resurrection (*1 En* 20:8; 81:1-4; see the
Excursus and cf. 92:3, "the righteous one will arise from sleep").
Second, while ostensibly addressed to Methuselah, the focus of
1 Enoch 82:1 and 82:2 is on the generations to come.   The books Enoch gives
to Methuselah (82:1d) are to be preserved and handed down to the

---

[50] On the wisdom motifs that permeate *1 En* 82:1-3, see in connection with our analysis
of the sixth vision of Enoch's Second Journey, the Tree of Wisdom (below, pp. 32-35).

"generations of eternity" (82:1e-f); so also wisdom (82:2a), from father to son to future sons, "to all the generations until eternity" (82:2b). Again, this image recalls the opening chapters of the Book of the Watchers. In *1 Enoch* 1:2, the target audience is identified as the "distant" generation. Enoch's revelation is possessed by those who will be saved on the day of judgment at the end-time.

Taken together, the two points highlighted above (the reception of life-giving wisdom by the generation of the end-time) indicate that the closing passage serves as an *inclusio* to chapters 1-5. Therefore, the angelic commission and Enochic fulfillment scenes reach beyond the Second Journey account itself (*1 En* 20-32 + 81:1-4) and function as the conclusion to the entire Book of the Watchers. By taking the reader full circle to the opening chapters, 81:5-82:3 indicate that the Book of the Watchers was constructed as Enoch's testament.

The Body

The body of testaments typically includes elements of biography, exhortation and prediction.[51] The patriarch retells an episode from his life that illustrates the vices or virtues he enjoins upon his children. The future of the tribe is then connected to their obedience or disobedience. There is great variety in how these elements are expressed.

First Journey Report

Setting: Angelic Descent and the Worthless Mystery (1 Enoch 6-11). Chapters 6-11 provide the background for biographical elements of Enoch's testament. These chapters retell the story of Genesis 6:1-4 in a way that incorporates a new motif: a worthless revelation is brought to earth by rebel angels. This motif serves as the counterpoint to the revealed wisdom Enoch will bring from heaven.

The investigation will proceed on the hypothesis that *1 Enoch* 6-11 combine two versions of the descent of a group of angels from heaven.[52] The first

---

[51] Hollander and de Jonge, *The Testaments: A Commentary*, 31-41.

[52] The identification of the two sources and plausible interpretations of their meaning are made by George W. E. Nickelsburg, "Apocalyptic and Myth in 1 Enoch 6-11," *JBL* 96 (1977) 383-405. For a differing explanation of the two versions, see P. D. Hanson, "Rebellion in Heaven, Azazel, and Euhemeristic Heroes in 1 Enoch 6-11," *JBL* 96 (1977) 195-233. See also the assessment of John J. Collins ("Methodological Issues in the Study of 1 Enoch: Reflections on the Articles of P. D. Hanson and G. W. Nickelsburg," *SBLSP* [1978] 315-22) and Nickelsburg's reply ("Reflections upon Reflections: A Response to John Collins' 'Methodological Issues in the Study of 1 Enoch,'" *SBLSP* [1978] 311-14).

concerns the angel Shemiḥazah, leader of a band of two hundred angels who came down to earth and intermarried with women. Their halfbreed offspring, the giants, wreaked havoc of such magnitude upon the earth that human beings were helpless before them and could only cry out for judgment. This version of the story did not originally contain the theme of revelation.

The second version involves the angel 'Asael. 'Asael and his cohort came down to earth to teach human beings forbidden arts. The result of this instruction was that godlessness—typified by the production of weapons, jewelry and cosmetics—spread upon the earth. In this version, human beings are viewed as responsible agents who are involved in sinful activities that derive from their reception of the unauthorized revelation of heavenly mysteries.

In the 'Asael material, the angel 'Asael himself is the subject of the verb "to teach" (אלף 4QEn^b 1 ii 26, διδάσκω; 8:1a); a verb used in parallel with "to show" (ὑποδείκνυμι G^g, δείκνυμι G^s, 8:1b; cf. 9:6). The content of 'Asael's instruction involves metallurgy and mining. But, in addition, there are a number of verses in chapters 6-11 in which the revelatory motif of the 'Asael material has apparently contaminated the Shemiḥazah version. Each of these verses contains explicit verbs for revelation (1 En 7:1de; 8:3; 9:8c; 10:7):

Shemiḥazah and revelatory activity:

1 En	7:1d	to *teach* them ...	(אלף 4QEn^a 1 iii 15)
	e	to *reveal* to them ...	(δηλόω G^g)
	8:3a	*taught* ...	(אלף 4QEn^a 1 iv 1, 4; 4QEn^b 1 iii 1, 2 [twice], 3, 4)
	i	to *reveal* mysteries ...	(ἀνακαλύπτω G^s)
	9:8c	and *revealed* to them ...	(δηλόω G^s)
	c	and *taught* them ...	(διδάσκω G^s)
	10:7c	the mystery which the Watchers *told*	(εἶπον G^s)
	c	and *taught* ...	(διδάσκω G^s)

In these verses from the Shemiḥazah version, the content of the revelation does not involve the skills related to metallurgy or mining ('Asael's proper domain; 1 En 8:1), but covers the areas of magic and astrology. This could reflect a third version of the story of angelic descent, but more likely represents a simple expansion of the scope of forbidden revelatory activity in the final redaction of chapters 6-11.[53] The net effect of this last redaction is to claim that the revelation brought by rebel angels leads to idolatry.

---

[53] Nickelsburg points out that the teaching of mining, on the one hand, and magic and astrology, on the other, can be found in the various versions of the Prometheus story, which probably influenced the 'Asael tradition and its coloring of the Shemiḥazah material ("Apocalyptic and Myth," 399-401).

Significantly, the character of Enoch is not yet mentioned in chapters 6-11. Rather, this retelling of Genesis 6:1-4 sets the context for elements of Enoch's biography, as *1 Enoch* 12:1-2 will immediately make clear.

Enoch's Ascent: The Vision of the Holy One and of Heaven (1 Enoch 12-16 and 17-19). These chapters integrate aspects of the life of Enoch into the context of the rebellion of the Watchers. The first two verses establish the basic chronological point that Enoch "was taken" (ἐλήμφθη, *1 En* 12:1) before the heavenly beings "took" wives (ἔλαβον, *1 En* 7:1) from the daughters of men (cf. Gen 5:24; 6:1-4).[54] Therefore, Enoch ascended to heaven and spent time with the holy ones before some of them rebelled and descended with unauthorized revelation. As stated in the Introduction, *1 Enoch* 12:1-2 interpret Genesis 5:24 in a penultimate sense.[55] Enoch is taken and walks with the holy ones for a period covering three hundred years. For this reason, he is in position to play a specific role vis-à-vis Shemihazah and 'Asael. The ensuing account, in the form of narrative, describes Enoch's role and interactions with the rebel Watchers.

Carol Newson carried out a literary analysis of the narrative in *1 Enoch* 12-16 and concluded that these chapters initially integrated the career of Enoch solely into the Shemihazah tradition (*1 En* 12:1-6; 13:3-16:1).[56] At a later point in time, namely when the 'Asael material was incorporated into chapters 6-11,[57] similar redactional passages were also added to chapters 12-16 (*1 En* 13:1-2; 16:2-3[4]).

If this analysis is correct, then at the level of the initial integration of Enoch into the Shemihazah material, Enoch is commissioned by faithful heavenly beings and by God himself to announce the permanent expulsion of Shemihazah and his band in order to restore and ensure order in heaven. In the process, Enoch also becomes the conveyor of speculative wisdom on the nature of angelic sin and its lasting consequences in the production of evil

---

[54] The correlation of the two Genesis passages was prompted by the verb לקח, which means "to take away" (Gen 5:24) and "to take a wife" (Gen 6:2).

[55] See above, pp. 10-11.

[56] Carol A. Newsom, "The Development of *1 Enoch* 6-19: Cosmology and Judgment," *CBQ* 42 (1980) 310-29.

[57] Newsom differs from Nickelsburg's view that the application of the teaching motif to the Shemihazah cycle is a secondary corruption from the 'Asael tradition. She argues that it is independent material which became attached to the Shemihazah story and itself later attracted the 'Asael tradition ("The Development," 313-14, 320-21.)

spirits upon the earth (*1 En* 15:3-16:1). At a later stage of redaction, namely, at the level of the 'Asael redaction, Newsom suggests Enoch's own reputation as a bearer of special wisdom attracted the teaching motif of the 'Asael material as a foil.

In any event, *1 Enoch* 13:1-2 and 16:2-3, which may well be redactional passages, contain verbs that underscore the revelatory activity of the rebel Watchers, as was the case also in the final redaction of chapters 6-11 (cf. esp. 16:2 with 8:3):

1 En 13:1 And, Enoch, go and say to 'Asael ...
    2 'And you will have no relief or petition,
        because of the unrighteous deeds which *you revealed* (δείκνυμι),
        [and because of all the godless deeds and the unrighteousness and
        the sin which *you revealed* (ὑποδείκνυμι)] to men.'[58]

1 En 16:2 And now (say) to the Watchers ...
    3 'You were in heaven,
        and no mystery *was revealed* to you (οὐκ ἀνεκαλύφθη);
        but a worthless mystery *you knew* (γινώσκω).[59]
        and this *you made known* (μηνύω) to the women
        in the hardness of your heart;
        and through this mystery the women and men are multiplying
        evils upon the earth.'

Once again the notion is reinforced that the practices previously outlined in chapters 6-11 (mining, metallurgy, cosmetology, magic and astrology) are sinful and originated from the revelatory activity of rebel angels. The content of the revelation is described here with adjectives such as "unrighteous," "godless" and "worthless."

Newsom's point that the portrayal of the worthless mystery serves as a counterpart to the true mystery revealed by Enoch is well-taken. This true mystery includes speculative knowledge on the nature of sin, given in Enoch's vision of the Holy One, and anticipates what he will be given in his vision of heaven (chaps 17-19; 20-32 + 81:1-4).

In chapters 12-16, the true mystery brought by Enoch is directly related to the biographical notes that identify him as a scribe. Assuming the validity of Newsom's analysis, this emphasis is present from the start, at the initial level of integrating Enoch into the Shemiḥazah tradition.

---

[58] The bracketed clause appears to be a doublet.

[59] The translation "worthless" in *1 En* 16:3 reflects the Ethiopic *mennuna*. Nickelsburg translates: "but a *stolen* mystery you learned." The Greek version reads "which did [not] happen from God" (τὸ ἐκ τοῦ θεοῦ γεγενημένον).

1 En 12:3 Enoch, the scribe   (*saḥāfi*, no Gk)
        4 Enoch, the scribe of   (ὁ γραμματεὺς τῆς δικαιοσύνης)
           righteousness
     15:1 Enoch, truthful man   (ἄνθρωπος ἀληθινὸς
           and scribe of truth   καὶ γραμματεὺς τῆς ἀληθείας)

The noun "scribe" has the root meaning of "one who writes," and is especially apropos for Enoch who is regarded elsewhere in Jewish tradition as the inventor of writing (*Jub* 4:17). However, in the present context, the word has both priestly[60] and prophetic nuances.

Enoch the scribe has a priestly role. At the request of the rebel Watchers, to whom Enoch had descended with a word of judgment (*1 En* 13:3), he wrote a "memorandum of petition" (*tazkāra se'lat*/ὑπόμνηματα ἐρωτήσεως, *1 En* 13:4) for them and their halfbreed sons. This memorandum was a request for forgiveness. As such, it recorded "the deeds of each one of them" (*la-la-'aḥadu megbāromu*; *1 En* 13:6). In essence, then, this was a book that listed the Watchers and their sinful deeds.[61] Enoch recited the book at the waters of Dan and, in a dream-vision, ascended to the divine throne. But God rejected the petition for forgiveness and commissioned Enoch to pronounce judgment. Enoch returned and wrote a document summarizing the incident: *The Book of the Words of Truth and the Reprimand of the Watchers Who Were From Eternity* (*1 En* 14:1).[62]

The documents written by Enoch have binding, judicial authority. Enoch wrote a petition that included a compilation of sins. When the petition was rejected, he then wrote a book that recorded this fact. But what specific sins were involved here? The Shemiḥazah myth (until contaminated by the 'Asael material) was about improper intermarriage. Nickelsburg suggested that the myth may have originally referred to the successors of Alexander, the Diadochi, who were warrior chieftains and some of whom were said to have

---

[60] In the period of the restoration, Ezra is called a priest and a scribe (Ezra 7:6, 11, 12, 21; Neh 8:1-2, 4, 9, 13). Interestingly, Ezra faced the issue of intermarriage. As a scribe, he knew the statutes of God, in particular, that intermarriage with foreigners was prohibited; as a priest, he made intercession for those who had sinned (Ezra 9; Neh 9). See Nickelsburg, "Enoch, Levi, and Peter," 585; and Martha Himmelfarb, *Ascent to Heaven in Jewish and Christian Apocalypses* (New York: Oxford University, 1993) 23-25.

[61] Cf. *1 En* 10:8b. An analogous concept is present in *1 En* 81:2, 4; although in the later passage the book contains the sinful deeds of human beings (see the Excursus).

[62] In 4QEn[c] I vi 9, the word ספר is used in *1 En* 14:1. This "book" serves as a legal document or bill of indictment, as in imperial Aramaic (so Milik, *The Books of Enoch*, 35, 193).

gods as their fathers.[63] The myth was then reinterpreted in Enochic tradition and served as a paradigm for a "corrupt" priesthood that violated the laws of purity as understood by the Enochic community.[64]

The suggestion is plausible and sheds light on the activity of scribes in this period. As David Suter explains: "The use of Enoch, the heavenly scribe, as the vehicle for the revelations in the Book of the Watchers suggests that the myth reflects scribal opinion of some sort, and one is reminded that in the third century B.C.E. the scribes are in the process of taking over the interpretation of the Torah from the priests."[65] It may be the case that scribes in the Enochic tradition find a model for dealing with a "corrupt" priesthood in the way that Enoch the scribe responded to the rebel Watchers.

The latter point is further supported by the inclusion of the explicit revelatory theme at the 'Asael level of redaction. The fact that the sins (the "corrupt" teaching and practices) are equated with magic and astrology should not necessarily be taken literally. The charge of practicing idolatry is standard rhetoric among rival teachers or traditions.[66]

In addition to the priestly overtones of Enoch's scribal work, prophetic nuances are also present. The book that Enoch writes contains an elaborate account of his ascent to the divine throne and subsequent divine commission.[67] The description of the commission draws elements from the prophetic commissioning form.

Walther Zimmerli describes two basic types of commission or prophetic call narrative in the Hebrew Bible.[68] One type is characterized by such elements as a very personal encounter between God and the one called, a dialogue, expressions of reluctance or objection by the one called, and God's response through personal promises or the granting of signs (e.g., Jer 1). The second type is not a narrative in the strict sense. The one called sees the Lord sitting on his throne with the heavenly host surrounding him, the Lord asks the divine council whom he should send, the heavenly beings suggest various pos-

---

[63] "Apocalyptic and Myth," 391, 396-97.

[64] Nickelsburg, "Enoch, Levi, and Peter," 575-600. See also David Suter, "Fallen Angel, Fallen Priest: The Problem of Family Purity in 1 Enoch 6-16," *HUCA* 50 (1979) 115-35. John J. Collins attributes this historical reapplication of the Shemiḥazah myth to "the essential polyvalence of apocalyptic symbolism" ("The Apocalyptic Technique: Setting and Function in the Book of Watchers," *CBQ* 44 [1982] 98).

[65] Suter, "Fallen Angel, Fallen Priest," 134.

[66] See below, p. 210, n. 499.

[67] For the ascent, see Chap. 3, pp. 112-15.

[68] Walther Zimmerli, *Ezekiel 1* (Hermeneia; Philadelphia: Fortress, 1979) 97-100.

sibilities, the one to be sent voluntarily steps forward, and God places his word in the agent's mouth (e.g. Isa 6; Ezek 1-2).

The account of Enoch's commission in *1 Enoch* 14-16 has close connections to several elements in the second type of call described by Zimmerli.[69] Enoch sees God's lofty throne in the form of a chariot (*1 En* 14:18), he describes the Great Glory who sits upon the throne and the heavenly host that stands before the Great Glory (*1 En* 14:20-23), and he hears directly from God the word that he is to take to the rebel Watchers (*1 En* 14:24-16:4). References to Enoch's trembling and fear before the throne (*1 En* 14:24; 15:1) reflect the element of a very personal encounter; an element common to Zimmerli's first type of prophetic call narrative, but not restricted to it.[70]

Like the prophetic call narratives, Enoch's commission is preserved in a book. It functions as the divine authorization for his message of reprimand to the Watchers.

In sum, authors in the Enochic tradition had both priestly and prophetic roles in mind when they called Enoch a scribe. In the body of testamentary literature, the virtues of the father are presented as models for the descendants. Therefore, it is safe to assume that Enochic authors were themselves scribes who patterned their roles on the biography of Enoch. The Enochic scribes claim to know the righteous and true interpretation of Torah and they reprimand, with prophet-like authority, those who violate this interpretation.

The true mystery revealed to Enoch includes not only what he heard before the divine throne but also what he learned about the places of heaven. Enoch's book of truth and reprimand was expanded to include chapters 17-19. These chapters contain visionary journey traditions that the reader has been led to expect. The introductory address in *1 Enoch* 1:2 summarized the present work as a "vision of the Holy One *and of heaven.*" Indeed, the vision of the Holy One (*1 En* 14) itself presupposed not only an ascent but a heavenly journey. This is indicated by the verbs of motion in chapter 14 and by the fact that

---

[69] The parallels between *1 En* 14-16 and Ezek 1-2 were brought together by Jansen (*Die Henochgestalt*, 114-17). Cf. Johannes Munck, *Paul and the Salvation of Mankind* (Atlanta: John Knox, 1959) 31-32. For the additional argument that *1 En* 14-16 represents an assimilation of Ezek 40-48 into Ezek 1-2, see Nickelsburg, "Enoch, Levi, and Peter," 576-82. A thorough description of the Book of the Watchers' indebtedness to Ezekiel can be found in Himmelfarb, *Ascent to Heaven*, 9-20, 72-74.

[70] Cf. Isaiah's cry, "Woe is me!" (Isa 6:5) and Ezekiel's prostrate position (Ezek 1:28). In the context of Enoch's vision, his trembling before the throne (*1 En* 14:24) is the recurrence of reactions he had as he made his way through the heavenly temple (*1 En* 14:9, 13-14). This reaction is indicative of his subjective involvement in the vision, a pointer to later Jewish texts of Merkavah mysticism (cf. Nickelsburg, "Enoch, Levi, and Peter," 580).

1 Enoch 14:25 refers to an accompanying angel who is conducting Enoch on his tour to the throne.   In addition, *1 Enoch* 17:1 begins abruptly with accompanying angels who are transporting Enoch, an image that seems related to 14:25.[71]

The completion of Enoch's first journey brings a satisfying resolution to the narrative in chapters 6-16.   At the end of this journey, Enoch sees the place where the rebel Watchers are held and punished until the day of the great judgment (*1 En* 18:6-19:2).   The creation is prepared for the future judgment.[72]   The vision form of the scene appears disjointed as compared to its doublet at the beginning of the second journey.[73]   In addition, the angel Uriel interprets the scene as the place of punishment for errant stars and rebellious angels.   This is striking because, to this point, the reader has learned only about rebel Watchers, nothing about stars that have gone astray.   The reference to stars presupposes the existence of an astronomical Torah among the heavenly mysteries revealed to Enoch.

The account of the first journey concludes with a statement that underscores Enoch's unique revelatory role.   The vocabulary of the statement ("Enoch," "saw," "visions") alludes to the introductory piece in *1 Enoch* 1:2, forming a nice *inclusio* at one stage of the redaction:[74]

1 En 19:3   And I, *Enoch*, alone *saw* the *visions*, the ends of all things.
          And no one of men has seen as I *saw*.

The emphasis here on Enoch's singular role as seer is not necessarily intended to contrast him with foreign culture heroes.[75]   Rather, the accent on the uniqueness of Enoch and his visions may explain why the bearers of Enochic traditions have privileged revelation apart from other groups within Judaism (cf. Dan 10:7; 4 Ezra 7:44; 12:36; 13:53).

---

[71] See Newsom, "The Development," 322.

[72] Cf. *T. Levi* 2:3-6:2.   Levi passed through three heavens, which an angel interpreted as ready for the day of judgment, and then arrived at the Lord sitting on this throne.   After this event, Levi was returned to the earth and commissioned by the angel to execute vengeance on Shechem for the sake of Dinah.   Enoch's first journey began with a vision of the Lord on his throne and a divine commission to pronounce judgment on the rebel Watchers (*1 En* 14:8-16:4).   The journey continued to the western reaches of the upper cosmos where Enoch saw, in effect, that heaven is ready for the day of judgment (18:6-19:2).

[73] For details, see Chap. 3, pp. 120-22.

[74] Nickelsburg, *Jewish Literature*, 54.

[75] Scholars have pointed to a parallel passage in the Epic of Gilgamesh (Newsom, "The Development," 326; VanderKam, *Enoch and the Growth*, 137).

Second Journey Report

The literary scheme of the seven vision traditions of the Second Journey (*1 En* 20-32 + 81:1-4) is reviewed in the Excursus.[76] It is our present task to investigate the one vision of this journey that bears directly on our theme of revelation.

Tree of Wisdom (1 Enoch 28-32).   The sixth vision of Enoch's Second Journey takes the following form:[77]

i.	Scene	28:1-32:3a
ii.	Description: Verb of Seeing	32:3b-4
iii.	Dialogue	
	Type I a)	32:5
	b)	32:6
iv.	Blessing	----

In the Description of the place at which Enoch has arrived, the verb "I saw" is used in *1 Enoch* 32:3b to relate two features about this locale. First, Enoch saw large and beautiful trees in the Garden of God and, among them, the Tree of Wisdom from which some persons or angels are eating. Second, Enoch saw in detail the unique characteristics of the Tree of Wisdom.[78]

The motif of a tall and beautiful tree in the Garden of God, which the other trees in the Garden cannot rival, comes from the ancient mythological concept of the world tree.[79] In *1 Enoch* 32, the position of the world tree is occupied by the Tree of Wisdom. This tree is later identified by the angel as the tree from which Adam and Eve ate; that is, the Tree of the Knowledge of Good and Evil (Gen 2-3). But, not only does this vision superimpose two

---

[76] Cf. *T. Levi* 8:1-19. In his second vision, Levi sees seven angels, each of whom clothes him with a different vestment of the priesthood. On this basis, Levi receives instructions related to the performance of his priestly duties (chaps. 9, 11-12).

[77] On the vision form, see Marie-Theres Wacker, *Weltordnung und Gericht: Studien zu 1 Henoch 22* (Würzburg: Echter, 1982) 101; and the Excursus. *1 En* 28:1-32:3a contains sight-seeing traditions about aromatic trees. It falls into the category of creation material and is discussed in Chap. 3, p. 119.

[78] Our analysis of the description of the Tree of Wisdom can be found in the comparative section at the end of Part I, pp. 93-94.

[79] See Ezek 31 and W. Zimmerli, *Ezekiel 2* (Hermeneia; Philadelphia: Fortress, 1983) 145-48.

myths about the large and beautiful tree in the Garden of God, it adds an entirely new feature to the biblical myth. This new feature takes us to the heart of the Enochic conception of revelation.

The added feature involves the act of consumption that Enoch witnessed at the Tree of Wisdom. There is a textual problem in *1 En* 32:3b, but we translate as follows:[80]

> *1 En* 32:3b   and I saw ... the Tree of Wisdom, whose fruit
>   < the holy ones > eat and learn great wisdom.

Enoch saw an activity that explained the origin of angelic knowledge and, thus, the source of the angelic interpretations he has received of the places on his journey. The holy ones have access to the Tree of Wisdom and, by eating from it,[81] they "learn great wisdom" and communicate this to Enoch. The content of the "great wisdom," then, is the angelic explanations of the other visions.[82]

The vision form continues with a Dialogue: an expression of astonishment by Enoch (*1 En* 32:5) and the angel Gabriel's interpretation (*1 En* 32:6). The latter reads as follows:

> *1 En* 32:6   "This is the Tree of Wisdom from which your father of old and
>   your mother of old, who were before you, ate and learned
>   wisdom. And their eyes were opened, and they knew that
>   they were naked, and they were driven from the garden."

The assumption here is that the Tree of Wisdom continues to function in a way that is analogous to the Genesis story. Two new factors, however, must

---

[80] The Greek is: καὶ ἴδον ... τὸ δένδρον τῆς φρονήσεως οὗ ἐσθίουσιν ἁγίου τοῦ καρποῦ αὐτοῦ καὶ ἐπίστανται φρόνησιν μεγάλην. The Ethiopic contains no word for "holy." The Aramaic is too fragmentary to read. The verb "they eat" is in the present tense and seems to imply the angels. Thus, ἁγίου may very well be a misreading for ἅγιοι. The alternative is to view the verb as an historical present and the plural number as a reference to Adam and Eve.

[81] Perhaps the tradition reads the words of the snake to Eve in Gen 3:5, "when you eat of it ... you will be like *'elohim*", as implying that the *'elohim* are angelic beings who eat from the Tree. This possibility is consistent with the idea that transgression originated with the angels and thus makes the Garden story's version of how evil entered the world less problematic for the Enochic tradition. For a different view, see Himmelfarb, *Ascent to Heaven*, 74.

[82] This "great wisdom" involves matters of cosmology (see Chap. 3) and judgment (see Chap. 5).

be taken into account; first, the inaccessibility of the Tree, and second, the specific content of the knowledge derived from it.

The Tree of Wisdom has become inaccessible to human beings. There is a dearth of wisdom upon the earth. However, the Tree still functions in the upper eastern extremity of the cosmos and Enoch can retrieve its wisdom. Adam and Eve "learned wisdom" (cf. Gen 3:6) by eating directly from the Tree themselves. This was possible because they lived in its environment: the Garden. Enoch, however, must journey to the Garden and he is not portrayed as eating directly from the Tree. Enoch is given "great wisdom" through the mediation of interpreting angels. Still, the Tree remains the source of revelation. God has preserved it and given Enoch special access to it.

Second, the content of Enoch's wisdom is unique by comparison to the Genesis myth. Adam and Eve were given a sexual awareness; Enoch receives knowledge about the places he visits on his cosmic journey. Through the interpreting role of angels, Enoch's eyes too are opened, as were the eyes of Adam and Eve (cf. *1 En* 1:5; 32:6).

Consistent with the interpretation of the Tree of Wisdom offered above, the blessing appended to the end of the Book of the Watchers is addressed to God who "show(ed) his *great* deeds *to his angels* and to the spirits of men" (*1 En* 36:4). The revelatory process starts with the role given to the angels (cf. Dan 9:22). Of course, Enoch is the first human spirit to be shown these things. Through the revealed wisdom that Enoch leaves as his testament, the heavenly mysteries of God's great deeds throughout the cosmos have been passed to the Enochic community.

The introductory chapters of *1 Enoch* prepared us to recognize that the distant generation will be "given wisdom" (*1 En* 5:8). The bearers of Enochic traditions view themselves as this generation. Enoch learned the "great wisdom" communicated to him by the angels, wrote it in books of wisdom, and passed it on to his children and the distant generation. As noted earlier, the author of the closing passage of Enoch's testament, *1 Enoch* 82, uses the wisdom theme to form an *inclusio* to the opening passage. *1 Enoch* 82 also draws on the imagery of Enoch's vision of the Tree of Wisdom:

1 En 32:3b   < the holy ones > *eat* and *learn great wisdom*
    32:6   your father of old and your mother of old *ate* and *learned wisdom*

1 En 82:3   and they will incline their ears to *learn* this *wisdom,*
          and it will be better for those who *eat* than good food.

The language of inclining the ears is used by sages to introduce wisdom instruction (Prov 4:20). The metaphor of eating, which occurs within a "better" proverb, is a traditional metaphor for learning wisdom. But in the context of *1 Enoch* 82:1-3, the reference to eating recalls for the reader the scene in chapter 32. Moreover, the wisdom learned in *1 Enoch* 82:3 is "this wisdom," namely, "this wisdom which surpasses their thought" (*1 En* 82:2c). That is, Enoch transmits a great wisdom that transcends human thought. This wisdom was first imparted to him by angels who had access to the Tree of Wisdom. The righteous can symbolically "eat" or "learn" this wisdom through Enoch's books, the testament he has left for the generations of eternity (*1 En* 82:1). It seems reasonable to conclude that Enoch's books of wisdom were taught in a setting of oral instruction.

Summary

The Book of the Watchers displays elements typical of testamentary literature (opening, body, closing). Like many other testaments, the Book of the Watchers uses the vocabulary and motifs of wisdom. However, in *1 Enoch*, wisdom is always the *revealed* wisdom that Enoch brings from heaven. This wisdom is life-giving in the sense that it guarantees salvation in the last judgment.

A NARRATIVE BRIDGE TO THE EPISTLE

1 Enoch 91:1-10, 18-19

In terms of the redactional history of *1 Enoch*, this passage is a bridge from the end of the Book of the Watchers (81:5-82:3) to the Epistle (chaps 92-105). It is common to regard chapter 91 as a kind of preface to the Epistle. Kolenkow, for example, treats *1 Enoch* 91-94 as a literary unit, a blessing-revelation testament. Indeed, *1 Enoch* 91:1, in which Enoch summons his children, reads like the opening passage of a testament. However, *1 Enoch* 91 actually recreates the closing scene from the end of the Book of the Watchers. Enoch calls his children together (91:1-2) and issues two exhortations (91:3-10, 18-19).[83]

The author who created the summons in chapter 91 was very perceptive in building on the original scene in *1 Enoch* 81:5-6. When Enoch was returned to his house and commissioned by the angels, he was told to impart revelation to his son Methuselah and all his (Enoch's) children (81:5-6). But

---

[83] The first exhortation has a motive clause that consists of a prediction of the future (91:5-9). See Chap. 5, pp. 178-79.

in the fulfillment passage of *1 Enoch* 82:1-3, the children are portrayed as a line of descendants reaching from Methuselah to the distant generation. This minor incongruity between the original commission and fulfillment scenes is corrected in the bridge passage. In *1 Enoch* 91:1, Enoch asks Methuselah to call his brothers and all the children of his mother. Thus, an additional fulfillment scene has been created that conforms more closely to the specific requirements of the commission in 81:5-6.

The verb "show" was used in the original commission scene and this verb also occupies a major place in *1 Enoch* 91. In addition, the author of the bridge passage supplies the one verb from the original commission that was not taken up in the original fulfillment scene in 82:1-3, viz., "to testify."

Original Commission Scene	Bridge Fulfillment Scene
81:5 Make known (*'ayde'a*) to Methuselah and show (*'ar'aya*) all your children	91:1f that I may show (*'ar'aya*) you
81:6 testify (*'asme'a*) to all your children	91:3d for I will testify (*'asme'a*) to you
	91:5a For I know (*'a'mara*) that
	91:18a And now I tell (*behla*) you b and show (*'ar'aya*) you c I will show (*'ar'aya*) you them again, that you may know (*'a'mara*) what is coming

Enoch, then, is once again put in the posture of transmitting his testament, this time as a testimony to all his children.[84] Before he does this, however, he explains his authorization:

1 En   91:1d   For a voice calls me,
         e   and a spirit has been poured out over me,
         f   so that I may show you everything that will happen to
                   you forever.

The image of a "voice" that "calls" reflects *1 Enoch* 14:24-15:2. After Enoch ascended to the divine throne, he related that "the Lord called me with

---

[84] The parallels with Deut 31 were noted by Nickelsburg (*Jewish Literature*, 151). God commissioned Moses to write and teach a song that would serve as a witness to God.

his mouth" (14:24). Enoch was then exhorted by God "to hear my voice" (15:1). The divine voice commissioned him with a message of judgment on the rebel Watchers (15:2). In *1 Enoch* 91:1, this imagery from the older divine commission is reused to lend authority to the exhortations of this chapter and, ultimately, to the Epistle that will follow. The new element in 91:1 is the reference to the outpouring of a spirit. It identifies Enoch as a prophet-like figure;[85] an identification that also recalls *1 Enoch* 14-16, chapters that displayed elements of the prophetic commissioning scene.

It is not only the case that the summons in *1 Enoch* 91:1-2 looks back to chapters 81-82 (the angelic commission) and chapters 14-15 (the divine commission),[86] the exhortations that follow, while quite general in nature, also recall material from the Book of the Watchers. The content of the exhortations may be approached through a consideration of their structure.

The literary form of the two exhortations in *1 Enoch* 91:3b-10 and 91:18-19 has three basic parts: the opening to instruction, the exhortation proper based on a two-ways theology typical of wisdom, and a concluding motive clause. The structure can be illustrated as follows:[87]

---

[85] The spirit is "put upon" (שׂים על, Num 11:17; נתן על, Num 11:25), "rests upon" (נוח על, Num 11:25) and "comes upon" (היה על, Num 24:2) those who prophesy. The expression "poured out upon" is found in eschatological contexts in which the spirit is promised to all Israel (יצק על, Isa 44:3; שׁפך על Ezek 39:29; Joel 2:28, 29 [Hb 3:1, 2]). *1 En* 91:1 implies that Enoch has a proleptic possession of the spirit of the end-time.

[86] Rau argues that *1 En* 91:1-10, 18-19 (indeed, the whole of *1 En* 91:1-94:5) also assumes the presence of the two dream-visions in chapters 83-90 (*Kosmologie*, 438-444). There are at least three aspects to his argument. 1) Enoch shows his children "everything that will come upon you forever" (*1 En* 91:1). This formula is picked up from *1 En* 90:41 and refers to the historical overview presented in the Animal Apocalypse. 2) The demand for attention in *1 En* 91:3 corresponds with *1 En* 85:2. 3) The expression "for I know that ..." (*1 En* 91:5; 94:5) represents an appeal to a vision. In particular, *1 En* 91:5-10, with its contrast between the first and second increase of evil, assumes the sequence of chapters 83-84 and 85-90.

We do not find these arguments persuasive. The phenomena Rau calls attention to in 1) and 3) can be accounted for if the author knows the Apocalypse of Weeks (*1 En* 93:1-10; 91:11-17). The force of 2) is mitigated by the fact that the demand for attention in *1 En* 91:3 is a stereotypical form for the introduction of wisdom instruction (cf. Prov 4:1, 20; 5:1; 7:24). Moreover, if *1 En* 85:2 is a framing passage that helps incorporate the Animal Apocalypse in its present location, the influence may very well have gone the other way (from 91:3 to 85:2). But again, the form is too fixed and common within wisdom traditions to prove dependency in either direction.

[87] Cf. *1 En* 94:1-5. On the two basic types of exhortation found throughout the Epistle, see Nickelsburg, "The Apocalyptic Message," 312.

1 En 91:3b-10		*1 En* 91:18-19	
Opening:			
3b-d	Hear, O sons of Enoch	18a-c	And now I tell you, my children
			and I show you the paths ...
		19a	And now hear me, my children
Exhortation:			
3e	Love the truth and	b	Walk in the paths of
	walk in it		righteousness
4a-b	and do not ...	c	and do not walk in the paths
c	But walk in righteousness		of violence
d	... in the paths of goodness		
Motive:			
5-10	For I know that ...	d-e	for they will perish forever ...

There are differences between the two units. First, the motive clause in the first exhortation is itself the introduction to an extensive piece that is an apocalypse in its own right (verses 5-10).[88] Second, the exhortation in 91:18-19 uses a double opening formula. Beyond these variations, the vocabulary of the two exhortations, particularly the terms that summarize the content of Enoch's testament, are similar and are drawn from the Book of the Watchers.

The terms used for the revealed wisdom in Enoch's testament include "truth" (91:3e, 4a), "righteousness" (91:4c, 4e, 18b, 19b; cf. 81:7b) and "goodness" (91:4d). This vocabulary recalls Enoch's earlier description as a scribe of righteousness and truth (*1 En* 12:4; 15:1) and the "Book of the words of truth ..." (14:1) that he wrote about his ascent to God's throne and his commission to pronounce judgment on the Watchers. The Book of the Watchers and the testimony derived from it (the Epistle) is the path of wisdom in which Enoch's children are to walk.

In contrast, the paths of violence and iniquity are to be avoided. If the way of righteousness and truth refers to the true mysteries revealed by Enoch, it follows that the way of violence and iniquity is analogous to the forbidden mysteries revealed by the rebel Watchers (the analogy is worked out in 91:5-10).

---

[88] It has been dubbed the "Methuselah" Apocalypse by VanderKam, *Enoch and the Growth*, 170.

THE EPISTLE OF ENOCH

The testamentary features of the Epistle, particularly in its opening chapters (*1 En* 92-94), were noted by Kolenkow.[89] These opening chapters may be divided into four sections and three of them—the superscription and introduction (92:1-5), the Apocalypse of Weeks (93:1-10; 91:11-17) and the two-ways instruction (94:1-5)—place Enoch in the posture of fulfilling the angelic commission, as he had done in 82:1-3.[90] The remainder of the Epistle (94:6-105:2) will occupy our attention insofar as the author applies wisdom vocabulary to himself and his opponents.

1 Enoch 92:1-5

In the commissioning scene that concluded the Book of the Watchers, Enoch was charged to write for his sons (*1 En* 81:6). Enoch carried out this command (82:1b) with the result that books of wisdom (82:1d) were given to Methuselah, books that were to be handed down to the generations of eternity. The superscription of the Epistle hearkens back to this scene.

1 Enoch 92:1 begins abruptly "That which was written by Enoch the scribe ...". The writing itself, which may be called an "Epistle,"[91] is addressed "to all my sons who will dwell upon the earth, and to the last generations who will observe truth and peace" (92:1). The stress falls on the "last generations."[92] The author of the Epistle, writing in the name of Enoch, addresses an audience that he believes is living in the end-time.

Like 82:1-2, which identified Enoch's books with wisdom, the superscription describes Enoch's writing as "this complete sign of wisdom."[93] Moreover, the wisdom envisaged in both passages is salvific and, therefore, those

---

[89] "The Genre Testament," 61-62. For the delimitation of the Epistle of Enoch, see Nickelsburg, "The Apocalyptic Message," 309, n. 2.

[90] Only the fragment preserved in *1 En* 93:11-14 does not reuse vocabulary from the commissioning scene. This passage is treated in Chap. 3, pp. 124-27.

[91] The term "Epistle" is appropriate because this is the self-designation employed in *1 En* 100:6.

[92] This is the case, even if we adopt the longer reading reconstructed by Milik on the basis of 4QEn^g 1 ii 22-24. This longer reading may mention Methuselah and his brothers, along with their descendants. In any event, the Aramaic does preserve the expression "to the last generations" (ולדריא אחריא[ו]). See Milik, *The Books of Enoch*, 260.

[93] See the Introduction, p. 11. If the reconstruction of the Aramaic by Milik is correct (*The Books of Enoch*, 260-62), then the superscription draws Enoch into the circle of the wise by describing him as "the wisest of men" (אנושא כים[וח]). See also VanderKam, *Enoch and the Growth*, 173-74.

who possess it are portrayed in much the same way. In 82:3a, those who understand the wisdom of Enoch will not sleep. The same motif appears within the introductory address (92:2-5) following the Epistle's superscription:[94]

1 En 92:3a-b   And the righteous one will arise from sleep,
                  he will arise and walk in the paths of righteousness.

In short, the Epistle's superscription and introduction stress that the righteous, living in the last days, can be assured that the wisdom revealed by Enoch will deliver them from their troubles, even if ultimate deliverance comes only by way of resurrection.

1 Enoch 93:1-10; 91:11-17

Kolenkow noted that the Apocalypse of Weeks supplies the typical testamentary element of the forecast of the future.[95] The periodized history of good and evil times and the prediction of future bliss for the righteous are explicitly based on what Enoch read from the heavenly tablets (cf. 81:1-2):

1 En 93:2g   I, Enoch, I have been shown [everything in a heavenly
                   vision,
         h   and from] the word of the Watchers and Holy Ones I have
                   known everything;
         i   [and in the heavenly tablets I] have read everything [and
                   understoo]d.[96]

The parallels between this passage and *1 Enoch* 1:2-3b, have been noted by scholars.[97] Both passages are introductory verses that refer to the vision of heaven and the role of interpreting angels. In addition, the opening lines of the introduction and the body of the Apocalypse begin with the expression "Enoch

---

[94] It is based on the Remiel tradition. See the Excursus.

[95] Kolenkow, "The Genre Testament," 60-61. We will not enter into the question of the textual evolution of the Apocalypse. For a critical response to the complicated theory of Ferdinand Dexinger (*Henochs Zehnwochenapokalypse und offene Probleme der Apokalyptikforschung* [SPB 29; Leiden: Brill, 1977], see James C. VanderKam, "Studies in the Apocalypse of Weeks (*1 Enoch* 93:1-10; 91:11-17)," *CBQ* 46 (1984) 513-18.

[96] Translation by Milik, *The Books of Enoch*, 264. The Ethiopic is substantially the same, except that it lacks the three occurrences of "everything." Cf. VanderKam, *Enoch and the Growth*, 150-51.

[97] Rau, *Kosmologie*, 350-51; VanderKam, *Enoch and the Growth*, 153.

took up his discourse" (93:1a, 3a),[98] an obvious allusion to 1:2a and 1:3b. In both contexts, the parable or discourse has reference to a previously hidden mystery about to be revealed.

There is one major difference, however, between the opening passage of the Book of the Watchers and the introduction to the Apocalypse of Weeks. In *1 Enoch* 1:2, the verb "to understand" applied collectively to what Enoch saw in the vision and heard explained by the angels. However, in 93:2, the same verb is used in conjunction with "to read" and has as its object the heavenly tablets. The heavenly tablets are not mentioned in 1:2.[99]

This difference can be accounted for if the introduction to the Apocalypse is incorporating vocabulary from *1 Enoch* 81:1-2. In the final vision of the Second Journey, Enoch carried out the angelic command to see, read and understand the tablets of heaven. As that scene gave support to what Enoch went on to say about the book of iniquity and the fate of the righteous dead, so the reference in 93:2 lends authority to the historical Apocalypse that follows.

Two further points relate the Apocalypse of Weeks to the commission and fulfilment scenes that originally concluded the Book of the Watchers (81:5-82:3).

First, the introduction to the Apocalypse incorporates lines that put Enoch in the position of carrying out what was commanded to him by the angels:

1 En   93:2d   these things I tell (*behla*) you
         e   and I make known (*'ayde'a*) to you, my children,
         f   I myself, Enoch.

The verb "to make known" was used when the seven angels commissioned Enoch (81:5; cf. 81:7) and is employed here with "to tell" to indicate yet another fulfillment of that commission (cf. 91:18, "And now I tell you and show you").

Along these same lines, the Apocalypse of Weeks, while ostensibly addressed to "my children," is aimed at the generations of eternity, as in the original fulfillment scene (82:2). In 93:2a-c, the target audience is called the "sons of righteousness," "the chosen ones of eternity" and "the plant of truth." These descriptive names allude to passages in the Book of the Watchers (e.g., 1:1; 10:16) and to a cast of characters present later in the Apocalypse itself; namely, those at the end of the seventh week, the very

---

[98] The Ethiopic reference to "books" in these two verses is secondary. The Aramaic is fully preserved in 4QEnᵍ I iii 23: נסב חנוך מתלה ("Enoch took up his discourse").

[99] Rau contends that this difference is somehow related to the stress placed on the throne vision in *1 En* 1:2 (*Kosmologie*, 151).

beginning of the eschatological scenario.[100] Thus, what Enoch makes known is intended especially for the last generation.

Second, the content of Enoch's revelation is equated with wisdom. This was the case in 82:1-3 (cf. 5:8; 32:3-6; 92:1) and is again in the eschatological context of 93:10. The righteous generation living at the end of the seventh week, that is, the author and his community in the beginning of the end-time, receive the gift of wisdom:

> *1 En* 93:10   And with its end] there shall be chosen the elect,
>   for witnesses to righteousness from the eternal plant of
>   righteousness,
>   [to whom] shall be given sevenfold wisdom and knowledge.[101]

In the Enochic corpus, the expression "to give/be given wisdom" (here in conjunction with knowledge: חכמה ומדע תתיה]ב) is a technical term for the reception of revelation. The adjective "sevenfold" may symbolize the completeness of the revelation or may even be an allusion to the seven visions of Enoch's Second Journey (*1 En* 20-32 + 81:1-4). This revelation not only secures safety in the judgment, it qualifies the elect to play a decisive role in it (91:11-17).

1 Enoch 94:1-5

This passage is another general exhortation to righteousness that uses two-ways theology (cf. 91:3-4, 18-19; 92:2-5). However, a feature that was just below the surface in other passages emerges more clearly here. The author warns against opponents of Enoch's revealed wisdom.

The passage is divisible into two sections, each of which opens with language that alludes to the testamentary setting: "And now I tell you, my sons/O righteous" (94:1a[102]/94:3a; cf. 91:18a; 93:2d). Furthermore, there are key terms and motifs in both sections that derive from the original fulfillment scene in 82:1-3.

In the first unit, the expression of two-ways theology in 94:1 is expanded by 94:2 to explain how it is that the righteous of the end-time can avoid the paths of iniquity:

---

[100] Nickelsburg, "The Apocalyptic Message," 315.

[101] Text and translation in Milik, *The Books of Enoch*, 265-66. See also Nickelsburg, "Revealed Wisdom," 75.

[102] This line is extant in Aramaic (Milik, *The Books of Enoch*, 270).

1 En 94:2   And to certain men of a generation the paths of violence and
                  death *will be revealed (kašata)*;
                  and they will keep away from them
                  and they will not follow them.

This verse was probably reformulated in the bridge passage in *1 Enoch* 91:18
("I *show* you the paths of righteousness *and the paths of violence*"). In any
case, the verb used in 94:2 (*kašata*) ties this unit to the original fulfillment
scene in 82:1: "I *have revealed* everything to you." The totality of Enochic
revelation means that the way of iniquity and violence is included within its
purview (cf. 81:5d; 104:10).

The second section in 94:3-5 also includes the theme that Enoch
knows what sinners will do:

1 En 94:5a   Hold fast in the thought of your heart,
         b   and do not erase my word from your heart.
         c   *For I know that* sinners will tempt men to make wisdom bad;
         d   and no place will be found for her,
         e   and none of the temptation will diminish.

As in the first unit, 82:1-3 lies in the background here. The exhortation
"hold fast (*'axaza*) ... and do not erase (*damsasa*)[103] my word" (94:5a-b)
corresponds to Enoch's charge to Methuselah in the original fulfillment
scene: "Keep (*'aqaba*) ... the books from the hand of your father"
(82:1).[104] Moreover, just as these books were equated with wisdom in
82:2, the same key term reappears in the present passage. In 94:5c, sinners tempt men to make wisdom "evil" (*'ekuy*). In view is a perversion of
wisdom by the opponents. From the standpoint of the author, this perversion is thorough (94:5d)[105] and persistent (94:5e).

The situation behind the two exhortations in *1 Enoch* 94:1-5 must be
one of great urgency and threat to the author's community. Is he losing
students to other wisdom teachers? At the very least, those whom the
author labels "sinners" who pervert wisdom are persons who offer a significant challenge to Enochic tradition. The author is claiming that Enoch
foresaw the challenge, revealed the content of what the sinners would teach

---

[103] Dillmann, *Lexicon*, 1089.

[104] On the parallels between *1 En* 94:5a-b, Prov 4:4-5 and Tob 4:19, see George W. E.
Nickelsburg, "Tobit and Enoch: Distant Cousins With a Recognizable Resemblance,"
SBLSP (1988) 63-64.

[105] The disappearance of wisdom may allude to the wisdom myth in *1 En* 42 (cf. 4 Ezra
5:9-10).

and warned about the consequences of following it. He urges his readers
to avoid the way that leads to death and choose righteousness and an elect
life so that they may live (94:4).[106]

1 Enoch 94:6-105:2

The elements of the genre testament become rather fuzzy in the major
addresses of the Epistle. Kolenkow apparently viewed these chapters as an
extension of the exhortatory element (with the inclusion of woes).[107] Nickelsburg has shown that the basic forms of the woe-oracle, exhortation and
description of the judgment have been altered through combinations with
explicit revelatory formulas,[108] a fact that comports well with the notion of
a blessing-revelation testament. Those revelatory formulas that contain the
verb "know" are worthy of further scrutiny. Following this task, a summary is offered of the wisdom vocabulary the author uses to portray himself and his opponents.

A quick review of how the verb "know" has been used to this point is
in order. "Know" was the leading verb in the angelic commission Enoch
received after his Second Journey ("Make known everything to Methuselah
your son," 81:5). While the fulfillment scene in 82:1-3 did not take up this
specific verb, later attempts to build on the scene did employ it (91:5, 18;
93:2; 94:5). In short, the verb "to know" has always applied to the
heavenly mysteries that Enoch revealed to his children (cf. *T. Levi* 4:1).[109]

There is a striking difference in the application of the verb "to know"
in *1 Enoch* 94:6-105:2. In the latter part of the Epistle, virtually every
occurrence of the active or passive imperative of the verb "to know" is
directed at sinners,[110] a group that is hardly within the purview of Enoch's
testament. Or is it? Kolenkow suggested that the genre testament was
apologetic literature.[111] A closer examination of the verses that contain the
revelatory formula "know" directed to sinners will aid in testing the
validity of this suggestion.

---

[106] For the idea of choosing in the context of the closing passage of a testament, cf. *T. Levi* 19:1-2.

[107] Kolenkow, "The Genre Testament," 62.

[108] "The Apocalyptic Message," 310-22.

[109] Nickelsburg, "The Apocalyptic Message," 315-16.

[110] The only exception is the exhortation to the righteous in *1 En* 97:2: "*Be it known* to you that ...".

[111] Kolenkow, "The Genre Testament," 64-70.

The following table contains the examples of the formula, along with an indication of the content and literary context associated with each:

TABLE 1
THE *KNOW*-FORMULA IN THE EPISTLE OF ENOCH

	Formula	Content	Context
1 En 94:10	Thus I say and *make known*	Creator will overturn and destroy	Woe-series
98:8	Henceforth, *know*	What is being written in heaven	Oath
98:10a	And now *know*	What is prepared	Woe-series
98:10b	[*Know*]	What is prepared	Woe-series
98:12	Now, *be it known*	Delivered into the hands of the righteous	Woe-series
100:10	And now *know*	What is searched out in heaven	*Rîb*
103:7	*Know* (cf. 103:2)	Distress in Sheol	Disputation

The *know*-formula is not an element of a single literary form. While it appears most often in the Woe-series (the first example is not an imperative, but is included because it is directed at sinners), it is also used in contexts of the Oath, *Rîb* and Disputation Speech. Common to all of these different literary contexts, however, is the basic content covered by the *know*-formula. The summaries of the content, provided above, indicate the essential point. The *know*-formula is used to exhort sinners concerning what Enoch learned on his cosmic journeys, as recorded in the Book of the Watchers; namely, that judgment has been decreed and places in creation have been made ready for it.

Perhaps the closest analogy to the Enochic *know*-formula is the messenger formula used in prophetic speech. The prophet, who has been made privy to the divine council, introduces his announcement of judgment with a *say*-formula: "Thus says the Lord."[112] According to David Aune,

---

[112] Claus Westermann, *Basic Forms of Prophetic Speech* (Philadelphia: Westminster, 1967) 149.

"The use of the messenger formula at the time the message is delivered has the effect of calling the recipients' attention to the earlier commissioning of the messenger by the sender of the message."[113] The same effect holds for the Enochic *know*-formula; it recalls the commission issued in *1 Enoch* 81:5. Enoch toured the upper reaches of the earth and was commissioned to impart esoteric knowledge. He does so with the *know*-formula, which may be characterized as a heavenly-messenger formula.

Because the sender of the message lies behind this formula, there may be some hope, however slight, that the recipients will heed the message and repent. It is true that polemic aimed at sinners has an indirect effect on the righteous as well; that is, a message of judgment on sinners is a comfort to the righteous. Still, one should not be too hasty and exclude the possibility that the *know*-formula is intended to bring about a change of heart in sinners, so that, for example, they will seek and choose for themselves righteousness and an elect life (*1 En* 94:4a). Such a view accords with Kolenkow's suggestion that blessing-revelation testaments contain implicit invitations for outsiders to choose between good and evil and join the righteous community.[114]

Our treatment of the revelation theme in the Epistle concludes with a review of how the author portrays himself and his opponents with the language of wisdom. Nickelsburg pointed out that this portrayal occurs almost exclusively in three passages: 98:9-99:10; the Apocalypse of Weeks (93:10 and 91:11); and 104:9-105:2.[115] The following is a synthesis of the major points of Nickelsburg's analysis.

1) The author belongs to a circle of the wise who "are teachers or preachers of some sort."[116] This circle is in conflict with individuals called fools, who not only do not listen to the wise (98:9), but also annul or teach others to disregard the words of the wise (98:14).[117] Thus, the setting reflected in the Epistle is one in which teachers of the revealed wisdom of Enoch face a serious challenge from other teachers.

---

[113] David E. Aune, *Prophecy in Early Christianity and the Ancient Mediterranean World* (Grand Rapids: Eerdmans, 1983) 89-90.

[114] Kolenkow, "The Genre Testament," 66-71.

[115] Nickelsburg, "The Epistle of Enoch and the Qumran Literature," *JJS* 33 (1982) 334-45.

[116] Ibid., 335.

[117] Nickelsburg states that "annul" (98:14) is "a legal technical term that denotes the nullification of a covenant or the disobeying or disregarding of laws and commandments" (ibid., 336).

2) The conflict between the wise and the fools involves "a written and not simply an oral phenomenon; the false teachers write down their lies."[118] This is clear from the Woe-oracle in *1 Enoch* 98:15 ("Woe to those who write lying words and words of error"). The fact that the challengers of Enoch's books of wisdom have a written corpus of their own suggests the existence of other wisdom books. The central issue in *1 Enoch* and these competing wisdom books revolves around which group or tradition advocates the correct interpretation of the Torah: "the author and his opponents are locked in a dispute over the interpretation of the Torah."[119] Among the verses supporting this thesis is the Woe-oracle in *1 Enoch* 99:2, which characterizes the addressees as those "who alter the true words and pervert the eternal covenant and consider themselves to be without sin." Interestingly, the author must acknowledge that what he regards as an alteration and perversion of the Torah, his opponents themselves consider faithful interpretation. However, in typical polemical fashion, the author identifies the practices of his opponents with idolatry (*1 En* 99:6-9).[120]

3) In the last days, the wisdom of the wise will show itself superior to the teaching of the opponents. The wisdom books of Enoch guarantee salvation in the last days and enable the wise to triumph over their adversaries. This thought permeates the Woe-series in *1 Enoch* 98:9-99:10, and comes to expression in the decisive seventh week of the Apocalypse of Weeks, in which the sevenfold wisdom and knowledge given to the elect enables them to overcome oppressive practices and false teaching ("uproot the foundations of violence and the structure of deceit," *1 En* 91:11; cf. 99:12, 14).

It should not be assumed, however, that the anticipated victory is viewed solely in terms of the destruction of false teachers and practices. Rather, the author of the Epistle holds out the hope that some will come over to the side of Enochic wisdom in the triumph of the last days (*1 En* 100:6, cf. 91:14). This hope emerges in the conclusion to the Epistle, a passage in which the three points summarized above come together (*1 En* 104:9-105:2):[121]

---

[118] Ibid., 338. Nickelsburg offers a brief survey of the vocabulary of falsehood in early Jewish and Christian texts.

[119] Ibid.

[120] The same equation may be present in the Woe-oracle of *1 En* 99:1 (ibid., 339).

[121] For the issues of textual criticism that inform Nickelsburg's translation of *1 En* 104:9-105:2, see his "Enoch 97-104: A Study of the Greek and Ethiopic Texts," *Armenian and Biblical Studies* (ed. Michael E. Stone; Jerusalem: St. James, 1976) 103, 134-35.

104:9   Do not err in your hearts, nor lie,
        nor alter the words of truth,
        nor falsify the words of the Holy One,
        nor give praise to your errors.
      For it is not to righteousness that all your lies
        and all your error lead, but to great sin.

  10   And now I know this mystery,
        that sinners will alter and copy the words of truth,
        and pervert many and lie and invent great fabrications,
        and compose writings in their names.

  11   And would that they would write all my words in truth
        and neither remove nor alter these words,
        but write in truth all that I testify to them.

  12   And again I know a second mystery,
        that to the righteous and pious and wise my books will be
          given for the joy of righteousness and much wisdom;

  13   Yea, to them the books will be given,
        and they will believe in them,
        and in them all the righteous will rejoice and be glad,
        to learn from them all the paths of truth.

105:1   In those days, says the Lord, they will summon and testify
        against the sons of earth in their wisdom.
      Instruct them, for you are their leaders and ... rewards over
        all the earth.

   2   For I and my son will join ourselves with them forever in the
        paths of truth in their life.
      And you will have peace.
      Rejoice, O children of truth. Amen.

In this concluding passage, the form of the Woe-oracle has been dropped and sinners are exhorted to stop their errors and lies (104:9). The basis for this appeal is the two mysteries that have been revealed to Enoch (104:10-11, 12-13). In essence, these two mysteries are the paths of violence/death and the paths of righteousness/truth mentioned earlier in the Epistle (94:2, 5; cf. 91:3e-10, 18). The difference is that in 104:10-13 the two-ways theology is explicitly related to the production and transmission of two kinds of books. Sinners compose books of their own, filled with lies and fabrications, rather than copy the words of Enoch. The righteous, pious and wise, however, are given the books of Enoch (cf. 82:1-3) from which they learn all the paths of truth.

The confrontation of the ways of the lie and the truth, based on two kinds of books, is resolved in the last days in favor of the revealed wisdom of the books of Enoch. Thus, the passage ends with the prediction of a final testamentary-type scene. The wise "will summon and testify" (105:1;

cf. 81:6; 91:1-3) to "the sons of earth" (cf. 92:1). The next verse is broken (105:1c-d), but it is clear that the wise will experience some success in instructing the sons of earth in the revealed wisdom of Enoch. In short, "The wise speak where they can be heard, and they testify to the truth in the hope that their message will be heeded and met with repentance. The Epistle of Enoch is part of this message and testimony and appeal."[122]

This point confirms what was said above in connection with the *know*-formula. An important aspect of the triumph of the wisdom books of Enoch in the last days is the positive response of humankind. Kolenkow's thesis regarding the apologetic purpose of testamentary literature finds support in the Epistle of Enoch.

Summary

Our study of the theme of revealed wisdom in the Epistle has illustrated the foundational significance of the testamentary closing passage in the Book of the Watchers (81:5-82:3). Discrete sections of the Epistle allude to the commission given to Enoch by the angels and recreate a fulfillment scene (92:1; 93:1-2; 94:1, 3). Indeed, the Epistle as a whole must be viewed from this perspective (105:1-2). The bridge passage, which linked the Epistle to the Book of the Watchers, adopted the same stance (91:1-3, 18).

This approach by the author(s) of the Epistle serves to reinforce the notion that the words of Enoch are grounded in what he learned from his tour of the upper, unseen world and in the authority he received to reveal it to his children and the last generation. In the Epistle, this perspective is used to shed needed light on a controversy between teachers who possessed Enoch's books of revealed wisdom and teachers who possessed books that advocated another way. Enoch foresaw the controversy and addressed it in the strongest possible terms. Those who follow another way are fools and idolaters. They must abandon their lies or they will perish in the judgment of God. Only the wisdom books of Enoch, the Epistle now included, reveal the paths of righteousness and truth, paths that lead to eternal salvation.

---

[122] Nickelsburg, "The Epistle of Enoch," 345.

THE ASTRONOMICAL MATERIAL

In terms of the redactional history of *1 Enoch*, chapters 33-36 are a summary of astronomical and meteorological lore used to conclude the Book of the Watchers. Their position at the end of the Book of the Watchers filled a lacuna or perhaps even caused the displacement of the original conclusion (81:1-82:3). The Astronomical Book (chaps 72-82) is itself a summary of more extensive material. Brief comments will be made on these two texts as they relate to the theme of revelation.

1 Enoch 33-36

Chapter 33 is apparently a partial summary drawn from the Astronomical Book. The angel Uriel shows Enoch the gates of heaven through which the lights of heaven come out (33:2; cf. 72:3). Chapters 34-36 contain another vision of gates; in this instance, the gates through which the winds blow and bring meteorological phenomena to the earth. This tradition differs in significant details from the parallel in the Astronomical Book (*1 En* 76).

The astronomical and meteorological materials appended in chapters 33-36 conclude with a blessing formula that Wacker identified as a standard closing element in the vision form.[123] The formula in 36:4, however, is intended to close the entire Book of the Watchers. In this secondary conclusion, Enoch "blessed the Lord of Glory" who had acted "to show his great deeds to his angels and to the spirits of men" (36:4; cf. 1:2).

1 Enoch 72:1-80:1 (+ 82:4-20)

The Astronomical Book portrays Enoch as the father of astronomy.[124] Enoch's description of the regularity of the movements and changes of heavenly bodies may owe its ultimate origins to Mesopotamian astronomy,[125] but if so, this "Judaized refraction," as VanderKam calls it, is truly revolutionary in the sense that the observed regularity excludes any forecasting of future events.[126]

---

[123] *Weltordnung*, 101.

[124] VanderKam, *Enoch and the Growth*, 89-90.

[125] Ibid., 91-101.

[126] Even primitive astronomy underwent paradigm shifts. See Thomas S. Kuhn, *The Structure of Scientific Revolutions* (Second edition, Enlarged; Chicago: University of Chicago, 1970). This fact is noted by VanderKam, *Enoch and the Growth*, 103.

The make-up of the Astronomical Book has been newly assessed on the basis of the Aramaic manuscripts from Qumrân.[127] These manuscripts attest to a text that existed independently and was more primitive and expansive than chapters 72-80; 82:4-20.[128] The fragmentary nature of the Aramaic manuscripts prohibits the drawing of any firm conclusions on specific points. Still, in terms of the theme of revelation, two important facts seem to be confirmed by the Aramaic evidence.

First, the astronomical material is presented in the context of revelations imparted to Enoch by the angel Uriel,[129] and as such, presupposes a heavenly journey of the kind depicted in chapters 20-32 (+ 81:1-82:3). Rau has shown that the formulae used in the framing passages are secondary to the astronomical data they introduce or conclude. He has dubbed these passages "Uriel-notices"[130] and "vision-notices"[131] and argues, successfully, that they are interchangeable.

The initial Uriel-notice in the superscription (72:1) identifies Uriel as "the holy angel who was with me ...". This language reflects that used of the accompanying angel in the journey reports. However, in the Astronomical Book, there is no explicit reference to a journey nor is there a dialogue between Enoch and Uriel. Rather, the vision form of the journey traditions has apparently generated stereotypical expressions. These expressions are used at strategic points to present astronomical data as the subject of revelation. In the summary passage of *1 Enoch* 80:1, the Uriel-notice employs the verb "reveal" (*kašata*) in parallel with the verb "to show" (*'ar'aya*).

Second, within the Astronomical Book are found two "Methuselah-notices" (*1 En* 76:14; 79:1), which, it is logical to assume, presuppose an angelic commissioning scene in which Enoch is charged to transmit revela-

---

[127] See Milik, *The Books of Enoch*, 273-97.

[128] Presumably, the Greek translator, followed by the Ethiopic, condensed, deleted and rearranged text.

[129] If Milik's reconstruction of 4QEnastr^b 25 4 is correct, the Aramaic witnesses to the Uriel-notice in *1 En* 78:10 (*The Books of Enoch*, 293).

[130] There are nine Uriel-notices of the basic form: "Uriel *showed to me* [Enoch]" (*'ar'ayani*): *1 En* 72:1; 74:2; 75:3; 75:4; 78:10; 79:2; 79:6; 80:1; 82:7. The reference in 80:1 is unique because it is a first person address by Uriel.

[131] There are ten vision-notices of the form "*I saw*" (*re'iku*): *1 En* 72:3; 73:1; 74:1; 74:9; 75:6; 75:8; 76:1; 77:4; 77:5; 77:8.

tion to his son Methuselah.[132] Of course, such a scene is present in the
closing passage of the Book of the Watchers; a scene that employs the verb
"show" as in the "Methuselah-notices" (81:5-6).

The key point that emerges from the two facts touched on above is
that the astronomical traditions are included among Enoch's books of
revealed wisdom. It is stated at one point, for example, that Enoch gives
this astronomical testament to Methuselah in written form (*ṣaḥafa*, [twice]
74:2; cf. 33:3-4). Of course, the present text carries the self-designation
"the *book* (*maṣḥaf*) of the revolutions of the lights of heaven" (72:1).
These references appear to play off the angelic commission "to write"
(81:6); a commission Enoch fulfilled by producing and transmitting
"books" (82:1).

Summary

Among the books of Enoch's testament, then, are traditions that comprise an astronomical Torah (a Torah of the stars was presupposed in *1 En*
17-19). The redactional position of chapters 33-36 suggests that the
astronomical Torah was understood as a vision tradition of Enoch's Second
Journey. Along the same lines, the editor who summarized the extensive
material in the Astronomical Book left indications that he assumed both a
journey tradition in which this material was revealed to Enoch and a commissioning scene in which Enoch was authorized to transmit the data to
Methuselah. The authors/editors of *1 Enoch* 33-36 and 72:1-80:1 share
these perspectives with the author of the Epistle. The astronomical
material, too, is grounded in the cosmic journey of Enoch and is conveyed
with the authority of heaven.

---

[132] These notices take the form "*I [Enoch] have shown to you*, Methuselah" (*'ar'akuka*).
Again, if we accept Milik's reconstruction of 4QEnastr[b] 23 2 (*The Books of Enoch*, 289),
we have Aramaic attestation to the notice of *1 En* 76:14. There seems to be little doubt
about the presence of 79:1 in 4QEnastr[b] 26 6 (ibid., 294).

2. BEN SIRA'S BOOK OF WISDOM

Passages that convey ben Sira's concept of revelation will now be gathered and analyzed. A specific concept of *revealed* wisdom lies behind much of what ben Sira means by the term "wisdom." The survey will begin with the myth of the descent of personified Wisdom in Sirach 24. This myth gives rise to a number of passages that employ the literary form of the *Liebesgeschichte* or Love Story.[133] The form presupposes the myth and enables ben Sira to express some of the dynamics in his concept of revealed wisdom. For example, the Story elements of pursuing and acquiring a lover are often decoded by ben Sira in terms of the quest for wisdom under his tutelage. Because this is true, it is necessary to include a selection of passages that are autobiographical;[134] passages in which ben Sira speaks of his role as a sage without explicitly enlisting elements of the *Liebesgeschichte*.

THE MYTH OF THE DESCENT OF WISDOM

Sirach 24

Sirach 24 is a poem in which wisdom is personified and speaks in the first person. Wisdom recites her heavenly origin, her search for a dwelling place and her eventual residence in Israel. Ben Sira then writes a kind of commentary on Wisdom's speech. The entire poem displays a chiastic structure:

---

[133] It is used more extensively than was initially indicated by Baumgartner ("Die literarischen Gattungen," 189-90). He called attention to Sir 14:20-27; 51:13-21 and the parallel in Wis 8:1-18.

[134] Skehan and Di Lella, *The Wisdom of Ben Sira*, 28-29. This form is not as frequent in the Hebrew Bible. Perhaps the closest parallels are in Prov 4:3-9 and Qoh 1:12-2:26 (see Crenshaw, "Wisdom," 256-58).

Sir 24:   1-7   A   Wisdom: "I went forth" (ἐξῆλθον)
           8-12   She quotes the Creator (εἶπεν)
           13-17   B   Wisdom's Growth
                               (use of plant similes)
           19-22   C   Wisdom's Invitation
           23-29   B'   Wisdom is Torah
                               (use of water similes)
           30-33   A'   Ben Sira: "I went forth" (ἐξῆλθον)
                           He quotes himself (εἶπα)

Taken together, Sirach 24:1-7 and 8-12 describe the origin and career of Wisdom. The two pieces are packed with literary allusions and have been analyzed from many different perspectives.[135] After being spewed from God's mouth, Wisdom describes a two-stage career: she searches the cosmos and then she is sent to Israel. The imagery of the second stage does not appear to have been noticed by the commentators. Wisdom has returned to heaven and is praising herself in terms that assume a prior commissioning scene. The scene to which Wisdom alludes is roughly analogous to a type of prophetic call narrative reviewed above in connection with *1 Enoch* 14-16.[136]

The particular elements of prophetic call in the allusions of Wisdom's speech belong to the second type defined by Zimmerli.[137] This type displays a great deal of freedom, but some of the more stable elements include: a vision of the Lord sitting upon a throne, the presence of the heavenly host, a question regarding who can fulfill the task at hand, the various possibilities raised by the heavenly beings, the selection of a special agent who may, in turn, express his own inadequacy, and finally, the Lord's command to go and speak.

There is no vision of the Lord on the throne in Sirach 24, but the parallel passage in Sirach 1:1-10 does refer to the "One who is wise, greatly to be feared, sitting upon his throne" (Sir 1:8). It is surely this One around whom the hosts are assembled in chapter 24 (cf. Sir 42:17c-d) and from whose mouth Wisdom previously went forth (24:3).

The other elements of the call are freely reshaped on the basis that this commission was not received by a human agent, but by a heavenly being.

---

[135] We suggest in Chap. 4 that Sir 24:1-7 is in large part a reprise of motifs in Sir 1:1-10 (see pp. 154-55). Examples of various approaches to this material can be found in Gerald T. Shepherd, *Wisdom as a Hermeneutical Construct: A Study in the Sapientializing of the Old Testament* (BZAW 151; Berlin/New York: de Gruyter, 1980) 19-71.

[136] See above, pp. 29-30.

[137] Zimmerli, *Ezekiel 1*, 97-100.

There is no question related to the search for a candidate, Wisdom is the obvious choice; there is no allusion to humility or inadequacy, Wisdom is worthy of the call and recites her qualifications (her cosmic travels); nor is it necessary in the act of commissioning for the Most High to place his words in his agent's mouth, Wisdom has come from the mouth of the Most High and is, therefore, the word. The only question to be raised is where or to whom the agent is sent. Wisdom herself takes the initiative and raises this question: "In whose inheritance should I abide?" (Sir 24:7b).[138]

At this point, Wisdom received a direct command from the Creator: "In Jacob make your dwelling, in Israel your inheritance" (Sir 24:8c-d). After she obeyed this command, Wisdom came to understand she was predestined for this role in Israel. Like the prophet who traces his call to before the time he was fashioned in the womb (Jer 1:5; cf. Isa 49:5), Wisdom states that she was created before the ages (Sir 24:9).

Wisdom received a command to dwell in the tent (Sir 24:8a-b), later described as the "holy tent" (ἐν σκηνῇ ἁγίᾳ, 24:10a). This was the moveable tent of the wilderness experience of Israel. As this tent gave way to the permanent structure of the temple in Jerusalem, so Wisdom came to reside there (Sir 24:10b-11). Here she "took root" (Sir 24:12). This new metaphor anticipates the description to follow.[139]

As Wisdom continues her self-praise for obeying the divine commission, she describes herself as the Tree of Wisdom (B-C). This Tree is unlike any ordinary tree and is depicted as sharing the characteristics of several trees and flowers. The imagery recalls a garden setting, a major motif of the Love Story.[140] Furthermore, the specific invitation to come and eat (Sir 24:19) is reminiscent of the Love Story (cf. Sir 6:19). The focus here, however, is on the Tree, a Tree that grows out from the Temple mount.[141]

Ben Sira's commentary on Wisdom's hymn (B') begins in verse 23 by identifying her with a book: "All this is the book of the covenant (βίβλος διαθήκης) of the Most High God." He then cites Deuteronomy 33:4 to show that this book is the Torah that Moses commanded Israel. In ben Sira's view, the Torah is a book full of wisdom from heaven.[142]

---

[138] Translation by Skehan (Skehan and Di Lella, *The Wisdom of Ben Sira*, 327). Even if we render the Greek without the interrogative, which is possible, the question is implied.

[139] In addition, the verb "to take root" (ἐρρίζω) recalls the imagery of the "root of wisdom" (Sir 1:6, 20).

[140] Sheppard notes the parallels to the Eden paradise and especially to Cant 4-6: "There a young woman appears in a garden ... rich with the same kinds of vegetation like that in Sir. 24 ..." (*Wisdom as a Hermeneutical Construct*, 53).

[141] We return to the Tree of Wisdom in the comparative section below, pp. 93-94.

[142] The Greek idea of παιδεία based on a book has influenced ben Sira. See Bickerman, *The Jews in the Greek Age*, 169-72.

This book possesses the same qualities as the Spirit of the Lord. The allusions to Isaiah 11:2 are unmistakeable: the book is full of wisdom (Sir 24:25), understanding (24:26), knowledge (24:27) and counsels (24:29).[143] The book is inspired, so much so that human beings cannot fully fathom the wisdom it contains. Who then can know it? The stage is set for ben Sira to describe his role as sage.

The activity of ben Sira in providing wisdom from the book of the covenant (A') is the subject of Sirach 24:30-33. He began his career with modest intentions (Sir 24:30-31b; cf. 33:16), but soon his teaching, like Wisdom herself, could not be contained (24:31c-33; cf. 33:16-17). The simile in verse 30 is a localized one ("like a rivulet"), but gives way in verse 32 to a universal one ("like the dawn," cf. 24:27). With this universal image, ben Sira gives the book of the covenant the leading role in the international pursuit of wisdom. This is his unique achievement.[144]

The concluding couplet to chapter 24 has a special bearing on the theme of revelation:

Sir 24:33a   Again, I will pour out teaching like prophecy,
     b   and leave it for the generations of eternity.

Two brief comments are in order. First, ben Sira likens his wisdom instruction to prophecy. This reference forms an *inclusio* with the prophetic commissioning scene alluded to at the beginning of the poem. Personified Wisdom fulfills her commission through an inspired book that is studied and taught by sages. The fact that ben Sira "pours out" (ἐκχεῶ) his teaching is consistent with the earlier water similes (24:25-26, 30-31) and means that he views himself as inspired by the Spirit as he engages in his work (cf. *1 En*

---

[143] A comparison of the Greek of Sir 24 with Isa 11:2 [LXX] shows that only the term "knowledge" differs between the two texts (παιδεία, Sir 24:27; γνῶσις, Isa 11:2).

[144] Therefore, we cannot agree with Martin Hengel's assessment of ben Sira's program. Hengel argued that the identification of wisdom and Torah meant that the universality of wisdom intended by Sir 1:1-9 and 24:3-6 was shattered. He concluded that "the original universal wisdom becomes the possession of a limited number of elect, the people of Israel or the pious devoted to the law" (Martin Hengel, *Judaism and Hellenism. Studies in their Encounter in Palestine during the Early Hellenistic Period* [trans. J. Bowden, 2 vols. in 1; Philadelphia: Fortress, 1974] I.161). But there is no curtailing of wisdom in Sirach 24. This was noted earlier by Robert H. Pfeiffer, who observed that wisdom "looms much more prominently in Sirach's book than the Law with which he identified it" (Robert H. Pfeiffer, *History of New Testament Times: With an Introduction to the Apocrypha* [New York: Harper & Row] 370). The point of the equation of Torah and wisdom in Sir 24:23 is not to restrict or nationalize wisdom (as happens later in Bar 3:9-4:4); rather, it is to universalize Torah.

91:1; Joel 2:28-29 [Hb 3:1-2]). As a result, the activity of ben Sira is prophet-like. Ben Sira himself does not claim to be a prophet, but he claims participation in an inspired process that is prophetic in origin and result.

Second, ben Sira describes his teaching as relevant "for the generations of eternity" (Sir 24:33b; cf. 1:15b; *1 En* 82:3). He envisions that his wisdom will be preserved and passed down from generation to generation. Indeed, it will itself comprise an inspired book that later generations will study (Sir 50:27).[145]

THE *LIEBESGESCHICHTE* AND THE SCHOOL

The dynamics of the process of attaining wisdom often come to expression within the form of the *Liebesgeschichte*. As suggested above, the personification of Wisdom and the myth of her descent in Israel is presupposed as the background to the Love Story, and more generally, to the teaching situation or activity in ben Sira's school.[146] In this section, passages that employ motifs from the Love Story are collected.

Sirach 4:11-19

This poem emphasizes the role of discipline in the pursuit of wisdom. In spite of the reference to "love" in verse 12 ("Those who love her ..."), commentators have not recognized elements of the *Liebesgeschichte* in this piece. This may be due to the fact that the poem opens in verse 11 with the image of

---

[145] John G. Gammie, along with others, has pointed out that what tied ben Sira to the prophets was not the typical critique of idolatry or social injustice, but his understanding of the divinely inspired process of creative composition ("The Sage in Sirach," *The Sage in Israel and the Ancient Near East* [ed. John G. Gammie and Leo G. Perdue; Winona Lake, IN: Eisenbrauns, 1990] 370-71).

[146] Our choice of the word "school" is based on Sir 51:23 ("house of research"). What ben Sira meant by this term, and the character of education previous to his time, continues to be a topic of debate. André Lemaire ("The Sage in School and Temple," *The Sage in Israel and the Ancient Near East*, 165-181) argues for schools as formal institutions whose origins can be traced to the First Temple period. Others, such as James L. Crenshaw (in reaction to an earlier book by Lemaire) offer caution about accepting claims for an elaborate system of schools: "considerable diversity characterized education in ancient Israel, and scholarly preoccupation with the existence or nonexistence of a school threatens to obscure this significant fact" ("Education in Ancient Israel," *JBL* 104 [1985] 615). We adopt Crenshaw's caution but retain the term "school" for any setting in which the giving and receiving of knowledge takes place (see Bickerman, *The Jews in the Greek Age*, 167).

Wisdom as mother.[147] But the Love Story can incorporate such an image (cf. 15:2). Our translation of Sirach 4:11-19 is based on the Hebrew (ms A):[148]

Sir 4:11   Wisdom teaches her sons,
                 and admonishes all who understand her.
      12   Those who love her love life,
                 and those who seek her gain favor from the Lord.
      13   Those who take hold of her find glory from the Lord,
                 and they encamp where the Lord's blessings rest.
      14   Those who serve the Holy One serve her,
                 (even) his (God's) tent is her place of entry.[149]
      15   "He who obeys me will judge truly,
                 and he who listens to me will encamp in the inner chambers,
      17a   For in disguise I will walk with him,
        c   and at first I will test him with trials.
        d   When his heart is filled with me,
      18   I will return and direct him,
                 and reveal to him my secrets.
      19   If he turns aside, then I will abandon him,
                 and I will bind him with fetters.
             If he turns aside, I will reject him,
                 and I will hand him over to the destroyers."[150]

The overall structure of this poem is marked by the shift from the third to the first person in verse 15.[151] In addition, a careful consideration of the content displays broad formal similarities to the outline of an unquestioned Love Story considered below, viz., Sirach 51:13-21:

---

[147] Di Lella writes: "Throughout the poem, Wisdom is personified as a woman deeply concerned about her children" (Skehan and Di Lella, *The Wisdom of Ben Sira*, 171).

[148] The Greek reads "will judge *nations*" in verse 15a and adds verses 16, 17b ("she will bring fear and dread upon him") and 17e ("and she will test him with her ordinances").

[149] The Hebrew is unintelligible and in need of restoration. Our restoration is based on the Syriac "his tent" and the notion of Wisdom's "entries" (מבואיה; as mentioned also in Sir 14:22). Thus, the mangled colon ואלהו במא ויהא is reconstructed as: ואהלו מבואיה . It would also seem that the Greek of 4:13b reflects part of this reading (καὶ οὗ εἰσπορεύεται); a fact that would explain the necessity to create a Greek reading *de novo* in 4:14b. The thought of the line as we have restored it is identical to 24:10. Note also the traditional connection between the tent of meeting and judgment (4:15). Perhaps the line became mangled because of the daring identification of the tent of meeting (4:14b) with Wisdom's bridal chamber (4:15b).

[150] It is possible that 4:19 contains a doublet. However, on the basis of Sir 6:32-33, one should not be too quick to assume this.

[151] Notice that the first person speech *begins* in Sir 4:15 ("He who obeys me") with the same note on which the first person speech of Wisdom *ends* in Sir 24:3-22 ("Whoever obeys me"). As we will see, literary links of this type are common in Sirach.

a)   The lover/student is to seek Wisdom (4:12b; 51:13c).
b)   Wisdom will discipline her lover/student (4:17; 51:17;
      cf. 51:26ab).
c)   If the lover/student stays devoted, Wisdom will reveal her
      secrets (4:18b; 51:19cd).

In Sirach 4:11-19, erotic overtones are not nearly as pronounced as they are later in Sirach 51:13-21. Still, this nuance is not altogether absent. The reference to the "inner chambers" in Sirach 4:15b may be an allusion to the bed chamber (חדר, cf. Cant 1:4; 3:4).

Verses 17-18 explain the process by which one eventually enters the enticing inner chambers. Wisdom dons a disguise ("in disguise"/בהתנכר) to test her lover with trials and only reveals her true self ("I will reveal to him my secrets"/וגליתי לו מסתרי)[152] after her lover has proven his faithfulness and diligence. The language of disguise/revelation is that of angelophany, applied here to the Love Story.[153] In the context of the latter, Wisdom's revelation of secrets in the bed chamber is matched by her lover's claim: "I perceived her hidden things [= nakedness]" (מערמיה אתבונן, Sir 51:19d).[154] Thus, Wisdom's revelation of secrets has a sexual nuance in this poem (cf. Gen 3:7; 1 En 32:6).

The content of the "secrets" disclosed by Wisdom is not decoded. However, the first line of Wisdom's address ("He who obeys me will judge truly," 4:15a) indicates that behind this poem is the discipline required by interpreters of Torah to find answers for current issues in society. The cultic allusion in 4:14 ("serve the Holy One")[155] may also suggest that such decision-makers have some relation to the priestly establishment (cf. Sir 7:29-31).[156]

---

[152] There is a Hebrew plural noun מסתרים derived from the root סתר. However, if we vocalize the traditional noun differently, ben Sira's term could be a transliteration of Greek μυστήρια.

[153] Suggested to me by George Nickelsburg. Among several examples: the goddess Athena appears to Telemachus disguised as Mentes (Homer, *Odyssey*, Bk 1) and Raphael is sent to Tobit disguised as Azarias (Tob 3:17; 5:3-13; 12:11-22).

[154] For this understanding of Sir 51:19d, see below, pp. 70-72.

[155] Box and Oesterley, "Sirach," *APOT*, 1.329.

[156] Bickerman points out that jurists had to rule on purely ritual controversies, as well as more secular matters. For examples of the "New Jurisprudence," see *The Jews in the Greek Age*, 192-200.

Sirach 6:18-37

The didactic essay in Sirach 6:18-37 is a further commentary on the role of discipline in the pursuit of wisdom. Like the Love Story that concludes the book, the present poem takes its point of departure from the period of youth (Sir 6:18a; 51:13a, 15d). In addition, both poems share a basic two-part structure: various poetic metaphors (Sir 6:18-31; 51:13-21) and their decoding in the teaching or school setting (Sir 6:32-37; 51:22-30). The high incidence of common vocabulary in these two poems is also quite striking. It is certainly true that the essay in Sirach 6:18-37 lacks "the delicate balance of literary ambiguity" characteristic of the acrostic poem in chapter 51.[157] Still, as will become apparent below, some elements of the *Liebesgeschichte* are unmistakeably present in this essay.

The text of Sirach 6:18-37 presents few difficulties:[158]

Sir 6:18 [My Son, from your youth up accept discipline,
                   and until you are gray] you will overtake Wisdom.
     19   As one who plows and reaps, draw near to her,
                   and wait for her abundant produce.
            For in her work for a short time you will work,
                   and in time to come you will eat her fruit.
     20   Harsh is she to the foolish,
                   and he who lacks sense will not hold her.
     21   Like a burdensome stone she will be upon him,
                   and he will not delay to cast her away.
     22   For discipline, like her name, so she is,
                   and she is not plain to many.

     23   [Listen, son, and receive my judgment,
                   and do not utterly reject my counsel.
     24   Set your feet into her net,
                   put your neck into her collar.]
     25   Spread your shoulders and lift her up,
                   and do not feel disgust for her cords.
     26   [With all your soul draw near to her,
                   and with all your might keep] her [ways].
     27   Search and investigate, seek and find,
                   and when you have hold of her, do not let her loose.

---

[157] J. A. Sanders, "The Qumran Psalms Scroll (11QPs^a) Reviewed," in *On Language, Culture and Religion: In Honor of Eugene A. Nida* (ed. M. Black and W. W. Smalley; The Hague: Mouton, 1974) 91.

[158] The Hebrew (ms A) is reproduced and in places restored from the Greek (vss 18, 23-24, 26, 34) by Patrick W. Skehan in an appendix to his article, "The Acrostic Poem in Sirach," *HTR* 64 (1971) 387-400. Our translation brackets verses not extant in Hebrew.

28 For afterward you will find her resting-place,
        and it will be turned for you into pleasure.
29 And her net will become for you a strong abode,
        and her cords, a garment of gold.
30 A yoke of gold is her yoke,
        and her fetters are a purple cord.
31 As garments of glory you will put her on,
        and as a crown of beauty you will crown yourself with her.

32 If you are willing, my son, you will show yourself wise,
        and if you set your heart to it you will be clever.
33 If you consent to listen,
        and incline your ear, you will be taught.
34 [Be present in the assembly of the elders,
        and cleave to their wisdom.]
35 Be willing to listen to every discourse,
        and do not let a parable of insight escape you.
36 Perceive whoever has insight and inquire of him,
        Let your foot wear out my doorsill.
37 Study the fear of the Most High,
        Meditate continually in his commandments.
    And he will cause your heart to understand,
        and he will give you the wisdom you desire.

Structurally, the didactic essay consists of three major units introduced with the address "[my] son" (6:18-22, 23-31, 32-37). This opening is typical of wisdom instruction. While it derives originally from the setting in the home, by ben Sira's time it was an indispensable cliché for the one who is taught wisdom by any teacher (cf. *1 En* 82:1 91:1, 3, 18, 19; 93:2; 94:1).

The first major section is framed by the word that is the main concern of the poem, "discipline" ($\pi\alpha\iota\delta\varepsilon\iota\alpha$, 6:18a; מוסר, 6:22a). This topic is initially explicated with the metaphor of farm labor (6:19). The promise is held out that those who are diligent will eat the fruit of wisdom, a metaphor that links this poem with Sirach 24:19-21. In the three bicola of verses 20-22, ben Sira contrasts the hardworking wise man with the fool (אויל) and the senseless (חסר לב) who cannot endure the rigors of such labor.

The second unit consists of two metaphors: the hunting and yoking of animals (vss 24-25) and the Love Story (vss 26-28). Di Lella sees only the first metaphor and argues that the hunting metaphor of verse 24 is continued in verses 26-28; at the same time, the figure of the hunter has shifted from Wisdom herself to the one who seeks Wisdom. The weakness of this interpretation is evident from verse 28, a verse he regards as portraying "the satisfaction one experiences at the end of a successful day's hunt."[159] In our view, a new

---

[159] Skehan and Di Lella, *The Wisdom of Ben Sira*, 194.

metaphor is introduced with the shift of subject in verses 26-28. This section draws its imagery from the *Liebesgeschichte* and describes the discipline it takes to find and keep a lover.

In verse 26, the parallel expressions "with all your soul" and "with all your strength" are drawn from Deuteronomy 6:5.[160] Ben Sira has daringly broadened the scope of the Shema to include not only love for the Lord your God, but love for Wisdom! The image of the lover drawing near to Wisdom and keeping her ways will be fully exploited in Sirach 14:20-27.[161]

Verse 27 contains three verb pairs. The first pair is "search and investigate" (דרש וחקר, cf. Sir 3:21). The verb דרש has a significant role in the *Liebesgeschichte*, as will be noted in our study of the final poem (Sir 51:14b, 23b). Sirach 6:27 demonstrates that the synonym חקר can also be used in the Love Story (cf. 14:22a). The second verb pair "seek and find" (בקש ומצא) is also present in the concluding poem (the *qoph* bicolon, which decodes Sir 51:13c, 16b, 20b). The final verb pair in Sirach 6:27, "take hold of her and do not let her go" (רפה/חזק hif.) is not used in the final acrostic of Sirach 51, but is vocabulary drawn from the Love Story. In Canticles, the maiden, in the context of seeking (בקש) and finding (מצא) her lover (3:1-4), says: "I held (אחז) him and would not let him go (רפה)" (3:4). In sum, all of the verbs in Sirach 6:27 are intelligible in the context of the *Liebesgeschichte*.

This interpretation of verse 27 is confirmed by verse 28. The "resting place" (מנוחתה) of wisdom is her house (cf. Ruth 1:9). The diligent search for Wisdom reaches its goal when one finds her and comes to live in her house (cf. Sir 4:15; 14:22-27). Here, she is transformed into "delight" (תענוג). Such "delights" involve not only the comforts and luxuries of her house, but the term also has a sexual overtone (cf. Cant 7:7-10 [Eng 6-9]; Qoh 2:8). Indeed, this word anticipates the erotic nuances so typical of Sirach 51:13-30.

Assuming the above interpretation of verses 26-28 is correct, something of this imagery might be expected to recur in verse 31. Skehan and Di Lella show that the hunting terminology of verse 24 is picked up again in verse 29, and the yoking imagery of verse 25 in verse 30. Similarly, the elements of the Love Story in verses 26-28 are recalled in verse 31. The "glorious apparel" (Sir 6:31a) is an allusion to the wedding garment (cf. Isa 61:10; Matt 22:11), and the "splendid crown" (Sir 6:31b) is the wedding crown (cf. Cant 3:11).[162]

---

[160] Ibid.

[161] See below, pp. 63-65.

[162] According to Marvin H. Pope (*Song of Songs* [AB 7C; Garden City, NY: Doubleday, 1977] 448), "In Jewish weddings crowns were worn by both the groom and the bride until the time of the war with Rome in A.D. 70, when the custom was abandoned as a sign of mourning." A common view of Sir 6:31 is that the imagery alludes to the attire of the high priest (cf. Sir 50:11a; 45:12a). But this breaks the symmetry with the metaphors of Sir 6:24-28.

The translation provided below is that of James A. Sanders.[171] The versification is from the LXX, but in a few places the Greek version lacks a colon that is extant in Hebrew. These cola are underlined in the translation.

Sir 51:13	א	I was a young man before I had erred when I looked for her.
14	ב	She came to me in her beauty and I explored her in depth.
15ab	ג	Even (as) a blossom drops when the grapes ripen, making glad the heart,
15cd	ד	(so) my foot trod in uprightness; for from my youth have I known her.
16	ה	I inclined my ear but a little; yet great, I found, was the persuasion.
17	ו	So she became for me a nurse, (even) a tutor, to whom I dedicated my ardor.
18	ז	I purposed to make sport; I yearned for pleasure and would not pause.
19a	ח	I burned in my desire for her and my passion did not abate.
20a 19b	ט	I bestirred my desire for her and on her heights I would not relax.
19cd	י	My hand opened her gate and I perceived her nakedness.
	כ	I cleansed my hand within her
20b		and discovered her in her purity.
20cd	ל	I acquired a heart for her from the start and because of that will I never forsake her.
21	מ	My loins would burn like a firepot from gazing upon her hence I took her as a pleasant possession.
22	נ	Yahweh has granted me the gift of elocution, so with my tongue do I honor him.
23	ס	Turn aside to me, O untutored men, and lodge in my house of study.

---

[171] Sanders is used because of his acute textual judgments. The problems in the passage are legion, and it would take us too far afield to enter into them all. Text and translation in James A. Sanders, ed., *The Psalms Scroll of Qumran Cave 11* (DJD 4; Oxford: Clarendon, 1965) 80-81 and idem, *The Dead Sea Psalms Scroll* (Ithaca, NY: Cornell University, 1967) 114-15. Modifications to his original translation can be found in two later articles: "The Sirach 51 Acrostic," *Hommages à André Dupont-Sommer* (Paris: Adrien-Maisonneuve, 1971) 429-38; and "The Qumran Psalms Scroll (11QPsª) Reviewed," 88-95.

24	ע	How long will you go lacking in all this and let your soul go thirsting?
25	פ	I have spoken boldly about her: (now) do you acquire Wisdom, gratis, for yourselves.
26ab	צ	Bring your necks under her yoke and let your soul bear her burden.
26c	ק	She is near to those who look for her; <u>and he who dedicates himself discovers her.</u>
27	ר	See for yourselves how young I was; yet I toiled within her and discovered her.
28	ש	Heed diligently my lesson from my youth and thus acquire silver and gold by my example.
29	ת	(Then) will my soul delight in my instruction; nor will you be ashamed of my song.
30	(פ)	Work your work in righteousness and he will grant you your reward in due season.

Ben Sira's autobiographical poem divides into two major parts. In the
first part (51:13-21), ben Sira opens with the independent first person pronoun
(אני) and recounts his early search for Wisdom, personified as a woman. He
proceeds to describe his life with her from the period of his adolescence to
mature manhood. In the second part of the poem (51:22-30), ben Sira decodes
the Love Story by issuing a parenesis for others to come and learn wisdom in
his school.[172] In what follows, the two parts of ben Sira's concluding acrostic
will be investigated from the point of view of what each conveys about activity
in his school.[173]

Verses 13-21

Ben Sira uses an allegory to depict his passionate attraction to wisdom as
he moved from adolescence (נער, vss 13a, 15d, cf. vs 28b; קטן, vs 27b) to
maturity. There are erotic overtones to much of the imagery in these verses,
although Sanders may have overstated the case at times.[174] The allegory
works so brilliantly because the poet has chosen to employ a number of key
terms that contain *double entendres*. He tells his reader as much in Sirach

---

[172] This structure is also reflected in Sirach 24:1-33: personified Wisdom traces her
career (24:3-22) and ben Sira relates this to his work as a sage (24:23-33).

[173] Celia Deutsch successfully argues that the sage is the focus of the entire poem ("The
Sirach 51 Acrostic: Confession and Exhortation," *ZAW* 94 [1982] 400-09).

[174] See Jonathan Goldstein, "Review of *The Psalms Scroll of Qumran 11 (11QPs^a)* by J.
A. Sanders," *JNES* 27 (1967) 307-08.

51:29, where the parallelism indicates that his instruction (יְשִׁיבָה, vs 29a)[175] is related to his love song (שִׁירָה, vs 29b). The attentive reader, however, will have picked up on this before coming to verse 29. Terms employed in the first part of the poem to depict the passionate search and acquisition of a lover, recur in the second part of the poem in the context of disciplined study of wisdom.

Perhaps this literary device is most apparent with the root דרשׁ. In an erotic image, the poet writes: "I explored her" (אדרושׁנה) in depth (vs 14b). The reader will meet this Hebrew root again in the second half of the poem. Ben Sira invites the untutored (or foolish) to lodge "in my house of study" (בבית מדרשׁי, vs 23b). In the latter context, "house of study" is more than a technical term; the expression draws on the notion of "explore" present in the verb of verse 14b. Therefore, the root דרשׁ in verse 23b refers to the activity of "exploring" (= "researching") Torah in ben Sira's school.

The literary phenomenon illustrated above is carried through with a number of other terms. Those that bear on the theme of revelation are:

בקשׁ. Ben Sira was a youth when he "looked for" a lover (ובקשׁתיה, vs 13c). He later assures those in his school that wisdom is near "to those who look for her" (למבקשׁיה, vs 26c). Thus, בקשׁ, like דרשׁ, is a term used for investigating and interpreting the Torah.

מצא. Ben Sira "discovered" Wisdom in her purity (מצאתיה, vs 20b; cf. vs 16b, also his recollection in vs 27), that is, when she was allowed to have sexual intercourse. When this metaphor is decoded in the school setting (in the second colon of the *qoph* verse, no corresponding Greek colon), it applies to the student: "he who dedicates himself discovers her" (ימצאה). Thus the verb מצא indicates the goal or result of the exegetical task.

קנה. This root is very similar to מצא. Ben Sira "acquires" or "takes" his lover as a "pleasant possession" (קניתיה קנין טוב, vs 21c; cf. vs 20c). In the second part of the poem, the root will recur when he invites his untutored students to "acquire" wisdom for themselves without cost (קנו, vs 25b; cf. vs 28c). Again, the goal of study is to possess wisdom.

על. The literary device of using key words in both parts of the poem may help us in translating the troublesome term ועלה in verse 17a (Sanders: "a nurse").

---

[175] Sanders (following Segal) interprets יְשִׁיבָה as a reference to "the doctrine of the wise man when he sits to teach" ("The Sirach 51 Acrostic," 437). Schechter and Taylor emend to שִׂיבָה ("old age"), but this destroys the parallelism (*The Wisdom of Ben Sira*, LIII, 68). Di Lella opts to read the Greek, "mercy" (Skehan and Di Lella, *The Wisdom of Ben Sira*, 573).

In verse 26a, ben Sira exhorts his students to put their necks "under her yoke" (בעולה). If verse 26a is alluding to verse 17a, as seems likely, this would support Goldstein's emendation of verse 17 to read: "And she became my yoke; I subjected my manhood to my goad"[176]. In any case, the poem is clear that discipline is essential for attaining wisdom.

The above examples demonstrate that several terms used in the poem have double meanings. The result is a very creative reciprocity. The reader hears intimations of exegetical activity in the Love Story and echoes of the Love Story in the invitation to study.

Because this is so prominent a literary feature, the careful reader will notice that one important erotic expression in the first part of the poem has no matching member in the second. The fact that this erotic phrase is not decoded in the school context is all the more striking because it has a *double entendre* and was used elsewhere in Sirach for the exegetical task of the school. Moreover, it is the one expression that makes it explicitly clear that this poem is about acquiring the hidden things of wisdom from the sage. The erotic expression is found in verse 19d:

Sir 51:19c My hand opened her gate
     d   and I perceived her nakedness.
                ([ו]מערמיה אתבונן)[177]

Again, because of the literary device ben Sira employs in this poem, the reader naturally looks for the verb בין in the second half of the poem. It is not found there.

However, not simply the term בין, but the entire expression may lie behind the Greek of Sirach 1:6b. The Greek noun τὰ πανουργεύματα (Sir 1:6b) recurs in Sirach 42:18, a significant fact because the Hebrew is extant in 42:18.[178] In the latter passage, this Greek noun is a rendering for מערם.[179]

---

[176] "Review of *The Psalms Scroll*," 307.

[177] The Greek translation of 51:19d is: καὶ τὰ ἀγνοήματα αὐτῆς ἐπενόησα ("and I thought upon her unknown things"). The Hebrew noun מערם means "nakedness, naked person" as in 2 Chr 28:15: "and with the spoil they clothed all that were naked among them" (וכל מערמיהם הלבישו מן־השלל).

[178] The parallel reference is incorrectly listed as 42:16 in Skehan and Di Lella, *The Wisdom of Ben Sira*, 137, n. 6.

[179] The Greek translator of Sir 1:6b and 42:18b has apparently read מערם as a form of the verb ערם "be subtle, crafty."

Thus, Sirach 1:6b can be retroverted into Hebrew with some degree of confidence:[180]

Sir 1:6b (cj)   מערמיה מי יתבונן
her hidden parts who perceives?

Sir 42:18b   ובמערמיהם יתבונן
and into their hidden parts he perceives

Sir 51:19d   [ו]מערמיה אתבונן
and her hidden parts (= nakedness) I perceive

A brief consideration of the contexts of Sirach 1:6b and 42:18 is in order here.[181] In the introductory poem (Sir 1:1-10), verses 1-4 make the point that no human being can fully comprehend the divine wisdom that is displayed in creation. The answer to the rhetorical questions of verses 2 and 3 ("Who can number these? Who can fathom these?") is apparently that no one can. However, there is a major shift in emphasis in verses 6-10. The Lord who fashioned wisdom has made it accessible to those who love (= fear) him.[182] Thus, the answer to the rhetorical questions of 1:6 ("To whom has wisdom's root been revealed? Who perceives its hidden parts?") is ben Sira and others like him.

Sirach 42:18 occurs within a Hymn of Praise to God the Creator. God searches out the abyss and human heart and "perceives their hidden parts." Unlike Sirach 1:6b and 51:19d, God is the subject here. However, the next verse immediately adds that God "reveals the deepest secrets" (42:19b; cf. Sir 4:18b). Thus, what God perceives (or to be precise, *part* of what God perceives), God allows others to apprehend by means of revelation. Who are the recipients of this revelation? The end of the long poem tells us:

Sir 43:32   Beyond these many things lie hid,
              only a few of his works have I seen.
      33   It is the Lord who has made all things,
              and to those who fear him he gives wisdom.

---

[180] Three different Greek verbs are used in these verses (γινώσκω, 1:6b; διανοέομαι, 42:18b; ἐπινοέω, 51:19b), but each means "perceive, understand, comprehend" and can translate the Hebrew בין (*hitp.*).

[181] See the more extensive treatment in Chap. 4, pp. 142-45 and 155-56.

[182] The reading "those who fear him" (Sir 1:10) is found only in a few Greek mss and the Syriac, but note the connection between Sir 1:6 ("To whom has wisdom's root been revealed?") and Sir 1:20 ("The root of wisdom is fear of the Lord").

The expression "gives wisdom" (ἔδωκεν σοφίαν, no Hb) is a technical term (cf. Sir 6:37d; *1 En* 5:8; 82:2) that matches the earlier "reveals the deepest secrets." The recipient of revealed wisdom is ben Sira, who expounds creation's hidden things and deepest secrets in this poem.

Against this background, the significance of Sirach 51:19 can be appreciated. Ben Sira speaks in the first person and uses an erotic image when he claims: "I perceived her hidden parts." The "hidden parts" denote her nakedness or the intimate details shared by lovers. Ben Sira does not decode this metaphor in 51:22-30. The question of how this applies to the teaching situation is not answered. But perhaps Sirach 51:19 supplies a direct answer to the rhetorical question posed in the introductory poem at Sirach 1:6. Ben Sira responds to his own earlier question and forms an *inclusio* around the entire book.[183] The point of 51:19d as it relates to the teaching situation must then be intuited by the reader. The point would seem to be that *this entire book* contains the hidden things revealed to ben Sira and taught in his school.

Verses 22-30

Most of the relevant passages in the second part of the poem have been referred to above. It is necessary, however, to comment on the important dialectic between "reward" and "work" in these verses. The second half of the poem is framed by the idea of God's "giving a reward" (שכר נתן, 51:22, 30), an expression that echoes "to give wisdom." The reward comes in the context of the teaching activity (vs 22) in ben Sira's school (vs 23). In this school, he boldly imparts wisdom so that his students may acquire it (vss 24-25). Such wisdom, however, does not come easily. Students must discipline themselves (vs 26), as ben Sira has done, in order to learn (vss 27-29). Only those who work hard will be given wisdom as a reward in due season (vs 30). On the one hand, wisdom always remains the possession and prerogative of God. On the other hand, God gives wisdom as a reward to those who work hard at acquiring it.

Summary

Ben Sira portrays personified Wisdom, through the motifs of the Love Story, as an attractive, desirable, and elusive lover. Suitors must exercise self-

---

[183] If the suggestion is correct and there is a linkage from Sir 51:19 back to 1:6, then this would confirm the view that ben Sira himself composed the acrostic poem to conclude his book. As we have indicated earlier, similar kinds of literary links are employed by ben Sira.

discipline to win her. The effort expended is well worth the outcome; when one finally gains her approval and marries her, one becomes privy to her secrets. These basic motifs are decoded in a way that relates directly to the school setting.

The identification of personified Wisdom with a book lies behind the decodification (Sir 24:23). The sage meditates on Torah (Sir 6:37; 14:20), handles it properly (Sir 15:1), and is able to teach (Sir 15:20; 51:22-30). Those who listen to him and retain what is taught will be given wisdom or shown hidden things in Torah.

ADDITIONAL PASSAGES
REFLECTING A SCHOOL SETTING

In addition to poems in which motifs from the *Liebesgeschichte* are employed and decoded in relation to the school, there are other discourses devoted more or less exclusively to the teaching situation. Like the passages reviewed above, these too are autobiographical in nature.

Sirach 3:17-29

The first discourse under this heading has a tangential point of contact with the *Liebesgeschichte* in that it refers to a revealed secret. This secret is set in contrast with other secret things that are forbidden. The poem is a didactic essay that divides into three strophes.[184] The following translation is based on the Hebrew.[185]

Sir 3:17 My son, in all your works walk in humility,
                and you will be loved more than a giver of gifts.
     18 My son, the greater you are, so shall you abase yourself,
                and in the eyes of God you will find favor.
     19 For many are the mercies of God,

---

[184] Di Lella's delimitation of this unit is confusing. He treats Sir 3:17-24 as a poem of seven bicola. Sir 3:25-29 is an independent poem, yet he ties it with the two that follow (Sir 3:30-4:6; 4:7-10). Di Lella recognizes that the latter two poems have little in common with Sir 3:25-29 or with one another, but suggests that this is an example of ben Sira's tendency to place unrelated bodies of material together (Skehan and Di Lella, *The Wisdom of Ben Sira*, 164). His suggestion is not convincing in this case. Our analysis will show that Sirach 3:25-29 is very closely related to what precedes in 3:17-19, 20-24.

[185] Ms C for vss 17b-18, 21-22; ms A for the remainder. The versification follows the Greek. For the translation of 3:17b and 3:26b, see T. Penar, *Northwest Semitic Philology and the Hebrew Fragments of Ben Sira* (BibOr 28; Rome: Biblical Institute, 1975) 7, 9.

and to the humble he reveals his secret.

21   Things too marvelous for you, do not investigate,
         and things too evil[186] for you, do not research.
22   On what is authorized, give attention,
         but you have no business with secret things.
23   And into what is beyond you, do not meddle,
         for that which is too great for you was shown you.
24   For many are the thoughts of the sons of men,
         evil and erring imaginations.

26   A hard heart will be abhorred at its end,
         and he who loves riches will be led on by them.
27   A hard heart has many sorrows,
         he writhes in pain who adds sin to sin.
25   Without a pupil in the eye, light is missing,
         and without knowledge, wisdom is missing.
28   Do not run to heal the wound of a scoffer
         for there is no healing for him,
         for from an evil planting is his planting.
29   A wise heart understands the parables of the wise,
         and the ear that listens to wisdom will rejoice.

The first strophe (Sir 3:17-19) is framed by the idea of humility.   Ben
Sira urges his student ("My son") to "walk in humility" (בענוה הלוך, vs 17a).
Of course, the teacher himself walks this path.   The connection between wisdom and humility is traditional (Prov 15:33).   There are textual problems in
the concluding colon of the strophe, but the Hebrew of ms A identifies the
"humble" (ענוים, vs 19b) as those to whom God "reveals his secret" (יגלה
סודו, cf. Sir 4:18; 42:19; Amos 3:7).   On the basis of the next strophe, it
appears that the humility required for this revelation involves the will to reject
unauthorized teaching and submit to the wisdom ben Sira dispenses.

Strophe two (Sir 3:21-24) may also have a literary frame.   In the parallelism of verse 21, ms C juxtaposes the "marvelous things" (vs 21a) with "evil
things" (vs 21b).   Skehan proposes that these terms may originally have been
singular and that the Hebrew in 3:21b may have been רם ("high").[187]   This
suggestion brings the bicolon into line with biblical parallels (Pss 131:1;
139:6).   While this is plausible, another possibility should be kept open.   It is
conceivable that ben Sira wants his readers to think of the biblical parallels

---

[186] Ms A reads "hidden."   Our reasons for following ms C will be explained below.
[187] Skehan and Di Lella, *The Wisdom of Ben Sira*, 159.   The Greek in Sir 3:21b reads:
ἰσχυρότερά.

with the first colon, and then deliberately puns them with the second colon.
The pun is that the "high things" (רמים)[188] are actually "evil things" (רעים, ms
C). The wordplay reflects his scorn for the forbidden material. In support of
the reading "evil things" is the fact that it forms an *inclusio* with the "evil and
erring imaginations" in the last colon of the stanza (vs 24b). Therefore, the
forbidden teaching is not *really* marvelous and "high" (vs 21), it is evil and
arouses the evil curiosity (vs 24).[189]

The internal structure of strophe two can be illustrated in the following
manner:

... פלאות ממך אל	21a	Things too marvelous for you, do not ...
... ורעים ממך אל	b	and things too evil for you, do not ...
... באשר הורשיתה	22a	On what is authorized ...
... אל יהי לך בנסתרות	b	you have no ... with secret things
... וביותר ממך אל	23a	And into what is beyond you, do not ...
... כי רב ממך	b	for that which is too great for you ...
... כי	24a	For ...
ודמיונות רעות מתעות	b	evil and erring imaginations.

The bicola in verses 21 and 23 are constructed in synonymous parallelism
and make use of the comparative (ממך) to claim that certain subjects or
materials are not to be studied. Verse 23b puts the final comparative in a
motive clause, which is expanded in verse 24. The verbs employed in verses
21 and 23a are in the form of a negative command expressed by אל with the
jussive ("do not"). In the motive clause of verse 23b, the verb (*hof.* pf.) refers
to the activity of rival teachers to which the students have been exposed.
Sandwiched between verses 21 and 23 is a bicolon written in antithetic parallelism. It contrasts legitimate objects of interpretation (vs 22a) with what is
strictly off-limits (vs 22b).

The subjects emphatically forbidden to ben Sira's students are characterized in verses 21 and 23 as "too marvelous," "too evil," "too far beyond,"
and "too great" (cf. *1 En* 82:2). The biblical parallels to such terms would
themselves justify ben Sira's warning (Pss 131:1; 139:6), but he supplies an
additional support in verse 22b by alluding to the "secret things" of
Deuteronomy 29:29a [Hb 28a] ("The secret things [הנסתרת] belong to the

---

[188] The closest parallel is Ps 131:1: "O Lord, my heart is not lifted up, my eyes are not
raised too high (רום, *qal*); I do not occupy myself with things too great (גדלות) and too
marvelous (נפלאות) for me." Cf. Ps 139:6: "Such knowledge is too wonderful (פלאיה) for
me; it is high (שגב, *ni.* ptc.), I cannot attain it."

[189] Sir 3:24 echoes the thought of Gen 6:5, but not the specific vocabulary (apart from
רע).

Lord our God"). Thus, there are limits to what God reveals; some subjects are beyond the ken of human knowledge by divine decree.

Given the antithetic parallelism of verse 22, it may be assumed that the authorized material (vs 22a) designates the "things that are revealed" (גלה, *ni.* ptc.) to Israel in the words of the Torah (Deut 29:29b [Hb 28b]). However, as ben Sira understands it, what God "reveals" (גלה) may also be called a secret (סוד, 3:19b). The instruction of the sage (like the forbidden knowledge!) goes beyond the actual words of the Torah.

The jussive verbs employed in strophe two are familiar from our survey in the preceding section. Two of the verbs were present in the *Liebesgeschichte* in Sirach 51:13-30. The root דרש (3:21b) was used to depict the sage's "exploration" of personified Wisdom (51:14b) and the "research" that takes place in his school (51:23b). In the present poem, it is used in synonymous parallelism with חקר, "to investigate" (3:21a; cf. 6:27; 14:22). The root בין (3:22a) occurred in ben Sira's Love Story at the very high point of the erotic imagery ("I perceived her nakedness" 51:19d; cf. 1:6b; 4:11; 6:36a; 14:21b). Here in strophe two, the antithetic parallel is "not to have business with" (ועסק אל יהי לך, 3:22b). The one remaining jussive verb in verse 23a is unintelligible.[190] The Greek version (μὴ περιεργάζου, "to be a busybody") suggests a wordplay on true work.[191] Finally, the verb in the motive clause in 3:23b (הראית, "it was shown you") indicates that ben Sira's students have had access to the teaching of his rivals.[192]

All of the verbs in strophe two refer to the activity of using texts for study. As the comparative passages demonstrate, the verbs fit the teaching situation and the context of ben Sira's school. The implication of the present poem is that the same method of study is used in other schools, only the subjects of study are different. Ben Sira stresses that his counterparts research unauthorized subjects. Apparently the forbidden material is somewhat attractive and has led to experimentation. Ben Sira urges his students to stay with his instruction.

---

[190] The expression is אל תמר. Taylor proposes "rebel not (by intruding into)" and points to Exod 23:21 and Col 2:18 (Schechter & Taylor, *The Wisdom of Ben Sira*, xvi).

[191] See W. Bauer, *A Greek-English Lexicon of the New Testament and Other Early Christian Literature* (2nd ed., revised and augmented by F. W. Gingrich and F. W. Danker; Chicago: University of Chicago, 1979) s.v. This play on words is present in 2 Thess 3:11.

[192] Alternatively, Skehan and Di Lella read Sir 3:23b as a reference to ben Sira's activity: "more than enough for you has been shown you" (*The Wisdom of Ben Sira*, 158, 160).

Strophe three (Sir 3:25-29), like one and perhaps two, has a literary frame. The precise nature of this frame depends on the placement of the bicolon in verse 25. If one adopts the placement of ms A and reads the bicolon between verses 27 and 28, then the literary frame consists of the contrast between the "hard heart" (vs 26a, 27a) and the "wise heart" (vs 29a).[193]

There are several indications that strophe three is tied to the preceding units: the "arrogant person" contrasts with the humble in strophe one (Sir 3:28a/3:17a, 19b), the "evil planting" symbolizes the evil teaching mentioned in strophe two (3:28c/3:21b, 24b), and the one who "understands" (בין) the parables of the wise is the one who practices the legitimate activity stated in strophe two (3:29a/3:22a). In sum, the teaching situation carries over into strophe three.

It follows that the terms "hard heart" and "wise heart" are used to characterize two kinds of students. The hard-hearted persons are rivals (cf. *1 En* 5:4; 16:3; 98:11) who study the secret things forbidden by God. Such persons can expect a bitter end (Sir 3:26) and a life filled with sorrows (3:27). As the blind lack *light*, these unknowledgeable persons lack *wisdom* (3:25; cf. *1 En* 5:8).

Sirach 3:28 is a tristich that may demonstrate once again how ben Sira can twist traditional formulations.

Sir 3:28a	אל תרוץ לרפאות מכץ
b	כי אין לה רפואה
c	כי מנטע רע נטעו

a	Do not run to heal the wound of a scoffer
b	for there is no healing for him,
c	for from an evil planting is his planting.

The language of verse 28c is very suggestive. Ben Sira charges his opponent with originating from an "evil plant." With this image, he may be intentionally distorting a claim made by some by his contemporaries. A number of pre-Qumranic texts refer to the chosen remnant as a plant that is righteous, true or eternal.[194] Ben Sira may be countering such a claim with scathing sarcasm in Sirach 3:28c. Moreover, if he does this with the word "evil" in

---

[193] If Sir 3:25 opens the stanza (as in GII, but read the Hebrew), then the term "wisdom" forms an *inclusio* (25b, 29b).

[194] *1 En* 10:16; 93:2, 5, 10; 1QS 8:5 (cf. CD 1:7). See George W. E. Nickelsburg, "*1 Enoch* and Qumran Origins: The State of the Question and Some Prospects for Answers," *SBLSP* (1986) 342-43.

3:28c, then this supports our earlier suggestion that he made a similar move in 3:21b (when he substituted the word "evil" in a traditional formulation). Ben Sira, then, is exhorting his students to keep their distance from those who study unauthorized subjects because such arrogant people are beyond help.

Over against the hard-hearted, ben Sira portrays the wise-hearted person in the closing bicolon of strophe three (Sir 3:29). The terms "understands" (בִּין, cf. 3:22a) and "listens" (קְשֵׁב, *hif.* ptc.; cf. 4:15b; 6:33, 35; 51:28) fit the teaching situation. The proper subject matter is defined as "the parables of the wise" (מִשְׁלֵי חֲכָמִים) and "wisdom" (חָכְמָה). To state the obvious, such expressions stand for the Torah interpretation of sages like ben Sira. God reveals his secret (3:19b) through their instruction. The result is that the attentive ear "rejoices" (שָׂמַח); an image that contrasts with the "sorrow" of the hard-hearted (3:27a) and anticipates the book's concluding poem ("My soul will rejoice in my instruction," 51:29a; cf. 51:15b; 15:6).

From the above analysis, it is reasonable to conclude that Sirach 3:17-29 is not a polemic against Greek learning, as is often asserted by scholars.[195] The allusion in Sirach 3:28 suggests that ben Sira is responding to Jewish groups that propound esoteric teaching. The controversy is fully intelligible as an intra-Jewish debate over the correct interpretation of Torah.

Sirach 32[35]:14-17;
33:16-18 [36:16a; 30:25-26][196]

These two passages open and close a long didactic essay (Sir 32:14-33:18). The body of the essay contains three units; the first two develop various contrasts, stated in the introduction, between the pious and the sinner (32:18-24; 33:1-6) and the third puts the contrasts into perspective with the doctrine of opposites (33:7-15).[197]

The two passages that frame the long essay (Sir 32:14-17; 33:16-18) employ the term "instruction/knowledge" (מוּסָר/παιδεία, 32[35]:14a; παιδεία,

---

[195] To cite a recent example, Di Lella states: "In vv 21, 22b, 23a, 24, Ben Sira cautions his readers about the futility of Greek learning, its goals and techniques, and also reminds them of what the Lord has bestowed on them (vv 22a, 23b)" (Skehan and Di Lella, *The Wisdom of Ben Sira*, 160). This view of the opposition can be traced back to R. Smend, who suggested that the "sons of men" in Sir 3:24 was a reference to Greeks (*Die Weisheit des Jesus Sirachs erklärt* [Berlin: Reimer, 1906] 222). The view was popularized by Martin Hengel, who, with his customary caution, said of Smend, "we may perhaps concede that he is right" (*Judaism and Hellenism*, 139).

[196] In the Greek mss, Sir 30:25-33:13a and 33:13b-36:16a were transposed. References to the Greek text will be placed in brackets.

[197] See Chap. 4, pp. 138-39.

33:18b [30:26b]) to form an *inclusio*. In addition, the closing passage is autobiographical, which suggests that the entire discourse bears a relation to the activity of the sage and the teaching environment. The following analysis will build on this perspective.

Sirach 32:14-17 describes two kinds of students. Our translation is based on the Hebrew (ms B):[198]

Sir 32[35]:14   He who seeks God receives instruction,
         and he who inquires of him gets an answer.
    15   He who researches the Torah finds it,
         but he who is a madman is ensnared by it.
    16   He who fears the Lord understands judgment,
         and brings forth guidance from darkness.
    17   A man of violence turns aside reprimands,
         and he drags the Torah off after his needs.

Students who study with ben Sira receive "instruction" (מוסר, 32:14a), a result that includes "an answer" (מענה, 32:14b). The latter term does not refer to an answer to prayer,[199] but to an exegetical answer. Apparently, the student has come with a question requiring an ethical judgment (משפט, 32:16a; cf. "to judge truly", 4:15). The answer or instruction is to be found through conducting research in a book. Thus, the "one who seeks God" (דורש אל, 32:14a) is also the "one who researchs Torah" (דורש תורה, 32:15a). The root דרש, used in the *Liebesgeschichte* with a double referrant (Wisdom and Torah), also has two objects here (God and Torah). It is a common verb for designating interpretive activity (cf. Sir 3:21a; 6:27a; 51:14b, 23b). Through the study of Torah in ben Sira's school, the student "receives" (לקח, 32:14a,b) his answer or "gains" (פוק, 32:15a)[200] instruction. As Sirach 32:16 puts it, the student "understands" (בין) the ethical judgment necessary and is therefore able to offer "guidance" (תחבולות) out of darkness. In other words, a hidden truth has been brought to light and can now be practiced.

In contrast to good students, there are others who disagree with the guidance offered in ben Sira's school. Ben Sira describes someone who spurns his instruction as a "madman" (מתלהלה, 32:15b)[201] who is ensnared by the Torah or by his answers derived from the Torah. The motif of the sinner not abiding

---

[198] There are doublets in verses 14, 15 and 16.
[199] As in the doublet of vs 14.
[200] A verb synonymous with מצא, see Prov 3:13.
[201] See להה and Prov 26:18.

the discipline of the Torah is common in school settings.[202] Moreover, Sirach
32:17 suggests that ben Sira had close contact with his rivals.

Sir   32[35]:17a   איש חמט יטה תוכחות
          b   ואחר צרכו ימשך תורה

          a   A man of violence turns aside reprimands,
          b   and he drags the Law off after his needs.

Ben Sira apparently warned the opposition, without effect. The content of the
warning may be reflected in 32:17b: the interpretations and practices of his
opponents are self-serving and shortsighted. The fact that ben Sira characterizes his opponent as a "man of violence" who distorts the Torah indicates that
the Torah was interpreted to support some sort of social, political or military
program.[203]

Ben Sira's confidence in his own role as an investigator of Torah and dis-
penser of guidance clearly emerges in the short autobiographical poem that
concludes the essay (Sir 33:16-18, ms E; cf. 24:30-33; 51:13-30):

Sir 33:16 [36:16a]   Now I, the last, was vigilant,
               [30:25a]   just like one gleaning after the vintagers.
      17 [b]   By the blessing of God, I too went in the front,
          [c]   and like a vintner I filled my wine-vat.
      18 [26a]   See that I have labored, not for myself,
          [b]   but for all who seek [instruction].

Ben Sira uses first-person speech to describe himself as the last in a long
line of teachers (Sir 33:16a), although he does not mean to imply that none will
come after him. His illustrious career had humble beginnings. He started like
one who gleans after the vintagers (Sir 33:16b). This metaphor applies to his
time of study under earlier wisdom teachers (cf. Sir 8:8-9). By the blessing of
God, ben Sira advanced to the forefront. At the present time, he is like a vint-
ner who has filled his wine-vat (Sir 33:17). That is, he adds to the wisdom
tradition through his own study, discovery and compositions (cf. Sir 15:10;
21:15).

As a result of his progress, students now come to study with ben Sira.
Thus, he can conclude that he labors for all who "seek" (בקש) instruction (Sir
33:18). The root בקש, like דרש in the opening lines (Sir 32:14a, 15a) is used
elsewhere to depict activity in ben Sira's school (cf. Sir 4:12b; 6:27b; 51:13b,

---

202 Sir 4:19; 6:20-22; 15:7-9; cf. 21:19.
203 On the expression "man of violence," see Chap. 6, p. 229, n. 545.

26c). For those who want answers related to contemporary issues, ben Sira's work as a wisdom teacher is indispensible.

Sirach 34[31]:1-8

This poem is ben Sira's polemic against dreams. It is included in the present group of passages because it illustrates that dream interpretation has no place in his teaching activity.[204] The Hebrew (ms E) breaks off in verse one, and therefore the Greek version is the basis for our translation:

Sir 34:1   Empty and false are the hopes of stupid men,
                   and fools are sent winging by dreams.
     2   Like one grasping at shadows and chasing the wind,
                   is the one who attends to dreams.
     3   The dream-vision is "this thing" means "that thing,"
                   what compares to some person means that person.
     4   From the unclean, what will be clean?
                   And from liars, what will be true?
     5   Divinations and omens and dreams are foolish,
                   and like a woman in labor, the heart fantasizes.
     6   Unless from the Most High it is sent as a visitation,
                   do not give your heart to them.
     7   For dreams have led many astray,
                   and those who hoped in them perished.
     8   Without deceit the Law will be fulfilled,
                   and perfect wisdom is in the mouth of the faithful.

The presupposition behind this didactic essay is that dreams have given *hope* to some Jews (34:1, 7), a hope with which ben Sira is not at all sympathetic. Ben Sira provides no specifics about the content of the dreams in question, but his satirical remark in 34:1b may provide something of a clue. The colon "fools *are sent winging* (ἀναπτερόω) by dreams" may be aimed at those who claim visionary ascents to heaven (cf. *1 En* 14:8). Ben Sira is aware of the "dream-vision" (ὅρασις ἐνυπνίων, *attrib. gen.*, 34[31]:3a) and its parabolic-like interpretation (ὁμοίωμα, 34[31]:3b). The fact that he belittles those who place their hope in dreams as "stupid men" and "fools" (34:1)

---

[204] On the widespread practice of dream interpretation in the ancient world see Naphtali Lewis, *The Interpretation of Dreams and Portents* (Toronto & Sarasota: Hakkert, 1976). Ben Sira's criticisms could reflect his difficulties with the general phenomenon of dreams. However, in view of his polemic against Jewish esoteric material (Sir 3:21-24), it is worthwhile to raise the question whether the present passage is aimed at dream visions like Enoch's.

should not prevent us from recognizing that those in question would have regarded themselves as pious Jews whose tradition of dream-visions reinforced their own interpretation of the Torah (cf. 34:8).

Ben Sira's criticisms of the dream as a mode of revelation are not very profound. He seems to argue that in the nature of the case dreams are too elusive (Sir 34:2) and their interpretation too arbitrary (34:3). The rhetorical question in 34:4a may imply that visionaries are ritually unclean. Have they separated themselves from the temple? The next verse goes even further. By linking dreams with "divinations and omens" (34:5a), ben Sira charges his adversaries with the idolatrous practices of the nations forbidden by the Torah (Deut 18:10-11). Of course, it should not be assumed that ben Sira's opponents really practiced divinations and omens. This is a stereotypical attack (cf. *1 En* 7:1; 8:3; 9:8), perhaps an attempt to trace the opposition to the mantic wisdom tradition.

The strongest criticism of the dream-vision is the argument from experience found in Sirach 34:7. Ben Sira seems to allude to a well known (but now obscure), past event in which the bearers of dream-visions were misled into taking a course of action that failed and resulted in their being "banished" or "driven out" (ἐκπίπτω, 34[31]:7b; cf. Sir 33:12).[205] For ben Sira, the failures of the past speak loudly against the legitimacy of dream interpretation.

For all of his criticisms, ben Sira remains ambivalent when it comes to dreams as a mode of revelation. He has to acknowledge that when dreams are sent as a visitation from God, one must pay attention to them (Sir 34:6).[206] The issue left unresolved by this concession is precisely how one determines whether a dream has been sent by God. In any case, the fulfillment of the Torah and the wisdom offered by faithful sages like ben Sira have no part in the deceit (ψεύδους, vs 8; an *inclusio* with ψευδεῖς, vs 1) typical of dream interpretation (cf. *1 En* 99:8-9).

Sirach 38:24-39:11

After an introductory couplet (Sir 38:24), this discourse consists of two major units that contrast the careers of various manual laborers (38:25-34b)

---

[205] This fits nicely with Tcherikover's interpretation of Sir 26:5 (*Hellenistic Civilization and the Jews*, 147).

[206] He has in mind more than just the dreams recorded in the prophetic corpus. From texts such as 1 Kgs 3:4-15 and Job 4:12-21, we know that dreams played a role in the wisdom tradition. In 1 Kgs 3:4-15, the deuteronomistic historian traces the origin of the Solomonic wisdom tradition to Solomon's request in a dream-vision at Gibeon; and in Job 4:12-21, Eliphaz appeals to a dream as a source of authority in his debate with Job.

with the career of the wise man (38:34c-39:11).[207] The introduction and second unit are autobiographical and contribute to an investigation of ben Sira's
activity as a teacher of revealed wisdom.

The opening couplet sets the theme of the discourse: the pursuit of wisdom requires leisure time.[208] Sirach 38:24 is extant in Hebrew (ms B):

Sir 38:24a   חכמת סופר תרבה חכמה

        b   וחסר עסק הוא יתחכם

> The wisdom of the *sôpēr* increases wisdom,
> and the one who lacks business makes himself wise.

Verse 24a is the only passage in which ben Sira refers to himself as a
סופר (*sôpēr*), usually translated "scribe."[209] But ben Sira was not a professional scribe, that is, a clerk, notary, accountant, copyist or elementary school
teacher. Moreover, the parallel colon indicates that this profession as such is
not in view since scribes were surely occupied with business. Some scholars
have concluded that for ben Sira the term scribe is the equivalent of sage.[210]
Others argue that the word scribe designates a particular aspect of the activity
of the sage.[211] If the latter is the case, then ben Sira uses the term סופר in a
non-professional, non-technical sense.

---

[207] It has often been compared to the Egyptian poem "The Satire on the Trades" (*ANET*,
432-34). For parallels to other Egyptian works, see Jack T. Sanders, *Ben Sira and Demotic
Wisdom* (SBLMS 28; Chico, CA: Scholars, 1983) 61-63.

[208] The first unit consists of five strophes that describe various occupations that do not
afford the necessary leisure time for study: the farmer (Sir 38:25-26), engraver (38:27),
smith (38:28), potter (38:29-30) and all skilled laborers (38:31-34b).

[209] The verb ספר, "count, recount/proclaim," occurs in Sir 42:7a, 15b, 17b; 43:24a;
44:15b; 51:1c; and the noun ספרה, "book," is found in Sir 44:4c. In Sir 42:15b and
51:1c, the verb is used, with ben Sira as subject, to introduce a composition.

[210] Skehan and Di Lella, *The Wisdom of Ben Sira*, 10. Box and Oesterley (*APOT*
1.455) titled Sir 39:1-11: "*The ideal scribe described.*" The error probably goes back to
Luther (Bickerman, *The Jews in the Greek Age*, 163).

[211] Gammie cautiously states this view: "the term for scribe—whether the Hebrew
sôpēr, the Aramaic *sāpar*, or the Greek *grammateus*—was used as an official designation of
a governmental official who performed duties of an administrative, financial, or judicial
sort ... the term scribe was a governmental title that may have become applied to students of
the biblical law derivatively" ("The Sage in Sirach," 367-68). J. Marböck argues that the
background for the term scribe should be sought in Ezra 7:6, 10, and 11; ben Sira has
developed and deepened the idea of the *study* of the Torah ("Sir., 38,24-39,11: Der schriftgelehrte Weise: Ein Beitrag zu Gestalt und Werk Ben Siras," *La Sagesse de l'Ancien Testament* [ed. M. Gilbert; BETL 51; Gembloux: Leuven University, 1979] 297, 302-03).

It is helpful to compare Sir 38:24a with Sir 44:4c (ms M):

Sir 44:4c   חכמי שיח בספרתם

                sages with discourse in their books

In the context of the Hymn to the Fathers, ben Sira is referring to David and Solomon in 44:4c. He praises the wise ancestors who wrote books because they left a name for themselves and their wisdom is recounted in the assembly (44:8-15). The same two themes appear in the conclusion of the discourse on the career of the sage in Sir 39:9-11. This suggests that the expression חכמת סופר in the opening colon (38:24a) also anticipates the allusion to David and Solomon and means something like "the wisdom of a writer."

The meaning "one who writes" is attested for סופר at Qumrân, also in connection with wisdom. In 11QPs[a], the prose insert on David's compositions begins as follows:[212]

11QPs[a] xxvii 1   יהי דויד בן ישי חכם ואור כאור השמש וסופר

                And David, the son of Jesse, was *wise*, and a
                light like the light of the sun, and *literate*

Ben Sira should be understood in Sir 38:24a as extolling the sage who writes compositions. Presumably there were sages who did not write; not because they could not, but because they insisted on the oral transmission of wisdom. Ben Sira, however, models his career on that of the wise ancestors (44:4c) and takes his obligation to write with utmost seriousness (cf. 50:27-29).

Sirach 38:24b states the basic precondition necessary if ben Sira's students will become wise. They must be free of business concerns. The idea is parallel to the Greek notion that leisure time is essential for acquiring wisdom.[213] Ben Sira himself has this leisure time, and he expects it of his students. The time allows for the work necessary to make oneself wise. The nature of this work is the subject of the second major unit.

Sirach 38:34c-39:11 consists of four strophes. Strophes one (Sir 38:34c-39:3) and three (39:6-8) will occupy most of our attention; we offer brief comments on two (39:4-5) and four (39:9-11). The opening couplet of strophe one

---

212 Text and translation in Sanders, *The Dead Sea Psalms Scroll*, 136-37.
213 Greek σχολή = Latin *scola* = English "school".

makes the transition from the first major unit.[214] The translation is based on the Greek:

Sir 38:34c	It is otherwise with the one who devotes himself,
d	and reflects on the Law of the Most High.
39:1a	He seeks out the wisdom of all the ancients,
b	and is busy with prophecies.
2a	He listens to the discourse of famous men,
b	and enters together with them into the turns of proverbs.
3a	He seeks out the hidden things of riddles,
b	and is busy with the enigmas of parables.
4a	He will serve among the greatest men,
b	and he will appear before rulers.
c	He will pass through the land of other nations,
d	for he tests good and evil among men.
5a	He will give his heart to rise early,
b	to <seek> the Lord who created him.
c	and before the Most High he will make supplication,
d	He will open his mouth in prayer,
e	and make supplication concerning his sins.
6a	If the great Lord is willing,
b	he will be filled with a spirit of understanding.
c	He will pour forth his words of wisdom,
d	and in prayer give praise to the Lord.
7a	He will set aright counsel and knowledge,
b	and in his (the Lord's) secrets he will reflect.
8a	He will show instruction in his teaching,
b	and in the Law of the Lord's covenant he will glory.
9a	Many will praise his understanding,
b	until eternity it will not be erased.
c	His memory will not fade,
d	and his name will live to all generations.
10a	His wisdom nations will describe,
b	and the assembly will proclaim his praise.
11a	When he lives, he is comparable to a thousand,
b	and when he goes to his rest, he bequeaths a name.[215]

---

[214] Skehan and Di Lella take Sir 38:34c-d as the concluding couplet of the first unit and regard it as forming an *inclusio* with Sir 38:24 (*The Wisdom of Ben Sira*, 445-53). But the opening couplet (Sir 38:24) is an introduction to the entire composition, not simply the first unit. In addition, there is no verbal link between Sir 38:24 and 38:34c-d.

[215] The Greek of Sir 39:11 is corrupt. See Skehan and Di Lella, *The Wisdom of Ben Sira*, 448.

In the opening line of strophe one, the expression "the one who devotes himself" (τοῦ ἐπιδιδόντος τὴν ψυχὴν αὐτοῦ, Sir 38:34c) contrasts with the dedication of manual laborers mentioned in the preceding unit (38:26a, 27e, 28g, 30c). Beyond this, the phrase, along with its parallel in 38:34d ("*and reflects on* the Law of the Most High"/καὶ διανοουμένου ἐν νόμῳ ὑψίστου), is vocabulary used elsewhere of the teaching situation ("devote," 6:32b; 14:21a; "reflect," 6:37a; 14:22a).[216]

The remaining verbs in strophe one illustrate the activity of the sage and his students. The verb "he seeks out" (ἐκζητέω, 39:1a, 3a) goes back to one, or possibly both, of the two most common Hebrew verbs for "research" in ben Sira's school.[217] In turn, both of the parallels to this verb are words that mean "is busy with" (ἀσχολάω, 39:1b; ἀναστρέφω, 39:3b). These expressions reach back to the idea of "busi-ness" in the introductory couplet (Sir 38:24).[218] The one who lacks business is introduced to a new kind of business in ben Sira's school: the business of researching books (Torah, wisdom, prophecies).

The verbs in Sirach 39:2 complete the picture. They fit a setting of oral instruction in which students are presented the subtleties of wisdom. The phrase "he listens to the discourse" (διήγησιν ... συντηρήσει, 39:2a) may go back to Sirach 6:35 (לשמע ... כל שיחה/"every discourse ... to hear").[219] The parallel verb "to enter into with" (συνεισέρχομαι, 39:2b) recalls the "entries" of personified Wisdom and the revelation of her secrets (4:14b; 14:22b).

Indeed, in terms of ben Sira's enumeration of the objects of study, it becomes increasingly clear that the sage works to discover hidden things. Strophe one uses a plethora of terms to designate the objects of study: Torah of the Most High, wisdom of all the ancients, prophecies, discourse of famous men, turns of proverbs, hidden things of riddles, enigmas of parables. The

---

216 The Hebrew idiom in Sir 6:32b and 14:21a (ms A) is : שים לב ("set your heart to," "devote yourself to"). A synonymous Hebrew expression (ונותן לב/נפשו) is used in Sir 50:28; 51:26c. Either idiom may lie behind the Greek of Sir 38:34c. The Hebrew word translated "reflect" in Sir 6:37a and 14:22a is בין (*hitp*).

217 The Greek verb (ἐκ)ζητέω can translate דרש (as in Sir 51:14b) or בקש (Sir 33:18; cf. 24:34).

218 The Hebrew idiom in Sir 38:24 is: יהי עסק לך (cf. Sir 3:22). The synonym (רטש, *hitp.* = ἀναστρέφω, pass.) is found apart from allusions to manual laborers in Sir 8:8:

8:8a   אל תטש שיחת חכמים
b   ובחידתיהם התרטש
8a   Spurn not the discourse of the wise,
b   but *busy yourself* with their riddles.

219 That συντηρέω can translate שמע is clear from Sir 41:14a ("listen to instruction"). On "listen/hear" in the school setting, see also Sir 4:15b; 6:33a-b; 51:28.

motif of hiddenness or obscurity, explicit in the latter examples, is implied in the former materials as well. Ben Sira has already said that the Torah must be researched for its hidden wisdom (24:23; 32:15).

It is difficult to know which Hebrew words lie behind the Greek παραβολή (39:2b, 3b) and παροιμία (39:3a). Either term can translate חידה ("riddle," cf. Sir 47:17 and 8:8) or משל ("proverb/parable," cf. Sir 3:29 and 6:35; 47:17). For the Greek translator, as for ben Sira, the Hebrew words are synonymous; the משל has the same character as the חידה. The parables or riddles in view are presumably interpretations that uncover the hidden truths of Torah. It is in this sense, too, that the authors of the wisdom Psalms use terms like wisdom, parable and riddle (Ps 49) and Torah, parable and riddle (Ps 78) to expound new paradoxes.[220] The fact that Torah, wisdom and prophecies contain hidden meanings indicates that the Greek notion of ὑπόνοια has entered the stream of Jewish interpretation.[221]

Strophe two (Sir 39:4-5) touches on the activity in ben Sira's school in two important respects. First, ben Sira emphasizes the role of travel in the sage's career (39:4cd; cf. Sir 34:9-13). The wisdom possessed by foreign cultures is valuable insofar as it passes the test of Torah. Several passages in Sirach show dependence on both Egyptian and Greek sources.[222] Second, ben Sira's insistence on the place of prayer is fully consistent with a dialectic expressed elsewhere: one works to make oneself wise and God gives wisdom (6:32, 37; 51:30). The sapiential work depicted in strophe one must be accompanied by prayer. The study of sacred texts is not simply a rational exercise that operates according to fixed hermeneutical rules. Rather, ben Sira's notion of research and interpretation borders on the mystical. The sage must be purged of sin in preparation for the revelatory gift of God.

In strophe three (Sir 39:6-8), ben Sira describes the results of the aforementioned study and prayer. The "filled/poured out" (39:6) metaphor was employed earlier (Sir 24:23-33; cf. Sir 4:17c). Torah was described in the language of Isaiah 11:2 as filled with the spirit of wisdom, understanding, knowledge and counsel; which, in a prophet-like manner, ben Sira then poured out. Sirach 39:6 builds on the same imagery. One of the attributes applied to the Torah in Sirach 24:26 ("understanding") is ascribed to the sage himself in Sirach 39:6b ("a spirit of understanding"). The remaining three attributes of the spirit-filled Torah in Sirach 24 ("wisdom" 24:25; "knowledge" 24:27; "counsel" 24:29) characterize the instruction of the sage ("words of wisdom"

---

[220] Bickerman, *The Jews in the Greek Age*, 168.
[221] Suggested to me by Dr. Helen Goldstein.
[222] See Sanders, *Ben Sira and Demotic Wisdom*.

39:6c; "counsel and knowledge" 39:7a). Ben Sira regards the sage as inspired by the same Spirit that fills the Torah (cf. *1 En* 91:1); thus the sage is equipped to pour out the hidden meaning of the Torah and his teaching shares in its attributes.

Each of the couplets in Sirach 39:6c-d, 7a-b and 8a-b displays a delicate balance. The first line describes the work of the sage directed toward others (39:6c, 7a, 8a) and the second shifts the direction toward God (39:6d, 7b, 8b). A brief discussion of each couplet follows.

Sirach 39:6c employs the metaphor mentioned above; the sage "*pours out words of wisdom.*" There may be an allusion to writing in this expression. The verb "pour out" is used in parallel with "written in this book" in Sirach 50:27. Moreover, in the present discourse, 39:6c echoes the introduction in Sirach 38:24: the sage who writes increases wisdom. In any case, the second line of the couplet (39:6d) states the role God played in the production of wisdom. The sage praises God in prayer for granting the petition referred to in strophe two (Sir 39:5). Such prayers could themselves become written compositions (cf. Sir 51:1-12).

The couplet in Sirach 39:7a-b implies the involvement of students in the process leading to revelation, in a manner seen previously. Students apparently come to the sage with their questions (cf. Sir 32:14; 33:18). The sage then "sets aright" ($κατευθύνω$, 39:7a) those matters requiring a proper decision or legal judgment.[223] As stated earlier, the questions may have involved ritual, social or political concerns. Assuming that the book of the Torah and the oral tradition provide no explicit answers for the issues raised, sages like ben Sira must set matters aright by finding God's hidden truth in the Torah. This is clear from the second line of the couplet. The sage "reflects on his (= God's) secrets" (39:7b).[224] The verb "reflects" was used in strophe one with reference to the Torah (Sir 38:34d). The words "his secrets" refer to the hidden things of God contained in the Torah. Such secrets are revealed through the activity of the inspired sage.

The couplet in 39:8a-b concludes the description of the sage's productivity. The first line uses the metaphor of wisdom shining forth ($ἐκφαίνω$, vs 8a) from the sage. The metaphor has an eschatological cast in Daniel 12:3.[225]

---

[223] The Greek $κατευθύνω$ probably translates the Hebrew ישׁר (*pi.*) "to set aright." Prov 1:3c LXX reads: $καὶ κρίμα κατευθύνειν$ ("to set judgment aright"), which appears to be a paraphrastic rendering of ומשפט ומישרים.

[224] The pronoun $αὐτοῦ$ refers to God (so also Skehan and Di Lella, *The Wisdom of Ben Sira*, 448, 452).

[225] See George W. E. Nickelsburg, Jr., *Resurrection, Immortality, and Eternal Life in Intertestamental Judaism* (HTS 26; Cambridge: Harvard University, 1972) 26.

In the present context, the couplet leads into strophe four with its stress on the lasting significance of the sage and his work. The second line states that the sage boasts in "the Torah of the covenant of the Lord," words that recall Sirach 24:23. It is the Torah as book that contains the lasting wisdom brought to light by the sage.

The final strophe on the work of the sage affirms that the reward of wisdom is reputation or a good name (Sir 39:9-11; cf. 44:8-15). This thought leads into the last passage of the present section, a passage in which ben Sira assigns his name to the revealed wisdom he has written.

Sirach 50:27-29

From a formal point of view, these verses can be viewed as the subscription to the book of Sirach.[226] The following translation is based on the Hebrew (ms B), apart from verses 27b and 29a which must be supplied from the Greek.

Sir 50:27a	Instruction in good sense and timely proverbs
b	were written in this book;
c	by Yeshua ben Eleazar ben Sira,
d	who poured (them) out in his understanding heart.[227]
28a	Blessed is the man who meditates on these things,
b	and he who lays (them) upon his heart will be wise.
29a	If he does them, he will be strong for all things,
b	for the fear of the Lord is (his) life.[228]

The content of ben Sira's book is summarized with the common wisdom terms "instruction" (מוסר, 50:27a) and "proverbs" (משלים, 50:27a). In addition, the metaphor "poured out" (נבע, 50:27d) was used earlier with reference to the inspired, prophet-like activity of the sage (Sir 24:33; 39:6; cf. 16:25; 18:29). All of this is as it should be; the reader expects the familiar in a summary statement. Even the mention of writing in 50:27b, if original, was

---

[226] A prayer of praise (Sir 51:1-12) and the autobiographical poem (51:13-30) were soon added, with the result that a new subscription, variously written in the mss, was secondarily appended after 51:30 (Skehan and Di Lella, *The Wisdom of Ben Sira*, 579-80).

[227] For this line, we have followed the Hebrew as reconstructed by Skehan (Skehan and Di Lella, *The Wisdom of Ben Sira*, 557). Perhaps the remaining Hebrew words in the colon reflect a corruption of verse 27b, which is missing in Hebrew. That is, אשר ניבע בפתור could be corrupt for an original אשר נכתב בספר ("which was written in [this] book").

[228] There is no need to emend the Hebrew. When 50:29a is supplied from the Greek, we have a fine parallelism between "strength" and "life" (cf. Qoh 7:12, 19).

anticipated earlier (38:24).[229] The colon is also consistent with his view of παιδεία based on book learning.

Sirach 50:27c is noteworthy. It is one thing for ben Sira to state that the sage leaves a good name; it is another thing to interpret this to mean he may sign his name to his book. This bold innovation elicited the following apologetic comment from Di Lella: "If, as seems to be the case, Ben Sira added these words himself, he was following the model of Prov 1:1-3 and Qoh 1:1, 12; 12:9-10; accordingly, he cannot be faulted for immodesty."[230] But the fact of the matter is that ben Sira does something quite novel as compared to Proverbs or Qoheleth. He personally autographs his book. The model for this should be sought in prophetic texts (Jer 25:13; Nah 1:1).

Sirach 50:28-29, like 50:27, draws upon familiar vocabulary. However, the traditional terms are given a subtle, new twist. A comparison of Sirach 50:28-29 with Sirach 14:20-21 and 15:1 will illustrate the nuances:

50: 28a	אשרי איש באלה יהגה blessed is the man who meditates on these things	14:20a	אשרי אנוש בחכמה יהגה blessed is the man who meditates on Wisdom
28b	ונותן על לבו יחכם he who lays them upon his heart will be wise	14:21a	השם על דרכיה לבו he who sets his heart upon her (Wisdom's) ways
50: 29a	ἐὰν γὰρ αὐτὰ ποιήσῃ (= אם יעשה אלה) if he does these things	15:1	כי ירא יי" יעשה זאת for he who fears the Lord will do these things
29b	כי יראת ייי... for the fear of the Lord		

The new cast given to the earlier formulations follows from the claim that an inspired sage has written a book of revealed wisdom. Whereas ben Sira earlier exhorted his students to "meditate" (הגה) on personified Wisdom (Sir 14:20a), here he tells them to "meditate" (הגה, Sir 50:28a) on "these things" (באלה, 50:28a); namely, the מוסר and משלים inscribed in his book. Similarly, "to set one's heart" on the ways of Wisdom (14:21a) becomes "to take to heart" what is written in ben Sira's book (50:28b). This line of thought

---

[229] Also, in the introduction to the Hymn to the Fathers, ben Sira praises "the sages with discourse in their books" (חכמי שיח בספרתם, Sir 44:4c) and "those who take up parables with writing" (ונשאי משל בכתב, 44:5b).

[230] Skehan and Di Lella, *The Wisdom of Ben Sira*, 559.

reaches its climax in Sirach 50:29. Traditionally, "to practice" wisdom is equivalent to "the fear of the Lord" (Sir 15:1). But here ben Sira implies that "to practice" what he has written in his book is "to fear the Lord" (50:29).

In short, ben Sira envisions his own book as an object of study. The Torah, infused as it is with Wisdom, is the principle book on which παιδεία is based; but ben Sira's book contains inspired essays that reveal the hidden meaning of the Torah. Therefore, his book too is authoritative and results in blessedness for those who meditate upon it and do what it says. The blessing in view is a good quality of life (Sir 50:29).

Summary

The passages in this section did not use the motif of the Love Story, yet the vocabulary of that Story, especially as it related to the teaching situation, was employed. The verbal or nominal form of the term "wise" was present in each passage. Wisdom comes through the activity of "research" (דרשׁ) in the Torah; the main task of ben Sira and his students (3:21; 32:15; cf. 39:1a, 3a). As a result of this activity, God reveals his secret (3:19b; 39:7b) and light shines from the sage (3:25; 32:16b; 39:8a). Ben Sira himself is an enlightened teacher of revealed wisdom. A common device for presenting this wisdom is the parable (3:29a; 39:3; 50:27). Indeed, the myth of personified Wisdom and the Love Story are examples of such parables.

Similar claims to possessing revealed wisdom, based on research in the Torah, must have been made by others; some of whom ben Sira regarded as apostate. He warns his audience of secret things that are pursued by evil and erring imaginations (3:21-24). The one who studies such things abuses the Torah and is variously labelled: hard-hearted, proud, madman, man of violence, senseless and fool. The latter two words occur in a context in which ben Sira rejects the dream-vision as an object of (or supplement to) research (34:1-8). The interpretation of such visions is false and leads people astray.

COMPARATIVE ANALYSIS OF THE REVELATION THEME IN *1 ENOCH* AND SIRACH

The close reading of passages in *1 Enoch* and Sirach that exhibit the theme of revelation has put us in position to offer a comparative analysis. This analysis will focus on the similarities and differences between the authors of the respective books in how they conceptualize and write about revelation.

In both traditions, the theme comes to expression as *revealed wisdom*. Therefore, the discussion below is oriented to the nature and function of wisdom. On the basis of the previous survey, four aspects of wisdom are worthy of a comparative analysis: wisdom is in heaven, wisdom is brought to the earth by a figure who descends from heaven, wisdom is identified with a book or books, and wisdom is life-giving.

The Heavenly Origin of Wisdom

Both traditions start with the conceptual premise that wisdom comes forth from God's mouth; it is the words of God (*1 En* 14:24; Sir 24:3). It follows that someone has to be present in heaven to hear God's words. In *1 Enoch*, a pseudepigraphic figure, Enoch, ascends to heaven for this purpose; in Sirach, the words of God are personified in the mythic figure of Lady Wisdom.

While in heaven, Enoch also travels to various sites that are interpreted for him by the holy ones (*1 En* 17-19; 20-32; 81:1-4). The words of angels, too, constitute wisdom; a point made when Enoch sees holy ones eating from the Tree of Wisdom (*1 En* 32). Lady Wisdom also tours the extremities of the cosmos (Sir 24:4-6), though she obviously has no need of interpreting angels. Rather, the angels listen to her (Sir 24:2) and she *does not interpret* what she sees. For ben Sira, revelation about heavenly places does not fall within the scope of wisdom. Presumably, such revelation is among the "secret things" that belong to the Lord (Sir 3:22).

The Role of a Revealer Figure

In both *1 Enoch* and Sirach, the figure who is in heaven appears in the divine assembly before God's throne and is commissioned for the task of revelation. In *1 Enoch*, elements from the literary form of the prophetic call narrative are used within a throne vision to recount the commission of Enoch (*1 En* 14:18-16:4). After his heavenly journeys, Enoch is returned to earth and commissioned again by the holy ones (*1 En* 81:5-82:3). He possesses divine authorization to reveal a great wisdom from God. Indeed, the author of the Epistle repeatedly uses a heavenly-messenger formula ("Know ...") that brings the commission to mind ("Make known ...", 81:5). In Sirach, personified Wisdom speaks in a Hymn of Praise about her fulfillment of a divine commission. The literary form of the call narrative is not used, but the echoes of a *prophetic* commissioning scene are detectable in the Hymn (Sir 24:3-7, 8-12). As Enoch was returned to his house, Wisdom was sent to reside in Israel.

The commissioning scenes, whether directly in view (*1 Enoch*) or merely reflected in the text (Sirach) provide a basis for sages to regard their own work in prophet-like terms. In *1 Enoch*, the authors of the bridge passage and the Epistle make frequent allusions to the earlier commissioning scenes (*1 En*

91:1; 92:1; 93:2). They regard themselves as sharing in the fulfillment of the commission. Ben Sira relates Wisdom's prophetic commission to himself when he compares his wisdom instruction to prophecy (Sir 24:33). Personified Wisdom's commission is partially fulfilled through his own activity. Understandably, therefore, sages in *1 Enoch* and ben Sira use the vocabulary of prophecy to describe their work (filled/poured out; *1 En* 91:1; Sir 24:33; 39:6; 50:27).

Another helpful way to approach the role of the revealer figure is to consider the utilization of the Tree of Wisdom in *1 Enoch* and Sirach. The description of the Tree in *1 Enoch* 32:3-4 and Sirach 24:13-22 indicates that the same Tree, the Tree of Wisdom, is in view. In both passages, the Tree is depicted as a composite or hybrid. The respective portraits may be juxtaposed to demonstrate the similarities:

	1 Enoch 32		Sirach 24
1.	The tree is like (ὅμοιον) the fir (στροβιλέᾳ) in height (τὸ ὕψος).	1.	Like (ὡς) a cedar (κέδρος) ... I am raised high (ἀνυψώθην)
2.	Its leaves (φύλλα) are like (ὅμοια) the carob tree (κερατίᾳ)	2.	... my branches (κλάδοι) like (ὡς) a terebinth (τερέβινθος)
3.	Its fruit (καρπὸς) is like (ὡσεὶ) clusters of a vine (βότρυες ἀμπέλου) very beautiful (šannāy ṭeqqa / ἱλαροὶ λίαν)	3.	I sprouted pleasure like a vine (ὡς ἄμπελος) and my blossoms are fruit (καρπὸς) of glory and wealth (δόξης καὶ πλούτου)
4.	Its fragrance (ὀσμή) reaches far (πόρρω) from the tree.	4.	Like cinnamon ... I give forth (δίεδωκα) a good fragrance (εὐωδίαν)

The two passages appear to draw upon a common tradition that describes four principle aspects of the Tree of Wisdom: its height, foliage, fruit and fragrance. Of course, these aspects neither occur in the same sequence nor show evidence of fixed terminology. Moreover, the description of the Tree in Sirach 24 is much more elaborate than indicated above, probably through influence of the garden motif from the Love Story (as suggested earlier). Still, by reducing the more cluttered picture in Sirach 24 to the basic images of *1 Enoch* 32, a number of correspondences emerge. The similarities may derive from an oral tradition antecedent to both accounts. The tradition likens the tree's height to a needleleafed conifer, its foliage to that of a broadleafed tree, its fruit to the fruit of the vine, and its fragrance to the bark of aromatic trees.

However, while the same Tree can be recognized, two fundamental differences emerge with respect to how the Tree of Wisdom functions in *1 Enoch* and Sirach. First, Enoch saw the Tree while on a journey to the outer Eastern reaches of the cosmos. It was not present on earth. In Sirach, Personified Wisdom envisioned herself as this tree, a tree plotted at the temple in Jerusalem.[231] Second, Enoch saw holy ones eating the fruit of the Tree of Wisdom. In contrast, Personified Wisdom invites all who desire her to eat her fruits.

The different locales of the Tree and the different consumers of its fruit point to divergent conceptions of how wisdom becomes available on the earth. In *1 Enoch*, the great wisdom represented by the Tree is inaccessible to ordinary mortals. It is made known to angels and they, in turn, communicate it to Enoch through interpretations of his visions. Enoch then brings this wisdom from heaven to the chosen and righteous, who "eat" it (82:3b). In Sirach, the wisdom represented by the Tree is present in Israel and is accessible to all who desire it. Wisdom emanates from Jerusalem to all humankind through the activity of sages like ben Sira.

A Book or Books of Revealed Wisdom

In both traditions, revealed wisdom is inscribed in a book or books. In *1 Enoch*, the books of wisdom are transmitted as the testament of Enoch, reserved for the end-time (1:1; 82:1-2; 93:10; 104:12; 72:1). The references to Enoch as scribe in the Book of the Watchers (12:3,4; 15:1) portrayed him in a professional, priest-like capacity: he wrote a legal petition for the rebel Watchers, took it before the Divine Judge, and then returned and wrote a bill of indictment. However, in the opening of the Epistle, the term scribe appears

---

[231] In fact, not only has the Tree taken root in Jerusalem, but ben Sira likens its fragrance to the anointing oil used on the priests (among others) and to the incense that burned in the tabernacle/holy place (Sir 24:15; for details, see Skehan and Di Lella, *The Wisdom of Ben Sira*, 334-35). Similar cultic nuances are also present in Sir 4:11-19. In the Enochic tradition, the Tree associated with the locale of the temple is the Tree of Life, which will be transplanted next to the temple only after the Lord comes in judgment to reward the righteous (*1 En* 25:5).

to be used in a non-professional way (92:1). In Sirach, personified Wisdom does not fulfill her commission by writing books, rather she hides in a book that is already written—the Torah (Sir 24:23). Motifs of the Love Story are used to portray how the sage seeks and discovers the secrets of Wisdom in this book. When ben Sira finds the hidden things of wisdom, he responds with written compositions (Sir 38:24a). Ben Sira is as serious as Enochic sages about the obligation to write a book of the wisdom revealed to him (50:27-29).

In both traditions, the books of wisdom contain what are called "parables" (1 En 1:2, 3; 93:1, 3; Sir 50:27; cf. 39:3; 3:29). Parables are understood in much the same way. They are interpretations or retellings of Torah that convey previously hidden truth through some explicit or implicit point of comparison. The comparison often requires the participation of the reader.[232] The fall of the Watchers is a parable; the readers are expected to make the connection to contemporaries (a corrupt priesthood). Enoch's heavenly journeys and visions are parables from which the chosen and righteous community is expected to draw analogies to their present situation. In Sirach, the personification of Wisdom and the Love Story are among the parables. The comparative point is that the one who would be wise is beckoned to the disciplined study of Torah with ben Sira.

In their parabolic interpretations, the authors of 1 Enoch and ben Sira do not make much of the Sinai event nor do they enjoin any specific legal requirements from the books of Moses. Of course, they do not disparage these things and to a certain extent, presuppose them (1 En 99:2; Sir 45:5); yet with their reader-involving paradigms or parables, sages from both traditions have mythicized the Torah. It is not the literal meaning of the Torah that interests them; it is getting behind the now obscure text into some deeper, hidden meaning.

This similar approach to the Torah, however, did not yield the same results. The authors of 1 Enoch and ben Sira are aware of rival sages who oppose the version of revealed wisdom contained in their respective books. The stereotypical rhetoric for opponents is used: hard-hearted, mockers, liars, fools (1 En 98:9, 11, 15; 104:10; Sir 3:26-27, 28; 34:1, 4). In addition, in both traditions the opponents are charged with idolatry for practicing divination and omens (1 En 7:1; 8:3; 9:8; Sir 34:5). These tactics are consistent with an intra-Jewish controversy. Each group in the dispute claims to possess

---

[232] Polk refers to this as the "extra-informational, behavior-affecting function of the *māšāl*" ("Paradigms, Parables, and *Mešālîm*," 570).

revealed wisdom and makes the most serious charge possible against its opponents.

Some of the specific polemical language found in one book calls the other to mind. Ben Sira warned his students not to study "things too wondrous" (Sir 3:21a), "what is beyond you" (3:23a), and "a thing too great for you" (3:23b). He may even have punned the notion that such "high things" were in reality "evil things" (3:21b). In any event, he did label them "evil and erring imaginations" (3:24) that come from an "evil plant" (3:28). The reference to erring or straying comes up again in the context of ben Sira's criticism of the dream-vision (34:7). He calls "hopes" derived from visions "false" (34:1a, 8a) and claims they led people to destruction in the past.

The vocabulary highlighted above also appears in *1 Enoch*. The author of the Epistle drew upon the heavenly vision traditions of Enoch to bring a message of "hope" to his community (*1 En* 96:1; 104:4), although he too is aware of the dashed hopes of the past (104:9-15). The visions upon which he based his exhortations of hope were known to him as a "great wisdom" (*1 En* 32:3), "great and glorious wonders" (36:4), and "this wisdom which is beyond (human) thought" (82:2). The community he exhorted was called "the plant of righteousness and truth" (10:16; 93:2, 5, 10). Finally, the author of the Epistle warns against those who "will make wisdom an evil thing" (*1 En* 94:5) and "falsify the words of the Holy One" (104:9)—precisely what ben Sira did to an opposing wisdom tradition.[233]

The authors of *1 Enoch* were also critical of the teaching and practices of their rivals. The Shemiḥazah version of the myth of the fallen Watchers was a criticism of the priesthood for violations of the laws of family purity. The teaching motif found in the 'Asael version of the myth, which became attached to the Shemiḥazah version, referred to the teaching of worthless mysteries; presumably the instruction offered by priests or sages who supported the temple establishment. Ben Sira is a contemporary sage who supports the priests (Sir 7:29-31) and the high priest (50:1-24). In addition, the author of the Epistle of Enoch knows the mystery that in the end-time, sinners "write books in their own names" (τὰς γραφὰς ἀν[αγρά]φουσιν ἐπὶ τοῖς ὀνόμασιν

---

[233] There are other possibilities too that come to mind. For example, one of the sources behind the Damascus Document (CD) is a pre-Qumranic text that Jerome Murphy-O'Connor calls the "Missionary Document" (CD 2:14-6:1). The bearers of this wisdom-like text claim that God made a covenant with them "to reveal to them the secret things (נסתרות) in which all Israel had gone astray" (CD 3:14). Does such a claim lay behind ben Sira's warning in Sir 3:22b ("you have no business with secret things")? For Murphy-O'Connor's discussion of the Missionary Document, see his article "An Essene Missionary Document? CD 2:14-6:1," *RB* 77 (1970) 201-09.

αὐτῶν, *1 En* 104:10). A plurality of opponents are in view here, but ben Sira has surely written a book in his own name (Sir 50:27).[234]

The specific polemic surrounding revelation in the books of Sirach and *1 Enoch* raises the distinct possibility that each tradition regards the other among its rivals.

The Life-giving Function of Wisdom

In the two traditions, the function of wisdom is to impart and sustain life. With an allusion to the fruit of the Tree of Wisdom (*1 En* 32:4), Enoch describes the wisdom of his books as "better for those who eat (it) than good food" (82:3). In Sirach, too, wisdom is "better to have than the honeycomb" (Sir 24:20) for the one who eats of it (24:21). Nourishment and strength for life are conveyed by these two better-than proverbs. In addition, authors in both traditions explicitly state that those who possess their wisdom will live (*1 En* 5:8; Sir 50:29).

This life-giving function of wisdom is also conveyed through the blessed-formula. In *1 Enoch*, those persons are *blessed* who listen to the words of the wise in the end-time (99:10). Ben Sira calls those *blessed* who study and practice the wisdom contained in his book (Sir 50:28). Moreover, if the target audience of Enoch's formula is the generation of the end-time (cf. *generations of eternity*, 82:2), then it must be remembered that ben Sira, too, envisions his wisdom being passed to *generations of eternity* (Sir 24:33).

There is also a similar openness in the respective wisdom traditions. Enoch's testament is apologetic literature that openly offers life. The author of the Epistle invites his readers to choose an elect life (*1 En* 94:4) and expects Enochic wisdom to be attractive to outsiders (100:6; 105:1-2). Ben Sira has packaged wisdom as attractively as possible (the lover) and likewise summons his readers to choose life (Sir 15:17).

The formulas and vocabulary relating the function of wisdom are remarkably similar, yet the two conceptions of life imparted by wisdom are radically different. The revealed wisdom of Enoch promises eschatological life, salvation at the final judgment (*1 En* 5:9). This life transcends death (81:4; 82:3). Ben Sira *never* speaks of life in this sense. For him, wisdom promises an improved quality of life, a happy and secure life, in the present time (Sir 4:12-13; 15:4-6; 24:22).

---

[234] Even if "the writings" (*1 En* 104:10) is a reference to "scripture or scripture's retelling" (Nickelsburg, "The Epistle of Enoch," 342) it is possible to think of ben Sira, for his parables are a retelling of scripture, as is his Hymn to the Fathers.

The comparative analysis has shown that revelation has essentially the same formal structure in *1 Enoch* and Sirach. Wisdom originates in heaven with God and is brought from heaven to a designated community by a revealer figure (Enoch and personified Wisdom). Wisdom comes to be identified with a book or books (in conflict with others) and these books promise life. It is not the formal character, then, but the content of revelation that sets *1 Enoch* and Sirach apart. The two major subjects of revealed wisdom are creation and the judgment. These themes are the focus of Parts II and III. The analysis will seek to carry forward a consideration of the possible adversarial relationship between the two traditions.

PART II

THE CREATION THEME IN *1 ENOCH* AND SIRACH

The presentation in this unit will be organized around two distinct aspects of creation: the observable and the hidden. On the one hand, the authors of *1 Enoch* and ben Sira appeal to observable aspects of the created order to lend support to their respective versions of revealed wisdom. Creation provides the legitimization for the tradition.[235] On the other hand, sages in the two traditions also appeal to hidden aspects of the created order. The sages reveal hidden things about creation that validate or reinforce the tradition. This is as much the case for ben Sira as it is for the Enochic wise man.

The terminology and literary styles associated with the creation theme will merit special attention. These features occur elsewhere in the genre Hymns of Praise in the Psalms, some of which are creation or nature Hymns. The creation Hymns are tied to the agricultural festivals and praise the Maker of heaven and earth for his continuous creative works (Pss 8; 19:1-6; 33; 104; 136:1-9; 139; 147-48; cf. 11QPsᵃ xxvi 9-15).[236] The three-part structure of Hymns of Praise, and in particular the body (second part), is characterized by

---

[235] The practice of enlisting creation for this purpose was standard in Israel and throughout the Ancient Near East. Motifs accenting the stability of the created order were appropriated, and in certain respects, transformed, by both the Davidic monarchy and the Jerusalem cult. See the discussion in B. W. Anderson, *Creation versus Chaos: The Reinterpretation of Mythical Symbolism in the Bible* (New York: Association, 1967) 63-74.

[236] E. Gerstenberger, "Psalms," *Old Testament Form Criticism* (ed. J. H. Hayes; San Antonio: Trinity University, 1974) 212-14; idem, *Psalms: Part I, with an Introduction to Cultic Poetry* (FOTL 14; Grand Rapids: Eerdmans, 1988) 16-19). For the text and a translation of 11QPsᵃ xxvi, see Sanders, *The Psalms Scroll*, 89-91.

a variety of literary styles.[237]   This stylistic variety (e.g., participial style, rhetorical questions, lists) is evident in several creation Hymns in the wisdom literature (Job 38-41; Prov 8; Wis 7:15-22a; 7:22b-8:1) and second Isaiah.[238]

---

[237] Gerstenberger outlines a three-part structure that fits most of the Hymns: "1) Call to praise (usually understood as an exhortation by a choir leader or the like to a group or the whole of the congregation, 2) Account of Yahweh's deeds or qualities (the body of the hymn may feature various styles and formulaic expressions) and 3) Conclusion (renewed call to praise; blessings; petitions; or other forms)" ("Psalms," 209).

[238] On the creation Hymns in Job and Isaiah, see C. Westermann, *The Structure of the Book of Job: A Form-Critical Analysis* (Philadelphia: Fortress, 1981) 72-74, 108-22; and idem, *Isaiah 40-66: A Commentary* (Philadelphia: Westminster, 1969) 24-26. Crenshaw ("Wisdom," 247-49) argues that a distinction be made between 1) creation Hymns in the wisdom literature, which may be compared with similar Hymns from nonwisdom literature, and 2) Hymns of praise to personified Wisdom as the contact between Yahweh and creation, which are a special wisdom genre. But if creation Hymns and Hymns of praise to Wisdom use similar words, motifs, and literary styles, surely the two may be compared.

3. THE CREATED ORDER IN THE ENOCHIC BOOKS OF WISDOM

OBSERVABLE ASPECTS OF THE CREATION

The two passages we discuss under this heading present various phenomena observed by the naked eye. The Enochic authors regard observable reality as a kind of cosmic parable and exhort their readers to draw the appropriate lesson.

1 Enoch 2:1-5:4[239]

This piece uses the vocabulary and *topoi* characteristic of the nature or creation Hymn. For example, it treats the works of God in heaven, earth and sea (*1 En* 2:1; 2:2; 5:3/ Ps 104:1-4, 5-23, 25-26); the watering of the trees and the marking of the seasons (*1 En* 2:3-5:1/Ps 104:16, 19); and the destruction of the wicked (*1 En* 5:4/Ps 104:35).

The unit is related to the one that follows (*1 En* 5:5-9), and the two have been identified as the two elements of a late prophetic form known as the "salvation-judgment oracle."[240] The first element, *1 En* 2:1-5:4, represents an expanded "reproach" or "accusation." The *topoi* of the creation Hymn are pressed into service in this element to urge sinners to understand the message(s) of creation before it is too late.

---

[239] Closure of a literary unit is marked in *1 En* 5:4 with a reference to those who speak "proud and hard (words)" (רברבן וקשין) against God. This same expression concluded the theophany in *1 En* 1:3c-9.

[240] Rau, *Kosmologie*, 106-24, esp. 115, 121; Nickelsburg, *Jewish Literature*, 49. For our treatment of *1 En* 5:5-9, see Chap. 5, pp. 173-74.

The text of *1 Enoch* 2:1-5:4 presents several problems and the translation
must have recourse to Aramaic, Greek and Ethiopic manuscripts:[241]

1 En   2:1   Contemplate all the works, and observe the works of heaven,
                how they do not alter their paths; and the luminaries <of>
                heaven, that they all rise and set, each one ordered in its
                appointed time; and they appear on their feasts and do not
                transgress their own appointed order.

    2   Observe the earth, and contemplate the works that come to pass
                on it from the beginning until the consummation, that
                nothing on earth changes, but all the works of God are
                manifest to you.

    3   Observe < the signs of summer and winter.· Contemplate the
                signs of> winter, that all the earth is filled with water,
                and clouds and dew and rain rest upon it.

    3:1   Contemplate and observe how all the trees appear withered and
                <how> all their leaves are stripped, except fourteen trees
                which are not stripped, which remain with the old until the
                new comes after two or three years.

    4:1   Observe the signs of summer, whereby the sun burns and
                scorches, and you seek shelter and shade from its presence,
                and the earth burns with scorching heat, and you are unable
                to tread on the dust or the rock because of the burning.

    5:1   Contemplate all the trees; their leaves blossom green on them,
                and they cover the trees. And all their fruit is for
                glorious honor.

        Examine and contemplate all these works, and understand that
                he who lives for all the ages made all these works. 2/ And
                his works come to pass from year to year, and they all carry
                out their works for him, and their works do not alter, but
                they all carry out his word.

    [3   Observe how, in like manner, the sea and the rivers carry out
                and do not alter their works from his words.]

    4   *But you changed your works and do not practice his word;*
                but you transgress against him with proud and hard words
                with your unclean mouth against his majesty.
                Hard of heart! There will be no peace for you!

---

241 Nickelsburg's translation, except for the italicized words. We add a word in 5:1:
"*Examine and* ..." (see the following note) and follow 4QEn^a in 5:4. The Aramaic texts
(4QEn^a, 4QEn^c) are found in Milik, *The Books of Enoch*, 145-47, 184-85. See also the
text-critical discussion in Knibb, *The Ethiopic Book of Enoch*, 2.60-65. *1 En* 5:3 is not
attested in Aramaic, but is present in Greek and Ethiopic.

The plural imperative forms of the verbs employed in *1 Enoch* 2:1-5:4 exhort the readers to study the works of creation and thereby learn from the Creator (5:1b). Fortunately, the Aramaic verbs in question are known, or can be conjectured, from the Qumrân manuscripts. The following table lists the verbs, along with their Greek equivalents.[242]

TABLE 2
ARAMAIC AND GREEK IMPERATIVE VERBS IN *1 EN* 2:1-5:3

		4QEnᵃ	4QEnᶜ	Greek
2:1	Contemplate ...	----	[אתבוננא]	κατανοήσατε
	and observe ...	----	[וחז]וא	----
2:2	Observe ...	ח[זו]	חזוא	ἴδετε
	and contemplate	וא[תבו]ננו	ואתבוננא	διανοήθητε
2:3	Observe ...	חזו	[חזוא]	ἴδετε
	Contemplate ...	----	[ואתבוננא]	----
3:1	Contemplate and	----	----	καταμάθετε
	observe ...	חזו	[חזוא]	ἴδετε
4:1	Observe ...	חזו	[חזוא]	----
5:1	Contemplate	[אתבוננוא]	[אתבוננוא]	----
	Examine and	[ ]	חק]רו]	διανοήθητε
	contemplate	ואתבוננו	[אתבוננא]	γνῶτε
	and understand	[ואשכילו]	[ואשכילו]	νοήσατε
5:3	Observe ...	----	----	ἴδετε

The two verbs חזה and בון are consistently employed (apart from the conclusion that begins in 5:1b) and provide both structure and semi-poetic quality.

---

[242] The table departs from Milik's readings of [חזו ודעו] "observe and enjoy" in *1 En* 5:1a and [הל]לו] "praise" in 5:1b. For the latter, on the basis of photo plate IX, we read חק]רו], "examine" (in agreement with Black, *The Book of Enoch or 1 Enoch*, 328).

Those addressed are charged to engage in study of the created order: heaven
(2:1), earth (2:2-5:1a) and sea (5:3).[243] The verbs used for study denote
empirical observation in this context. However, the meaning of the two verbs
cannot be narrowly restricted; there is a mystical nuance to them. The root
חזה is often used for a vision or the visionary,[244] and בין represents the special
understanding that comes by way of such supernatural channels.[245] This is not
to suggest that esoteric creation material be read into *1 Enoch* 2:1-5:4,[246] but it
is to allow for some degree of continuity between the study of observable
phenomena, described in this passage, and the study of hidden things conveyed
in others.[247]

What is the message to be learned from the observation of the created
order? The passage carries two messages; one explicit, the other more subtle.

First, the observer is asked to consider how the works of God on each
level of the tripartite creation do not disobey. The luminaries "do not alter"
(οὐκ ἠλλοίωσαν) their paths and "do not transgress" (ולא מעברין/οὐ
παραβαίνουσιν) their appointed orders (2:1). Things on earth "do not
change" (לא ל[אשניה/οὐκ ἀλλοιοῦται, 2:2). The seas and rivers "do not alter"
(οὐκ ἀλλοιοῦσιν) their works (5:3). The idea that the works of God in creation
"do not transgress" was most often applied to the sea in the Hebrew Bible (Ps
104:9; 148:6; Jer 5:22; Prov 8:29; Job 38:10-11).[248] Only in Jeremiah 5,

---

243 In terms of redaction history, it is possible that the original subunit on the earth has
been expanded by the addition of the section on the signs of summer and winter (2:3-5:1a).
Furthermore, the last section on the sea (5:3) may be a later addition. Rau's analysis of the
background and development of the traditions in 2:1-5:4 is highly speculative (*Kosmologie*,
68-75).

244 The root חזה may have come into Hebrew as an Aramaic loanword. "It has a wide
range of meanings, referring both to the natural vision of the eyes and to supernatural
visions of various kinds" (Jepsen, "חזה," *TDOT* 4 [1980] 281-82).

245 The various Hebrew and Aramaic forms of the root can refer to the ordinary human
act of perceiving; however, the root can also denote the perception or understanding that
comes by way of special revelation (Dan 8:5, 15, 16, 17, 27; 9:2, 22, 23; 10:1, 11, 12,
14; 12:8, 10) (see Ringgren, "בין," *TDOT* 2 [1975] 99-107).

246 Scholars have noted the connections between *1 En* 2:1-5:4 and the Astronomical
Book. Black mentions possible terminological links between 2:1 and 79:5; 82:9, 10 (*The
Book of Enoch or 1 Enoch*, 109-10). Milik considers the material about the signs of summer and winter in 2:3-5:1 to be dependent on 82:15-20 and 4QEnastr^d I i (*The Books of
Enoch*, 148, 296-97). Even the injunction to observe the sea and rivers in 5:3 could allude
to Enoch's visions of the abyss and rivers (*1 En* 77:3, 5-7; cf. 17:8). Still, we should not
run ahead of the author of *1 En* 2:1-5:4. At this point, he is asking sinners to study observable phenomena, not the hidden things revealed in the books of Enoch!

247 See below, pp. 117-18.

248 The biblical references are discussed by Rau, *Kosmologie*, 83-90, 114-15.

however, is this obedience of the sea set over against human disobedience.[249] The sea that does not "transgress/pass over" (עבר) its sandy barriers (Jer 5:22, twice) is contrasted with people of a stubborn and rebellious heart who "have turned aside (סור) and gone away (הלך)" (Jer 5:23; cf. 5:28: "they overflow [עברו] with evil matters"[250]).

Like Jeremiah 5:22-23, *1 Enoch* 2:1-5:4 contrasts disobedient sinners and the obedient works of creation. In the summary in *1 Enoch* 5:2, the author returns to the theme of obedience with a wordplay. The works of God come to pass from "year to year" (שנה [ושנה, 5:2a) and "do not change" (לא ישניון, 5:2c).[251] This sets up the contrast in 5:4: sinners are emphatically addressed ("But you," ואנתן) as those who changed ("you changed," שניתן) their works. In addition, the parallel statement that sinners "transgressed" (ותע[ברון, 5:4) against God forms an *inclusio* with the luminaries in *1 Enoch* 2:1. The luminaries "do not transgress" ([ולא מעב]רין) their appointed orders.

The idea of transgression supplies the key to the explicit message of the piece: *The works of creation do not change/transgress, but you do!* The implication is that sinners have forsaken the ordinance of God and must return to the norms practiced by the elect community. This point is reinforced in the second element of the salvation-judgment oracle (*1 En* 5:5-9). The elect "will sin no more (οὐ μὴ ἁμαρτήσονται ἔτι) through godlessness or pride ... nor will they transgress (οὐ μὴ πλημμελήσουσιν), nor will they sin (οὐδὲ μὴ ἁμάρτωσιν) all the days of their life" (5:8c, f-g; cf. 5:6e). These statements follow immediately upon the eschatological gift of wisdom (5:8a-d) and the "*understanding*" (νόημα, 5:8e; cf. 5:1 νοήσατε) possessed by the wise man. The wise man understands the created order, joins with it in obedience to the Creator's word (as practiced by the elect community), and is free from transgression. *1 Enoch* 2:1-5:4 is an invitation to come to the same understanding or, failing this, to be accused by the rest of creation.

The second message in *1 Enoch* 2:1-5:4 is not explicitly stated by the author but must be intuited by the reader.[252] The author includes material

---

[249] Rau noted the correspondence between Jer 5:23 and *1 En* 5:4 (*Kosmologie*, 114), but claimed that the meaning of *1 En* 5:4 was not primarily a question of contrasting the obedience of the works of creation with the disobedience of the wicked (ibid., 92). The Aramaic of *1 En* 5:4 now indicates otherwise.

[250] Translation suggested in F. Brown, S. R. Driver and C. A. Briggs, *A Hebrew and English Lexicon of the Old Testament* (Corrected edition; Oxford: Clarendon, 1907/1977) 717. Various emendations have been suggested for the problematic phrase in question: גם עברו דברירע (Jer 5:28). In our view, the emendations are unnecessary because the figurative meaning is attested (cf. Ps 73:7b).

[251] The Aramaic words in this paragraph are found in 4QEnᵃ.

[252] On this aspect of parables, see Chap. I, p. 20, n. 40.

about the "signs" (דגלי, 2:3 [twice]; 4:1) of summer and winter (2:3-5:1).[253] The signs involve a combination of the *climatic conditions* of winter and summer and the *accompanying response* of human beings (in summer only) and the trees: in winter, when moisture is abundant, the trees are stripped of their foliage; in summer, when the sun and the earth burn, human beings try to escape the heat; in summer, when the heat is severe (and moisture scarce), the trees blossom and are fruitful.[254]

What is the message conveyed by these signs? A literary clue is offered in the second part of the salvation-judgment oracle. As indicated above, some motifs in *1 Enoch* 5:8 resonate with the creation piece (no more sin, new understanding). It comes as no surprise, therefore, that the same holds true for 5:9. In *1 Enoch* 5:9a, the chosen are assured that "they will not die *in the heat of wrath* (ἐν ὀργῇ θυμοῦ)."[255] The (botanical) images of growing (αὔξω) and increasing (πληθύνω) follow this statement (5:9c-d). In short, the salvation of the elect community is pictured with motifs that recall the signs of summer in 2:3-5:1.

In the summer season, when the sun "burns and scorches" and the earth "burns," human beings seek shade and cannot walk on the ground because of the "burning/heat" (4:1).[256] The reader intuits the meaning: one must escape the heat of wrath poured out in the final judgment. In summer, when moisture is scarce, the trees blossom and bear fruit (5:1). Again, intuition tells the reader that the elect will flourish at the time of the judgment. If the reader

---

[253] The term has been understood as referring to "'natural, regular and cyclical phenomena'; cf. אותות in Hebrew" (Milik, *The Books of Enoch*, 148) and "'weather sign', 'token of changes of weather and times', e.g. Jer. 10.2 אותות השמים, LXX σημεῖα τοῦ οὐρανοῦ" (Black, *The Book of Enoch or 1 Enoch*, 111). But the point in Jer 10:2 is that the nations "are terrified" (חתת, *ni.*) at the signs of the heavens. Our discussion assumes that weather signs bear some relationship to the interpretation of the times (cf. Lu 12:54-56; par. Matt 16:2-3).

[254] Rau calls attention to the antithetical relationship between two phenomena within one season: in winter, the dampness of the earth stands over against the withering of the trees; in summer, the heat stands over against the foliage and fruit-bearing of the trees. Yet, Rau appeals to *1 En* 82:15-20 and argues that together the four phenomena correspond to the four quarters of the year, in the sequence fall, winter, summer, spring. He concludes that the passage is about the unchanging rhythm of the events of nature (*Kosmologie*, 72-75, 91). Nickelsburg refers to the "paradoxical order" of the phenomena on earth ("The Place of the Astronomical Book in the Enochic Corpus," *unpublished paper*).

[255] In Isa 42:25 LXX ὀργὴν θυμοῦ αὐτοῦ translates חמה אפו ("the heat of his wrath").

[256] The Aramaic verbs are rare (see Black, *The Books of Enoch or 1 Enoch*, 112), unless we read the last occurrence in 4:1 as חמת[א/ה (Milik, *The Books of Enoch*, 146, 185). The Greek is not extant.

truly understands the signs of summer, he will seek refuge with the Enochic community and will not die in the judgment.

If the above analysis is correct, one may at least speculate about the meaning of the signs of winter. There is an abundance of water in the winter season (2:3)—an indication of the blessing of God—yet most trees appear withered and loose their leaves (3:1). Does this sign apply to the community of godless sinners whom the author is addressing? Are sinners, who have changed their ways as compared to the Enochic community yet believe themselves to be righteous, portrayed as spiritually barren by the image of the withering of the trees? Perhaps, but this conclusion is impossible to demonstrate. It may be the case that 2:3-3:1 simply sets the context for 4:1-5:1; after all, the human response is only introduced in the latter.

1 Enoch 101:1-9[257]

The second Enochic passage occupied with the observable phenomena of creation also occurs in a context of judgment. The context is introduced by a series of Woe-oracles (*1 En* 100:7-9). Two units employing creation motifs follow. The first gives the created elements a role in the judgment (100:10-13); the second exhorts sinners to understand a lesson(s) taught by creation (101:1-9). The context closes with a description of the final judgment (102:1-3). In the analysis of *1 Enoch* 101:1-9 below, there will be reason to refer briefly to the preceding section (100:10-13).[258]

1 En   101:1   So contemplate, O sons of men, the deeds of the Most High
         and fear to do evil in his presence.
     2   If he closes the windows of heaven,
            and withholds the dew and the rain from descending because
            of you, what will you do?
     3   If he sends forth his wrath against you and your deeds,
            will you not be entreating him?
         Why do you speak with your mouth proud and hard things
            against his majesty?
         You will have no peace.
     4   Look at the captains who sail the sea!
         Their ships are shaken by wave and storm.
     5   And being beaten by the storm, they all fear,
            and they cast out into the sea all their goods and possessions.

---

[257] Greek text in Bonner, *The Last Chapters of Enoch in Greek* (Studies and Documents 8; London: Christophers, 1937) 54-59. For text-criticial decisions informing Nickelsburg's translation, see his "Enoch 97-104," 100-101, 120-21.

[258] On *1 En* 100:7-9, see pp. 208-09; on 100:10-13 and 102:1-3, see pp. 182-84.

And in their heart they are apprehensive
   that the sea will swallow them up, and they will perish
   in it.
6   Are not all the sea and all its waters and all its movement
      the work of the Most High?
      and he constituted it from the waters,
      and bound it together and confined it by the sand.
7   And at his rebuke they fear and dry up,
      and the fish die and all that is in it;
      but you sinners upon the earth do not fear him.
8   Did he not make the heavens and the earth and all that is in
      them?
      And who gave knowledge and wisdom to all that move on the
      earth and to all that are in the sea?
9   Do not the captains fear the sea?
      But the sinners do not fear the Most High.

1 Enoch 101:1-9 offers a reprise of many of the motifs present in *1 Enoch* 2:1-5:4.[259] The imperatives "contemplate" and "look" are taken up again (101:1a, 4a).[260] As in the earlier piece, 101:1-9 directs the observer to the "works of the Most High" (τὰ ἔργα τοῦ ὑψίστου, 101:1, cf. 101:6/ἔργα θεοῦ, 2:2; τὰ ἔργα αὐτοῦ, 5:2); namely, the works of heaven and earth that God "made" (ἐποίησεν, 5:1/101:8 [no Gk]). The "works" of the sea and rivers, mentioned briefly in 5:3, receive expanded treatment in 101:4-9. The expansion builds on the contrast between the obedience of the sea and the disobedience of sinners, and its language even more closely parallels that of Jeremiah 5:20-31.[261] Finally, the addressees in both passages are characterized as those who speak proud and hard words against God's majesty (101:3/5:4).

The expressions "fear to do evil" (101:1b) and "fear the Most High" (101:9b) form an *inclusio* to the passage. This vocabulary was not used in 2:1-

---

[259] This point was made by Rau and Nickelsburg, see the following two notes.

[260] Rau noted that the verb "contemplate" in *1 En* 2:1-5:4 is found only here (101:1a) in the whole of Enochic tradition (*Kosmologie*, 87). The Greek is κατανοήσατε (as in 2:1). The verb "look" (101:4a) is probably [ἴδε-]τε (as in 2:2, 3; 3:1; 5:3). Bonner proposes reading [ὁρᾶ-]τε (*The Last Chapters of Enoch in Greek*, 55), but we see no reason not to prefer the verb commonly used in *1 En* 2-5. Further, we may conjecture that the Aramaic verbs are בין and חזה.

[261] This was pointed out by Nickelsburg, "The Place of the Astronomical Book in the Enochic Corpus." Jer 5 includes references to the fear of God (5:22, 24), the sand as a boundary (5:22), the tossing of the waves (5:22; but see below), and the giving of the rains (5:24). Cf. also the question "what will you do?" (Jer 5:31/*1 En* 101:2).

5:4, but it is traditional in Hymns of Praise and the wisdom literature.[262] The motif of fear is developed in two major ways in 101:2-3 and 101:4-9.

First, the rhetorical questions in *1 Enoch* 101:2-3 refer the reader back to the preceding unit (100:10-13). The first question looks back to 100:11-12 and the second to 100:13:[263]

1 En 100:10 And now know that the angels will search out your deeds in
heaven,
from the sun and from the moon and from the stars,
concerning your sins;
because on earth you execute judgment on the righteous.

11 And every cloud and mist and dew and rain will testify
against you;
for they will all be withheld from you, so as not to
descend upon you,
and they will be mindful of your sins.

12 Therefore, give gifts to the rain, lest it be withheld from
descending to you,
and to the dew and cloud and mist pay gold, that they may
descend.

13 For if the snow and the frost and its cold hurl themselves
upon you,
and the winds and their chill and all their scourges,
then you will not be able to endure before the cold and
their scourges.

The imagery of 100:10-11 is that of the covenant lawsuit.[264] Sun, moon and stars witness the deeds of covenant violators. Here, additional elements of creation also have this function,[265] in particular, the meteorological elements of the winter season ("every cloud and mist and dew and rain," 100:11; cf. 100:12/"clouds and dew and rain," 2:3) testify by virtue of the fact that they are withheld from descending (100:11, 12). The verbal expression "withhold from descent" ($\kappa\omega\lambda\acute{\upsilon}\omega$ $\kappa\alpha\tau\alpha\beta\tilde{\eta}\nu\alpha\iota$) is taken up again in the rhetorical question of 101:2. Sinners are helpless before the accurate and powerful testimony of meteorological elements. They should regard this aspect of creation as a parable and learn the lesson: fear to do evil.

---

[262] E.g., Pss 33:18; 111:10; Prov 3:7. See Roland E. Murphy, "Religious Dimensions of Israelite Wisdom," *Ancient Israelite Religion* (ed. Patrick D. Miller, Jr., Paul D. Hanson, and S. Dean McBride; Philadelphia: Fortress) 452-53.

[263] See Nickelsburg ("Enoch 97-104," 99, 151) for the textual criticism informing his translation.

[264] See Chap. 5, pp. 182-83.

[265] This was not as apparent in 2:1-5:4, although Hartman raises the possibility that the covenant lawsuit is in the background (*Asking For A Meaning*, 28-30).

The second rhetorical question in 101:3 alludes to 100:13. The idea, "if" God "sends forth" (ἐὰν ἀποστείληται) his wrath "against you" (ἐφ᾽ ὑμᾶς, 101:3), echoes what was previously said of the elements and their scourges: "if (they) hurl themselves against you" (ἐὰν ἐπιρρίψῃ ἐφ᾽ ὑμᾶς, 100:13). In contexts of judgment, God is commonly portrayed as pouring out or hurling fire (cf. *1 En* 102:1). However, because *1 Enoch* 100:11-12 dealt with the meteorology of the winter season, 100:13 carries this imagery forward. God sends a winter blizzard before which sinners are unable to endure (100:13). The elements of snow, frost and cold become instruments of God's judgment. Again, sinners should contemplate this phenomena as a parable and fear to do evil.

The theme of fear is developed in a second major way in *1 Enoch* 101:4-9. This section contains an expanded picture of the work of God on the sea. In addition to the similarities with Jeremiah 5 noted above, the imagery in 101:4-5 and 101:9 parallels Psalm 107:23-30.

Psalm 107 is a Hymn of Praise offered by pilgrims who came to Jerusalem for a major festival.[266]   After an introduction (107:1-3), four strophes follow, each of which concludes with a two-part refrain (107:4-9, 10-16, 17-22, 23-32). The first part of the refrain is identical: "Let them thank the Lord for his steadfast love, for *his wonderful works* (נפלאותיו) *to the sons of men*" (107:8, 15, 21, 31; cf. *1 En* 101:1).[267]

Psalm 107:23-30 offers one example of the "works" of the Lord: his works on the sea. This strophe shares a similar structure with the others: a description of humankind's distress, the cry to the Lord and his deliverance, and an exhortation to thank the Lord (the refrain). For purposes of comparison, Psalm 107:23-30 is juxtaposed to the related imagery in *1 Enoch* 101:4-5:

Psalm 107	*1 Enoch* 101
Humankind's distress	
23 Some went down to the sea in ships ...	4a Look at the captains who sail the sea!

---

[266] On the category "Pilgrim Songs" within the Hymns of Praise, see Gerstenberger, "Psalms," 210-12.

[267] The fifth and concluding strophe (Ps 107:33-43) offers a variation on the refrain: "Whoever is wise, let him give heed to these things; *let* people *consider* (יתבוננו) the steadfast love of the Lord" (107:43). While this concluding strophe is usually not regarded as original to the Pilgrim Song, this is not significant for our purposes. Note the connection between the verb "consider/contemplate" in Ps 107:43 and *1 En* 101:1.

24	they saw the deeds of the Lord, his wonderful works in the deep.		Their ships ...
25	... he raised the stormy wind, which lifted up the waves of the sea.	4b	... are shaken by wave and storm.
26a	They mounted up ... they went down ...	5a	And being beaten by the storm ...
			... they all fear, and they cast out into the sea all their goods ...
26b-27	their courage melted away ... they reeled and staggered ... and were at their wits' end.	5b	And in their heart, they are apprehensive, that the sea will swallow them up, and they will perish in it.

Cry and deliverance

28-30	Then they cried to the Lord ... and he delivered them ... he made the storm be still, and the waves of the sea were hushed ...

Exhortation to praise

31	... for his wonderful works to the sons of men!

The basic difference between the two accounts is the lack of the last two elements in *1 Enoch*. In Psalm 107, pilgrims on the storm-tossed sea cried to God for deliverance and were rescued. In *1 Enoch* 101:4-5, these elements do not follow the picture of human distress. The distress itself is further developed by the common practice of throwing goods overboard. This particular feature is related to "fear" (101:5a) and has a parabolic significance the reader must intuit. The reader who fears God must dispossess himself of (ill-gotten) material gain or perish.

The human response is part of the situation of distress in *1 Enoch*. The passage does not contain cries for deliverance and God's rescue. Rather, these particular hymnic motifs have given way to the didactic intention of the piece. Sinners must show they fear God by acting decisively in the present distress before it is too late and they perish. The point is dramatically reinforced through a connection to the judgment scene that follows in *1 Enoch* 102:1-3.

The "shaking" ($\sigma\alpha\lambda\varepsilon\acute{\nu}\omega$) of the ship at sea (101:4) anticipates the "shaking" ([$\sigma\nu\sigma$]$\sigma\varepsilon\acute{\iota}\omega$) of the sinners, the heavens, the earth and all of humankind in final judgment (102:1d, 2a, 2b, [3c]).[268]

Summary

In *1 Enoch* 2:1–5:4 and 101:1-9, the observable phenomena of creation are regarded as objects to be contemplated. The idea that one should study the created works of God is found in creation Hymns and the wisdom literature, but both passages are more indebted to Jeremiah 5. In *1 Enoch*, the creation theme is joined to the prophetic announcement of judgment. Creation offers explicit and implicit lessons that warn sinners of the coming judgment and how they may escape. In both 2:1-5:4 and 101:1-9, the implicit lesson is found in a typical human response to a distressing aspect of created reality (summer heat/storm at sea). The way to escape judgment is to seek shelter with the Enochic community and practice their "fear of God." For both authors, it remains an open question whether sinners will recognize the parabolic messages of creation.

HIDDEN ASPECTS OF THE CREATION

This section is devoted to passages that relate another aspect of the created order: phenomena that are hidden from the naked eye but have been seen and (sometimes) experienced by Enoch. These phenomena, too, authenticate the practices of the Enochic community and have a role in the judgment. The investigation begins in the Book of the Watchers, moves to one passage in the Epistle (*1 En* 93:11-14), and concludes with the Astronomical Book.

1 Enoch 12-36

In this portion of the Book of the Watchers, the hidden elements of creation come into play in four ways. They are found in connection with the ascent of Enoch, the material of the heavenly temple, the sight-seeing reports of his journeys, and the places of eschatological significance to which he journeys.

---

[268] The Greek text of *1 En* 102:1-3 is corrupt in places. It moves the "shaking" of heaven and the luminaries (vs 2a) after verse 3a, thereby displacing what is predicated of the sons of earth in verses 3b-c (including their "shaking"). See G. Zuntz, "Notes on the Greek Enoch," *JBL* 61 (1942) 197-201.

The Ascent of Enoch

A single verse, *1 Enoch* 14:8, describes the created elements involved in the ascent of Enoch:[269]

1 En 14:8   And in (the) vision it was shown to me thus:
Behold, clouds in the vision were summoning me, and mists were crying out to me;
and shooting stars and lightning flashes were hastening me and speeding me along;
and winds in my vision made me fly and lifted me upward and brought me to heaven.

The passage emphasizes what Enoch "was shown" ($\delta\varepsilon\acute{\iota}\kappa\nu\nu\mu\iota$, pass./*'astar'aya*) in his "vision" ($\ddot{o}\rho\alpha\sigma\iota\varsigma$/*rā'y*, 3 times). He is shown clouds, mists, shooting stars,[270] lightning flashes, and winds. While these elements of nature might also be seen from the earth,[271] here they are objects of revelation and function in a supernatural way. Enoch is conducted to the presence of God by the various created elements. Each of the elements mentioned is the subject of a verb of beckoning or motion. Together, they are portrayed as obedient servants of God engaged in something other than their usual capacity.

The Material of the Heavenly Temple

After the created elements summon and transport Enoch into heaven, he still does not find himself immediately in the presence of God. Rather, *1 Enoch* 14:9-17 records his movements, perceptions, and experiences, once

---

[269] For Nickelsburg's translation and accompanying text-critical notes, see his "Enoch, Levi, and Peter," 578, n. 17. *1 En* 14:8 belongs to the earliest stratum of chapters 12-16, chapters that introduce Enoch into the myth of Shemihazah and the Watchers. Enoch has written a book (*1 En* 14:1-16:4) telling the story of his ascent to the divine throne and his prophet-like commission to pronounce judgment on the fallen angels. The book opens with a brief summary section (14:2-7), after which 14:8 begins the narrative of the visionary experience by describing how Enoch was transported to heaven.

[270] The idiom is $\delta\iota\alpha\delta\rho\rho\mu\alpha\grave{\iota}$ $\tau\tilde{\omega}\nu$ $\dot{\alpha}\sigma\tau\acute{\varepsilon}\rho\omega\nu$/*ruṣata kawākebt* (*literally*, "the runnings of the stars").

[271] The elements may ultimately derive from an onomasticon or list. Such lists were adapted to many different literary forms. We will return to the use and development of such lists below.

again employing elements of the created order. Enoch's approach to God recalls the temple tour in Ezekiel 40-48.[272]

In the Enochic conception of the temple, as opposed to Ezekiel's, there is no mention of outer and inner courts, nor of a vestibule as such.[273] The focus is on the temple proper. In terms of the basic layout of the temple, the nave and inner room of Ezekiel's temple are pictured as adjoining houses, with the second or inner house greater than the first. Finally, the account in Ezekiel contains many specific details involving measurements, materials and decorative designs. The Enochic temple tour lacks any reference to measurements, but does describe the material of the two houses, which consists of created elements.

Two comments are in order regarding the function of these created elements in the heavenly temple. First, although a few of the specific images are obscure, it is obvious that the elements of fire and snow dominate. The outer wall is built of hailstones wrapped in tongues of fire (*1 En* 14:9). Similarly, the first house is constructed of hailstones; its walls and floor are made of snow (14:10). The ceiling is depicted by two elements that played a role previously in the ascent; "the ceiling was like shooting stars and lightning flashes" (14:11; cf. 14:8). Finally, the walls and doors of this first snowhouse are enveloped in fire, as was the case with the outer wall of the complex (14:12).

Curiously, the elements of hailstone/snow disappear in the material of the second, greater house, which is totally constructed of tongues of fire (14:15). Perhaps the intention of the narrative is to call attention to the throne within, which is said to have an appearance "like ice" (14:18). In addition, the Great Glory who sits on the throne has raiment "whiter than much snow" (14:20). Flashes of lightning and shooting stars again appear in the second house, but as the material of its "upper part" (τὸ ἀνώτερον/*mal'elt*, 14:17b) rather than the ceiling, which is flaming fire (14:17c).

The combination of the elements of fire and snow, elements not associated in nature, conveys the idea that Enoch has entered another realm. The

---

[272] In Chap. I (p. 30, n. 69), we noted scholars who argue that Enoch's approach to God draws upon the temple tour in Ezek 40-48 and the vision of the divine throne in Ezek 1-2. Nickelsburg, in particular, suggests that the latter passage supplies phenomena for the material of the temple in *1 En* 14:9-17 ("Enoch, Levi, and Peter," 582.)

[273] The Enochic version moves from the wall (Ezek 40:5) directly to the nave (Ezek 41:1), bypassing the outer court (Ezek 40:17), the inner court (Ezek 40:28) and the vestibule (Ezek 40:38). In this respect, the Enochic account has closer ties to the layout of Solomon's temple as described in 1 Kgs 6, though the latter has a vestibule.

extreme opposites of created phenomena are joined in this realm to reflect its supernatural and transcendent character.[274]

A second comment concerns Enoch's experience during his temple tour. The lack of any reference to an accompanying angel at this stage of the tour may not be too significant[275] but it certainly helps the narrative to focus on the unique experience of Enoch. At each stage of the tour, Enoch is struck with fear: at the wall (ἐκφοβέω, *1 En* 14:9), at the first house (φόβος ... καὶ τρόμος, 14:13c; σειόμενος καὶ τρέμων, 14:14a) and at the second house (τρέμων, 14:24). Enoch's fear is directly related to the two extremes of created phenomena, fire and snow. He experiences hot and cold, and is terrified (14:13).

There are limits to Enoch's experience. It does not appear, for example, that Enoch entered the greater house (nor did Ezekiel enter the nave). Enoch received his prophet-like commission after being picked up from the floor and brought to the door of the second house (*1 En* 14:25). The restriction at the threshold was also observed by the angels (14:21).[276] Enoch would not proceed where angels feared to tread!

Both the description of the temple and the point of cessation of the tour serve to validate the message of judgment Enoch will convey to the Watchers. Because the rebel Watchers once inhabited the heavenly sanctuary (*1 En* 15:3), they will recognize the created phenomena Enoch saw and experienced.[277] The terror-inspiring, hidden elements of the heavenly realm authenticate his mission to the Watchers.

The Sight-Seeing Reports

Under this heading, the esoteric creation traditions preserved in the journey reports (*1 En* 17:1-18:5; 28-31) will be investigated. The treatment of 17:1-18:5 will also include a brief discussion of chapters 33-36.

Carol Newsom has called attention to the parallels between chapters 17-18 and chapter 14.[278] As Enoch toured the heavenly temple before approaching the throne to hear God's verdict on the Watchers, so Enoch later tours heaven itself (17:1-18:5) before moving beyond the mountain throne to see the

---

[274] Nickelsburg, "Enoch, Levi, and Peter," 582.

[275] Cf. Ezek 40:3-4. An angel steps into view for the first time in *1 En* 14:25 in connection with the commissioning scene.

[276] Our discussion of the Enochic account of the angelic presence around the throne (*1 En* 14:20-23) is reserved for the comparative section below, pp. 161-62.

[277] Nickelsburg, *Jewish Literature*, 52-53.

[278] "The Development," 324.

place where God's verdict will be carried out.[279]   What hidden phenomena does Enoch see in his tour of heaven?

After a brief introductory statement in *1 Enoch* 17:1-2 previewing the ultimate destination, two literary units of esoteric creation tradition follow (17:3-7; 18:1-5). For our purposes, the mythic geography present in the first major unit may be left aside (17:4-7).[280]   What remains is primarily references to the luminaries (17:3). The second unit is largely about the winds (18:1-5).[281]

1 En   17:3   And I saw the place of the luminaries
               and the treasuries of the stars and of the thunders,
               and to the depths of the ether, where the bow of fire and the
               arrows and their quivers (were) and all the lightnings.

        18:1   I saw the treasuries of all the winds. I saw how through
               them he ordered all created things.

           2   And I saw the foundation of the earth and the cornerstone of
               the earth. I saw the four winds bearing the earth and the
               firmament of heaven. 3/ And I saw how the winds stretch
               out the height of heaven. And they stand between earth and
               heaven; they are the pillars of heaven.
           4   I saw the winds of heaven that turn and bring to (their)
               setting the disc of the sun and all the stars.
           5   I saw the winds upon the earth bearing the clouds.
               I saw the paths of the angels.
               I saw at the ends of the earth the firmament of heaven above.

The verb "I saw" (ἴδον/re'iku) dominates the two sections. The imperative of this verb was used in *1 Enoch* 2:1-5:4 and 101:4 to exhort sinners to "observe" the works of God in heaven, earth and sea. The ascended Enoch looks at hidden phenomena in the same way. That is, as there was a message in the observable works of creation, so also in the hidden works of heaven.

---

[279] From the point of view of redaction history, chapters 17-19 are a later addition to chapters 6-16. The goal of the journey in these chapters is the place of punishment for the the Watchers (*1 En* 18:6-19:2). This place is considered shortly under the category of places of eschatological significance.

[280] The parallels to ancient Near Eastern and Greek mythology have been discussed by many scholars. See, for example, VanderKam, *Enoch and the Growth*, 137-39.

[281] Nickelsburg's translation is based on Greek and Ethiopic. The luminaries and winds emerge again at the conclusion of the Book of the Watchers (chaps 33, 34-36). In fact, *1 En* 33:1 also contains a description of mythic beasts that may serve as a parallel to the mythic geography of *1 En* 17:4-7.

A major lesson to be learned from the hidden elements of creation relates to the luminaries. In the first unit of sight-seeing material, the luminaries and stars occupy the leading position: "I saw the place of the luminaries and the treasuries of the stars ..." (*1 En* 17:3). The second unit begins with a parallel expression: "I saw the treasuries of all the winds" (18:1a).[282] The leading emphasis in the second unit is on the ordering function of the winds (18:1b),[283] including the manner in which the winds provide order for the sun and all the stars. Enoch sees how the winds rotate the heavens and conduct the luminaries on their paths: "I saw the winds of heaven that turn (heaven) and bring to setting the disc of the sun and all the stars" (18:4).[284] Finally, 18:5b ("I saw the paths of the angels") implies, in this context, that the angels are leaders of the stars.

The emphasis on the luminaries and the regularity of their movements was also present in *1 Enoch* 2:1, and thus 17:3 and 18:4, 5b should be viewed in connection with that passage. In fact, the esoteric sight-seeing material in *1 Enoch* 18 displays motifs found in 2:1:

	1 Enoch 2		*1 Enoch* 18
1b	*Observe* the works of *heaven*	4a	*I saw* the winds of *heaven*
c	they do not alter their *paths*	[5b	*I saw* the *paths* of the angels]
d	and the *luminaries* of heaven	4b	and bring to *setting*
e	they *all* rise and *set*		the disc of the *sun*
			and all the stars
f	each one *ordered* in its	1b	*he ordered all* created things
	appointed time (τάσσω, twice)		(κοσμέω)
g	they appear on their feasts		
h	do not transgress their *order* (τάξις)		

A major difference is that *1 Enoch* 18:4, 5b places the phenomena of *1 Enoch* 2:1 under the control of the winds and the angels. The result is that

---

[282] That the stars and the winds have "treasuries" is a biblical image; but one that is not utilized elsewhere in early Enochic tradition, neither in the Astronomical Book nor in chapters 33, 34-36 (but cf. 41:5).

[283] The ordering function of the winds in *1 En* 18:1-5 is much different from functions ascribed to them in either the Astronomical Book (*1 En* 76) or chapters 34-36. Here, the winds provide support for earth and heaven, and insure the regularity of the movements of the luminaries. In the Astronomical Book (*1 En* 76) and chapters 34-36, the winds have a meteorological function. The only meteorological allusion in 18:1-5 is in verse 5a.

[284] In this respect, there is at least a point of contact with early Enochic tradition: "the wind blows the chariots on which it (the sun) ascends" (*1 En* 72:5).

as Enoch journeys to the place of punishment for the Watchers, he sees that all is well in heaven as far as the luminaries are concerned. Their treasuries are intact and their movements are regulated.

There was no explicit statement in the preceding chapters that suggested anything had gone awry with the luminaries. Why is order stressed in this sight-seeing report? *1 Enoch* 17:3 and 18:4, 5b anticipate the punishment of erring stars at the destination of Enoch's first journey (18:15-16). The lesson, therefore, is that order exists in heaven in spite of the fact that some stars and angels have rebelled and will be punished. The sight-seeing reports offer assurance about the stability of the upper world.

The interpretation of 17:3 and 18:1-5 offered above receives support from the two literary units that close the Book of the Watchers (chaps 33, 34-36).[285] These closing reports seem to have been included with an eye toward *1 Enoch* 17:1-18:5, forming an *inclusio* to Enoch's journeys. Like the opening two sight-seeing sections, these two units also treat the stars and the winds. The difference is that in the units prefacing the first journey, Enoch is at the ends of the earth in the West; in chapter 33 he has arrived at the ends of the earth in the East. If Enoch previously saw the "setting" (*1 En* 18:4) of the sun and all the stars, here he states: "I saw how the stars of heaven come forth" (33:3). The action of setting gives way to rising because he is in the East.

The same emphasis on orderliness is present in *1 Enoch* 33-36, although it is ascribed to a different factor; namely, gates. In *1 Enoch* 33, the stars come forth through gates on the eastern horizon. In *1 Enoch* 34-36, the winds blow through gates at each of the cardinal compass points. After Enoch circumambulates earth's disk to survey the wind gates,[286] he arrives once again in the East where he sees that above the gates of the winds are small windows through which the stars pass "and they proceed westward on the path that is shown them" (*1 En* 36:3; cf. 75:6-7). This reference to "the path" shown to the stars may allude to "the paths of the angels" in *1 Enoch* 18:5b.

Thus, the Book of the Watchers closes by reiterating the point that no significant disruption has occurred with respect to the heavens. From West (*1 En*

---

[285] In terms of redaction history, these chapters, which offer an abbreviated summary of the Astronomical Book, are secondary. The original ending of the Book of the Watchers can be found in *1 En* 81:1-82:3. See the Excursus.

[286] The account of Enoch's circumambulation of earth's disk to survey the gates of the winds assumes his starting position in the East. Therefore, Enoch has to journey to the North (*1 En* 34:1) before he can survey the wind gates with the same orientation given in *1 En* 76 (north, west, south, east). See Neugebauer's diagram and assessment of the wind gates in chapters 34-36 ("The 'Astronomical' Chapters of the Ethiopic Book of Enoch [72 to 82]," in Black, *The Book of Enoch or 1 Enoch*, 406).

17:1-18:5) to East (*1 En* 33:3; 36:2-3), Enoch sees that the luminaries remain in an ordered state.

1 Enoch 28:1-32:2 is a sight-seeing report that focuses on the special trees and plants that Enoch sees on his way to Paradise and the Tree of Wisdom (32:3-6). The text is broken in places,[287] but it is clear that these trees and plants provide exotic spices and perfumes.[288] The beauty and fragrance of the trees prepare Enoch for Paradise, whose trees are even larger and more beautiful (*1 En* 32:3). The Tree of Wisdom is largest and most beautiful; two qualities drawn from the World Tree of ancient mythology.[289] The Tree of Wisdom also has a fragrance (32:4d) that is obviously intended to contrast with the aroma of the spice trees seen *en route*.[290]

While *1 Enoch* 28:1-32:2 describes the trees Enoch saw ("I saw," 29:2; 30:1, 3; 31:1; "I was shown," 31:2),[291] the implication is that he also *smells* the sweet aromas of the spice trees. Likewise, the fragrance of the Tree of Wisdom "penetrates far from the tree" (32:4d), presumably far enough to reach Enoch. Thus, Enoch is having a pleasurable experience as he journeys to Paradise.

Enoch gives a report about sweet-smelling trees on his journey to tree-filled Paradise. If the sight-seeing material about the luminaries offered a reassuring message about the heavens, then the hidden phenomena of these trees contains a comforting message about the earth. As the heavens did not collapse due to the rebellion of the Watchers, neither will the earth succumb to total devastation because of the disobedience of humankind. Heaven and earth have endured some serious blows, but Enoch sees hidden realities that guarantee the recovery of both. In terms of the earth, Enoch sees that its productivity and associated pleasures are held in reserve for the chosen (cf. *1 En* 10:18).

---

[287] Aramaic fragments (4QEn⁰ I xxvi 3-6, 14-21; 4QEn⁰ I xii) in Milik, *The Books of Enoch*, 231-32, 201. See the text-critical discussion in Knibb, *The Ethiopic Book of Enoch*, 2.116-22.

[288] Milik's attempt (*The Books of Enoch*, 25-28) to relate the information in *1 En* 28:1-32:2 to actual geographical places and trade routes has been questioned by many. See VanderKam, *Enoch and the Growth*, 137, n. 99.

[289] See Chap. I, p. 32, n. 79.

[290] Curiously, the trees in Paradise are not said to be "sweet-smelling" (*1 En* 32:3 Gk; Ethiopic does read "sweet-smelling" [*dĕnāhomu šannāy*]; see Dillman, *Lexicon*, 1309). This is odd because there are fragrant trees in the *mountain* Paradise of God, in comparison to which the Tree of Life is said to have a sweeter fragrance (*1 En* 24:3-4).

[291] The verbs are חזית and אחזיאת (31:1, 2; 4QEn⁰ I xii 26, 27).

Places of Eschatological Significance

The goal of the journey traditions in the Book of the Watchers is places of eschatological import. The destination of the first journey is the prisons of the stars and angels (*1 En* 18:6-19:2). The second journey begins here (*1 En* 21:1-6, 7-10)[292] and includes stops at hidden places reserved for humankind. The subject of this subheading is the hidden places creation holds for the stars and humankind.

The material on the stars at the end of the first journey is confined to *1 Enoch* 18:12-16:[293]

1 En   18:12   And beyond this chasm I saw a place where there was neither
                 firmament of heaven above, nor firmly founded earth
                 beneath it. Neither was there water upon it, nor bird;
                 but the place was desolate and fearful. 13/ There I saw
                 seven stars like great burning mountains.

         14   To me, when I inquired about them, the angel said, "This
                 place is the end of heaven and earth; this has become a
                 prison for the stars and the hosts of heaven. 15/ And the
                 stars that are rolling over in the fire, these are those
                 that transgressed the command of the Lord in the beginning
                 of their rising, for they did not come out in their
                 appointed times. 16/ And he was angry with them and bound
                 them until the time of the consummation of their sins—ten
                 thousand years."

These verses may be an insertion into a vision form that originally applied only to the angels.[294] The following diagram illustrates the literary disjunction:

---

[292] Nickelsburg, *Jewish Literature*, 55.

[293] Nickelsburg's translation is based on Greek and Ethiopic. The Aramaic evidence (4QEne1 xx, xxi) is too fragmentary to be useful (Milik, *The Books of Enoch*, 228).

[294] Nickelsburg suggests that the original order of the passage is 18:6-11, 19:1-2, 18:12-16, and 19:3 (*Jewish Literature*, 66, n. 28). On the vision form, see Wacker, *Weltordnung*, 101.

TABLE 3
THE PUNISHMENT OF STARS AND ANGELS:
THE VISION FORM IN THE JOURNEY REPORTS OF ENOCH

		Journey 1		Journey 2	
		Stars (18:12-16)	Angels (18:6-11; 19:1-2)	Stars (21:1-6)	Angels (21:7-10)
i.	Scene	------	18:6-10	21:1	21:7a
ii.	Verb(s) of Seeing	[18:12-13a]	18:11	21:2-3	21:7b
iii.	Dialogue				
	Type I				
	a)	[18:13b]		21:4	
	b)	[18:14-16]		21:5-6	
	Type II				
	a)		------		21:8
	b)		------		21:9a
	c)		------		21:9b
	d)		19:1-2		21:10

The opening words of 18:12, "And beyond this chasm, I saw," look suspiciously secondary (cf. 18:11: "And I saw a great chasm"). The statement that the place was desolate and fearful (18:12) recalls images from the first house of the divine temple ("no delight of life was in it"/"Fear enveloped me", 14:13). Finally, the reference to "seven stars like great burning mountains" (18:13) could be formed on analogy to the seven mountains mentioned in 18:6.

If 18:12-16 is secondary, the material was most likely inserted at the same time chapters 17-19 were appended. As indicated above, the opening two sight-seeing reports provide assurance about the regularity of the stars (17:3; 18:4, 5b) to prepare the reader for what will be said about them at journey's goal (18:15-16).

The disobedient and imprisoned stars are described in language that recalls 2:1:

1 Enoch 2:1	*1 Enoch* 18:15
the luminaries "all rise (ἀνατέλλει)	they "transgressed (οἱ παραβάντες)
and set, each one ordered	the command of the Lord
in its appointed time	in the beginning of their rising
(ἐν τῷ τεταγμένῳ καιρῷ)	(τῆς ἀνατολῆς αὐτῶν)
... and do not transgress	for they did not come out
(οὐ παραβαίνουσιν)	in their appointed times
their appointed order."	(ἐν τοῖς καιροῖς αὐτῶν)"

While it may appear from the perspective of earth that the stars do not transgress, Enoch sees otherwise in heaven. Even so, heaven has not been disrupted; the transgressing stars are imprisoned.

The insertion of 18:12-16 into the place of punishment for the rebel Watchers indicates that astronomical errancy is being tied to the older tradition about the fall of the Watchers.[295] A linkage has been made between the stars that "transgressed" and the older tradition of "the angels who mingled with the women" (19:1).

That the threat of astronomical errancy is an ongoing one is presupposed in the second journey report. The statement that the stars transgressed the command of the Lord is repeated, but the words "in the beginning of their rising" (a possible reference to creation) are eliminated (21:6). In addition, the vision material associated with the angel Raguel (*1 En* 20:4; 23:1-24:1) indicates that he is on duty in the West to oversee the pursuit and punishment of erring luminaries.[296] In this way, the continuing threat of transgression is met.

In sum, the Enochic community found an explanation for the astronomical miscalculations of the dominant society by relating them to the hidden phenomena of transgressing stars. The erring luminaries will be punished along with the rebel Watchers, a fact guaranteed by the place Enoch sees and the holy one in the West, Raguel, who acts as God's avenger.

The second journey of Enoch includes hidden places of eschatological import for human beings; including the mountain of Sheol (*1 En* 22:1-14), the

---

[295] Newsom suggests that 19:1-2 is secondary and that the punishment of the Watchers has been assimilated to that of the erring stars ("The Development," 323). We are arguing that the assimilation went the other way.

[296] Raguel is described as the holy angel who "takes vengeance" (ἐκδικῶν) on the world of the luminaries (*1 En* 20:4). When Enoch arrives at the fire of the West (23:1-2) and asks for an interpretation (23:3), Raguel informs him that this fire "pursues" (ἐκδιώκω) all the luminaries of heaven (23:4). The sense of this verb is "pursue to take vengeance." In the LXX, both Greek terms given above can translate the Hebrew נקם, *hitp.* (Jer 5:9, 29; 9:9; Ps 44:16).

mountain paradise of God and the Tree of Life (*1 En* 24:2-25:7), and the holy mountain at the center of the earth with its adjacent accursed valley (*1 En* 26:1-27:5). The author's description of these places emphasizes that they have been *created* for the future judgment of humankind. This is the case in two of the three visions mentioned above, Sheol and the Tree of Life.

When the angel Raphael interprets the hollow places in the mountain of Sheol, he tells Enoch "they were created" (*tafaṭru*)[297] to gather the souls of humans (*1 En* 22:3). And again, "they were made" (ἐποιήθησαν; 22:4, 9) in order to "separate" (χωρίζω; 22:9) the souls of the dead until the judgment. Subsequently, when Raphael interprets the function of each of the four hollow places, his interpretation is introduced by alternating expressions: "this has been separated" (χωρίζω/*falaṭa* β; 22:9, 12) and "this has been created" (κτίζω/*faṭara*; 22:10, 13). Creation language is used throughout the vision of Sheol to reinforce the notion that the cosmos was structured in anticipation of the coming judgment.[298]

Creation language is also present in Enoch's vision of the mountain paradise of God and the Tree of Life (*1 En* 24:2-25:7). In the last member of the vision form, Enoch responds to what he has seen by blessing God "who has prepared (ἡτοίμασεν) such things for men (who are) righteous and has created (ἔκτισεν) them and promised to give (them) to them" (25:7). God has prepared and created the salvific benefits the righteous will experience when God descends on the holy mountain and transplants the Tree of Life beside the temple (cf. *1 En* 103:3).[299]

The creation theme in *1 Enoch* 22 and 25 is taken up again in the (secondary) conclusion to the Book of the Watchers. Enoch blesses God who has done "wonders" (*ta'āmerāta*) to show the "greatness of his work" (*'ebaya gebru*) to angels and to the spirits of men, so that[300] they might glorify "his work and all his deeds" (*gebro wa-kʷello tagbāro*). In his tour of the upper cosmos, Enoch saw the wonders and the work of God; namely, the *created places* of eschatological significance. In effect, the Book of the Watchers

---

[297] The Greek is ἐκρίθησαν ("they were separated"), an apparent corruption of ἐκτίσθησαν, since throughout this passage the Ethiopic *faṭra* translates κτίζω (*1 En* 22:10, 13).

[298] George W. E. Nickelsburg, "The Apocalyptic Construction of Reality in *1 Enoch*," *Mysteries and Revelations: Apocalyptic Studies since the Uppsala Colloquium* (JSPS 9; ed. J. J. Collins and J. H. Charlesworth; Sheffield: JSOT, 1991) 56.

[299] See Chap. 5, pp. 187-88.

[300] The purpose clause at the conclusion of *1 En* 36:4 appears to contain a doublet in Ethiopic (our only witness).

closes with an invitation for angels and humankind to bless God for having
revealed the hidden places of creation.

1 Enoch 93:11-14

The Epistle of Enoch contains a passage in which Enoch reviews the hidden things he has seen and made known. *1 Enoch* 93:11-14 presents a number of textual problems for the translator, and it is best to rely on the Ethiopic:[301]

1 En   93:11   For who is there of all the sons of men who is able to hear
                         the words of the Holy One and not be terrified;
                   and who is able to think his thoughts?
                   And who is there of all men who is able to look at all the
                         works of heaven,

         12   ....[302]
                   Or to see a soul or a spirit
                         and is able to [return and][303] tell?
                   Or to ascend and see all their ends,
                         and to consider them or make (something) like them?

         13   Or who is there of all men who is able to know what is the
                         width and length of the earth;
                   and to whom has the size of all them been shown?

         14   And who is there of all men who is able to know the length
                         of the heavens,
                   and what is their height and upon what they are founded?
                   And what is the number of the stars,
                         and where all the luminaries rest?

1 Enoch 93:11-14 combines the literary features of rhetorical questions and a catalogue of the hidden aspects of creation.[304] Wisdom texts, such as

---

[301] Words and phrases from the fragment discovered at Qumrân (4QEng I v 15-23; Milik, *The Books of Enoch*, 269-70) do not always correlate with the Ethiopic. The problem is compounded by the fact that, in those places where it can be determined that the Aramaic text read differently, the Qumrân manuscript is too damaged to reconstruct the full reading. See Knibb, *The Ethiopic Book of Enoch*, 2.225-26.

[302] Ethiopic contains a doublet here: "And how is anyone able to look at heaven, and who is able to understand the works of heaven?"

[303] Our addition to Nickelsburg's translation. 4QEng 1 5 19 has the word למתב (ל + infinitive = "to return"), although whether the line as a whole corresponds to anything in the Ethiopic of 93:12 is impossible to determine.

[304] Michael Stone, "Lists of Revealed Things in the Apocalyptic Literature," *Magnalia Dei: The Mighty Acts of God* (ed. F. M. Cross, W. E. Lemke and P. D. Hanson; Garden City, NY: Doubleday, 1976) 415-52.

Job 38-39 and Proverbs 30:1-4, also combine rhetorical questions and lists of places and things.[305] The combination in Job and Proverbs makes the point that humankind cannot fathom the profound character of God's works in much of creation.

In so-called apocalyptic literature, however, such combinations serve an entirely different purpose. Michael Stone suggests that some primitive formulaic lists were first modified by verbs and then expanded by references to regularity and proportionality.[306] In *1 Enoch* 93:11-14, the speculative content of such lists has been further adapted to the interrogative formulation of the wisdom tradition.[307] The rhetorical questions imply that human knowledge of (esoteric) created phenomena is now possible because it was revealed to Enoch and has been imparted to the righteous as an eschatological gift.

Stone's analysis serves to strengthen the long-standing claim of scholars that *1 Enoch* 93:12 refers to the heavenly journeys of Enoch.[308] The following observations lend additional support to the view that *1 Enoch* 93:11-14 involves the speculative content of Enochic tradition.

First, the passage opens with imagery that recalls the parameters of the journey traditions: the divine commission (*1 En* 14-16) and the testamentary fulfillment scene (82:1-3).

The language of hearing the voice of the Holy One (*sami'a qālo la-qeddus*) and not being terrified (*'i-yethawwek*, 93:11a)[309] immediately suggests

---

[305] The device of asking rhetorical questions about places and things is much older than its appearance in the Hebrew Bible. Von Rad traces it to the catechetical mode and encyclopaedic scope of instruction in ancient Egyptian scribal schools. For details, see his "Job XXXVIII and Ancient Egyptian Wisdom," *Studies in Ancient Israelite Wisdom* (ed. J. L. Crenshaw; New York: Ktav, 1976) 267-77.

[306] See his treatment of *1 En* 41:1-7; 43:1-2; 60:11-13, 14-22; *2 En* 23:2; 40:1-13 ("Lists of Revealed Things," 414-19).

[307] Ibid., 423-26. This conclusion is more persuasive than that offered by Black, who dubs *1 En* 93:11-14 "A Nature Poem" and comments: "The whole pericope can, in fact, be explained as a poem on natural theology which could have come from a source quite independent of Enoch" (*The Book of Enoch or 1 Enoch*, 286).

[308] See Charles, *APOT*, 2.264. Milik states that *1 En* 93:12 is "an allusion to the ultra-terrestrial journeys of Enoch, in particular to that in the abode of souls, En. 22" (*The Books of Enoch*, 271). *Pace* Black, who argues that "to ascend" imitates Prov 30:4 (*The Book of Enoch or 1 Enoch*, 286).

[309] Nickelsburg points out that the question in *1 En* 93:11 echoes Deut 4:33 ("Did any people ever hear the voice of a god speaking and still live?"). He concludes that "Enoch's vision of God's throneroom is likened to the event at Sinai, and his cosmological teaching supplements the Mosaic Torah" ("The Place of the Astronomical Book in the Enochic Corpus").

the ascent and commission in *1 Enoch* 14-16. After his ascent (14:8) and temple tour (14:9-23), Enoch arrives at the threshold of the inner sanctuary and the divine throne. References to hearing the word/voice of the Lord occur three times in the ensuing context (*1 En* 14:24; 15:1a, 1c), and the Lord's commission begins, "Fear not, Enoch ..." (μὴ φοβηθῇς/ '*i-tefrāh*, 15:1b). Thus, the related motifs of hearing and not being terrified in 93:11a apply to Enoch.

Moreover, the parallel clause in *1 Enoch* 93:11b employs the vocabulary "to think his thoughts" (*yahalli xellinnāhu*). This expression echoes the testamentary setting from the original ending of the Book of the Watchers (*1 En* 82:1-3). Enoch gives wisdom to his descendants, wisdom beyond "their thoughts" (*hellinnāhomu*, 82:2). Enoch's wisdom surpasses human thought because God has revealed the meaning of hidden places in creation. If *1 Enoch* 93:11b implies that Enoch's wisdom represents God's thoughts, this is merely the corollary to 82:2.

Second, that the rhetorical questions in *1 Enoch* 93:11-14 receive a positive answer from Enoch is suggested by the recurring formula: "Who is there of all (the sons of) men who is able to ..." (*1 En* 93:11, 11c, 13, 14).[310] The formula appears to reflect *1 Enoch* 19:3: "And I, Enoch, *alone* saw the vision, the ends of all things. *And no one of men* has seen as I saw."[311] A further pointer to Enoch is the fact that the various verbs used to complete the formula (who is able "to hear/think/look/see/tell/consider/know") have parallels in the Book of the Watchers.[312]

Third, the knowledge pertaining to earth (*1 En* 93:13), heaven (93:14a-b), and the stars (93:14c-d) recalls aspects of the sight-seeing material in *1 Enoch* 17:3 (place of the luminaries) and 18:1-5 (foundation of the earth/height of heaven). Different from 93:13-14, the emphasis in the sight-seeing material was on structure and stability, not dimensions and numbers. Still, Enoch knows the dimensions of heaven and earth in the sense that he experienced them in his travels. The specific reference to the "number" (*xʷalqomu*) of the

---

[310] There is no Aramaic for the opening words in 93:11, but from what is extant in 93:11c, 13 and 14 (4QEnᵍ I v 17, 20, 22) it is clear that the expression is: מנו הוא כול אנוש די יכל.

[311] The Greek (Gᵍ¹) reads: κἀγὼ Ἐνὼχ ἴδον τὰ θεωρήματα μόνος, τὰ πέρατα πάντων, καὶ οὐ μὴ ἴδῃ οὐδὲ εἷς ἀνθρώπων ὡς ἐγὼ ἴδον.

[312] Examples: hear (*samʿa*, 14:24; 15:1a, 1c); think/consider (*xallaya*, noun in 82:2); look (*nassara*, 81:1-2); see (*reʿya*, *passim*); tell (*nagara*, 82:1); know/understand (*'a'mara*, 5:1; 25:1-2; 81:1-2).

stars (93:14c) has a parallel in 33:3 ("according to their number"/*ba-xʷalqomu*).[313]

In our view, *1 Enoch* 93:11-14 offers a summary of the hidden aspects of creation against the background of the Book of the Watchers. The rhetorical questions point to the uniqueness of Enoch as a revealer of wisdom. The content of his wisdom includes hidden phenomena throughout the cosmos. Enoch's knowledge of hidden things insures the validity of the Epistle's eschatological message.

1 Enoch 72-80; 82:4-20

The traditions compiled in the Astronomical Book offer precise, schematic accounts of the movements of the sun, moon and stars. The specific astronomical and meteorological details need not preoccupy us.[314] The general character of cosmic order portrayed in the Astronomical Book may be summarized by two observations.

First, Enoch sees fixed structures and fixed laws. These two components of the upper reaches of the cosmos complement one another. Together they establish and guarantee the regularity of the heavens and the seasons.

Of course, the fixed structures are not observable from the earth and therefore the fixed laws, the precise numerical schemes, could not have been arrived at apart from revelation. The peculiar emphasis of the Astronomical Book is illustrated from the start by the fact that the unseen structures through which rising and setting occur (nouns of place; 72:1, 2) are mentioned before the (presumably) perceptible rising and setting (verbs; 72:3, cf. 2:1).[315] The complementarity follows from the fact that the "law" (*te'zāz*) of the sun, moon and stars is now an arithmetic function of their position when rising and setting

---

[313] For references to counting the stars in the speculative tradition, see Stone, "Lists of Revealed Things," 426-29. According to Stone, the origin of the idea lies in the hymnic praises of God's activity in nature (Ps 147:4-5; Isa 40:26) and was adapted to stress what was beyond human ken (Gen 15:5; 22:17; Jer 33:22).

[314] See Neugebauer, "The 'Astronomical' Chapters," 386-419. It is unfortunate that Neugebauer does not comment on 80:2-8. He places this passage with the following unit (81:1-82:3) and labels the entire body as an intrusion of "apocalyptic" material. But the astronomical material in 72:1-80:1 has itself been "apocalypticized," that is, made the object of revelation, and 80:2-8 is more closely related to it than to 81:1-82:3.

[315] Nouns of place: *1 En* 72:1, *wa-mulādātihomu* ("and their places of origin"); 72:2, *muḍā'u ... wa-me'rābihu* ("its place of origin ... and its place of setting"). The activity of rising and setting: *1 En* 72:3, *yewadde' ... ya'arreb* (the sun "rises ... sets"); 72:3, *yešarreq wa-ya'arreb* (the moon "rises and sets," and the leaders of the stars together with those whom they lead). Cf. *1 En* 2:1, *yešarreq wa-ya'arreb* (each light "rises and sets").

in one of six "gates" on the eastern and western horizon (72:2-3; 75:6). Moreover, the position of the sun and stars when rising and setting in these gates also marks the "times" or seasons of the year.[316]

The author of *1 Enoch* 2:1 was aware of hidden astronomical phenomena revealed to Enoch, but called sinners to observe the *prima facie* regularity of the paths,[317] risings and settings, appointed times[318] and laws[319] of the heavenly bodies. The Astronomical Book accounts for such movements by relating them to the notion of structure, with its concomitant laws. The movements have a calculated value. A computation table becomes possible because the hidden, created structures have been seen by Enoch.

The structures involved in the rising and setting of the luminaries are symmetrical (six gates on each horizon), a characteristic that carries over to other places in the upper reaches of the cosmos. The number twelve is used for the gates of the winds (*1 En* 76). However, the gates through which the winds blow encircle the earth's horizon and are not the same twelve gates through which the luminaries rise and set.[320] Still, this symmetrical structure also provides order; specific meteorological phenomena are associated with each gate.

In short, all of the traditions collected in the Astronomical Book combine to leave an indelible impression of the symmetrical emplacements and orchestrated rhythms of the heavens and the seasons.[321]

A second observation about the astronomical traditions involves the palpable incongruity between the "revealed" structures and laws, on the one hand, and the "perceptible" movements of the luminaries, on the other. At times, scholars may have been too quick to allege problems between these

---

[316] Neugebauer ("The 'Astronomical' Chapters," 395, 402-03, 414) comments on this role for the sun (*1 En* 72:13, 19) and the stars (75:3, 6; 82:16, 19).

[317] The Ethiopic term *fenāw* in the sense of "(astronomical) path" occurs only in 2:1; 36:3 and 80:6 (but see also 18:5b: "I saw the paths of the angels"). The synonym *meḥwār* ("journey, course, orbit") is the preferred term in the Astronomical Book (72:33, 34, 35; 74:1, 4).

[318] 2:1 *ba-ba-zamanu*; 72:1 *wa-ba-ba-zamanomu*.

[319] 2:1 *te'zāzomu* (β mss). This is the term in 72:2, 35; 73:1; 74:1; 76:14; 79:2. The common synonym is *šer'at*, "rule" (78:10; 79:1, 2, 5; 82:9).

[320] Neugebauer suggests there may have originally been eight wind directions and that the expansion to twelve gates may have been influenced by the number of gates for the luminaries ("The 'Astronomical' Chapters," 404).

[321] This applies to mythic geography as well, where the number seven dominates (*1 En* 77).

primitive astronomical data and perceptible reality;[322] still, the artificial constructions imposed on many of the data is quite apparent.

An initial answer to this lack of fit with "perceived" reality must begin with the recognition that it is not the vantage point of earth that informs these schemes. The perspective of heaven has been gained to impart the structures and formulas. In the nature of the case, therefore, these are data that must be accepted on the authority of revelation. For the bearers of these traditions, the revealed data are the "real" data, and something has occurred to alter humankind's perceptions from the earth.

It is safe to assume that the Enochic community recognized the lack of fit between their revealed data and their world and that they had an explanation for this. How does the Enochic tradition itself explain the "glitches" in the system as viewed and experienced from the earth? Why was the cosmos malfunctioning? Why was it not operating in full accord with their revealed (idealized) schemes? The author of *1 Enoch* 80:2-8 provides an explanation.

In its present location, this piece has been attached to the final Uriel-notice (*1 En* 80:1) as a kind of appendix to the preceding astronomical material.[323] The opening words, "But in the days of the sinners ..." (*1 En* 80:2a), clearly intend to contrast what will follow with the earlier data. Our translation is based on Ethiopic:[324]

---

[322] For example, when commenting on *1 En* 75:6-7, which states that the stars rise and set in the same gates as the sun and moon, Neugebauer writes: "This makes little sense since the stars rise in all points of the eastern horizon" ("The 'Astronomical' Chapters," 402). But perhaps a distinction between real and perceptible rising and setting, similar to that found in Greek and hellenistic thought, is presupposed by Enochic tradition. That is, the place where a star *really* rises and where it is first *visible* are two separate questions. For a discussion of this distinction see G. R. Mair, "The *Phaenomena* of Aratus: Introduction," *LCL*, 377.

[323] *Contra* Rau, who begins the passage with 80:1. He reads the subjunctive "that you may see ..." in 80:1 as looking ahead to vss 2-8 (*Kosmologie*, 279). In our view, the verb sums up the purpose of chapters 72-79.

[324] The only textual problem in *1 En* 80:2-8 is in verse 5. Charles bracketed vss 5a and 5b as an interpolation dealing with the sun and pointed out that excising them leaves a tristich relating to the moon in vss 4a-b, 5c (*The Ethiopic Version of the Book of Enoch* [Oxford: Clarendon, 1906] 153). Black, following Knibb, moves vs 5b to the end of vs 2. The mention of "drought" in vs 5b then logically follows the reference to the withholding of the rains at the end of vs 2 and vss 5a and 5c are regarded as describing the moon, not the sun (Black, *The Book of Enoch or 1 Enoch*, 69, 252). Rau also reads 80:5a and 5c as referring to the moon, but he does not move vs 5b. Rather, he considers vs 5b a secondary expansion on the background of the hellenistic-babylonian astrology in which extra-ordinary events on earth are tied to changes in heavenly bodies (*Kosmologie*, 286-87). We prefer the position of Rau, which is intelligible without recourse to his tradition-history explanation of vss 5a and 5c (he argues that the salvific sign in *1 En* 91:16 has been restamped in 80:5a, 5c as a disaster sign).

1 En 80:2   But in the days of the sinners the years will be shorter,
              and their seed will be late on their land and on their
                  fields.
              And all events on the earth will change,
                  and will not appear at their times.
              And the rain will be withheld,
                  and heaven will cause (it) to cease.

        3   And in those times, the fruit of the earth will be late,
                  and it will not grow at its time,
              and the fruit of the tree will be withheld at its time.

        4   And the moon will change its fixed patterns,
                  and it will not appear at its time.

        5   And in those days, it will appear (in) heaven,
                  and drought will arrive on great chariots in the west.[325]
              and it will shine with more than the prescribed brightness.

        6   And many of the heads of the stars will stray from the
                  command,
                  and these will change their paths and their actions,
              and will not appear at their times which are commanded for
                  them.

        7   And the entire law of the stars will be closed to sinners,
                  and the thoughts of those upon earth will go astray over
                  them.
              And they will turn from all their ways,
                  and they will go astray and will liken them gods.

        8   And there will be much evil upon them,
                  and punishment will come on them to destroy all.

Rau argues that many of the images in *1 Enoch* 80:2-8 result from a sapiential reformulation of the eschatological signs traditionally associated with the "Day of the Lord."[326] This is extremely unlikely. It is significant that the sun is not mentioned at all in 80:2-8. The "darkening" of the sun plays a major

---

[325] The Ethiopic text is corrupt. See Knibb, *The Ethiopic Book of Enoch*, 2.185-86. Black moves this line to the end of verse 2 (*The Book of Enoch or 1 Enoch*, 69, 252).

[326] He appeals to *Sib. Or.* 3.88-92, *4 Ezra* 7:39-44, and Lactantius, *Epitome of the Divine Institutes* 66[76], which describe the Day of Judgment in conjunction with the cessation of the seasons and the absence of luminaries (*Kosmologie*, 289-93). But themes of cessation and absence are not present in 80:2-8, and the passage is open to other interpretations. Cf. Carroll D. Osburn's suggestion that 80:2-8 provides metaphors for the characterization of sinners in the book of Jude ("*1 Enoch* 80:2-8 (67:5-7) and Jude 12-13," *CBQ* 47 [1985] 296-303).

role in contexts of eschatological judgment.[327] In addition, 80:2-8 as a whole, is not about the *termination* of the created order.[328]

Our exposition takes a point of departure from the similarities between *1 Enoch* 80:6-8 and 18:15-19:1. If a perspective can be gained from the similarities, then perhaps 80:2-5 will also fall into place.

A comparison of *1 Enoch* 80:6-8 and 18:15-19:1 yields the following result:

1 En 18:15-19:1		*1 En* 80:6-8
15 stars ... in the fire, these are transgressed the command ...	6a	And many heads of the stars will stray from the command,
	b	and these will change
in the beginning of their rising for they did not come out in their appointed times	c	their paths and their actions and will not appear at their times ...
16 bound for ten thousand years		
	7a	law of the stars closed
1 There stand the angels ... their spirits ... lead astray	b-c	(men) will go astray/will turn
(men) to sacrifice	d	And they will go astray
to demons as to gods		and will liken them gods
until the day of the	8	much evil/punishment will
great judgment ...		come on them to destroy all

The fact that both passages cover the same *topoi* in the same order suggests that they share a common tradition. The differences are easily explained. On the one hand, *1 Enoch* 18:15-19:1 is found in the context of Enoch's vision of the prison of the stars and angels, which accounts for the imagery of fire (18:15) and binding (18:16) as well as the language "these are .../There stand ..." (18:15/19:1). On the other hand, *1 Enoch* 80:6-8 is ostensibly a prophecy about the law of the stars (80:7a), that is, the law revealed in the Astronomical Book.

1 Enoch 80:6-8 makes explicit what was implied in 18:15-19:1: the stars have "heads" or angelic leaders, some of whom have violated the laws of the

---

[327] Rau accounts for the absence of any reference to the sun by suggesting that the passage was formulated under the influence of *1 En* 74:12: the moon conducts the years (*Kosmologie*, 286).

[328] There may be a hint of this in *1 En* 80:8b; but if so, it represents the culmination point, not the leading tendency of the passage. At issue is the word "all" in 80:8b. Rau takes this as a reference to the entire creation; thus in his view the eschatological alteration of earthly and heavenly events is nothing less than the termination of the orders of creation, a counterpoint to the new creation promised in 72:1 (ibid., 299-301).

Creator. Apparently, the rebellion of the Watchers (*1 En* 6-11) had disastrous results not only on human history, but on astronomy as well. The assumption at work is that the Watchers had stellar responsibilities that were abandoned upon the occasion of their descent. Angels insure that the stars exit their gates properly and stay on the right path (cf. 18:5b and 36:3; 82:10). Obviously, those stars whose leaders have departed will behave erratically and stray (= transgress).

The number of rebel angels and their respective erring stars is finite,[329] and certainly infinitesimal given the vast quantity of each. The important point to be remembered is that the reference to transgressing stars in *1 Enoch* 18:15-16 did not invalidate the notion of astronomical order expressed in 2:1. The same point is present in the Astronomical Book: the laws of the stars are not overturned simply because some heads of the stars and sinners err over them. *1 Enoch* 80:6 opens with the prophecy that "many" of the heads of stars will err. The number implied by the word "many" is finite. The same applies to the sinners who err (80:7a).

In the context of the Astronomical Book, the error relates to the determination of the calendar (80:7a-b; 75:2; 82:4-20). At issue is the validity of the 364-day solar year and its division into the four seasons.[330]

This analysis makes immediate sense of the preceding section, 80:2-5. Verse 2 opens: "But in the days of the sinners, the years will be shorter." If one does not intercalate the four days of the equinoxes and solstices (in the 360 day calendar) or a month about once every three years (in the lunisolar calendar), then from the perspective of the 364-day calender, the years will be shorter.[331] Planting (80:2b) and harvest (80:3) will be later every year. The rains will not fall at the right time (80:2e-f). It is by no means an overstatement for the author to claim that every event on earth will be adversely effected because, from his perspective, it will not occur at the right time (80:2c-d). The only solution for setting the created order aright would be periodic intercalations. This was certainly the practice of those who used the 360

---

[329] The number "seven" in *1 En* 18:13 is symbolic and probably dependent on 18:6. *1 En* 6:7 states that there were two hundred angels who took part in the descent.

[330] VanderKam points out that the calendar opposed in the Astronomical Book is not lunar, but one that consists of twelve 30-day months ("The 364-Day Calendar in the Enochic Literature," *SBLSP* [1983] 163-64; idem, *Enoch and the Growth*, 91). But the prophecy in 80:2-8 implies opposition to a shorter calendar, whether 360 or 354 days (the lunar calendar).

[331] Since the year is actually 365 1/4 days, the Enochic calendar produces the same result, though at a somewhat slower pace.

and 354 day calendars,[332] but our piece is entirely silent about such stopgap measures.

1 Enoch 80:2-8 does not foretell the total collapse of the operations defined in *1 Enoch* 72:1-80:1. The prophecy is not about the termination of all the luminaries and their related functions. Therefore, the signs of the end-time are not the subject of 80:2-8. After all, the sun endures. Planting and harvesting continue, although they are late from the perspective of the Enochic calendar. The moon shines with more than its prescribed brightness, an ominous "meteorological" sign to be sure, but it does shine nonetheless. Many stars err, but not all of them. In the days of the sinners, society lives out of synchronization with the created order, but the righteous do not.

Summary

The common verb in the passages dealing with the hidden phenomena of creation is "to see." This is the same verb used to exhort sinners to observe creation (*1 En* 2:1, 2, 3; 3:1; 4:1; 5:3; 101:4). In his heavenly journeys, Enoch "sees" hidden things much as a person on earth "sees" the observable works of heaven, earth and sea. Enoch sees distant things close up or other things that cannot be viewed at all from the perspective of earth. More than this, he experiences the terrors and joys of creation in ways that are unknown on earth, but will be known at the judgment.

Many of his visions and experiences combine to reinforce the message that God maintains control of the stars. Some leaders of the stars have transgressed, causing humankind to go astray. But Enoch sees prisons and future judgment for the disobedient. He also sees the cosmic structures, different at times, which provide for the proper operation of the luminaries. The righteous who regulate their lives by the astronomical laws revealed by Enoch are assured of the eschatological blessing of God, for the cosmos provides for this as well.

---

[332] In the Egyptian solar calendar of 360 days, five days were added at the end of the year (VanderKam, *Enoch and the Growth*, 97); in the Jewish lunisolar calendar of 354 days, a month was added either biennially or trienially (Herr, "The Calendar," *The Jewish People in the First Century* [CRINT 1.2; ed. S. Safrai and M. Stern; Philadelphia: Fortress, 1976] 838, n. 5).

4. THE CREATED ORDER IN
BEN SIRA'S BOOK OF WISDOM

The creation theme in Sirach can be explicated under the same two categories relevant for *1 Enoch*. In common with various Psalms, the book of Job, and Second Isaiah, ben Sira rehearses the observable works of creation.[333] The literary form he adapts for this purpose is the Hymn of Praise, or to be more specific, the Hymn of Praise to the Creator (Sir 16:24-17:14; 33[36]:7-15; 39:12-35; 42:15-43:33).[334] But ben Sira also employs the Hymn and its motifs to treat the hidden things of creation (Sir 1:1-10; 24:1-7). In the latter case, he uses the stylistic features of rhetorical questions and first person speech.

OBSERVABLE ASPECTS OF THE CREATION

The Doctrine of Opposites

The passages gathered below display hymnic motifs turned to didactic ends. When ben Sira looks at or is shown the works of creation, he discerns a built-in polarity. His elaboration of creation's structural polarity has been

---

[333] See above, pp. 99-100, nn. 236-38.

[334] Baumgartner ("Die literarischen Gattungen," 169-77) classified the passages mentioned in this paragraph under the category "Hymns and Hymnic Motifs," with one exception. He regarded Sir 33[36]:7-15 as part of a didactic poem. But as Baumgartner himself stressed, the Hymns and hymnic motifs are turned to didactic purposes. In our view, Sir 33[36]:7-15 is another example of this tendency.

called the doctrine of opposites.[335] Simply stated: every element in creation
obeys God and carries out the purpose for which it was designed, either for
good or bad; sometimes the same element has the capacity to function either
way. The scholarly discussions of this doctrine often subsume it under other
theological topics such as divine retribution, theodicy, or determinism and free
will. The emphasis of our treatment is on aspects of the doctrine itself.

Sirach 16:24-17:14

This hymnic piece draws a parallel between the works of heaven and
humankind. A wisdom introduction (16:24-25) stands in the place of the traditional hymnic call to praise. The body of the hymn expounds two works of
God: the creation of the luminaries (16:26-28) and humankind (17:1-14; 17:10
includes the note of praise). By observing the luminaries, ben Sira has learned
a lesson for humankind, and for Israel in particular. The hymn closes with his
didactic point: "Turn from all evil" (17:14a).

How did ben Sira arrive at this lesson? What did he see when he looked
up at the heavens?[336]

Sir   16:26   When God created the first of his works
              and, after he made them, distinguished their tasks,
      27   He ordered for all time their deeds,
              and their domains[337] unto their generations.
              They were not to hunger, nor grow weary,
              nor ever abandon their deeds.
      28   Each one should not crowd its neighbor,
              nor should they ever disobey his word.

When ben Sira looks up at the first of God's works, the luminaries, he
sees that they are ordered by God and do not disobey God's word (cf. *1 En*

---

335 This expression is used by Roland E. Murphy, *The Tree of Life: An Exploration of
Biblical Wisdom Literature* (ABRL; New York: Doubleday, 1990) 75. Hengel called it the
doctrine of the purposefulness of creation (*Judaism and Hellenism*, I.145); Marböck, *die
Ambivalenz und Doppeldeutigkeit alles Geschaffenen* (*Weisheit im Wandel* [BBB 37; Bonn:
Hanstein, 1971] 153); Di Lella, the doctrine of equilibrium in creation (Skehan and Di
Lella, *The Wisdom of Ben Sira*, 460).

336 Apart from the opening words (ms A), our translation of Sir 16:26-28 follows the
Greek.

337 Greek: τὰς ἀρχὰς. Cf. Jude 6: "And the angels that did not keep *their own domain*
(τὴν ἑαυτῶν ἀρχὴν) but abandoned their proper dwelling ..." The term is also used for
heavenly powers or rulers (Rom 8:38; 1 Cor 15:24; Eph 3:10; Col 1:16). The imagery of
Sir 16:27c-28, along with 17:32, suggests that ben Sira regards the angels as ruling the
domains of the stars (cf. *1 En* 75:1; 80:6; 82:4-20).

2:1; 18:1, 4). In the next unit, he states that God "showed" (ὑπέδειξεν) humankind "good and evil" (17:7b) when God "showed" (δεῖξαι) them "the splendor of his works" (17:8b). The parallelism between 17:7 and 17:8 indicates that the opposites of good and evil have been projected unto the heavens. It is good that the luminaries obey God; evil when they do not.

Ben Sira draws several parallels to humankind.[338] Among them, he describes the word God gave to Israel as law of life (Sir 17:11b), everlasting covenant (17:12a), and his commandments (17:12b). In the latter case, he says God "showed" (ὑπέδειξεν) his commandments to them. The revelation of the Torah to Israel is related to the "torah" one sees in the heavens. Just as "each" (ἕκαστος) luminary is ordered not to crowd "its neighbor" (τὸν πλησίον αὐτοῦ, 16:28a), so also God gives commands "to each" (ἑκάστῳ) Israelite "pertaining to his neighbor" (περὶ τοῦ πλησίον, 17:14b).

In projecting a torah unto the heavens from which humankind can learn to turn from evil (17:14a), ben Sira presupposes that there is not only goodness, but evil in the heavens. Indeed, this assumption comes forward in the next poems (Sir 17:15-24, 25-32). The "ways" (17:15a, 19b) and "deeds" (17:19a) of Israel will be requited as they deserve (17:23). The luminaries also have "deeds" (16:27a, 27d) and can expect recompense:

Sir 17:32a He himself holds accountable the hosts of highest heaven,
     b   and all humans are dust and ashes.

The reference to "the hosts of highest heaven" refers to the luminaries and their leaders (Sir 16:26-28; cf. 1 En 18:14).[339] The angelic leaders of the stars are apparently held to a higher standard than mere mortals, but the lesson of disobedience and accountability is not lost. The idea that some angels disobey and will be punished reflects an older Jewish tradition about an angelic revolt in heaven (Isa 14:12-14; 24:21; 1 En 6-11).[340]

In sum, as ben Sira understands the doctrine of opposites, both luminaries/angels and humankind are given commands and prohibitions and

---

[338] The many parallels between Sir 16:26-28 and 17:1-14 were noted by Schökel, "The Vision of Man in Sirach 16:24-17:14," Israelite Wisdom: Theological and Literary Essays in Honor of Samuel Terrien (ed. J. G. Gammie et al.; Missoula: Scholars, 1978) 235-45. On this passage as a creation commentary, see Sheppard, Wisdom as a Hermeneutical Construct, 72-83.

[339] Di Lella states that hosts are the sun, moon and stars, but that ben Sira probably had in mind the angels also (Skehan and Di Lella, The Wisdom of Ben Sira, 285.

[340] The same tradition has informed Sir 16:7. See Chap. 6, p. 230.

possess the freedom to do good or evil.[341] All will be punished or rewarded as they deserve.

Sirach 33[36]:7-15

This poem uses motifs from the Hymn of Praise to the Creator. It lacks an introduction because it has been joined to other poems that contrast the one who fears the Lord and the sinner (Sir 32:14-17, 18-24; 33:1-6).[342] In Sirach 33:7-15, ben Sira states yet another lesson he has learned from the luminaries; in this case, the sun and the moon. The operations of these two heavenly bodies bring the two categories of individuals depicted in the preceding poems within the purview of the doctrine of opposites:[343]

Sir	33:7a	Why is one day superior to others,
	b	all light of the days of the year is from the sun?
	8a	By the knowledge of the Lord they are separated,
	b	he made different times and feasts.
	9a	Some of them he blessed and they are made holy,
	b	and some of them he appointed as days for counting.
	10a	And all humankind is from vessels of clay,
	b	and from dust humankind was formed.
	11a	The wisdom of the Lord separated them,
	b	and made their ways different.
	12a	Some of them he blessed and exalted,
	b	and some he made holy and brought near to himself.
	c	And some of them he cursed and laid low,
	d	and he exiled them from their place.
	13a	As clay in the hands of the potter,
	b	for being kneaded according to his will,
	c	so is humankind in the hands of its Maker,
	d	for standing in front of his Creator.[344]
	14a	As evil is the opposite of good,

---

[341] G. Maier (*Mensch und Freier Wille: Nach den jüdischen Religionsparteien zwischen Ben Sira und Paulus* [WUNT 12; Tübingen: Mohr (Siebeck), 1971] 62-84) finds two lines of thought in Sir 17:1-10: humankind's lowliness (17:1; cf. Gen 2:7) and dominion (17:2-10; Gen 1:26-28). The former line leads to predestination; the latter, to freedom of the will. However, the development was likely more complex. For example, Nickelsburg noted the close relationship between Sir 16:26-17:7 and 1QS 3:15-18 and suggested that ben Sira knew an early version of the latter's determinism (*Resurrection*, 164, n. 121).

[342] See Chap. 2, pp. 78-80, for our discussion of Sir 32:14-17.

[343] Our translation is based on ms E. In places where the reading is unintelligible, we employ the Greek (this includes vss 7-8 and 11b).

[344] For the philological evidence supporting this translation, see Penar, *Northwest Semitic Philology*, 55-56. He points to the connection with Jer 18:6.

b   and life is the opposite of death,

c   so a good man is opposite of the wicked.

15a   Behold all the works of God,

b   all of them are in pairs, this corresponding to that.

Ben Sira draws an analogy between the days of the year and human beings. The analogy assumes a lunisolar calendar in which the ordinary days of the year are counted with reference to the sun, and months and special days are marked by the phases of the moon (Ps 104:19; Sir 43:6-8).[345] As the days are separated (διεχωρίσθησαν, Sir 33:8a) and made different (ἠλλοίωσεν, 33:8b), and only some are blessed and made holy (ב[ר]ך והקדשו, 33:9a), so too humankind is separated (διεχώρισεν/בדל hif., 33:11a) and made different (ἠλλοίωσεν, 33:11b), and only some are blessed and made holy (... [ברך] הקדיש, 33:12a, 12b).[346] Like the opposition between ordinary and holy days in the calendar, the contrast between sinners and the just can only be ascribed to the inscrutable wisdom of God (33:8a, 11a; cf. 42:18-21).

In no respect does ben Sira intend to suggest that God is responsible for sin. The language of blessing and cursing comes from Deuteronomy 27-28 and implies that humankind will be judged by its deeds. This thought is confirmed by Sirach 33:13 which echoes the judgment context of Jeremiah 18:6. Ben Sira teaches that the *categories* of sinners and the just have their place within the opposite (נוכח) phenomena of creation (Sir 33:14). As there are opposites of evil and good, death and life, so sinners and the just (cf. 11:14). The category to which a particular individual belongs is determined by that person's deeds.[347]

The concluding couplet to this passage is an invitation to "behold" (נבט, hif.) the works of God and thus see that "all of them are in pairs, this corresponding to that" (כולם שנים שנים זה לעומת [זה], 33:15). This vocabulary will be used in Sirach 42:24-25 to introduce a major creation Hymn. Here, it concludes ben Sira's effort to compare the calendric functions of the sun and moon with two opposite categories of individuals.

---

[345] Harmonization requires the periodic intercalation of a month (Herr, "The Calendar," 834-39).

[346] The Hebrew in Sir 33:8 and 33:11b, though garbled, does not appear to work out the analogy with the same full terminological precision. The Greek translator has obviously picked up on the point of the passage.

[347] It is otherwise in 1QS 3:15-4:26. See P. Winter, "Ben Sira 33[36]:7-15 and the Teaching of 'Two Ways'," *VT* 5 (1955) 315-18; cf. Maier, *Mensch und Freier Wille*, 98-112, 222-63.

Sirach 39:12-35

This Hymn of Praise to the Creator displays the major elements of the form. The wisdom introduction includes the call to praise and a statement of the theme (39:12-16). The works of God touched on in the body of the Hymn are wide-ranging, and it has been suggested that ben Sira employs a catalogue of various phenomena in nature. The lists are adapted to illustrate a didactic point. Finally, the conclusion restates the point and renews the call to praise in the same language used in the introduction (39:32-35).[348] Our translation begins with the statement of the theme in the last couplet of the introduction:[349]

Sir 39:16a The works of God are all good;
         b   for every need in its time he abundantly supplies.

         17a   At his word, the waters stand as though in a bottle,
         b   and by what issues from his mouth, storehouses.
         18a   By his command, he causes his pleasure to prosper,
         b   and nothing can hinder his deliverance.
         19a   The works of all flesh are before him,
         b   and nothing is hidden before his eyes.
         20a   From eternity to eternity he sees,
         b   is there any way to count up his acts of deliverance?
         c   Nothing is too little or insignificant for him,
         d   and nothing is too wonderful or difficult for him.[350]
         21a   No one can say: 'Why is this or that?'
         b   because everything for its need is chosen.
         22a   His blessing is like the Nile when it floods,
         b   like the Euphrates it drenches the earth.
         23a   Likewise, his curse drives out the nations,
         b   and he turns drinking water to salt.
         24a   His ways are upright to the perfect,
         b   to foreigners they are obstacles.
         25a   Good to those who are good he allotted from the beginning,
         b   just as to those who are evil, good and evil.
         26a   Chief of all needs for the life of humankind
         b   are water and fire and iron and salt,
         c   the kernel of the wheat, milk and honey,

---

[348] The minor differences in the Hebrew of Sir 39:16 and 39:33 allow us to restore the original couplet with some measure of confidence: מעשי אל כלם טובים לכל צורך בעתו יספיק. The verb ספק (= שפק) means "to suffice, to abound" (cf. Sir 15:18, where the subject is the wisdom of God).

[349] Translation from ms B, except for parts of vss 27-32 which are based on ms M and Yadin's restoration (*The Ben Sira Scroll*, 12-13, 39).

[350] On Sir 39:20c-d, see Penar, *Northwest Semitic Philology*, 66-67.

d	the juice of the grape, and oil and cloth.
27a	All these things are good for those who are good,
b	just as for those who are evil they are turned into evil.
28a	There are winds created for judgment,
b	and in their anger they remove mountains.
c	And in the time of destruction they pour out their power,
d	and the spirit of their Maker they appease.
29a	Fire and hail, famine[351] and plague,
b	these also for judgment are created.
30a	Carnivorous beasts, scorpion and viper,
b	and the sword of vengeance to annihilate the wicked;
c	all these too are created for their needs,
d	they are in his storehouse for the time they are appointed.
31a	When he commands, they rejoice,
b	and in their tasks they do not disobey his mouth.
32a	Therefore, from the beginning I took my stand,
b	and I understood and put in writing:
33a	the works of God are all good,
b	for every need in its time he abundantly supplies.
34a	No one can say: 'This is worse than that'
b	for everything in its time excels.
35a	Now with all (your) heart shout for joy,
b	and bless the name of the Holy One.

The thematic statement in Sirach 39:16 and 39:33 contains two key words that will also appear in 42:22-25; namely, all the works of God are "good" (טובים) and meet a "need" (צורך) in creation. The "needs" are basically twofold, depending on whether God will bless (39:22) or curse (39:23, 28; cf. 33:12).

Ben Sira adapts nature lists to define some of the "good things" and "bad things" used to bless and curse. Among the "good things" are: water, fire, iron, salt, wheat, milk, honey, wine, oil and cloth (39:26). There is a dual aspect to these good things. While they benefit the good, they turn out evil to the wicked.

The list of "bad things" begins with an expanded treatment of the "winds created for judgment" (39:28); the type of expansion found later in Sirach 43:13-26. The catalogue then continues with fire (cf. 16:6), hail, famine, plague, carnivorous beasts, scorpions, vipers and the sword of vengeance (39:29-30).

---

[351] In Sir 39:29a (and 40:9b), we follow the many scholars who emend רע to רעב on the basis of the Greek (most recently, Skehan and Di Lella, *The Wisdom of Ben Sira*, 457, 466).

To this list of "bad things," the different list in Sirach 40:8-10 should be compared:

Sir 40:8a Among all flesh, from humankind to beast,
    b   and upon sinners seven times more, come these:
    9a   plague and bloodshed, heat of fever and drought,
    b   violence and ruin, famine and death.
    10a   For the guilty, evil was created,
    b   and on his account destruction hastens.

Plague (דבר) and famine (λιμὸς/רעב cj.) appear in both lists. The new terms in 40:9 are phenomena brought on by the harsh conditions of nature (heat of fever and drought) or warfare (violence and ruin), or both (death).

In both of the above lists of "bad things," ben Sira emphasizes that the phenomena were originally made for the purpose of cursing the wicked. Such things were "*created* for judgment" (39:28 B^mg; 39:29 M), "*created* to meet their need" (39:30c) and "*created* for the wicked" (40:10). In each case, the verb is ברא (*ni.*). The verb alludes to Genesis 1:1 (cf. Isa 45:7). God provided good and bad things "from the beginning" (Sir 39:25). Indeed, the thematic statement that all of God's works are "good" (Sir 39:16a, 33b) itself goes back to the refrain in Genesis 1 ("and God saw that it was good").

Ben Sira has adapted lists of phenomena occurring in nature or warfare to his doctrine of opposites in order to answer some who questioned the justice of God. No one is to say "Why is this or that?" (זה למה זה, 39:21a) or "This is worse than that" (זה רע מזה, 39:34 B^mg).[352] The person tempted to question God's justice must learn that the "need" will be met "in its own time" (בעתו, 39:16b, 33b, 34b) or "for the time appointed it" (לעת יפקרו, 39:30d). Ben Sira teaches that at the opportune time, a time set by God, God will use the created elements for blessing or wrath. This is his contribution to the theodicy debate.[353]

Sirach 42:15-43:33

This poem displays the structure of the Hymn of Praise to the Creator. The introduction lacks the element of a call to praise, but such a call appears in the conclusion (43:28). The body of the Hymn treats the luminaries, meteorological phenomena, and the ocean. The analysis below will show that

---

[352] It is common to quote opponents in the Disputation Speech. See Chap. 5, p. 185, and Chap. 6, p. 220.

[353] Gerhard von Rad, *Wisdom in Israel* (Nashville: Abindgon, 1972) 251-54; Hengel, *Judaism and Hellenism*, I.144-45.

the entire presentation is shaped by the didactic purpose of demonstrating the doctrine of opposites.

<u>Introductory Stanza.</u>   The introduction is framed by references to "seeing" (חזה, 42:15b/נבט hif., 42:25b):[354]

Sir 42:15a	Let me now recall the works of God;
b	and what I have seen, I will repeat.
c	By the word of the Lord are his works;
d	and they accept the doing of his will.[355]
16a	As sunlight floods everything,
b	so the glory of the Lord fills his works.
17a	Yet even God's holy ones do not suffice
b	to recount all his wonders,
c	Though the Lord has given his hosts the strength
d	to stand firm before his glory.
18a	The Abyss and the heart he searches deeply,
b	and their secrets, he understands,
c	for the Most High knows all knowledge,
d	and sees what is coming forever.
19a	He announces what has passed by and what will come to pass,
b	he reveals the depths of hidden things.
20a	Understanding is not lacking with him,
b	a single detail does not escape him.
21a	He directs the mighty deeds of his wisdom,
b	he is one from eternity.
c	Nothing to be added nor taken away,
d	and he has no need for any counselor.
22a	How beautiful are all his works,
b	delightful to gaze upon and a joy to behold!
23a	Everything lives and stands forever;
b	for everything there is a need, and everything is preserved.
24a	All of them are in pairs, this corresponding to that;
b	and he has not made any of them in vain.
25a	One upon another, their goodness passes by;
b	and who can get enough of seeing their splendor?

---

[354] Our translation is based on ms M (Yadin, *The Ben Sira Scroll*, 26-28, 43) with the refinements suggested by Strugnell, "Notes and Queries on 'The Ben Sira Scroll from Masada'," *Eretz-Israel* 9 (1969) 116-17.

[355] The text reads: ופעל רצנו לקחו (ms M). Yadin translates: "And His doctrine—an act of His grace" (*The Ben Sira Scroll*, 45). Di Lella calls attention to the Syriac ("and all his creatures do his will") and suggests either the translation adopted above or "he accepts the one who does his will" (reading לקח B^mg) (Skehan and Di Lella, *The Wisdom of Ben Sira* 484, 487).

In addition to the two verbs of seeing in the frame, ben Sira employs the terms צוץ (Sir 42:22b) and ראה (42:22b; 43:11, 32). What he sees is the glory of creation as displayed in the doctrine of opposites. The introduction builds up to the thematic statement in 42:24.

In the opening lines, ben Sira contrasts what he is about to do with the task of angels. He "will repeat" (שנה, 42:15b) the glories he has seen in creation; the holy angels themselves do not suffice to "recount" (ספר, 42:17b) such glories. The parallel between the activity of angels and ben Sira reflects the angel/humankind analogy in 16:26-17:14. The call to praise in the conclusion of the present Hymn also alludes to this analogy. The exhortation "Do not grow weary" (אל תלאו/ μὴ κοπιᾶτε, 43:30d) takes up a metaphor used earlier of the luminaries (οὔτε ἐκοπίασαν, 16:27c).

However, it appears that in this introductory stanza the angels function as a foil to highlight the greatness of God's works. Even the angels who stand before God's glory are inadequate to the task ben Sira is about to undertake (42:17a-d). The reference is to the angelic hymns of praise around God's throne and to the limitations of angelic knowledge.[356] Ben Sira has seen something in creation that the angels themselves do not fully fathom.[357]

Ben Sira goes on to stress God's comprehensive knowledge and active role in superintending the works of creation. God "searches out" (חקר) the abyss and human heart and "understands their hidden things" (ובמערמיהם יתבונן, 42:18a-b). Because God then "reveals" (ומגלה) the depth of these "secret things" (נסתרות, 42:19b), ben Sira can include a stanza on the ocean and its effect on sailors (43:23-26). In the fullness of God's understanding, God has shown a profound secret about the abyss and human heart—a secret that is applicable to other parts of creation.[358]

---

[356] For the latter thought, cf. 11QPs^a xxvi 12: "When all his angels had witnessed (it) they sang aloud; for he showed them what they had not known."

[357] There is no hint here that ben Sira is polemicizing against the role of the *angelus interpres* in other traditions. For further discussion of ben Sira's picture of the angels around the throne, see the comparative section below.

[358] In Chap. 2, pp. 70-72, it was pointed out that Sir 42:18b ("their hidden things he understands") is parallel to Sir 1:6 and 51:19. The rhetorical question in 1:6 ("her hidden parts who understands?") is answered by both God (42:18b) and ben Sira (43:32-33; 51:19). In addition, 42:18a takes up the language of 1:3b and turns its rhetorical question ("the depths of the abyss who can fathom?") into a declarative sentence in which God is the subject ("he searches deeply the abyss").

It follows that the language of Sir 42:18d and 42:19a should be applied to creation, not history. The "things that are to come forever" (אתיות עולם, 42:18d; cf. 39:20a) and the "things that have passed and will come to pass" (חליפות ונהיות, 42:19a; cf. 42:25a) refer to phenomena in heaven, earth and sea. What has passed is the way God constituted the creation from the beginning. What will come to pass are God's works of providence in which the righteous are blessed and the wicked cursed.

Ben Sira also emphasizes God's active participation in all aspects of crea-tion. God "directs" (תכן, 42:21a)[359] the mighty deeds of his wisdom and, for this reason, has no need of a counselor (42:21d).

A thematic statement of the doctrine of opposites follows from God's complete knowledge, his revelation to ben Sira, and his active control. What ben Sira has seen with such delight and joy is stated in 42:23-25. The created order is stable, enduring and purposeful. Everything in the creation is in place, and remains in place, in order to meet any "need" (צרך, 42:23b) that may arise. All things come "in pairs, this corresponding to that" (שנים שנים] זה לעמת זה [זה, 42:24a). All things have an inherent goodness (טובם/ "*their goodness,*" 42:25a) because all fulfill a divine purpose when carrying out their functions. The vocabulary was present in preceding hymns (33[36]:15; 39:16, 21, 33-34). As we will see, the lesson here will be like that taught in 16:26-17:14: fear God and avoid evil. The duality of creation should put the fear of God in the human heart and motivate one to obey God.

The Sun and Moon. The body of the Hymn begins with a stanza on the works of God in heaven. Ben Sira treats the firmament, sun, moon, (stars), and rainbow (43:1-12). The sun and moon are two works of heaven that receive the most sustained treatment and the qualifier "to be feared" or "awesome" (נורא, Sir 43:2b, 8b):[360]

Sir 43:1a   The beauty of heaven and the brightness of the firmament,
    b   heaven is mighty, the sight of its radiance.
    2a   The sun shines fully when it comes out,
    b   an awesome object, the work of the Most High.
    3a   In its noontime, it brings the world to a boil,
    b   and before its heat, who can endure?
    4a   Like a flaming furnace, a work of cast metal,
    b   a ray of the sun burns up the mountains.
    c   A tongue of fire consumes the inhabited land,
    d   and the eye is scorched from its fire.
    5a   For great is the Lord who made it,

---

[359] For this meaning of תכן (*pi.*, Sir 42:21a) see Isa 40:13: "Who has *directed* the Spirit of the Lord, or as his counselor has instructed him?"

[360] Translation based on ms M (Yadin, *The Ben Sira Scroll*, 28-31, 43-44) with attention to the suggestions of Strugnell, "Notes and Queries," 117.

b and by his word, he directs its journey.[361]
6a And the moon also prescribes the times,
b ruling the seasons, and an eternal sign.
7a By it is the appointed time and from it, the festival,
b a light that takes pleasure in its waning.
8a The new moon like its name ever renews itself,
b how awesome in its changes.
c An instrument of the host of water-skins on high,
d it paves the firmament with its shining.
9a The beauty of heaven and glory of the stars,
b a shining ornament[362] in the heights of God.
10a At the word of the Lord, it stands as prescribed,
b and does not hang low in their night-watch.
11a Behold the rainbow and bless the one who made it,
b for it is very grand in its glory.
12a The vault of heaven it encompasses in its glory,
b and the hand of God stretched it out in might.

With a variety of verbs, ben Sira highlights the sun's fitness as an instrument of wrath (43:2-5). He begins by taking up a term used earlier in one of his lists of "bad things:" "who can endure its *heat*?" (חרב, 43:3b; cf. 40:9a, where it means "drought"). The sun "burns" (רתח, *hi.*) the earth (43:3a), "kindles" (נסק, *hi.* = נשק) the mountains (43:4b), "consumes" (ג[מר]) the inhabited world (43:4c), and the human eye "is burned" (כוה, *ni.*) by it (43:4d). Humankind cannot tolerate the fierceness of the sun's heat. This explains why ben Sira calls it a "fearful instrument" (43:2). The sun has a punishing capacity as it carries out the word of the Lord (43:5b).

Ben Sira had earlier said that all of humankind experiences "drought" (or: "searing heat"), but sinners seven times more (40:9a). The fact that individuals experience God's wrath as meted out by this fearful instrument informs one of ben Sira's metaphors. Elsewhere he used the metaphor of the sun's heat in connection with his wisdom instruction. The *blessed* person (Sir 14:20) pursues *Wisdom* until he finds her place and "takes refuge from the *heat* in her shade" (14:27a). The doctrine of opposites teaches one to join ranks with the wise and experience blessing rather than God's wrath.

---

361 Instead of the last Hebrew word in Sir 43:5b (אבירין), we read the Greek (πορεία). Note the similar statement about the moon in Sir 43:10. Di Lella proposes taking the last Hebrew word as the stallions or steeds that pull the sun's chariot (*The Wisdom of Ben Sira*, 488). Might it not also be translated "its mighty deeds," i.e., the deeds of the sun as outlined in Sir 43:3-4?

362 Instead of reading עד ומשריק with Yadin, read עדי משריק ("a shining ornament") with Di Lella (Skehan and Di Lella, *The Wisdom of Ben Sira*, 489).

Ben Sira's description of the function of the moon must also be understood against the background of the doctrine of opposites. The moon marks the passing of "times" (עתות, 43:6a) and each "season" (קץ, 43:6b) as an enduring sign. As he did in 33[36]:8-9, ben Sira is commenting on the role of the moon in the lunisolar calendar. Its special function is to designate the "sacred times" (מו[ע]ד) and "festivals" (חג, 43:7a). In addition to this function, which ben Sira exploited earlier for his doctrine of opposites, there is a second way in which the moon brings the blessing of God to the righteous.

Like the sun which burns up the earth, the moon too has a meteorological function. The lunar alterations or changes are awesome (43:8b) because they have a weather effect for the inhabitants of earth. Commentators have long noted that the expression "instrument of the host" (כלי צבא, 43:8c) in combination with "shining" (זהר, 43:8d) is a metaphor for "the fire signal or beacon which in front of the camp or army serves to control and direct its movements."[363] Thus, the moon signals "the host of water-skins on high," or an army of clouds, to pour down rain. The idea is related to the hellenistic notion that the moon can be watched for signs of impending rains (cf. *1 En* 80:4-5).[364] The rains can be either severe or gentle, they can curse or bless, as will be apparent in the following stanza. As with the sun, the moon carries out its functions in obedience to the word of the Lord (43:10; cf. 43:5b).

Meteorological Phenomena. In the second stanza of the body of his Hymn to the Creator, ben Sira offers an extended treatment of various weather phenomena. The stanza divides topically into three subunits:[365]

Sir	43:13a	His rebuke marks the hail,
	b	and directs the flashes of judgment.
	14a	For a purpose he lets loose the storehouse,
	b	and he makes the clouds fly like birds of prey.
	15a	His might strengthens the clouds,
	b	and breaks in pieces the hailstones.
	17a	The sound of his thunder makes his earth tremble,
	16a	and by his strength he shakes the mountains.
	b	At his word the south wind causes reproach,
	17b	whirlwind, hurricane and gale.

---

[363] Box and Oesterley, "Sirach," *APOT* 1.475.

[364] Aratus, *Phaenomena*, 778-818.

[365] Translation from ms M (Yadin, *The Ben Sira Scroll*, 31-33, 44), except for the lacuna in 43:20c-d, 21 (ms B). Cf. Strugnell, "Notes and Queries," 117-18.

   c   Like flocks of birds he lets out his snow,
   d   and like locusts settling is its descent.
18a   Its impressive whiteness puzzles the eyes,[366]
   b   and its showers confuse the mind.
19a   And also the hoarfrost he pours out like salt,
   b   and it sprouts like thornbush blossoms.
20a   The cold north wind, he brings back,
   b   like a clod, he congeals the fountains.
   c   He covers every pool of water,
   d   and like armour the pool puts (ice) on.

21a   He kindles the mountain growth with heat,
   b   and withers the new growth with flames.
22a   The healing of all is the dripping of the cloud of dew,
   b   it is let loose to revive from parching heat.

Storms and the South Wind. The first subunit begins with the imagery of hail and lightning (43:13) and ends with thunder and the "south wind" (תימן, 43:17a-16b).[367] The mention of the south wind introduces three synonyms for destructive storm winds (43:17b): "whirlwind" (עלעול), "hurricane" (סופה) and "gale" (וסערה). Within the boundaries of 43:13a and 17b, there are two references to "clouds" (עבים, 43:14b; ענן, 43:15a) and one to God's "storehouse" (אוצר, 43:14a).

With this imagery, ben Sira is describing the meteorology of the south winds as a "bad thing" within his doctrine of opposites (cf. 39:28). "Hail" was included in an earlier list of "bad things" that God kept "in his storehouse for the appointed time" (באוצרו לעת, 39:30d; cf. 39:17). The same idea is present here when ben Sira says that for "his own purpose" (למענו) God opens "(his) storehouse" (אוצר, 43:14a). The time and purpose for using the storehouse is related to the execution of judgment. This is evident from several terms associated with the weather phenomena, such as "rebuke"

---

[366] The Hebrew verb הגה in Sir 43:18a makes no sense and we may thus adopt the Greek reading (Strugnell, "Notes and Queries," 118). The Greek verb ἐκθαυμάζω implies grudging admiration, and Yadin suggested it be translated "will puzzle" (*The Ben Sira Scroll*, 32). If the verb תמה in 43:18b ("to be benumbed, stunned, confused") offers a clue, the couplet may be applying the language of covenant curse to a blizzard. Deut 28:28 pictures the Lord striking the disobedient "with madness, blindness and confusion of mind" (בשגעון ובעורון ובתמהון לבב).

[367] Di Lella regards Sir 43:16a as a reference to earthquakes (Skehan and Di Lella, *The Wisdom of Ben Sira*, 493-94). But the Biblical parallel to which he appeals (Ps 18:6, 18; cf. Judg 5:4-5) is a thunderstorm. The couplet in 43:17a/16a is also best regarded as descriptive of such a storm.

(גערה, 43:13a), "flashes of judgment" (זיקות משפט, 43:13b), and "reproach" (חרף *hi.*, 43:16b). The emphasis on the punishing capacity of meteorological phenomena is carried forward into the next subunit.

Storms and the North Wind. This subsection opens with a reference to snow (43:17c) and concludes with the "north wind" (צינת רוח צפון) and its effects (43:20a-d). Ben Sira traces his theme of opposites and divine judgment into the winter season. Di Lella suggests otherwise; while the south winds are a sign of God's anger, the snow and north winds are to be regarded as tokens of God's blessing.[368] Certainly, snow can be a sign of blessing, but it appears that in this case ben Sira is emphasizing its fearful capacity as a tool of judgment. Two considerations point in this direction.

First, the similes used in connection with the snow and north winds are harsh and have negative connotations. The initial comparison of flying snow to "flocks of birds" (רשף, 43:17c) seems innocent enough, especially since earlier the storm clouds were explicitly likened to "birds of prey" (עיט, 43:14b). However, that ben Sira has not shifted the focus to blessing is apparent from the next colon in which snow is said to descend and settle like "the locusts" (ארבה, 43:17d). With this image, ben Sira alludes to one of the plagues of Egypt (Exod 10:4-6) and one of the curses for disobedience to the covenant (Deut 28:38, 42).[369] Similarly, when ben Sira talks about the frost, the initial comparison to salt appears to be neutral (43:19a; cf. 39:26). But when he goes on to say that frost glistens like "the thornbush with blossoms" (כסנה צצים, 43:19b), his intention becomes clear. The combination of desert shrub and salt land is used in Jeremiah 17:5-6 to depict God's curse upon the disobedient (cf. Deut 29:23). Finally, the simile of the "armor" with which the north wind clothes bodies of water (43:20d) is taken from warfare. The term brings to mind the "sword of vengeance" in one of ben Sira's lists of "bad things" (39:30b). The similes of this subunit illustrate winter's capacity as a tool of judgment.

A second reason for reading the imagery of the winter season in continuity with the summer season is that what ben Sira says about the snow and

---

[368] In Di Lella's view, God's snow flies "serenely" to earth and settles down "in an orderly fashion." In addition, ben Sira emphasizes "the beauty of its whiteness." As for the cold north winds that clothe the ponds with armor, Di Lella only offers that "Ben Sira enjoyed the sight of a frozen pond" (Skehan and Di Lella, *The Wisdom of Ben Sira*, 494). In our view, ben Sira is not describing a winter wonderland!

[369] Di Lella's remark that "the locust swarm was considered well organized; cf. Prov 30:27" (Skehan and Di Lella, *The Wisdom of Ben Sira*, 494) is hardly sufficient to turn this into a positive image.

human eyes (43:18a) echoes what he said earlier about the sun and the eyes (43:4d). The power of the sun, with its capacity to burn the eyes, leaves human beings helpless. The snow has a power of its own with a similar effect on the eyes. Blizzards blind the eyes and throw human beings into confusion so that they seek shelter indoors. In this respect, snow functions like the sun; it is an instrument of judgment.

The Gentle Rain. With this third, short subunit on meteorological phenomena, a transition does occur. Ben Sira juxtaposes the sun as an instrument of wrath, on the one hand, and the clouds and dew as instruments of blessing, on the other. He begins in 43:21 by reusing vocabulary from his depiction of the sun (43:3-4). He had previously asked who could bear the sun's "heat" (חרב, 43:3b), a heat so powerful it "kindles" the mountains (יסיק, 43:4b). He returns to this imagery by describing the mountain growth "as though kindled with heat" (כחרב ישיק, 43:21a) and the meadows "as though with flames" (כלהבה, 43:21b).

Ben Sira has returned to the earlier imagery for the purpose of now contrasting it with the blessing of God. The "dripping clouds" (מערף ענן, 43:22a) and the "loosely hanging dew" (טל[ו] פורע, 43:22b) are instruments that bless (cf. Deut 32:2; 33:28); they "heal" (רפא) and "revive" (דשן) a scorched earth. The reader inevitably thinks of the function of the moon, which signals the clouds for blessing.

The Abyss and Sea. The last major topic in ben Sira's Hymn to the Creator returns to an element of creation broached in the introductory stanza (42:18a). The abyss/ocean and and sea are brought into the perspective of the doctrine of opposites. God, in his wisdom and power, directs even the great sea monsters to execute his wrath:[370]

Sir	43:23a	By his plans, he stilled the great waters,[371]
	b	and he planted islands in the ocean.
	24a	Those who go down to the sea tell of its extent,
	b	when our ears hear, we are awestruck.
	25a	Therein are marvels, his astounding works,
	b	all species of living things, and Rahab's mighty ones.

[370] Yadin questions his placement of a very fragmentary piece here (Yadin, *The Ben Sira Scroll*, 33-34, 44), as does Strugnell ("Notes and Queries," 118). The translation is based on ms B.

[371] See Box and Oesterley, "Sirach," *APOT* 1.477. It is not necessary to emend רבה("great [waters]") to רהב ("Rahab"). The Greek reads ἄβυσσον, as in 42:18a.

26a   Because of him (God), the messenger is successful,
  b   and by his words, what he wills is done.

The passage shares some of the vocabulary and imagery of Psalm 107:23-30:

	Sirach 43			Psalm 107
23a	the great waters רבה	23b		on the great waters במים רבים
24a	Those who go down to the sea יורדי הים	a		Some went down to the sea יורדי הים
25a	Therein are marvels שם פלאות	24b		his marvels in the deep ונפלאותיו במצולה
	his astounding works תמהי מעשהו	a		the works of the Lord מעשי יהוה
26a	because of him, the messenger is successful,	25a		For he commanded, and raised the stormy wind ...
b	and by his words, what he wills is done	29a		He made the storm be still ...

Different from Psalm 107, in Sirach 43:26a the messengers of God are not the storm and the wave, but the creatures mentioned in the preceding line: "all species of living things and the mighty ones of Rahab" (43:25b). Ben Sira has already elaborated on how God uses the storms, therefore he adapts Psalm 107:23-30 by incorporating the great sea creatures. The point he makes with the sea creatures is identical to that of the land beasts mentioned in his earlier list of "bad things" ("carnivorous beasts, scorpions, vipers", 39:30a). The ocean too, particularly its "edge," contains frightful creatures that ensure God's will is done (43:26b; cf. 42:15d, "they accept the doing of his will").

Ben Sira states that he and others are "awestruck" (שמם, *hitp.*, 43:24b) when they hear the sailors tell about God's marvels in the sea.[372] As was the case in previous stanzas of the Hymn, such awe includes a proper recognition that God uses creation, here the great fish of the sea, to carry out his judgment.[373]

---

[372] The sailors are doing what the angels do; the latter too "tell" the "wonders" of God (Sir 42:17a-b).

[373] As we interpret Sir 43:23-26, the message is very similar to that of the Leviathan passage in Job 41. In the latter, God has made this fierce creature before whom humankind cowers and, therefore, God can ask: "Who then is he that can stand before Me?" (Job 41:10b). In effect, ben Sira has earlier used this question with reference to the sun (Sir 43:3b), but it is apropos of the monsters of Rahab as well.

Concluding Stanza.   The concluding stanza of this Hymn contains
standard exhortations to praise and magnify God because of his works displayed throughout creation:[374]

Sir 43:27a   More than this cannot be added,
          b   the end of the matter: He is the All.
       28a   Let us continue to extol the Everlasting One for never
                    shall we reach the limits,
          b   since he is greater than all his works.
       29a   The Lord is to be exceedingly feared,
          b   his might is marvelous.
       30a   You who extol the Lord raise your voice,
          b   with all your strength for he is the Everlasting.[375]
          c   You who exalt him renew your strength,
          d   do not grow tired for you cannot reach the limits.
       31a   Who has seen him and can describe it?
          b   Or who can praise him as he is?
       32a   Many more things than these are hidden,
          b   I have seen a few of his works.
       33a   All things the Lord made,
          b   and to the pious he gave wisdom.

Ben Sira's adaptation of the typical closing motif of praise can perhaps
best be approached through the key word "all" (כל). The term is used to
frame the stanza: God is "the all" (הכל, vs 27b) in the sense that God has
made "all things" (הכל, vs 33a). In the context of this Hymn, we must recall
that "all of God's works" (כל מעשיו, 42:22a) are depicted as lovely because
"all of them" (כלם, 42:24a) come in twos. Therefore, the term "the all" in the
conclusion is intended to embrace the opposites of creation as elaborated in
this poem.[376]
      The emphasis on opposites is also apparent from the way in which God is
compared to his works. Just as the sun and moon had been described as
instruments "to be feared" (נורא, 43:2b, 8b), ben Sira now concludes that the
Lord is "to be exceedingly feared" (נו[רא ... מ[אד מאד, 43:29a). The superla-
tive follows naturally upon the statement that the Lord is greater "*than all* his

---

[374] Translation based on ms B and Greek (for 43:31, 33b).

[375] For the translation of Sir 43:28 and 43:30a-b, see Penar, *Northwest Semitic Philology*, 73-74.

[376] Hengel finds a suggestion of Stoic influence in ben Sira's use of the concept of the
"all" (*Judaism and Hellenism*, I.147-48).

works" (מכל מעשיו, 43:28b). If the created instruments of blessing and wrath generate fear, how much more the unfathomable Creator himself!

Ben Sira also employs the term "all" in the human response to God. The student is exhorted to exalt the Lord "*with all* your strength/you are able" (בכל תוכלו, 43:30b). The human response here is similar to the angelic response in the introduction of the Hymn (42:17c-d). Although ben Sira's students are exhorted to employ all of their abilities to this end, they, like the angels, never fully succeed in "reaching the limits" or "fathoming" God (43:28a, 30d; cf. 18:4-7). Unlike the works of creation, God himself is never seen (43:31).

The last two couplets of the conclusion strike an important balance. On the one hand, ben Sira acknowledges that even what he has seen in the creation amounts to but "few" of God's works, "many" things remain hidden (43:32a-b). On the other hand, ben Sira and his students experience success in their ongoing task of discerning the operations of the created order because the Lord who has made "all things" (43:33a) is the selfsame one who "gives wisdom to the pious" (43:33b).[377] Just as God is actively involved in directing "the mighty deeds *of his wisdom*" (42:21a), so too God actively dispenses *wisdom* so that humankind may properly apprehend those deeds. The duality of creation is unveiled to those individuals to whom God gives wisdom.

Summary

The passages surveyed above all use the language of "seeing" or "being shown" the "works of God" (Sir 17:8; 33:15; 39:33-34; 42:15, 25; 43:32b). What ben Sira sees in creation has been revealed to him (42:19) and to the wise (43:33) and in this sense is something new; yet it was present in creation from the beginning and through ben Sira's instruction is there for all to see. Creation is constituted in terms of the opposites of good and evil (17:7; 33:14, 15b; 39:25; 42:24); and even the evil is "good" because of the need for judgment that it serves (39:16, 33; 42:25). Ben Sira uses nature lists within his Hymns to provide examples of what he means by good and bad things.

The polarity of creation holds for heaven, earth and sea. Ben Sira looks at the heavens and concludes that the luminaries and angels must obey God or they will be held to account. He appeals to the luminaries in two distinct ways to illustrate how opposites affect humankind. As calendrical (33[36]:7-12) or meteorological tools (43:1-12; 21-22), God uses sun and moon to bless or curse humankind. As with the luminaries, other created elements are used for the same purpose. From the firmament of heaven, from the compass points of

---

[377] The Greek reads: καὶ τοῖς εὐσεβέσιν ἔδωκεν σοφίαν.

the winds (43:13-20), from the edge of the ocean (43:23-26), the all-wise and all-powerful Creator directs all created phenomena to bless or curse humankind.

Therefore, humankind should "fear" the Creator (17:8; 43:29). In the context of the doctrine of opposites, this means to avoid evil and obey the commandments. The observable phenomena in creation should engender awe (43:2b, 8b, 24b) because they display obedience and the potential to be used by God for judgment.

HIDDEN ASPECTS OF THE CREATION

Ben Sira has written two Hymns in praise of Wisdom that treat Wisdom's relationship to the creation (Sir 1:1-10 and 24:3-7). In these poems, he refers to hidden aspects of the creation. It appears that the two Hymns are closely related to each other, as the following parallels indicate:

	Sir 1:1, 3, 10		Sir 24:3-7
1a	All wisdom is from the Lord (παρὰ κυρίου)	3a	From the mouth of the Most High (ἀπὸ στόματος ὑψίστου) I came forth
3a	Heaven's height ... (ὕψος οὐρανοῦ)	4a	In the heights of heaven (ἐν ὑψηλοῖς) I dwelt
		5a	The vault of heaven (γῦρον οὐρανοῦ) I encircled alone
3c	the depths of the abyss (ἄβυσσον)	5b	through the deep abyss (ἐν βάθει ἀβύσσων) I walked
d	who can fathom?		
3b	earth's breadth ... (πλάτος γῆς)	6a	Over the waves of the sea, over all the earth ... (ἐν πάσῃ τῇ γῇ) I ruled
10a	With all flesh ... (μετὰ πάσης σαρκὸς)	7a	With them all ... (μετὰ τούτων πάντων) I sought a resting place

In the opening poem, the dimensions of the tripartite creation are presented, followed by the rhetorical question: "Who can fathom these?" (1:3).[378] The question assumes the inability of humankind to comprehend the great expanse of creation. In 24:3-7, the dimensions of creation are found in a first person speech by personified Wisdom. In effect, she answers the question put in 1:3. Wisdom conducts the search implied in the rhetorical question. Thus, the two passages, 1:1-10 and 24:3-7, are conceptually related, although it is impossible to determine the direction of dependency.[379]

Sirach 1:1-10

The opening and closing lines of this Hymn indicate its dynamic. These lines frame the Hymn by describing the movement of wisdom from God to the creation. Wisdom that is *with the Lord* comes to be *with humanity*:[380]

Sir 1:1a All wisdom is from the Lord,
    b and *with him* ($\mu\epsilon\tau$' $\alpha\dot{\upsilon}\tau o\hat{\upsilon}$) it is forever.
    2a The sand of the seas and the drops of rain
    b and the days of eternity: who can number?
    3a The height of heaven and the breadth of earth
    b and the abyss and wisdom: who can fathom?
    4a Before all things wisdom was created,
    b and wise understanding from eternity.
    6a To whom has wisdom's root been revealed?
    b Who knows her hidden things?
    8a One is wise, to be feared very much,
    b seated upon his throne: the Lord.
    9a He himself created her,
    b and he saw her and counted her out,
    c and he poured her forth upon all his works,
    10a *with all flesh* ($\mu\epsilon\tau\grave{\alpha}$ $\pi\acute{\alpha}\sigma\eta\varsigma$ $\sigma\alpha\rho\kappa\grave{o}\varsigma$) according to his gift,
    b he has lavished her on those who love him.

---

[378] The Greek verb $\dot{\epsilon}\xi\iota\chi\nu\iota\acute{\alpha}\zeta\omega$ (Sir 1:3) probably translates the Hebrew חקר, "to search out." Cf. Sir 42:18: "(God) searched out ($\dot{\epsilon}\xi\iota\chi\nu\epsilon\acute{\upsilon}\omega$/חקר) the abyss and human heart."

[379] Cf. Marböck, *Weisheit im Wandel*, 17-80. Di Lella regards Sir 24 as the beginning of the second major division of the book, and suggests that it serves as a parallel to 1:11-30 (Skehan and Di Lella, *The Wisdom of Ben Sira*, 331). Our view of the similarities between Sir 24:3-7 and 1:1-10 is a more compelling argument for the claim that Sir 24 opens the second half of the book. Of course, the position of a poem in the book does not settle the issue of priority.

[380] Translation from the Greek. Vss 5, 7 and 10c-d are secondary.

Sirach 1:9 is especially important for delineating the dynamic. Verse 9a returns to the theme of 1:4, which stated that *"before* all things wisdom *was created."* The allusion in 1:4 is to Proverbs 8:22-31 ("The Lord *created* me [ἔκτισέν] ... *before* [πρὸ] the beginning of the earth ..."). As in Proverbs, for ben Sira wisdom is God's first creation. However, ben Sira's development of this thought in 1:9 moves far beyond the imagery of Proverbs. In Proverbs 8:22-31, personified Wisdom is simply present at the creation ("I was there," 8:27/ "I was beside him ..." 8:30). Ben Sira envisions a more active involvement of wisdom in creation. God "saw" (εἶδεν) wisdom and "counted" her "out" (ἐξηρίθμησεν, Sir 1:9b). The vocabulary of "seeing" and "counting" has a parallel in Job 28:25-27.[381] In Job, this activity is ascribed to God in connection with a list of created things involving weights, measures and amounts.[382] Ben Sira applies God's activity to personified Wisdom herself before she is poured out on all God's works (1:9c).

The language of counting in Sirach 1:9b alludes to the amounts and measurements mentioned in 1:2-3. Indeed, 1:2 contains its own list of created things (sand of the seashores, drops of rain, and days of eternity) and asks the rhetorical question: "who can number (ἐξαριθμήσει) these?" One answer to this question is supplied by 1:9b-c. God saw and numbered Wisdom before he poured her out on all his works. Personified Wisdom, then, knows the humanly incomprehensible data of creation. She claims as much for herself in 24:3-7.

The recurrence of the language "hidden things" (Sir 1:6b) in Sirach 42:19b and 51:19d was discussed earlier.[383] The root of wisdom, an image that itself implies hiddenness, has been revealed to ben Sira and Israel (1:6a; cf. 1:20a; 24:12). The result is not that ben Sira comprehends the dimensions of the tripartite cosmos, but he does understand phenomena that issue from the reaches of the cosmos. Sirach 1:6 provides a foundation for the revelation of opposites. Ben Sira's inspired instruction of the polarity throughout creation is a major example of the abundant supply of wisdom in Israel (1:10b).

---

[381] Box and Oesterley, "Sirach," *APOT* 1.318.

[382] "When he gave to the wind its weight, and *counted out* (ἠρίθμησεν/תכן pi.) the waters by measure; when he made a decree for the rain, and a way for the lightning of the thunder; then *he saw* it (εἶδεν/ראה) and declared it; he established it, and searched it out" (Job 28:25-27).

[383] See Chap. 2, pp. 70-72.

Sirach 24:3-7

In Chapter 2, it was suggested that the description of the origin and career
of Wisdom in Sirach 24:1-7 and 8-12 alludes to a previous commissioning
scene.[384] Verses 3-7 deserve further comment because they appear to echo
parts of 1:1-10. In 24:3-7, personified Wisdom is portrayed in relation to hidden
den aspects of the creation.

Verses 1-2 provide the context for the first person speech found in verses
3-7. The scene is heaven, or more specifically, the divine throneroom. Personified
sonified Wisdom speaks in the presence of the angelic assembly to proclaim
her own worth:[385]

Sir	24:3a	I came forth from the mouth of the Most High,
	b	and like a mist covered the earth.
	4a	I dwelt in the heights,
	b	and my throne (was) in a pillar of cloud.
	5a	The vault of heaven I encircled alone,
	b	and in the depth of the abyss I walked.
	6a	In the waves of the sea and in all the earth,
	b	and in every people and nation I ruled.
	7a	With all of these I sought a resting place,
	b	in whose inheritance I may abide.

It is not our intention to comment on the history-of-religions background
to this passage.[386] Perhaps particular elements of ben Sira's presentation are
indebted to the syncretism of hellenistic religious thought, but there is no way
to demonstrate this with any degree of certainty.[387] Whatever ben Sira may
have adapted is fully intelligible within the context of his own tradition, particularly
ularly when the close relationship to 1:1-10 is recognized.

The dynamic present in 1:1-10 is also found in Sirach 24:3-7. Wisdom,
whose origin is "from" ($\pi\alpha\rho\grave{\alpha}$) the Lord (1:1a), now herself claims to have

---

[384] See pp. 54-55.

[385] Translation from the Greek.

[386] Hans Conzelmann ("The Mother of Wisdom," *The Future of Our Religious Past* [ed.
James M. Robinson; London: SCM, 1971] 230-43) argued that Sir 24:3-7 is a hymn to Isis
that ben Sira has adopted with minor alterations. The arguments he advanced have been
challenged by Sanders, *Ben Sira and Demotic Wisdom*, 45-50.

[387] We must be extremely cautious in claiming that elements of Isis theology influenced
ben Sira because the parallels usually cited from the Isis aretalogies come from texts that
are much later. Given the fact that the book of Sirach was translated very early in Egypt,
there is every likelihood that some influence went the other way. After all, Isis is more of
an imitator than an innovator.

come out "from" (ἀπὸ) the mouth of the Most High (24:3a). In the opening Hymn, Wisdom's movement culminates in her presence "with" (μετὰ) all flesh (1:10a), so here Wisdom says she sought a resting place "with" (μετὰ) all peoples and nations (24:7a).

The common dynamic indicates that ben Sira is again tracing Wisdom's movement from God to humanity. Personified Wisdom speaks in the first person and reviews her qualifications for the commission she received from God. Wisdom's credentials are based on her personal travels to the extremities of the tripartite creation.

In the course of her movement from God to humanity, Wisdom conducts the search implied in the rhetorical question of 1:3. Wisdom fathoms all parts of created reality: heaven, the abyss and the earth. To establish this point, ben Sira portrays personified Wisdom as moving about throughout the cosmos. She "dwelt/pitched her tent" (κατασκηνόω) in the heights (24:4a), "encircled" (κυκλόω) the vault of heaven alone (24:5a),[388] "walked around" (περιπατέω) in the depths of the abyss (24:5b), and "ruled" (ἡγέομαι) in the waves of the sea and in all the earth (24:6). Wisdom knows the humanly incomprehensible dimensions of creation from firsthand experience.

Summary

The hidden and humanly incomprehensible aspects of creation play a programmatic role in ben Sira's thought. The two passages reviewed above probably introduce two major parts of the book, an indication that this creation material has foundational significance. Ben Sira touches on the hidden reaches of creation not only to imply that the Creator is great and worthy of praise, but to show how Wisdom, created before all things, is present and active in every aspect of creation. There is no height nor depth nor breadth in creation with which she is not personally familiar.

Wisdom does not reveal these dimensions to the sage. Rather, her experience guarantees the truthfulness and authority of the other things she does reveal about the created order. For ben Sira, prominent among these other things are the opposites in creation; the works of God in the heavens, abyss and earth serve as instruments of recompense.

---

[388] Sanders points out that ben Sira's picture of the circle of heaven is something of a reversal of the imagery of the circle of the abyss found in older wisdom texts (Job 26:10; Prov 8:27). He comments: "I take the difference in expression to be due to the widespread interest in astrology in Ben Sira's day, which has provided the concept of the circle of the heavens ..." (*Ben Sira and Demotic Wisdom*, 48).

COMPARATIVE ANALYSIS OF THE
CREATION THEME IN *1 ENOCH* AND SIRACH

The investigation above has shown that *1 Enoch* and Sirach contain vocabulary and motifs from the Hymn of Praise. Authors in both traditions state what one may "see" of the "works of God" from the perspective of earth (*1 En* 2:1, 2; 5:1-2; 101:1-9; Sir 17:8; 33[36]:15; 39:16; 42:15),[389] or what Enoch and personified Wisdom see up close in their cosmic travels. The body of the traditional Hymn of Praise allows for the variety of creation motifs in these texts. Stylistic features such as lists of created elements and rhetorical questions are present in both traditions.

Creation as Observed from Earth

What the sage sees from the perspective of earth is that phenomena throughout the tripartite creation obey the Creator. One can look up at the heavens and see that the luminaries carry out God's word (*1 En* 2:1; Sir 16:26-28; 43:1-10). There is a lesson here for humankind, though it is applied in different ways. In *1 Enoch*, the obedience of the luminaries (along with God's works on earth and sea) contrasts with the disobedience of sinners and serves as an indictment (*1 En* 5:2-4; 100:10). The luminaries will become agents of judgment when they are shaken in the final cosmic catastrophe (102:2). In Sirach, the obedience of the luminaries contributes to the opposites in creation. Sun and moon distinguish regular from special days and bring good and bad weather. Their obedience qualifies them as daily instruments of blessing or the curse.

In both *1 Enoch* and Sirach, the one who contemplates the works of God in heaven is asked to learn much the same lesson: fear to do evil or avoid evil (*1 En* 101:1; Sir 17:14). Of course, it is by following the respective wisdom traditions that one is assured of doing this.

In addition to stressing the obedience of God's works in heaven, both traditions also project evil unto the heavens (*1 En* 18:15; 21:6; Sir 17:32a). The projection occurs against the background of God's judgment, which has maintained order (*1 En* 17:3; 18:16; 23:4; 33:3; 36:3; cf. Sir 16:7). Here, too, is a lesson for humankind. If the angels of heaven are subject to judgment, so too are human creatures.

---

[389] The connection between these passages was noted by Rau (*Kosmologie*, 88).

The works of God on the earth are easily observable and include the seasons and meteorological phenomena. Winter is regarded as a sign of blessing because of the abundant moisture (*1 En* 2:3; Sir 43:8c, 22). The two traditions also assert that God uses the snow, frost and cold of winter storms for judgment; but in *1 Enoch* the blizzard is adapted to eschatological judgment (100:13), and in Sirach it is a created opposite used for temporal judgment (43:17c-20).

The summer season is a time when the sun burns. There appears to be a specific parallel between *1 Enoch* 4:1 and Sirach 43:3b, 21. Both passages use the image of the burning heat of the sun before which human beings cannot endure.[390] In Sirach, this phenomenon illustrates one of creation's opposites; the capacity of the sun to be used as an instrument of judgment. In *1 Enoch* too, the withholding of rains or drought is indicative of the judgment of God (100:11-12).

Different from ben Sira, the author of *1 Enoch* 2:3-5:1 highlights a paradox within the two seasons. In winter, when moisture is abundant, deciduous trees are stripped; in summer, when it is dry, fruit bearing trees prosper.[391] Why call attention to the paradox? Does the Enochic author regard the doctrine of opposites as a too simplistic means of comprehending God's works on earth? *1 Enoch* 4:1 takes phenomena at home in the doctrine of opposites and shows, via paradox, that reality is more complex. Possibly the paradox is offered in response to a doctrine of opposites like ben Sira's.

The works of God on the sea are developed in both traditions. The brief reference in *1 Enoch* 5:3 is elaborated in 101:4-9. Similarly, the bare mention of the abyss in Sirach 42:18a-b is expounded in a later stanza (43:23-26). The Enochic authors and ben Sira have adapted vocabulary and motifs from Psalm 107:23-30. The motifs of cry and deliverance are absent in *1 Enoch* 101. Imagery from Jeremiah 5 was joined to Psalm 107 in order to contrast the obedience of the sea and the disobedience of sinners. In ben Sira's adaptation of Psalm 107, the place of the storm is occupied by the sea creatures who perform God's will (43:23-26; cf. *1 En* 101:8b). Like the land animals, sea creatures too have a function in the doctrine of opposites.

---

[390] Rau, *Kosmologie*, 73.

[391] Rau mentions the antithetical relationship between phenomena in the two seasons, but does not make much of it. He suggests that the references to the trees (*1 En* 3:1; 5:1) have their parallel in Sir 14:18 (ibid., 73-74). The falling off, and then sprouting, of green leaves is a traditional paradigm for the rhythm of nature. But, as Baumgartner pointed out long ago, Sir 14:18 uses a lament motif about the transience of human existence ("Die literarischen Gattungen," 183-84).

Whether the tradition focuses on the waves or the sea creatures, the effect of God's works on the sea (as with all of God's works) is to engender fear (*1 En* 101:1b, 5a, 7c, 9b; Sir 43:24b). That the two traditions mean something different by the concept of fear is especially clear from the passages about the sea. In *1 Enoch* 101:5a-b, fear is tied to the casting of goods into the sea. Those who fear God show a willingness to forsake wealth and accept the wisdom taught by the Enochic community. In Sirach 43:23-26, the report of the sailors about the creatures from the edge of the sea leaves the listener awestruck because the sea monsters carry out God's will.[392] Those who fear God recognize the dual purpose of created things as taught by ben Sira.

Creation as Observed from Heaven

In both *1 Enoch* and Sirach, the hidden works of God in heaven have been seen close up by Enoch and personified Wisdom, respectively. Esoteric creation knowledge is prominent in *1 Enoch*. In *1 Enoch*, the created elements obey God in supernatural ways. Created phenomena beckon Enoch and transport him to heaven (14:8) and created opposites are found together in the material of the heavenly temple (14:9-17). In the course of his heavenly journeys, Enoch is conducted to places of eschatological significance. He describes what he sees along the way, and an angel interprets for him what he sees upon arrival at each place. These descriptions and interpretations of hidden places have no parallel in Sirach.

However, the appearance of Enoch with the angels before the divine throne does resonate with a passage about the angels in Sirach. For purposes of comparison, *1 Enoch* 14:20-23 is juxtaposed to Sirach 42:15c-17, 21d:

1 Enoch 14		Sirach 42
	15c	By the word of the Lord are his deeds
	d	...
20a The Great Glory sat ...	16a	As the shining of the sun ...
b ... like the appearance of the sun	b	so the glory of the Lord fills his works.
c ...		

---

[392] Ben Sira's depiction of the monsters has a parallel in Enoch's report about the great beasts and birds that he saw at the ends of the earth (*1 En* 33:1; cf. 34:1). Both traditions refer to mighty creatures from the edge, beyond the normal reach of humankind; creatures that fill humankind with dread.

21a And no angel could enter	17a God's holy ones do not suffice
... because of the splendor	b to recount all his wonders.
and glory ...	
b ...	
22a ... a great fire stood by him	c the Lord has given his hosts the
b ... those about him ...	strength
c Ten thousand times ten	d to stand firm before his glory
thousand stood before him;	
d and he needed no counselor	21d and he has no need for any
his every word was deed.	counselor

Commentators have noted the similarities between *1 Enoch* 14:22d and Sirach 42:21d, 15c.[393] What has passed unnoticed, however, is the remarkably similar contexts in which the statements occur in the respective texts. Enoch is about to be commissioned to pronounce judgment on the rebel Watchers. Before Enoch hears God's word of judgment, the author provides an expanded account of the angels around the heavenly throne. As noted earlier, one purpose of this account is to verify to the Watchers that Enoch was indeed in their realm. What he sees, however, is that the angels who stand before God are hindered by God's glory and do not advise God about his deeds. Perhaps the implication is that God's announcement of judgment and God's creation of hidden places of judgment could not have been anticipated even by the angels (cf. *1 En* 36:4: God shows his great deeds *to his angels* and to the spirits of men). The wisdom and power of God establish the truth of what Enoch hears and sees in heaven.

Sirach 42:15-43:33 is a Hymn about the glory of God displayed in all his works. Early in the Hymn, ben Sira uses the angels as a foil. The holy ones stand before God's glory but they do not suffice to recount God's wonders (42:17). God alone has the wisdom and power to search creation, perceive its hidden things and reveal its secrets (42:18-21). These points lead up to a thematic statement of what God has revealed to ben Sira, namely, the doctrine of opposites (42:22-25)—the subject of this Hymn.

Therefore, in both *1 Enoch* 14 and Sirach 42, a scene with the angels underscores the inscrutable wisdom and almighty power of God and, in this way, prepares the reader for the message the sage is about to reveal. Enoch hears the divine judgment that restores order to heaven and earth, and then travels to places in the cosmos to see the hidden realities that confirm this judgment (*1 En* 17-19; 20-32 + 81-82). Ben Sira refers to the hidden reaches

---

[393] E.g., Black, *The Book of Enoch or 1 Enoch*, 150.

of the cosmos (heaven, treasuries, abyss; 43:1-26) only to the extent that such places contain the elements God uses to carry out his judgment. For ben Sira, this is not esoteric knowledge. The works of God that issue from hidden places have a capacity for judgment that is visible to all.

Both traditions view the created order as originally constituted for the necessity of judgment. In the journey reports of Enoch, the verb "created" and its synonym "prepared" are employed to stress that God designed the cosmos with temporary and permanent holding places for sinners and the just (*1 En* 22:3-4; 25:7; cf. 103:3). In Sirach, the verb "created" is used for the good and bad things in creation that God uses to bless the righteous and punish the wicked (Sir 39:28, 29; 40:10). Enoch sees *opposite places*, created and reserved in heaven for the righteous and sinners; ben Sira sees *opposite phenomena*, created and employed on earth to bless or curse.[394] As noted above, the Enochic tradition also recognizes that created phenomena are tools of judgment, but it applies such phenomena to the final judgment (4:1; 100:10-13).

When treating the hidden aspects of creation, both traditions employ the stylistic combination of onomastica and rhetorical questions. *1 Enoch* 93:11-14 may be compared with Sirach 1:3. The rhetorical questions related to cosmology can be answered by Enoch because he alone of all the sons of men journeyed throughout creation (*1 En* 19:3). Similarly, the question in Sirach 1:3 about who can fathom the dimensions of the cosmos is taken up and answered by personified Wisdom in 24:3-7. Wisdom alone has traversed the creation (24:5).

The conceptual closeness of the cosmic journeys of Enoch and personified Wisdom may be illustrated by the following example:

1 Enoch 17:7	Sirach 24:5b
And I departed (for) where no flesh *walks*. I saw the wintry winds of darkness and the gushing of all *the waters of the abyss*.	And in the *depths of the abyss* I *walked*.

1 Enoch 17:7 occurs in the context of sight-seeing material. The recently commissioned Enoch is witnessing the order that prevails in the cosmos as he

---

[394] In *1 Enoch*, the created places are reserved "until the time" of the great judgment; whereas, in ben Sira's view, the time of punishment or blessing comes during the course of one's life or at the moment of one's death. See Chap. 6.

journeys to the place where God reckons with disorder (18:6-19:2). Sirach 24:5b also presupposes a commissioning scene. But personified Wisdom, in contrast to Enoch, possesses cosmic credentials *before* she is commissioned for her special task. Still, she too acquired her knowledge of the cosmos by means of walking throughout its expanse. In both traditions, a unique figure (Enoch, personified Wisdom) experiences the hidden order of the cosmos through a journey. The difference is that Enoch reveals what he sees, personified Wisdom does not. Sirach 24:3-7 could even be read as a denial of the possibility of esoteric creation knowledge.

The hidden knowledge revealed to Enoch includes the astronomical data that supports a solar calendar of 364 days.[395] Enoch sees the structures and laws that validate this calendar (*1 En* 72-80:1) and prophesies about what happens when it is not followed (80:2-8). In contrast, ben Sira uses a lunisolar calendar (= 354 days; Sir 43:6-8) which requires periodic intercalations. The difference between the two calendars concerns not only the length of the year and the issue of intercalation, but inevitably involves the question of whether the sun or the moon is to be used to designate religious days. The observance of festival days is important in both traditions (*1 En* 2:1; Sir 33[36]:8; 43:7) and rival calendars would obviously result in observances on different dates. Enoch is portrayed as bringing the solar calendar from heaven and he charges those who do not follow it with erring. Ben Sira, for his part, puts the lunisolar calendar in the context of opposites thereby enabling it to distinguish the just and the wicked.

The comparative analysis has demonstrated that the conceptual framework for treating creation is remarkably similar in *1 Enoch* and Sirach. God's works throughout creation, whether observable or hidden, teach the importance of obedience. Authors from each tradition have enlisted the created order to lend confirmation to their own beliefs and practices. The constitution and maintenance of creation guarantees that judgment will fall on those who disobey and deviate from the tradition. Moreover, there are indications that each tradition views the other among the disobedient: the paradox of the seasons in *1 Enoch* plays off the doctrine of opposites, the cosmic journey of personified Wisdom in Sirach does not result in a revelation of esoteric knowledge, and the two traditions follow different calendars.

---

[395] The Astronomical Book does describe the variable illumination of the moon in a lunar month and also attempts to relate lunar years to the solar year (Neugebauer, "The 'Astronomical' Chapters," 396-401).

PART III

THE THEME OF JUDGMENT IN
1 ENOCH AND SIRACH

In this section, passages in *1 Enoch* and Sirach that exhibit the theme of the coming judgment are surveyed. In both books, the theme is presented through identical genres and literary forms. These include the Divine Warrior Hymn, the Disputation Speech and the Woe-oracle. Each of these literary structures displays basic constituent parts or characteristic motifs and standard vocabulary. The choice of passages and the scope of the analysis is again determined by the comparative aim of this study. Our effort concentrates on adaptations of literary traits insofar as these changes assist a discovery of how the judgment theme is conceptualized in each book.

5. JUDGMENT IN THE
ENOCHIC BOOKS OF WISDOM

THE DIVINE WARRIOR HYMN

The genre Divine Warrior Hymn originated in Canaanite and Mesopotamian cosmic conflict myths.[396] The genre was utilized in Israelite tradition to portray the exodus and conquest (e.g., Exod 15; Deut 33:2-5, 26-29; Judg 5) and the unassailability of the royal cult (e.g., the royal Psalms). There are several motifs associated with the genre, although the number and arrangement of the motifs varies. The common motifs, along with the passages in *1 Enoch* where they occur, may be listed as follows:[397]

---

[396] See Frank Moore Cross, *Canaanite Myth and Hebrew Epic: Essays in the History of the Religion of Israel* (Cambridge, MA: Harvard, 1973); and Patrick D. Miller, Jr., *The Divine Warrior in Early Israel* (HSM 5; Cambridge, MA: Harvard, 1973).

[397] The various combinations of Warrior Hymn motifs found in the biblical literature are illustrated by Hanson, *The Dawn of Apocalyptic*, 300-315. The same motifs were earlier identified in *1 Enoch* by Lars Hartman as elements of a pattern of thought present in several Jewish apocalyptic texts (*Prophecy interpreted: the Formation of some Jewish Apocalyptic Texts and of the Eschatological Discourse Mark 13 par.* [Lund: Gleerup, 1966] 23-49, 55).

TABLE 4

DIVINE WARRIOR MOTIFS IN *1 ENOCH*

	1:3c-9 5:5-9	10:11-11:2	25:3-6	91:5-9	99:3-10 100:1-6	100:10-13 102:1-3
Threat				x		
Combat-Victory over enemies	x	x		x	x	x
Victory Shout	x	x				
Theophany	x		x	x	x	x
Salvation of the Nation	x	x	x		x	
Fertility, new creation	x	x	x			
Universal Reign	x	x		x	x	
Procession to the Temple		x	x			
Banquet			x			

As the table illustrates, the above passages, taken together, present a full complement of the motifs associated with the Divine Warrior Hymn. Each of the texts listed above will be examined.

<u>1 Enoch 1-5</u>

In the opening chapters, motifs from the Divine Warrior Hymn are present in the description of the theophany (*1 En* 1:3c-9) and the alternating words of salvation and judgment (*1 En* 5:5-9).[398] The theophany is placed immediately after the superscript and introduction, and serves as a literary frontispiece to the entire corpus.[399]

The superscript sets the context for the theophany, which will take place "on the day of tribulation" (εἰς ἡμέραν ἀνάγκης /ba-'elata mendābē; *1 En*

---

[398] *1 En* 5:5-9 is the second part of a "Salvation-Judgment Oracle" (see Chap. 3, p. 101, n. 240). It should also be regarded as an elaboration of the twofold application of the theophany in 1:8-9.

[399] This forward placement leads Rau to argue that *1 Enoch* opens like a prophetic book (cf. Mic 1:2-4; *Kosmologie*, 40).

1:1).[400] The genitive in the phrase is an attributive genitive ("on the distressful day") and refers to the disaster that the Day of the Lord will bring for the enemies of the righteous.[401] This Day is designated "for the taking away" (ἐξᾶραι) of all enemies (*1 En* 1:1), a theme that recurs in the theophany to follow (1:9).

The introduction (*1 En* 1:2-3b) identifies the Holy One whom Enoch saw in a vision (1:2c), namely, the Great Glory encircled by fire and a myriad of angels (*1 En* 14:20-23), as the God (the Great Holy One) who descends in the theophany with his mighty host and before whom the high hills melt like wax (1:3c-4, 6). In addition, it was this God who commissioned Enoch to pronounce a word of judgment upon the rebel Watchers (*1 En* 14:24-16:4), a judgment realized through the theophany (1:5). However, the scope of the judgment in 1:3c-9 is expanded to include all of humanity.

The full description of the theophany reads as follows:[402]

1 En 1:3c   The Great Holy One will come forth from his dwelling,
     4   and the Eternal God will tread from thence upon Mount Sinai.
         And he will appear with his army,
           yea, he will appear with his mighty host from the heaven of heavens.
     5   And all the watchers will fear and quake,
           and those who are hiding in all the ends of the earth will sing;
         And all the ends of the earth will be shaken,
           and trembling and great fear will seize them (the watchers) unto the ends of the earth.
     6   And the high mountains will be shaken and fall and break apart,
         and the high hills will be made low and melt like wax before the fire;

---

[400] The expression alludes to the prophetic concept of "the Day of the Lord" as the time of final judgment. On the connections between the Day of the Lord and Holy War, see Gerhard von Rad, *Old Testament Theology* (New York: Harper & Row, 1965) II.119-25. For the phrase "day of tribulation" (*1 En* 1:1), compare Zeph 1:14-16: "the great day of the Lord" (ἡ ἡμέρα κυρίου ἡ μεγάλη) is "a day of distress and tribulation" (ἡμέρα θλίψεως καὶ ἀνάγκης).

[401] The expression "day/time of distress" is also used in the Hebrew Bible to refer to the distress of the righteous (Nickelsburg, *Resurrection*, 15, n. 26); thus, if this was the sense in *1 En* 1:1 it would not represent a new linguistic usage (*pace* Rau, *Kosmologie*, 37).

[402] The text presents several problems for the translator, but the biggest problem has now been settled by the Aramaic fragments, viz., whether to read "and those who are hiding in all the ends of the earth will sing; And all the ends of the earth will be shaken" in verse 5. These two lines are not present in Ethiopic and Charles regarded them as an interpolation by a later scribe (*The Ethiopic Version*, 3). However, the presence of these lines is confirmed by 4QEnª I i 7, although Milik's reconstruction suggests that the Greek translator misunderstood the Aramaic text (*The Books of Enoch*, 145). The English translation here and in passages below (unless otherwise noted) is that of George W. E. Nickelsburg.

7   And the earth will be wholly rent asunder,
    and everything on the earth will perish,
    and there will be judgment on all.

8   And with the righteous he will make peace,
    and over the chosen there will be protection,
    and upon them will be mercy.
    And they will all be God's,
    and he will grant them his good pleasure.
    And he will bless (them) all,
    and he will help (them) all.
    And light will shine upon them,
    and he will make peace with them.

9   Behold, he comes with the myriads of his holy ones,
    to execute judgment on all,
    and to destroy all the godless,
    and to convict all flesh
      for all the deeds of their godlessness which they have done,
      and the proud and hard words which godless sinners spoke
    against him.

This account draws on biblical descriptions of theophany in every respect but one;[403] namely, the presence and reaction of the Watchers in verse 5. The Watchers assume the posture ("fear and quake", vs 5a; "trembling and great fear", vs 5d) usually taken by human sinners.[404] However, in Enochic tradition, the origin of evil in the world is a consequence of the deeds of the Watchers and thus it is appropriate that final judgment begin with them.[405] The Watchers fear and quake because they know they are guilty of rebellion against God. Their petitions of forgiveness had been rejected by God (*1 En* 14:1-7; 16:2-4).

Verse 5b contains further adaptations of traditional Divine Warrior images. First, the combat motif characteristically includes warnings to human sinners that though they flee, there is no place for them to hide from God's judgment (Amos 9:2-4; *1 En* 102:1-3; Rev 6:15-17).[406] Here the Watchers are depicted, in line with their earlier human-like trepidation, as "hiding in all the

---

[403] A list of the biblical parallels is offered by Hartman, *Asking for a Meaning*, 23-26.

[404] See Gerhard von Rad, *Holy War in Ancient Israel* (Grand Rapids: Eerdmans, 1991 [orig. 1958]) 46-47.

[405] In *1 En* 1:3c-9, the Watchers (1:5) are mentioned before humankind (1:7c). Contrast the Apocalypse of Weeks, in which humankind experiences judgment (*1 En* 91:11-14) before the Watchers (91:15).

[406] For the background of this image in the Baal theophany, see Miller, *The Divine Warrior*, 146-47.

ends of the earth." The image is ironic. By virtue of God's decree, the Watchers have been bound in prisons under the earth from which they await the great judgment (*1 En* 10). Moreover, on his cosmic journey Enoch saw the prison of the Watchers at "the end of the great earth" in the Northwest (*1 En* 18:10). Thus, the Watchers are in a hiding place of sorts, but not because they *fled* on the Day of the Lord, rather they were previously *bound* in these places because of their rebellion.

A second adaptation relates to the motif of the victory shout. Traditionally, the human righteous sing the victory song when God comes in judgment. The ancient motif is here applied to the Watchers, who are forced to acknowledge God's righteous judgment. The scene is analogous to that present in *1 Enoch* 27 where *human* sinners *bless* God in the days of their judgment.

In sum, while the theophanic description in 1:3c-7 is portrayed from a stock of biblical images and results in universal judgment, a few motifs have been adapted to portray final judgment on the Watchers. The rebel Watchers occupy roles typically filled by humankind.

Of course, the "judgment on all" (1:7c) envisions humankind as well. The objects of the judgment are divided in verses 8 and 9 into the two groups mentioned earlier in the superscript: "the righteous"/ "the chosen" (1:8a-b; cf. "the righteous chosen ones"/"the righteous," 1:1) and "all the godless"/"all flesh"/"godless sinners" (1:9; cf. "all the enemies," 1:1). The final judgment results in the salvation of the Enochic community and the destruction of their enemies.[407]

The twofold application of the theophany has a parallel in Third Isaiah.[408] Because the imagery in *1 Enoch* 1:8-9, and other Enochic passages surveyed below, is related to Isaiah 56-66, a brief summary of the eschatology of the latter is in order.[409] Third Isaiah wrote after returning to Judea from the Babylonian exile. The high hopes expressed in Isaiah 40-55 had not been realized, largely, in the view of Third Isaiah, because of the sins of the people and their leaders. Bitterly disillusioned, the prophet drew upon traditional Divine Warrior motifs in his call for God to intervene. The motifs used include

---

[407] Hartman points out that in some texts judgment is equated with punishment, in which case judgment upon "all" means "all except the righteous;" in other texts the judgment of "all" means "all," including the righteous. He places *1 En* 1:7 in the former category (*Prophecy interpreted*, 44, n. 59; 72). But the "judgment on all" (1:7) is applied to the righteous (1:8; "all" 3 times) and the godless (1:9; "all" 4 times). Only in 1:9 does "judgment on all" mean punishment on all the godless.

[408] Hartman calls attention to how *1 En* 1:9 associates Jer 25:31 and Isa 66:15-16 (ibid., 117-18).

[409] See George W. E. Nickelsburg, "Eschatology (Early Jewish)," *ABD* II.581-82.

theophany (with a verb of descent or coming, earthquake and fire), human trembling, bloody battle, new creation, fertility and procession to the temple (Isa 59:15c-20; 63:1-6; 63:19b-64:2; 65:17-25; 66:14b-16, 22-23). Many of these passages describe how God will judge between the righteous and godless *within Israel* (cf. Jer 25:30-38). The focus of much of the polemic of Third Isaiah is on the leaders and practitioners of the normative cult who are blamed for the failed restoration program and the present evil times, although the judgment he anticipates is universal in scope.[410] Only God's intervention in final judgment and re-creation can rectify the situation.[411]

In the Divine Warrior contexts of Third Isaiah, terms such as "enemies," "adversaries" and "the wicked" are employed with reference to the established cultic community. For example, "our adversaries" (צרינו) who have trodden down the sanctuary (63:18) are the adversaries against whom the divine Warrior will fight ("your adversaries," צריך 64:2b [Hb 1b]; cf. "his adversaries," צריו 59:18).[412]

Like the opponents in Third Isaiah, "the enemies" and "the godless" in *1 Enoch* 1:1 and 1:9 may include representatives of a corrupt cult and priesthood. A criticism of the cult may be present in an early stratum of the Book of the Watchers.[413] In addition, in the immediate context of *1 Enoch* 1:8, the salvation of the righteous carries overtones of the Aaronic benediction.[414] However this may be, the polemic in *1 Enoch* is broader than cultic,[415] as it is also in Third Isaiah.

---

[410] Hanson demonstrated that the later prophets, Third Isaiah among them, drew upon motifs from the Warrior Hymn, often fusing them with other forms, to carry the polemic of one Israelite group against another (*The Dawn of Apocalyptic*, 32-208, esp. 98, 123-26, 183-84). The exception is Isa 63:1-6, in which the nations are judged. Hanson places this text late in the life of Second Isaiah or immediately thereafter (ibid., 207). But see also the references to the "nations" in 64:2 and "all flesh" in 66:16, 23.

[411] The fact that the eschatology of a text is shaped by mythic or dualistic rather than historical images, does not of itself qualify it as *apocalyptic* eschatology (Nickelsburg, "Eschatology [Early Jewish]," 581-82, 592-93). We accept Hanson's analysis of a polemical debate between prophetic/levitical and hierocratic/Zadokite groups without agreeing that the views of the prophetic/levitical group(s) become increasingly detached from historical reality and therefore can be plotted to yield the developmental stages of proto-, early-, middle- and late-apocalyptic. As Hanson himself acknowledges, texts such as Third Isaiah and Second Zechariah never totally abandon history for myth.

[412] Hanson, *The Dawn of Apocalyptic*, 96-98. Cf. "the wicked" (רשעים) in Isa 57:20-21 and "his enemies" (איביו) in 59:18; 66:6, 14.

[413] See Chap. I, pp. 28-29.

[414] Hartman, *Asking for a Meaning*, 25.

[415] The opponents are rival sages who interpret the Torah and its requirements in ways that the Enochic tradition regards as blasphemous and idolatrous. See Chap. I, pp. 46-47.

Alternating words of salvation and judgment (*1 En* 5:5-9) conclude the opening chapters of *1 Enoch*. Hanson showed that in late prophecy various motifs of the Divine Warrior Hymn undergo adaptations toward and fusions with the Salvation-Judgment Oracle.[416] *1 Enoch* 5:5-9 represents the second part of the Salvation-Judgment Oracle, called the announcement of salvation and judgment. The passage displays various motifs from the Divine Warrior Hymn.

The motif of salvation for the chosen and righteous is depicted with several terms used in the earlier Day of the Lord (1:1) and Divine Warrior (1:8) passages; including mercy (ἔλεος 5:6e; 1:8c), peace (εἰρήνη 5:6e, 7a; 1:8a, 8i), salvation (σωτηρία 5:6f; cf. 1:1) and light (φῶς 5:6f, 7a; 1:8h).[417] The single new term introduced to portray the Salvation of the group is "kindness" (ἐπιείκεια 5:6e), a synonym for mercy.[418] This new word appears in a colon that accents the "forgiveness of sins" received by the chosen (5:6e).

In addition to the reuse of earlier vocabulary to express salvation, several other Hymnic motifs are introduced in *1 Enoch* 5:5-9. The motif of the victory shout,[419] a motif adapted to the defeated Watchers in the theophany (1:5), is present here in the rejoicing and joy (χαίρω, χαρά) of the chosen (5:6d, 7a, 9d). The universal reign of God comes to expression in the promise that the righteous "will inherit the earth" (5:6g, 7b). The fertility of the new order is evident as the chosen now complete the number of their days and experience growth and increase in salvific benefits all the days of their life (5:9b-e).[420]

A radically new notion is supplied to the motif of fertility. The righteous not only complete their days, but they do so without sinning because they have been "given wisdom" (5:8a-c, 8f-g). The expression "to give wisdom" is a technical reference to the revelation imparted to Enoch and recorded in his

---

[416] According to Hanson, the Warrior motifs in Isa 59:15b-20; 65:16c-25; 66:15-16 and Zech 14:1-2 are related to the Salvation-Judgment Oracle (*The Dawn of Apocalyptic*, 120, 143, 163, 372).

[417] Hartman provides the biblical parallels to these terms. As was the case in 1:8, the Aaronic Benediction (Num 6:24-26) is in the background. Among other parallels, Hartman suggests that Ps 80:3, 7, 19 ("let your face shine, that we may be saved") had more influence in 5:5-9 than was the case in 1:8 (*Asking For A Meaning*, 33).

[418] Notice that Hartman lists Num 6:25 as parallels for both words: "mercy" is a virtual quotation, whereas the choice of "forbearance" has been influenced by Num 6:25 (ibid.). In Bar 2:27, the latter word is used in parallel with οἰκτιρμόν ("pity/compassion").

[419] The victory shout consists of the singing of praises and rejoicing on the part of the saved. Hanson (*The Dawn of Apocalyptic*, 305-06) lists many examples from the royal Psalms (cf. Pss 47:1, 6-7; 48:10-11; 97:8-9).

[420] The language echoes Exod 23:26; Deut 30:5, 16, 20; Ps 37:11 (Hartman, *Asking For A Meaning*, 37).

books.[421] The eschatological phenomenon of living without sin is tied directly to the possession of the books of Enoch. In a striking metaphor, the wisdom conveyed by these books is described as the divine light of eschatological salvation. The chosen are "enlightened" with "light" (5:8d, cf. 1:8h; 5:6f, 7a). Enochic wisdom, then, imparts the "light" of salvation.[422] As such, it brings fertility to the chosen: a sinless life after the judgment.

In those parts of *1 Enoch* 5:5-9 that announce judgment on the sinners, a basic term from the earlier Divine Warrior context is also reused. The years of the life of the godless "will perish" (ἀπολεῖται, 5:5a; 1:7b, cf. ἀπολέσαι, 1:9c) and they will experience "destruction" (ἀπώλεια, 5:5b). In addition, sinners are denied the eschatological gifts promised to the righteous; no mercy, peace or salvation for them (5:5c, 6h).[423]

The new expression that defines the portion of sinners in the judgment is the "eternal curse" (κατάρα αἰώνων, 5:5b, 6a, cf. 5:6i, 7c). It provides a contrast to the blessings enjoyed by the righteous (1:8f). Late prophecy supplies one example of a Divine Warrior Hymn that incorporates the motif of the "curses of the covenant" for God's enemies.[424] However, the Enochic author has moved beyond the biblical exemplar. The "eternal curse" (singular) is the fiery abyss that awaits the sinners. In *1 Enoch* 26-27, Enoch sees the "cursed valley" reserved for the "cursed." This vocabulary is also prominent in the Epistle, in passages to be considered below (*1 En* 97:10; 98:4; 102:3).

The notion of the curse takes a unique turn in *1 Enoch* 5:6a-c. Not only will the names of sinners become an eternal curse for all the righteous (5:6a),[425] but everyone, including "all the sinners and ungodly," will curse the names of sinners (5:6b-c). The picture of sinners "cursing" sinners is a reversal of what occurs in the present time, when sinners "bless" sinners (*1 En* 103:5-6).

---

[421] Chap. I, pp. 20 and 23.

[422] Cf. 1 QS 2:3: "May he lighten your heart with life-giving wisdom and grant you eternal knowledge!" (Hartman, *Asking For A Meaning*, 36). Other relevant parallels include Sir 24:32 and Dan 12:3.

[423] Hartman, ibid., 20.

[424] Zech 14 (Hanson, *The Dawn of Apocalyptic*, 372). For a typology of curse styles in the prophets, see D. Hillers, *Treaty-Curses and the Old Testament Prophets* (BibOr 16; Rome: Pontifical Biblical Institute, 1964).

[425] Charles (*The Ethiopic Version*, 10) points to parallels in Ps 102:9; Jer 29:22 and Isa 65:16. ·Hartman (*Asking For A Meaning*, 32) sees Isa 65:15-18 as influencing *1 En* 5:6.

1 Enoch 10:11-11:2

In this passage, God commissions the angel Michael to bind Shemiḥazah and the other Watchers[426] in the valleys of the earth until the eternal judgment (10:11-12), at which time they will be led away to the fiery abyss (10:13). The valleys are also designated as the holding place for the halfbreed sons of the Watchers and everyone who is condemned (10:14-15). This commission lies in the background to the description of the theophany in *1 Enoch* 1:3c-9. The major focus of God's commission, however, as it continues in 10:16-11:2, relates not to the Watchers but to the earth and its inhabitants.

Hartman has illustrated that the language and motifs of the Noah story in Genesis 6-9 have colored this passage.[427] The Enochic author reads the story of Noah as a prefigurement of the end-time. Noah stands for the righteous, the Flood for the judgment, and Noah's escape and renewed life on the earth for the eschatological salvation of the righteous. As Hartman notes, because the author of *1 Enoch* 10:11-11:2 is interpreting biblical texts, passages from outside the Noah story, but containing related motifs, are also brought into his exposition.[428] Among the motifs from non-Noahic passages are those with ties to the Divine Warrior Hymn.

A verbal link in *1 Enoch* 10:16 connects this passage to the theophany. Michael's commission "to destroy" ($\dot{\alpha}\pi\acute{o}\lambda\lambda\upsilon\mu\iota$) all perversity (10:16) is most likely the basis for the same language in the opening theophany: the myriads of holy ones come with the Divine Warrior "to destroy" ($\dot{\alpha}\pi\acute{o}\lambda\lambda\upsilon\mu\iota$) all the godless (1:9; cf. 1:1). In the present passage, it is not primarily wicked *persons*, but wicked *deeds* that are in view (10:16, 20, 22).

In addition to the task of purging the earth of all forms of sin, Michael and the angels may also have a role to play in enabling all the righteous to escape (10:17a). The role of angels in separating the wicked and the righteous will become explicit in Divine Warrior contexts in the Epistle of Enoch.

The group that escapes in the judgment has apparently appeared at about that very time. "Let the plant of righteousness and truth (re-)appear ($\dot{\alpha}\nu\alpha\phi\alpha\acute{\iota}\nu\omega$ 10:16c) ... and now all the righteous will escape" ($\dot{\epsilon}\kappa\phi\epsilon\acute{\upsilon}\gamma\omega$ 10:17a). The origin of the plant is ascribed to the time of Noah, who was himself taught how to "escape" ($\dot{\epsilon}\kappa\phi\epsilon\acute{\upsilon}\gamma\omega$) the deluge (10:3). However, the

---

[426] The tradition related to the binding of 'Asael in *1 En* 10:4-8 (bind 'Asael/on the day of judgment he will be led away to the burning conflagration/heal the earth) is a later redaction and shows dependence on the sequence in *1 En* 10:11-11:2.

[427] Lars Hartman, "'Comfort of the Scriptures'—an Early Jewish Interpretation of Noah's Salvation, I En. 10:16-11:2," *SEÅ* 41-42 (1976-77) 87-96.

[428] There are allusions to Deut 28, Ps 85 and Isa 65 (Hartman, ibid., 92).

emphasis in the present passage is on the reappearance of the plant immediately before the judgment.[429] The plant, then, is a metaphor for the righteous who will be present on the Day of the Lord (*1 En* 1:1), namely, the "distant" generation represented by the author and his community (*1 En* 1:2).

The fertility motif is expressed not only by the fact that the righteous complete their life in peace (10:17c, cf. 5:9), but also by the renewed productivity of the earth inherited after the judgment (10:18; cf. Isa 65:20-25). The heightened fertility of both humankind and the earth is portrayed through hyperboles that utilize the number "thousand(s)" (10:17b, 19; cf. Isa 60:22; 2 Bar 29:5).

The motif of God's universal reign emerges when, on the renewed earth, all of humankind worships God:

1 En   10:21   And all the sons of men will become righteous;[430]
              and all the peoples will worship (me);
              and all will bless me and prostrate themselves.

In the background is the motif of the procession to the temple. Although the temple is not explicitly mentioned here, this is not unusual (cf. Isa 66:23). It is often identified as the place where all the peoples will come to worship.[431] Also in the background, and left unexplained, is precisely how all of humankind will undergo a transformation to righteousness after God's judgment within Israel. An answer will emerge from other Divine Warrior passages treated below.

1 Enoch 25:3-6

This passage is found in the context of Enoch's heavenly journeys. The motifs from the Divine Warrior Hymn are employed in the literary form of the vision. Enoch has just seen the mountain throne of God and the Tree of Life. The *angelus interpres* is Michael, the same angel who was commissioned in *1 Enoch* 10:11-11:2. In *1 Enoch* 25:3-6, Divine Warrior motifs are adapted in the explanation attributed to Michael. This takes place in a very compressed fashion, as illustrated in the table above. In fact, these few verses contain a greater number of Divine Warrior motifs than any other context in *1 Enoch*.

---

[429] In the Apocalypse of Weeks, the plant that appears prior to the judgment (93:10) is first mentioned in connection with Abraham (93:3).

[430] Ethiopic: *wa-yekunu kʷellu weluda sab' ṣādeqāna*. This colon is missing in Greek.

[431] Cf. Zech 14:16; Mic 4:1-3; Isa 2:2-4; *1 En* 25:5; 91:13; 90:28-36.

The mountain throne of God is interpreted as "the seat where the Great Holy One, the Lord of Glory, the King of eternity, will sit, when he descends to visit the earth in goodness" (*1 En* 25:3). The title, "The Great Holy One," is reflected in the theophany (1:3c). However, as compared to the theophanic account in *1 Enoch* 1, a different verb is used in 25:3 to describe the coming of the Divine Warrior ("descend" [καταβαίνω], rather than "come forth" [ἐξέρχομαι, 1:3c] or "tread" [πατέω, 1:4a]); but the verbs in both passages are traditional.[432]

The combat or battle motif is not elaborated in this passage, an indication of the flexibility of the genre,[433] yet a reference to judgment on the enemies is present: "there will be vengeance on all" (25:4; cf. Isa 59:17; 63:4). In addition, in marked contrast to the theophany in *1 Enoch* 1:3c-9, the present passage mentions neither the shaking and leveling of the earth nor the fate of the Watchers. Rather, the result of the theophany is focused entirely on its salvific effect. The expression "to visit the earth in goodness" (ἐπισκέψασθαι τὴν γῆν ἐπ᾽ ἀγαθῷ/ yaxawweṣā la-medr ba-šannāy, 25:3) signifies the eschatological salvation given to the righteous.[434]

In sum, with a relatively brief interpretation of the mountain throne in 25:3-4, the author has combined the motifs of theophany, triumph over enemies, salvation and universal reign ("the King of eternity").

The interpretation of the Tree of Life continues the process of drawing on images from the ancient Divine Warrior Hymn. The Tree of Life will only become accessible at the judgment when it is transplanted next to the house of God. In this way, the motifs of rejoicing and procession to the Temple are tied closely to the Tree itself (25:5b-6b). In addition, the motifs of the banquet and restored fertility are linked to the Tree of Life. The righteous and pious eat its fruit (25:5a) and its fragrance enters their bones (25:6c). As a result, they live a long life free of hardships (25:6d-f; cf. 5:9; 10:17).

The vision form concludes with the seer blessing God for what God has prepared and created for the righteous (25:7). Enoch understands that the mountain throne of God and the Tree of Life have been explained to him in a way that shows how the creation is ready for the descent of the Divine Warrior and the gift of eschatological salvation to the righteous.

---

[432] "Descend" in Ps 18:9; Mic 1:3; Isa 64:1 [Hb 63:19]; "come forth/come" in Mic 1:3/Isa 66:15; "tread" in Mic 1:3.

[433] Hartman describes *1 En* 25:3-6 as a variant of the ordinary pattern because it does not contain all of the elements (*Prophecy interpreted*, 59-60).

[434] Cf. the similar expressions in *1 En* 98:9; 99:1; 103:3; 104:1. Especially close is 99:1, in which those who perish are denied "salvation for good" (σωτηρία εἰς ἀγαθόν). The expression "in goodness" in 25:3 also alludes to 20:5, a text in which Michael is introduced as being in charge of "the good ones of the people."

1 Enoch 91:5-9[435]

This passage is part of a narrative bridge that may have originally connected the Book of the Watchers to the Epistle.[436]   Enoch addresses Methuselah, along with all of his brothers (91:1-2). The opening two-ways instruction (91:3-4) is based on revelation, as indicated by the messenger formula ("For I know that ..." 91:5a). The so-called Methuselah apocalypse that follows displays motifs from the Divine Warrior Hymn.

Like *1 Enoch* 10:11-11:2, the present passage emphasizes what becomes of sin in the judgment. Iniquity in the days of Noah (91:5) serves as a type of the greater iniquity present in the last days (91:6). Iniquity will appear "again" (*kā'eba*, vs 6a-b) and it "will increase" (*lehqa*, vs 7a-b). Indeed, the depiction of sin in 91:6-7b recalls the motif of the threat from the Divine Warrior Hymn. In the traditional motif of the threat, the nations assemble for an assault on Zion. Here iniquity and its allies amass on a scale that exceeds their destructive power in antediluvian days. The allies are portrayed through the use of a number of synonyms for iniquity (91:6-8). The synonyms are drawn from *1 Enoch* 10:20.[437] In addition to this stock of terms, a few new words for iniquity have been incorporated into *1 Enoch* 91:6-8.[438] In this way, the dire threat facing the earth is heightened.

As is typical in the context of Warrior motifs, the response to this threat is the theophany of God. God "comes forth" (*wad'a* 91:7c-d; 1:3c) to battle his enemies. God's combat victory is defined in 91:8-9 through the traditional verb "destroy" (*hagala*, 91:8; *hagʷala* 91:9; cf. 1:9; 10:16). In addition, the verb *gazama* ("cut off," "uproot") serves as a metaphor for the thoroughness of God's victory (91:8a; cf. 91:5d; Luke 3:9, par. Matt 3:10). The latter verb may indicate the author's dependence on the Apocalypse of Weeks.[439]

The motif of God's universal reign is depicted through the response of the nations. In *1 Enoch* 10:21, the judgment resulted in all the peoples becoming righteous and worshiping God. Some of the details lacking in the earlier portrait are supplied here:

---

435 The text is only extant in Ethiopic translation. Verse 10 is a later gloss.

436 The testament setting of *1 En* 81:5-82:3 is recreated and expanded in 91:1-10, 18-19. See Chap. I, pp. 35-36.

437 These include *'ammadā* ("iniquity"), *gefʿ* ("violence"), *xāṭi'at* ("sin") and *rekʷs* ("pollution"). Only the term *rasi'* ("impious") in *1 En* 10:20 is not reused in 91:6-8.

438 The words in 1 En 91:6-8 without parallel in 10:20 include: *'abbasā* ("sin"), *ṣerfat* ("blasphemy"), *'elwat* ("perversity") and *gʷehlut* ("deceit").

439 The verb "uproot," along with the terms "violence" and "deceit," are present in 91:11. See Black, *The Book of Enoch or 1 Enoch*, 281.

1 En 91:9   And all the idols of the nations will be given up;
 and the tower(s) will be burned with fire.
 And they will remove them from all the earth,
 and they will be cast into the fiery judgment.
 and they will be destroyed in fierce, eternal judgment.

It would appear that all the idols of the nations are surrendered (*yetwahhab*, 91:9a) when the nations see God destroy iniquity in Israel (91:8). The idols are removed and burned (though we are not told by whom; the angels?), thus clearing the way for the universal worship of God (cf. 10:21; 91:14).

1 Enoch 99:3-10 and 100:1-6[440]

The next grouping of Divine Warrior motifs is found in the Epistle of Enoch. *1 Enoch* 99:3-10 and 100:1-6 invite joint treatment because of their proximity and complementary nature. The relationship can be illustrated as follows:[441]

	1 Enoch 99:3-10	100: 1-6
Prayer for the judgment	3	-- (but cf. 99:16d)
Signs of the end	4-5	--
The bloody battle	6	1-3
Theophany	--	4
Victory over enemies	7-9	4
Salvation		
Inner-Jewish	10	5
Gentiles	--	6

---

[440] For a discussion of the textual corruptions in these two passages, see Nickelsburg, "Enoch 97-104," 97-98, 108-112, 119, 138-39, 146.

[441] Both passages are preceded by a series of Woe-oracles (98:9-99:2; 99:11-16). The relationship of Warrior motifs to the Woe-oracles will be considered below (see p. 209). The idea that the righteous present their petitions as a reminder (μνημόσυνον) to the Most High and thereby trigger the judgment is expressed in 99:3. The series of Woes in 99:11-16 ends on the note that the righteous will remember (μνημο]νήσουσιν) the deeds of sinners (99:16d). *1 En* 100:1-6 uses the connection supplied by 99:16d (note also the Warrior imagery in 99:16a-c) to return to the earlier Divine Warrior motifs (99:3-10). It does so by elaborating on the bloody battle mentioned in 99:6 and bringing forward the theophany that was in the background in 99:7-10. In addition, as the outline indicates, the second passage expands on the motif of salvation, explaining how it relates to the Gentiles. Hartman, in his treatment of 100:1-9, referred to the "shifting of emphasis" among the elements of the pattern (*Prophecy interpreted*, 56).

The notion of prayer in *1 Enoch* 99:3 (and 99:16d) is most likely modeled on a motif found in the Book of the Watchers. It is true that in traditional Divine Warrior Hymns, the earthly king may call out to God for help (cf. Ps 18:6). Moreover, in the late prophets, this cry is transformed into a communal lament over the dire situation at hand.[442] Still, the closest analogy to 99:3 comes from the Book of the Watchers. The human spirits of those who were killed by the halfbreed giants cry out for judgment (*1 En* 8:4; cf. 7:6). The angels hear their cry and bring their petitions before God (*1 En* 9:1-11). God responds by killing off the giants in a war of mutual destruction, binding the Watchers until the final judgment and sending the Deluge. Thus, the suit of humanity in the antediluvian age of the giants supplies the paradigm for the prayer of the righteous in 99:3. The petitions of the righteous will trigger the arrival of the Day of the Lord (cf. 97:3, 5).

The idea that the nations are thrown into confusion on the day of battle is common to the combat motif,[443] but in 99:4-5 this confusion is singled out as a precursor to the battle itself. The confusion, evidenced by birth signs, serves as an indicator that the final battle is about to be joined. Signals preceding the advent of the Day of the Lord are further elaborated in later Jewish litera- ture.[444]

The battle itself is graphically depicted as a day of ceaseless bloodshed (99:6). The emphasis on the shedding of blood is typical in Divine Warrior contexts (cf. Isa 63:1-6). In 100:1-3, this aspect of the final battle is pictured in gruesome detail. Rivers of blood flow from family members who kill one another.

The motifs of God's victory and the salvation of the righteous as expressed in 99:7-10 presuppose a theophany to decide the battle. Without mentioning the theophany, the standard vocabulary for depicting its results is used. Sinners are "destroyed" ($\dot{\alpha}\pi\acute{o}\lambda\lambda\upsilon\mu\iota$, 99:9b; 1:9) and the righteous are "saved" ($\sigma\acute{\omega}\zeta\omega$, 99:10e; 1:1). The theophany stays in the background for the moment because the author wishes to focus on these two groups.

Those defeated on the "day of destruction" include the nations who were thrown into confusion (99:4-5) and those Jews against whom the author previously issued a series of Woe-oracles (98:9-99:2). Indeed, the verb "perish/be destroyed" permeates this prior series of Woes (98:9, 16; 99:1).

---

[442] A good example is the lament in Isa 59:9-15a which triggers the theophany in 59:15b-20 (Hanson, *The Dawn of Apocalyptic*, 122). See also the lament in Isa 63:7-64:12 which incorporates a prayer for God to "come down" (64:1).

[443] Cf. von Rad, *Holy War*, 48-49.

[444] Cf. 4 Ezra 5:8-9 and 6:20-24.

The addressees in the oracles are characterized as rival sages and teachers who do not accept Enochic wisdom (98:9, 14; 99:2) and who lead others astray (98:15).[445]

The author takes up God's victory in *1 Enoch* 99:7-9 and equates the errant activity of his opponents with the idolatry of the nations that will be destroyed on the Day of the Lord. The strategy of charging a rival group with idolatrous practices has antecedents in post-exilic prophecy.[446] The response and fate of these rival Jewish wise men in the judgment is worse than that of some idolaters from the nations. The author's Jewish opponents hope to find help from what they worship, but none is forthcoming (99:7; cf. Isa 57:13). The nations, in contrast, give up their idols and worship God (91:9; 10:21). Apparently, the nations learn from Jewish "idolaters" that the idols cannot deliver.

The community portrayed in 99:10 as recipients of salvation consists of "all," presumably Jews and Gentiles, who will listen to the sages of Enochic tradition and thus learn to obey God. The Gentiles will be brought explicitly within the circle of this saved community in 100:6.

Leading up to 100:6, a description of the theophany is supplied in 100:4-5. In particular, the author highlights the role of the angels with respect to the two groups separated at the judgment. The angels descend and gather the sinners into one place for judgment (100:4). They then serve as a "guard" ($\phi\nu\lambda\alpha\kappa\eta$) over all the righteous and holy, who are "kept/guarded" ($\tau\eta\rho\epsilon\omega$) as the apple of the eye until an end is made of evil and sin (100:5a-c). This role of the angels in the context of Divine Warrior motifs has been implicit in some of the passages studied above. The righteous will be present on the Day of the Lord (1:1), but they will have "protection" ($\sigma\nu\nu\tau\eta\rho\eta\sigma\iota\varsigma$ 1:8), most likely from the angels (cf. 1:4), and thus they will "escape" (10:17).

The ancient Warrior Hymn motif of God's universal reign is conveyed in 100:5d-e by the metaphor of "sweet sleep" and the absence of an enemy "to frighten." This motif is carried forward into 100:6, when the circle of the saved is enlarged to include all peoples ("the wise among men"/"the sons of the earth").

The emphasis in 100:6 is not on the fact that the Gentiles will give up their idols, although this is obviously assumed. In keeping with the emphasis

---

[445] See the reference in Chap. I, p. 46, n. 115.

[446] The levitical-prophetic group charges the hierocratic party of the Zadokites with idolatrous practices in Isa 57:3-9, 13; 65:3-7, 11-12; 66:3-4; Zech 13:2 (Hanson, *The Dawn of Apocalyptic*, 198-202, 367). That the Zadokites returned the charge is evident from the Zadokite revision in Ezek 44:10-14, which charges the Levites with going astray after idols (ibid., 265-67).

of the two preceding Woe-chains, the salvation of the nations is tied to their acceptence of Enochic wisdom. In particular, the Gentiles are given access to "these words of this epistle" (100:6b) which enables them to perceive the truth and recognize what can and cannot save them when iniquity collapses. Therefore, the conclusion drawn above in connection with *1 Enoch* 91:9 must be modified slightly. It is not solely the case that the nations will observe how God's judgment discriminates within Israel and so will give up their idols. In addition, the Gentiles are actually given a book of Enochic wisdom that explains the judgment and how to escape it. The Epistle of Enoch functions in 100:6b precisely as did the wisdom given to the elect in *1 Enoch* 5:8. The books of Enoch impart a wisdom that results in eschatological salvation.

1 Enoch 100:10-102:3[447]

Our survey of Divine Warrior motifs in *1 Enoch* now comes full circle, as illustrated by a comparison with the first unit treated under this heading:

Salvation-Judgment Oracle
Accusation:	Lessons of Creation	2:1-5:4
Announcement:	Alternating Words	5:5-9
	(Draws from theophany)	(1:3c-9)

Judgment Oracle
Accusation:	Creation supports *rîb*	100:10-13
	Lessons of Creation	101:1-9
Announcement:	Theophany	102:1-3

There are two notable differences from the opening sequence in the passages under consideration here. First, the Accusation has been expanded. It is introduced by the messenger formula common in the Epistle ("And now know that ...", 100:10).[448] Elements of creation that were earlier described from the perspective of earth as obedient to God—the luminaries, the signs of winter, such as clouds, dew and rain (2:1-5:4)—are here the objects of Enoch's heavenly knowledge of the judgment. He has learned and now reveals that the works of creation will participate in a covenant lawsuit against sinners (100:10-13). Second, the description of the theophany (102:1-3) is part of the Oracle itself. In *1 Enoch* 1:3c-9, the theophany precedes the Salvation-

---

[447] The differences in the ancient translations of *1 En* 100:10-13 and 102:1-3 are resolved by Nickelsburg, "Enoch 97-104," 99, 140, 150-51.

[448] On the significance of this formula, see Chap. I, pp. 44-46.

Judgement Oracle and supplies much of the language for the announcement in 5:5-9. In addition, there are no words of salvation in the theophanic account in *1 Enoch* 102:1-3. Rather, the Announcement focuses entirely on the fate of sinners as it does in the classic Judgment Oracle. This fate was already anticipated in the preceding Woe-series (100:7-9).[449]

The two differences indicated above merit further discussion. The section on the role of the created elements in witnessing and implementing God's covenant lawsuit against sinners (100:10-13) serves to underscore the seriousness of the appeal that follows (101:1-9). The theme of the heavens witnessing God's controversy (*rîb*) with Israel for her violations of the covenant is traditional (cf. Deut 32:1; Isa 1:2). In fact, the specific idea that God will withhold rain from descending upon sinners (100:10-11) appears in the context of Divine Warrior motifs in Zechariah 10:1-12.[450] In Enochic tradition, it is presupposed that the luminaries and meteorological phenomena are qualified to play the accusatory role because of their obedience to God's word (2:1-5:3; 72:1-80:1). The withholding of the waters seems to mark the beginning of an irreversible process that will culminate in the final judgment.[451] Consistent with the context, the picture of the final judgment is adumbrated here not through the fire and heat commonly associated with theophany, but through snow, frost and cold (100:13; cf. 17:7: "I saw the wintry winds"). When the withheld moisture finally arrives, it takes the form of a destructive winter blizzard.

The theophany in *1 Enoch* 102:1-3 does employ the traditional fire and earthquake imagery,[452] as in 1:3c-9. However, in contrast to the description in *1 Enoch* 1, the Watchers are not in focus at all in 102:1-3. Rather, human sinners, especially those addressed in 100:7-9, are the respondents to the theophany. They "flee," "shake/tremble" and "fear." Unlike the ironic picture of the Watchers hiding from God, these individuals really do attempt to hide themselves from the presence of the Great Glory (102:3b). The attempt is

---

[449] On the connection between 100:7-9 and 102:1-3, see below, pp. 208-09.

[450] In Zech 10:1-3, the false leaders are exhorted to "ask rain from the Lord" because the rains are being withheld in judgment (Hanson, *The Dawn of Apocalyptic*, 329-30).

[451] The same scenario is reflected in *1 En* 80:2-8. In the "days of the sinners," creation begins its active role of testifying. A chief indicator of this time is that the rain is withheld (80:2; cf. 100:11).

[452] On the textual problems, see Zuntz, "Notes on the Greek Enoch," 197-201. Hartman points out that while there is no explicit reference to God's "coming," this is true also of some theophanic texts in the Hebrew Bible such as Isa 30:30-33, to which the present passage is related (*Prophecy interpreted*, 73-74).

futile because the angels find them (102:3a; cf. 100:4). There is no place to flee and "be saved" (102:1b).

The description of the theophany ends on a note that takes the reader all the way back to 5:5-9, again indicating that we have come full circle. *1 Enoch* 102:3d-e ("And you sinners will be cursed forever; you will have no peace") draws its vocabulary from the announcement of judgment in *1 Enoch* 5:5 ("eternal curse"/"no mercy or peace").[453]

Summary

Enochic authors employ all of the traditional motifs of the Divine Warrior Hymn. Many of the motifs remain relatively unchanged, especially those drawn from Third Isaiah. The days are evil and Israel itself is divided into the righteous and the enemies of God. God "comes" or "descends" with a heavenly host in fire, storm and earthquake. Sinners attempt to flee but are confounded, routed and destroyed. A decisive end is made to the old era. God creates a new earth upon which the righteous live long and productive lives, and all humanity worships God.

These older motifs, however, have an entirely new context in *1 Enoch*. This is especially apparent from the way the Enochic authors have adapted several elements: the rebel Watchers occupy the place of human respondents, Enoch sees that the hidden Tree of Life will supply the banquet and give renewed fertility to humankind, and the saved—both Jews and Gentiles—owe their salvation to Enochic wisdom. The adaptations are based on Enoch's heavenly knowledge. This is true not only of the vision tradition in 25:3-6, but the theophany in 1:3c-9 is informed by *1 Enoch* 6-19 (Enoch hears judgment pronounced on the rebel Watchers and sees the place where they are bound), the commission in 10:11-11:2 takes place in heaven, the Methuselah apocalypse is introduced in 91:5 with the (heavenly-)messenger formula, and the "wise" who are saved in 99:10 and 100:6 possess the eschatological gift of revealed wisdom (5:8; 82:1-3). In short, traditional Warrior motifs and their adaptations are set in the context of the heavenly visions of Enoch. Elements old and new have been transposed into the key of apocalyptic eschatology.[454]

---

[453] It is common for announcements of disaster to end with a "concluding characterization." This may be the function of *1 En* 102:3d-e. See March, "Prophecy," 160.

[454] Nickelsburg, "Eschatology (Early Jewish)," 583.

THE DISPUTATION SPEECH

Scholars apply the genre Disputation Speech (*Streitgespräch*) to passages in both the prophetic and wisdom literature.[455] The origins of the form in these respective bodies of literature are different,[456] but through mutual influence later types of the genre are very similar. The literary form remains flexible in the discourse of prophet and sage, yet the following structural elements are often present:

1) An Introduction. This can be a simple address or an elaborate instruction that anticipates the citation to follow (Isa 40:12-26; Job 11:1-3; Prov 1:8-10).

2) The Citation of an Opponent, often with some form of the verb "to say" (cf. Isa 40:27; Job 11:4; Prov 1:11). This is usually a lament, complaint or dispute about divine justice.

3) The Author's Answer, which often contains an appeal to knowledge or wisdom (Isa 40:28; Job 11:5-6a, 7-12; Prov 1:15-18).

4) The Conclusion. Like the introduction, this element can vary considerably. It often consists of an exhortation or a summary (Isa 40:29-31; Job 11:6b, 13-20; Prov 1:19).

The pattern listed above will inform our analysis of the Disputation Speeches in *1 Enoch*. All of the Speeches occur in the Epistle of Enoch. We begin with the four Speeches that constitute a major literary unit (*1 En* 102:4-104:8) and conclude by analyzing two further examples (*1 En* 97:8-10; 98:4-8).

1 Enoch 102:4-104:8[457]

The structure and content of the four Disputation Speeches in this section (102:4-103:4; 103:5-8; 103:9-104:6; 104:7-8) have been analyzed by Nickelsburg.[458] The structure of the Speeches corresponds to the elements listed

---

[455] For the former, see Westermann, *Basic Forms of Prophetic Speech*, 201; for the latter, Murphy, *Wisdom Literature*, 18.

[456] In the prophetic literature, the Disputation Speech is traced to a judicial setting (March, "Prophecy," 168), whereas in the wisdom literature it goes back to the school setting (Crenshaw, "Wisdom," 254).

[457] There a number of corruptions in our witnesses to this passage (Nickelsburg, "Enoch 97-104," 101-03, 109, 121-34, 140, 146-49).

[458] "The Apocalyptic Message," 318-322.

above from the prophetic and wisdom literature.[459] The content of the author's answer is a point for point response to the issues contained in the introduction and citation.[460]

An additional aspect to the content of the author's reply in the four Disputation Speeches is discernible. In Chapter I, the presence and function of the messenger-type formula that introduces the replies was discussed (*1 En* 103:1-2; 103:7; 104:1; 104:8), but the substance of the reply was only briefly summarized.[461] In the Disputation Speeches, the content of the reply involves the author's knowledge *of the judgment*, a judgment whose broad outlines and specific details derive from the visions Enoch received on his journey through the cosmos (*1 En* 20-32; 81:1-4). This dependency on the visions can be detected in the citations and replies in each of the four Disputation Speeches.

First Disputation (102:4-103:4)

The introduction identifies the addressees as the righteous who have died in grief (102:4-5). The citation that follows (102:6-11), which the author wishes to dispute, concerns what the sinners say about this death. When sinners see the righteous die in grief, they question the benefit to be gained from a righteous life (102:6-7, 10-11). The assumption at work is that a death with grief is appropriate to the unrighteous. Therefore, if it happens to the righteous, there is no advantage to being upright. The sinners conclude they may as well continue to sin; especially since they prosper when they do so (102:9; cf. Prov 1:11-14). The only possible exception to this line of reasoning, namely, that the righteous do have something to gain, is raised and dismissed in verse 8:[462]

1 En 102:8   Henceforth, let them arise and be saved
                ([καὶ ἔτι] ἀ[να]στήτωσαν καὶ σωθήτωσαν)
                        and they shall forever see (the light).
                But, behold, they have died,
                        and henceforth forever they will not see the light.

---

[459] Ibid., 319. In addition, Nickelsburg makes the perceptive and persuasive suggestion that the speeches to the righteous dead (*1 En* 102:4-103:4) and the sinful dead (103:5-8) are expansions of the typical Enochic exhortation and woe, respectively (ibid., 320-21). This is a fine example of the fluidity of the genre Disputation Speech.

[460] Ibid., 320-22.

[461] See above, p. 45.

[462] For the restoration of the text, see Nickelsburg, "Enoch 97-104," 123-24.

The sinners deny in the strongest possible terms the idea of judgment and reward beyond death. The language of salvation and light is combined elsewhere in Enochic tradition to describe the experience of the righteous at the future judgment.[463] In *1 Enoch* 102:8a-b, this language is explicitly linked to resurrection.[464] The phrase "let them arise and be saved" expresses the ultimate hope of the righteous for vindication in the judgment. In the speech of the opponents, it is ironic mockery. The reader knows that the citation alludes to the domains of the angels Michael and Remiel as defined in the Book of the Watchers (cf. *1 En* 20:5, 8). Indeed, the author will exploit this allusion in his reply, to which we now turn.

The reply is introduced by a solemn oath that contains the messenger formula "I know this mystery" (103:1-2a). The mystery concerns what lies ahead for the righteous dead; namely, salvation in the future judgment (103:3-4). The author's description of the lot of the righteous dead in the coming judgment draws its vocabulary from the angel Michael's interpretation of Enoch's vision of the mountain throne of God and the Tree of Life in *1 Enoch* 25:3-7:

1 En 25:3-7

God will descend to visit the earth "in goodness" (ἐπ᾽ ἀγαθῷ/ ba-šannāy, vs 3). At that time, the Tree of Life "will be given" (δοθήσεται/yetwahhab, vs 4) to the righteous. The righteous "will rejoice greatly and be glad" (εὐφρανθήσονται εὐφραινόμενοι καὶ χαρήσονται/ yetfēššehu ba-feššehā wa-yethassayu) and "they will live" (ζήσονται/ yahayyewu, vs 6) a long life upon the earth. Enoch blesses God who "has pre-pared" (ἡτοίμασεν/ 'astadāllawa) such things and promised "to give" (δοῦναι/ yahabbewwomu, vs 7) them to the righteous.

1 En 103:3-4

The author refutes the citation with his knowledge that "good things (ἀγαθά/šannāy) and joy (χαρὰ/feššehā) ... have been prepared (ἡτοίμασται/ tadallawa) ... and much good will be given (wa-bezux šannāy yetwahhab)" (vs 3a-c) to the righteous. The souls of the pious who have died "will live (yahayyewu) and they will rejoice and be glad (χα[ρή]σονται καὶ [ἀγαλλιάσ-ονται][465]/ yetfēššehu wa-yet-haššaya)" (vs 4a-b).

---

[463] "And for them there will be salvation, a good light" (*1 En* 5:6b).

[464] The linkage of resurrection and light was present already in the Epistle's opening exhortation: "And the righteous one will arise from sleep; *he will arise and walk ... and he will walk in eternal light*" (*1 En* 92:3-4).

[465] This Greek verb is the suggestion of Nickelsburg ("Enoch 97-104," 147). In view of the many linguistic parallels to *1 Enoch* 25, we should retain the possibility that the verb is εὐφρανθήσονται.

The statement that the souls of the righteous dead "will live" (103:4a; 25:6) is part of the answer to the mockery of the sinners who said "let them arise and be saved" (102:8). The sinners assume, correctly, that the righteous must be raised out of Sheol (cf. 103:11: "descended into Sheol") to be saved; something the sinners consider an impossibility. But in *1 Enoch* 25:3-7, the righteous who "live" a long life after the judgment were those formerly housed in a separate compartment of Sheol (*1 En* 22:9b). Presumably, they are raised from Sheol at the time of the judgment in order to receive the gift of life (cf. *1 En* 22:13).

This presumption is confirmed by the tradition associated with the angel Remiel, "whom God has put in charge of them that rise" (*1 En* 20:8). In the Excursus, the case is made that the Remiel tradition, the last stop on Enoch's cosmic tour, survives in fragmentary form in *1 Enoch* 81:1-4. The nature of Remiel's work includes oversight of the tablets of heaven (81:1-2a). These tablets of heaven are mentioned in the expanded revelatory formula (*1 En* 103:2b-d) as the basis for the author's reply. According to the Remiel tradition, among the tablets are books that record the sinful deeds of men (81:2b), deeds that contributed to the death of the righteous (81:4; cf. 81:9). The heavenly record keeping of death by persecution guarantees the future resurrection of the righteous from Sheol. Because of the books, the memory of the righteous dead will never fade from the presence of the Great One (103:4c-d).

In conclusion, the author's knowledge of the judgment as expressed in *1 Enoch* 103:3-4 reflects a combination of two earlier vision traditions. The descriptive vocabulary of the judgment is drawn from *1 Enoch* 25, but the basic audience and issue at stake (the righteous who have died in grief and their future resurrection from Sheol) is given by the Remiel tradition in *1 Enoch* 81:1-4.

Second Disputation (103:5-8)

The analysis above will serve as a key to the remaining Disputation Speeches in this unit. Our investigation will focus on the extent to which the author's knowledge of the judgment is dependent on the vision traditions in the Book of the Watchers.

The audience addressed in the Second Disputation Speech is the dead sinners (103:5a). The citation consists of what living sinners say about their fellows who have died (103:5b-6). Consistent with their earlier reproach of the righteous dead, the sinners here pronounce a blessing on the sinful dead. The blessing is premised on the fact that the sinners were prosperous throughout life right up to the moment of death and at no time were subject to persecution. It is thus indisputable that "judgment was not executed on them in their life" (κρίσις οὐκ ἐγενήθη ἐν τῇ ζωῇ αὐτῶν/ kʷennanē 'i-tagabra lomu ba-ḥeywatomu, 103:6d).

As in the first Speech where the issue was a future judgment for the righteous dead, the issue here revolves around a future judgment for dead sinners. Is there recompense after death? The author's answer (103:7-8) begins with a messenger formula and again draws from Enoch's vision traditions.

The reply can hardly dispute the fact that dead sinners did not experience judgment in their lifetime. However, the author knows that Sheol contains a separate compartment for precisely such sinners and that their experience, therefore, in no way militates against the reality of future judgment. The citation concerning a lack of judgment and the author's reply are grounded in Enoch's vision of the Mountain of Sheol (*1 En* 22) and, more specifically, on the angel Raphael's interpretation of a compartment that has been created for a special class of sinners (22:10-11). This compartment is reserved for sinners who died and "judgment has not been executed on them in their life" (κρίσις οὐκ ἐγενήθη ἐπ' αὐτῶν ἐν τῇ ζωῇ αὐτῶν/kʷennanē 'i-kona ba-lā'lēhomu ba-ḥeywatomu, 22:10c). The citation in *1 Enoch* 103:6d is a virtual reprise of *1 Enoch* 22:10c. The author's revealed knowledge of the true state of affairs was derived in part from the description of this category of dead sinners in Sheol.

The author's answer emphasizes the punishment dead sinners will experience in Sheol as they await the reality of the great judgment. The author claims to know that the souls of the dead sinners are in "great distress" in Sheol (103:7). This is apparently an encroachment of the "great torment" (22:11a) that lies ahead for them in the judgment. The author has reinterpreted *1 Enoch* 22:11a to fit the context of this Second Disputation Speech; the afflictions that escaped the sinners in life await them immediately in Sheol after death.

A similar tendency can be detected in the author's depiction of the nature of Sheol itself. Common to both *1 Enoch* 22 and 103:8a are the traditional notions of "darkness" (σκοτεινοὶ/ṣalimāt, 22:2; ἐν σκότει/ba-ṣelmat, 103:7) and a prison ("pits ... of their confinement", 22:4; "in a trap", 103:8a). But the author of the Second Speech also refers to "a flame of fire" (103:8a; cf. Luke 16:24), a feature that has no parallel in *1 Enoch* 22. Again, this would seem to be an aspect of the future judgment (cf. *1 En* 99:11b; not present in

1 En 26-27) that has encroached into the depiction of the Sheol experience
because of the author's desire to stress the torment of sinners in Sheol.

In line with this analysis is the fact that the author's statement about the
future judgment itself lacks any descriptive images, apart from the terse comments that it will be a "great judgment" (103:8a; cf. 22:4, 11) and will last
forever (103:8b; cf. 22:11). Apparently the Sheol experience of dead sinners
(as reinterpreted in 103:7) will be made to last forever.

Third Disputation (103:9-104:6)

The first two Speeches were addressed to groups that were separated in
Sheol. To the righteous dead (*1 En* 22:9b), the author applied the language
and thought of *1 Enoch* 25:3-7 and 81:1-4; to the sinful dead who escaped
judgment in their lifetime (*1 En* 22:10), he reinterpreted the Sheol experience
as a tortuous one. The third Disputation Speech combines language used of
the remaining two groups in Sheol (*1 En* 22:12, 13). Once again, the author's
knowledge of the judgment involves him in a creative reinterpretation of
aspects of Enoch's visions.

The introduction of the Third Disputation identifies the addressees as the
living righteous (103:9a). The citation begins abruptly with the ancient debate
formula, "Do not say ..." (103:9a). The speech that follows is uttered by the
righteous themselves (the only example in this unit) and is a lament consisting
of a long litany of injustices (103:9b-15). The litany includes expressions that
resonate with the earlier description of a death "with grief" (102:5; cf. 103:9d-
11a, 15). Yet, it is the living who are complaining here; the survivors among
the righteous. The substance of their complaint is that they live a life with
grief; that is, they are complaining about being persecuted by sinners. In
103:11b-13, the lament portrays the suffering righteous under the metaphor of
abused slaves who plot an escape and fail. As in the case of such slaves, the
righteous are subjected to severe punishment. The situation becomes so
desperate that the righteous complain to the rulers and appeal for help (103:14-
15). However, the appeal only makes the situation worse because the rulers
aid their persecutors.

In a couple of instances the language of the lament has points of contact
with the description of those in one of Sheol's hollow places:

1 En 22:12

1 En 103:14-15

One of Sheol's compartments is reserved "for the spirits *of them that make suit* (τῶν ἐντυγχανόντων/ *'ella yesakkeyu*) ... when they were murdered (φονευθῶσιν/ *taqatlu*) ...". The same language was used earlier of the spirit of Abel (22:5-7). Enoch saw and inquired about Abel's spirit, which "makes suit" (ἐντυγχάνω, 5x /*sakya*, 3x) because he "was murdered" (ἐφόνευσεν/ *qatala*) by Cain. Abel functions as a paradigm for the description of the spirits in 22:12. The latter are further characterized as "those who make disclosure about the destruction" (οἵτινες ἐνφανίʒουσιν περὶ τῆς ἀπωλείας/ *'ella yāre''eyu baenta ḥegʷlat*).

A persecuted righteous group "made suit" (*sakya*, vs 14a) to the rulers about their tribulation. They cried out, but the rulers did not receive "the suits" (τὰς ἐντεύξεις/ *serāḥa*, vs 14c). In the terms of this citation, there is an added injustice on the part of the rulers. The rulers "did not disclose" (οὐχ ὑποδεικνύουσιν, vs 15e) the iniquities of the oppressors "who murdered us" (περὶ τῶν πεφονευ-μένων ἡμῶν/ *yeqatteluna*, vs 15f).

In *1 Enoch* 22:12, a compartment of Sheol is reserved for the martyrs who cry out to God about the injustice of their deaths. The citation in *1 Enoch* 103:9b-15 reuses the scene from 22:12—the righteous make suit when they are murdered—but this material is now adapted to the living righteous and incorporates a negative role for the rulers. The author tells the living righteous not to lament (103:9a) the injustice of dealing with the rulers. The suits that the rulers ignored will be heard in Sheol and justice will be served at the judgment (104:3c-d).

The author's reply begins with a solemn oath that the persecuted are remembered "for good" and "your names are written" before God. Again, it is the author's knowledge of future recompense for the righteous ("for good") and of heavenly books that informs his reply. The book of the names of the martyrs is the counterpart to the book of iniquity written against their persecutors (*1 En* 81:4).

The reply continues with a number of exhortations that at some points reuse motifs of the Divine Warrior Hymn present elsewhere in *1 Enoch*. These motifs include the cry of the righteous that triggers the descent of God and his host (104:3a-b; cf. 9:2, 10; 97:3; 99:3); the image of not hiding like the sinners on the day of judgment (104:5; cf. 1:5; 100:4; 102:3); and the experience of great joy after the combat victory (104:4b; cf. 5:6d, 7a, 9d; 25:6a).

The traditional motif of the salvation of the righteous is reinterpreted or intensified as applied to the persecuted righteous. The salvation imparted to the righteous after the descent of the Divine Warrior is often portrayed as light (1:8h; 5:6f, 8d; cf. 102:8). The traditional idea that the darkness of Sheol is replaced by the light of a new existence on earth is not present in 104:2-6. Rather, the image is transformed so that the persecuted righteous themselves shine like lights and have the gates of heaven open to them (104:2c-e; cf. Dan 12:3). In the context of the third Disputation, this reinterpretation of the lot of a class of righteous persons is dictated by their harsh experience on earth (104:2b), much like the author earlier reinterpreted the lot of a class of sinners in Sheol because of their good experience on earth (103:6). The point of the reinterpretation in the present passage is not to make the persecuted righteous into astral deities. However, they are clearly in a unique category that puts them closer to angels than to fellow human beings.[466]

In fact, this notion supplies the basis for the concluding exhortation (104:6). The author exhorts the righteous not to be the companions of sinners because they are destined to be companions of the host of heaven. While the issue of choosing companions with care is a typical wisdom *topos*, the many other allusions to *1 Enoch* 22 create the liklihood that the language of companionship derives from the description of the fourth compartment in Sheol (*1 En* 22:13). The angel Raphael tells Enoch that the last hollow place is for those who "will be companions with the lawless" (μετὰ τῶν ἀνόμων ἔσονται μέτοχοι/wa-mesla 'abbāsiyān yekawwenu kamāhomu, 22:13) and that their fate is to remain in Sheol forever. In *1 Enoch* 104:6, the suffering righteous, who see the sinners prospering (cf. 102:9; 103:6), are exhorted not to be "their companions" (μέτοχοι αὐτῶν/sutufāna meslēhomu) for their destiny is to be "companions" (sutufāna) of the host of heaven. Companions of sinners will remain in the darkness of Sheol (22:13), companions of the angels will shine like heavenly lights (104:2c-e).

Fourth Disputation (104:7-8)

The final Disputation Speech is the shortest of this unit. Using the ancient debate formula, "Do not say ...", the author identifies the addressees as sinners (104:7a). From the citation that follows (104:7b), it is clear he is refer-

---

[466] Nickelsburg (*Resurrection*, 119-22) argues that the spirits of the righteous ascend to heaven.

ring to sinners who are living. The dispute centers on what sinners have to say about themselves as they pursue their lifestyle of sin. It would appear that this citation and the author's reply represent an abbreviated version of the Disputation Speech in *1 Enoch* 98:6-8, a passage treated below. As in the other Speeches of this unit, the basic issue here too concerns the reality of recompense after death.

In the citation, the sinners deny the basis of future judgment by taking the position that "None of our sins will be searched out and written down" (104:7b). The author's reply begins with the idea of recorded sins. With an allusion to the book of iniquity over which the angel Remiel has charge, the author states "They are writing down all your sins day by day" (104:7c; cf. 81:1-4, esp. vss 2d-f, 4). As was the case in the previous Disputations, the author's knowledge of the coming judgment is again grounded in a journey report of Enoch. The only difference is that our author presents as an ongoing activity that which Enoch saw as an end product.

From the second part of the author's reply, it would appear that he does more than simply restate older tradition. A messenger formula ("And now I show you ...") introduces the assertion that "light and darkness, day and night observe all your sins" (104:8). It is significant that aspects of the creation that relate directly to the luminaries are mentioned. The author may be deliberately inverting the imagery of *1 Enoch* 2:1. If sinners will not "observe" (הזח, *1 En* 2:1) the works of heaven, they can be sure that the works of heaven will "observe" (ἐποπτεύω/ re'ya, *1 En* 104:8b) their works (cf. 100:10). So thorough is creation's observation (the moon and stars, too, fulfill this role), sinners cannot presume that darkness hides their deeds.

1 Enoch 97:8-10[467]

Before concluding the discussion of the Disputation Speeches in the Epistle of Enoch, two additional passages must be considered. The structure of *1 Enoch* 97:8-10 conforms to the basic pattern of the Disputation Speech:

1)	Introduction:	*Woe to you who acquire gold and silver unjustly*	97:8a
2)	Citation:	*and say ...*	97:8b-9
3)	Author's answer:	*You err! For ...*	97:10

---

[467] Textual corruptions are addressed by Nickelsburg, "Enoch 97-104," 93, 112-13. See also idem, "Riches, the Rich, and God's Judgment in *1 Enoch* 92-105 and the Gospel according to Luke," *NTS* 25 (1979) 329-30.

Like the second Disputation considered above (103:5-8), *1 Enoch* 97:8-10 is an expanded Woe-oracle. However, this Disputation is addressed to living sinners; more specifically, the wealthy who have acquired their riches "unjustly" (οὐκ ἀπὸ δικαιοσύνης/*za-'i-kona ba-ṣedq*, 97:8a; cf. ἀδίκως/*ba-'ammaḍā*, 97:10d). The citation consists of the boast of sinners in the great wealth they have amassed and in their freedom to do whatever they wish.

The author responds to this boast with an image of reversal. The wealth accumulated by sinners will be taken away "quickly" (ταχὺ) and they will be delivered to a great curse. The great judgment is imminent and will strip the wealthy. The image that sinners "*will be delivered* (παραδοθήσεσθε) to a great curse" (97:10e) resonates with the scene at the accursed valley in *1 Enoch* 26-27. The interpreting angel informed Enoch that "here *will be gathered* (ἐπισυναχθήσονται) all the cursed" (27:2). In addition, the boast of wealthy sinners (97:8-9) is an example of speaking improper words against the Lord (27:2). The wealthy are among the blasphemers whom the angels will take to the accursed valley at the great judgment.

1 Enoch 98:4-8[468]

This passage too can be analyzed in terms of the Disputation Speech. Indeed, as suggested above, it is probably the source for the fourth Disputation in *1 Enoch* 104:7-8. As a Disputation, *1 Enoch* 98:4-8 is unique compared to the other examples because the citation consists of what sinners *think* in their heart (98:7a). This change allows the author to preempt the speech of sinners. The Disputation displays the standard structure:

1)	Introduction:	Addressees are living sinners	
		I swear to you, sinners ...	98:4-5
		I swear to you, sinners ...	98:6
2)	Citation:	*Do not suppose to yourself*	98:7
		nor say in your heart ...	
		(μὴ ὑ[πο]λάβητε τῇ ψυχῇ ὑμῶν	
		μηδὲ ὑπολ[ά]βητε τῇ καρδίᾳ ὑμῶν)	
		('*i-tāmselu ba-manfasekemu*	
		wa-'i-tebalu ba-lebbekemu)	
3)	Author's Reply:	*Henceforth know ...*	98:8

---

[468] For a reconcilation of the ancient versions, see Nickelsburg, "Enoch 97-104," 113-18, 137, 145-46.

The introduction consists of a twofold instruction that anticipates the citation to follow. In the first instruction, the author asserts human responsibility for sin; and in the second, the knowledge of all sin on the part of heaven.

The instruction on human responsibility clarifies Enochic tradition regarding the origin of evil in the world. The tradition is open to misunderstanding on this point. In an earlier piece that is itself an attempt at theodicy, *1 Enoch* 15-16, Enoch hears a disquisition from God on the origin of evil. The rebel angels brought evil to the earth. The spirits of their halfbreed offspring survive the deaths of their bodies and afflict the earth as evil spirits until the great judgment. The present Disputation Speech makes it clear, however, that this older tradition is not intended to absolve human beings of responsibility for sin. Sin was not ordained by God, rather humankind created lawlessness "by themselves" (ἀφ' ἑαυτῶν/ *'em-re'somu*, 98:4f). Therefore, sinners are justly destined for a great curse (98:4g; cf. 97:10 above).

The second instruction is related to the first. If humankind is responsible for sin, it follows that heaven observes and records all sins. Yet the latter is not merely a theological deduction. From the author's reply, it is apparent that his knowledge of this aspect of the judgment comes from an earlier journey tradition of Enoch. The rejoinder to the claim that heaven neither sees nor records the unrighteous deeds of sinners opens with the messenger formula, "Henceforth know ...". The author continues: "all your unrighteous deeds are written down day by day until the day of your judgment" (98:8). This reply is informed by the tradition of the angel Remiel and the heavenly tablets (*1 En* 81:1-4). On the last stop of his journey, Enoch read the heavenly tablets which included a book in which was written "all the deeds of men" (81:2), namely, the "book of iniquity" (81:4). For our author, this earlier tradition settles the dispute regarding heavenly record keeping and, by extension, human responsibility for sin.

Summary

The Disputation Speeches in the Epistle of Enoch have been heavily influenced by the reports of Enoch's journey into the hidden reaches of the cosmos (*1 En* 20-32; 81:1-4). The author of the Epistle is not slavishly tied to these older reports; he reuses them in creative ways. The messenger formula marks his appeal to revelation. The content of his revealed knowledge of the judgment is largely an adaptation from reports of Enoch's vision of Sheol, the accursed valley, the mountain throne of God and the books of heaven. Our author clearly assumes that these entities are as much constituent features of creation as, for example, day and night. Both the hidden and the observable works of creation contribute to the author's knowledge of the coming judgment, though the emphasis falls on the former in the Disputations. In disputes about the unjust experiences of life and circumstances of death, the author of the Epistle draws on the vision traditions of Enoch to argue that justice will prevail in a post-mortem judgment.

THE WOE-ORACLE

The structure of the Woe-oracle, unlike its original *Sitz im Leben*,[469] is relatively clear. In its basic form, the interjection הוֹי is followed by a participle, adjective or noun that describes those being addressed. The offense of the addressees is then specified, often by means of another participial clause and a sentence with a finite verb. A threat usually concludes the oracle.[470]

Waldemar Janzen has refined this view of the structure of the Woe-oracle by making a helpful distinction between the *hôy*-formula itself and the *hôy*-pericope.[471] The formula is stable and consists of interjection and participle or noun; the pericope, the delimitable unit of prophetic speech in which the formula stands, defines what Janzen calls the contextual content within which the prophet considers the formula to be fitting. Janzen identifies three fairly characteristic features of this contextual content:

> (1) A characterization of the addressee ... as one who acts in self-reliant independence of the sovereignty of Yahweh. This may manifest itself simply in false security, or in group behavior defiant of covenant obligations towards the poor and needy, or in acts of national-political disloyalty to Yahweh. (2) A "Day of the Lord"-context within which the self-styled sovereignty will be confronted by the greater sovereignty of Yahweh in a terrifying visitation. (3) This confrontation is often expressed in a manner approximating the *Talionsstil*, the style of declaration of revenge, frequently to the point of "reversal of imagery" ...[472]

---

[469] Origins for the Woe-oracle have been sought in the covenant curses (Westermann, *Basic Forms of Prophetic Speech*, 190-98), in wisdom circles (E. Gerstenberger, "The Woe-oracles of the Prophets," *JBL* 81 [1962] 249-63) and in funeral laments (R. J. Clifford, "The Use of *Hôy* in the Prophets," *CBQ* 28 [1966] 458-64; J. G. Williams, "The Alas-oracles of the Eighth Century Prophets," HUCA XXXVIII [1967] 75-91).

[470] The structure is summarized in this manner by March, "Prophecy," 164-65. See also Aune, *Prophecy*, 96-97.

[471] Waldemar Janzen, *Mourning Cry and Woe Oracle* (BZAW 125; New York/Berlin: de Gruyter, 1972) 81.

[472] Janzen, *Mourning Cry and Woe Oracle*, 81-82.

The features of the contextual content as summarized by Janzen will prove helpful for analyzing the Woe-oracles in our study. In addition, the correspondence pattern between sin and judgment, while "often expressed" in the *Talionsstil*, can show up in other characteristic ways. Patrick D. Miller, Jr. has described and categorized two additional patterns of correspondence between sin and judgment.[473] The correspondence patterns of the Woe-oracle not only involve explicit *talionic* features, but may entail other aspects related to content and literary style.[474]

The Epistle of Enoch

The Woe-oracles in *1 Enoch* are all found in the Epistle and occur in chains,[475] as they do often in the prophets. At times the correspondence pattern occurs in the narrower context of the particular oracle or Woe-chain; at other times, however, the correspondence emerges from the extended context beyond the Woe-chain. Our investigation of the Woe-chains in the Epistle will concentrate on those features identified by Janzen and Miller; namely, the characterization of the addressees, the Day of the Lord context and the correspondence pattern between sin and judgment. There are a total of seven Woe-series.

---

[473] He classified the patterns based on primary attention to talionic features, meaning and content, and stylistic features (*Sin and Judgment in the Prophets: A Stylistic and Theological Analysis* [SBLMS 27; Chico, CA: Scholars, 1982], esp. pp. 111-19).

[474] Miller identified the following examples of the correspondence of *meaning* and *content*: A) the victim of the sin brings about the judgment on the sinner, B) what one did not think would happen does happen, C) correspondence is related to sin, judgment, *and salvation*, and D) a more general principle or theological statement of correspondence is included or related to the specific example. Among his examples of correspondence based on *stylistic* features are: A) repetition of words, B) figures of speech, such as simile, metaphor and wordplay, C) correspondence via common idea or subject without repetition or figure of speech, and D) correspondence worked out in surrounding narrative (ibid.).

[475] The only Woe-oracle not part of a chain has been expanded into a Disputation Speech (*1 En* 103:5-8).

Series 1[476]

1 En   94:6   Woe to those who build iniquity and violence,
                     and lay deceit as a foundation;
                 for quickly they will be overthrown,
                 and they will have no peace.
          7   Woe to those who build their houses with sin;
                 for from all their foundations they will be overthrown,
                 and by the sword they will fall.
                 And those who acquire gold and silver will quickly perish in
                     judgment.
          8   Woe to you rich, for in your riches you have trusted;
                 and from your riches you will depart,
                 because you have not remembered the Most High in the days
                     of your riches.
          9   You have committed blasphemy and iniquity;
                 and you have been prepared for the day of bloodshed
                 and the day of darkness and the day of great judgment.
          10   Thus I say and make known to you ...

The addressees are characterized as "those who build iniquity and violence" (*yaḥannesewwā la-'āmmaḍā wa-la-gef'*, 94:6a; cf. vs 7a) and "lay deceit
as a foundation" (*yešārerewwā la-gʷeḥlut*, 94:6b), or simply, the "rich"
(*'ab'elt*, 94:8a). The expanded element of threat in 94:7d identifies the subjects as those who "acquire" (*'aṭraya*) gold and silver. In 94:9, the author
adds the charge of blasphemy to his earlier charge of iniquity. In his view, the
wealth of his adversaries has been gained by unjust means and has left them
with a false security (94:8).

On the Day of the Lord, this false security will be confronted with a ter-
rifying visitation from the Creator. The threat stated in 94:9 uses three separate synonyms for this Day. Moreover, the Day of the Lord supplies the background for the correspondence patterns present within the oracles themselves.
Each of the three Woes in this series displays the general "reversal of
imagery" pattern. Those who build iniquity "will be overthrown" (*yetnaššatu*,
94:6c, 7b) and those who acquire gold and silver "will depart" (*tewaḍḍe'u*,
94:8b) from their riches. The adverb "quickly" (*feṭuna*), present in the first
oracle (94:6c) and the threat of 94:7c, stresses the suddenness of the reversal
of fortunes on the Day of the Lord.

---

[476] This Woe-series, along with Series 2 and Series 3, are extant in Ethiopic only. For a
discussion of *1 En* 94:6-10, see Nickelsburg, "Riches, the Rich, and God's Judgment,"
327-29.

Other patterns of sin and judgment are present in the extended context of this series (94:10; 95:3). The second Woe-oracle expands on the reversal imagery of overturning buildings by means of the added clause "and by the sword they will fall (*wadqa*)" (94:7c). The combination "overturn/fall" is reused in 94:10 after the messenger formula. The Creator himself will "overturn" (*gafte'a*) the wealthy and for "your fall (*deqatekemu*)" there will be no compassion" (94:10b-c). This is an example of what Miller called *stylistic* correspondence. But there is even more going on here, as evidenced by the reference to the "sword" (94:7c). One of the correspondence patterns identified by Miller portrays the victim of the sin as the one who executes judgment on the sinner (cf. Hab 2:6b-8). Thus, the exhortation to the righteous (the victims) that concludes the extended context of the Woe-series (*1 En* 95:3) is offered in the guise of an oracle of holy war.[477] The Lord delivers the wealthy into the hands of the righteous, an image that suggests a role for the righteous in bearing the sword.[478] Those who have been exploited will fell the wealthy on the day of bloodshed.

Series 2[479]

1 En	95:4	Woe to you who utter anathemas that you cannot loose; healing will be far from you on account of your sins.
	5	Woe to you who repay your neighbor with evil; for you will be repaid according to your deeds.

	6	Woe to you, lying witnesses, and those who weigh out
		        injustice;
		    for quickly you will be destroyed.

	7	Woe to you sinners because you persecute the righteous;
		    for you will be handed over and persecuted because of
		        injustice;
		    and their yoke will be heavy upon you.

The addressees are again characterized as those who commit sins (95:4b, 7a), although here the victims of this sin are identified as "your neighbor" (95:5a). The term "neighbor" suggests sinners are violating the Torah (Exod 20:16-17; Lev 19:13-18). In addition, the nature of the violations is highlighted. Sinners "utter anathemas" (*tāwaggezu gezatāta*, 95:4a) that are harmful to the righteous. Apparently, the righteous are ostracized in some

---

[477] Nickelsburg, "The Apocalyptic Message," 317.

[478] Cf. *1 En* 91:12; 98:12. von Rad, *Holy War*, 42-44.

[479] On the second and fourth members of the series (*1 En* 95:5, 7), see Nickelsburg, "The Apocalyptic Message," 310-11.

way.[480] The addressees are further portrayed as harming the righteous in ways more direct than mere ostracism, they "repay" (*tefaddeyu*, 95:5a) their neighbors with evil. The one specific example provided in the third oracle relates to the judicial system. Sinners pervert justice, serving as "lying witnesses" (*samā'ta ḥassat*) and corrupt judges ("those who weigh out injustice"/*la-'ella yedallewewwā la-'ammaḍā*, 95:6a). The final Woe-oracle categorizes the addressees as a class of "sinners" (*xāṭe'ān*, 95:7a) who persecute the righteous through their unjust practices and policies.

Only the superior sovereignty of the Lord on the great day of judgment will rectify this defiant behavior toward the righteous. The correspondence pattern between sin and judgment in the second and fourth Woe-oracles is in the *Talionsstil*. The fourth oracle is expanded, with the result that the victim of the sin executes judgment on the sinner ("their yoke will be heavy upon you", 95:7c). The first and third Woe-oracles initially appear to be patternless, until the broader context is considered.

The punishments mentioned in the first and third oracles look ahead to the extended context of the present series in which the author turns to exhort the righteous:

1 Enoch 95:4b	*1 Enoch* 96:3a-b
Woe ...	And fear not, you who have suffered;
healing (*fawwes*) will be far	for you will receive healing (*fawwes*)
from you on account of your sins.	

1 Enoch 95:6b (cf. 94:7d)	*1 Enoch* 96:1a-b
Woe ...	Be hopeful, O righteous;
for quickly	for quickly will the sinners
(*'esma feṭuna*)	(*'esma feṭuna* ...)
you will be destroyed.	be destroyed before you ...
(*tethagʷgʷalu*)	(*yethagʷgʷalu* ...)

In conjunction with this shared vocabulary, two correspondence patterns emerge in the extended context of the exhortations. First, a "reversal of imagery" pattern of sorts is present here because the healing denied to sinners earlier is promised to the righteous. Second, victims of the sin are present

---

[480] The חרם of the synagogue ban comes later. Still, the idea of uttering anathemas is that something or someone is "delivered up to divine wrath, dedicated to destruction and brought under a curse," an action that has practical, negative consequences (Behm, "ἀνάθεμα," *TDNT* 1:354-55).

("before you", 96:1b), even involved ("you will have authority over them as you desire," 96:1c), when this influential class of sinners is destroyed.

Series 3[481]

1 En   96:4   Woe to you, sinners, for your riches make you appear to be
                     righteous,
                  but your heart convicts you of being sinners;
                  and this word will be a testimony against you,
                  a reminder of (your) evil deeds.
         5   Woe to you who devour the finest of the wheat,
                  and drink [wine from the krater],
                  and tread on the lowly with your might.
         6   Woe to you who drink water [from every fountain];
                  for quickly you will be repaid, and cease and dry up,
                  because you have forsaken the fountain of life.
         7   Woe to you who commit iniquity and deceit and blasphemy;
                  it will be a reminder against you for evil.
         8   Woe to you, mighty, who with might oppress the righteous one;
                  for the day of your destruction will come.
                  In those days, many good days will come for the righteous
                  —in the day of your judgment.

The addressees are again characterized as "sinners" (xāṭe'ān, 96:4a) who use their wealth and power in defiance of their obligations to the poor and lowly. The portrait of the sinners here is a combination and extension of the sketches of the previous two series.

The internal relationship among the various Woe-oracles of this chain is significant. The first and fourth Woe-oracles are linked by the term "reminder." The term occurs in a statement normally given to the threat of punishment:

1 En 96:4c-d   and this word will be a testimony against you,
                       a reminder (tazkār) of evil deeds.
      96:7b   it will be a reminder (tazkār) against you for evil.

The usual structure of the Woe-oracle is varied. The threat of destruction is implied and its place is occupied by a statement that guarantees the punishment. Sin is recorded and this record, whether preserved orally by those in Sheol (1 En 22:12) or in written form in the book of iniquity (81:4), will be used at the final judgment.

---

[481] The emendation of the Ethiopic in 1 En 96:5b ("and drink wine, quaffing it from the krater") is suggested by Nickelsburg, "Riches, the Rich, and God's Judgment," 329.

The *stylistic* pattern of word repetition emerges in the broader context. The Woe-series is followed by two exhortations to the righteous, the second of which reads in part:

1 En 97:2a   Be it known to you that the Most High
                    remembers (*yezzēkkar*) your destruction

The destruction of the righteous was due to the evil and oppressive deeds of those addressed in the previous Woe-chain (96:4-8). God "remembers" this destruction and will vindicate the righteous because sin has its "reminder," its record in heaven (cf. 97:2b; 100:10; 1QH 1:24). Thus, the correspondence pattern of word repetition involves a technical term for the record that will be disclosed at the judgment.

The second and fifth Woe-oracles are also related through a key word. Curiously, the second oracle uses the element of sin characterization without including any threat of punishment or guarantee of punishment (96:5). However, the last line of the characterization ("and tread on the lowly *with your might* [*ba-xāylekemu*]", 96:5c) links the oracle to the fifth member of the series ("Woe to you, *mighty* [*xāyyālān*], who *with might* [*ba-xāyl*] oppress the righteous one", 96:8a). The fifth oracle, in turn, does have the typical punishment clause, which is itself expanded to produce a reversal and contrast pattern ("for the *day of your destruction* will come", 96:8b; "*many good days* will come for the righteous", 96:8c).

This leaves the central Woe-oracle of the series (96:6). It is the only example that provides a self-contained correspondence pattern. Sinners drink water from every fountain, but they will soon cease and dry up. The image is that of reversal. The expression introducing the reversal, "for quickly you will be repaid" (*'esma tetfaddayu fetuna*, 96:6b), recalls earlier oracles (94:6c, 7d; 95:5b, 6b) and reiterates the notion that only the sudden intrusion of the Day of the Lord will reverse the present state of affairs.

Series 4[482]

1 En   97:7   Woe to you, sinners, who are in the midst of the sea and
                    upon the dry land;
                there is an evil reminder against you.
         8   Woe to you who acquire gold and silver unjustly and say "...
         9   ..."

---

[482] Woe series 4-7 are extant in Greek and Ethiopic translation. The expanded Woe-oracle in *1 En* 97:8-10 is a Disputation Speech. See above, pp. 193-94.

10   You err!
      For your wealth will not remain,
         but will quickly ascend from you;
      for you have acquired everything unjustly,
         and you will be delivered to a great curse.

The characterization of the addressees as "sinners" (οἱ ἁμαρτωλοὶ/ xāṭe'ān, 97:7a) is typical of the Enochic oracles. The significance of locating them on the sea and the dry land is difficult to assess. Perhaps, in view of the second characterization (97:8a), the author intends to imply that sinners use the shipping and caravan routes to acquire gold and silver. In any event, the second characterization is a reprise from the Epistle's first Woe-series (94:7d). Thus, the second oracle of this short series brings the reader full circle; a literary clue that there may be a shift in emphasis in the remaining Woe-chains.

The punishment clause of the first oracle is again replaced by a statement that guarantees the punishment ("a reminder [is] against you [for] evil"[483], 97:7b, cf. 96:4c-d, 7b). The variation emphasizes that sin is recorded and will be disclosed on the day of judgment.

The second oracle has been expanded into a Disputation Speech. The author's reply (97:10) employs the general *reversal* pattern of punishment, as did the oracle against the wealthy in *1 Enoch* 94:8. The notion that the wealth of sinners will ascend "quickly" (ταχὺ/ feṭuna, 97:10c) is the standard allusion to the imminent nature of the Day of the Lord.

Series 5[484]

1 En   98:9   Woe to you, fools;
                     for you will be destroyed because of your folly.
                  And you do not listen to the wise;
                     and good things will not happen to you,
                     but evils will surround you.
          10   And now know that ...
                     [Know] that ...
          11   Woe to you, stiff-necked and hard of heart,
                     who do evil and consume blood.
                  Whence do you have good things to eat and drink and be satisified?

---

[483] My translation of the Greek: μνημόσυνον εἰς ὑμᾶς κακόν.

[484] Textual corruptions in *1 En* 98:9-99:2 are discussed in Nickelsburg, "Enoch 97-104," 93-94, 106-08, 118-19, 137-38. See also Nickelsburg's analysis of the Woe-oracles of this series in "The Epistle of Enoch," 334-39.

from all the good things which the Lord, the Most High,
   has abundantly provided upon the earth.
And you will have no peace.

12   Woe to you who love the deeds of iniquity;
   why do you have good hopes for yourselves?
   Now be it known to you that ...

13   Woe to you who rejoice over the troubles of the righteous;
   your grave will not be dug.

14   Woe to you who annul the words of the righteous;
   you will have no hope of salvation.

15   Woe to those who write lying words and words of error;
   they write and lead many astray with their lies, when they
      hear them.
   You yourselves err;

16   and you will have no peace but will quickly perish.

99:1   Woe to you who commit erring acts
   and who by false deeds receive honor and glory;
   you will perish, you will have no salvation for good.

2   Woe to you who change the true words
   and pervert the eternal covenant
   and consider themselves to be without sin;
   they will be swallowed up in the earth.

In this Woe-chain, the characterization of the addressees focuses primarily on rival sages and interpreters of Torah.[485] The individual oracles of the series are interspersed with heavenly messenger formulas (98:10, twice; 98:12c) and various additional threats (98:9c-e, 11e, 15c-16a). Language stressing the suddenness of the Day of the Lord, typical in earlier Woe-chains, is found in 98:16a: "you will have no peace but *will quickly perish*" ($\tau\alpha\chi\acute{\epsilon}\omega\varsigma$ $\dot{\alpha}\pi o\lambda\epsilon\widehat{\iota}\sigma\theta\epsilon$).

The striking feature about this Woe-series, the longest in the Epistle, is that there is no straightforward example of the most common correspondence pattern between sin and punishment, the *Talionsstil*.[486] By using the first oracle as a point of departure, an overall appreciation can be gained for the kinds of patterns that are utilized.

---

[485] See Chap. I, pp. 46-47, on rival sages in the Epistle of Enoch.

[486] Reversal patterns can be found if we combine various verses. For example, the combination of *1 En* 98:11 and 99:2 yields the following: those who "consume" ($\check{\epsilon}\sigma\theta o\nu\tau\epsilon\varsigma$) blood (98:11b) have changed the Torah and "will be devoured" ($\kappa\alpha\tau\alpha\pi o\theta\acute{\eta}\sigma o\nu\tau\alpha\iota$) in the earth (99:2d). Or again, the "stiff-necked" (98:11a) will be delivered into the hands of the righteous and "they will cut off your necks" (98:12c-d).

Two correspondence patterns are present in the oracle and appended threat in *1 Enoch* 98:9. The Woe-oracle employs the *stylistic* pattern of word repetition to link the addressees ("fools"/ἄφρονες, 98:9a) among those who will be destroyed at the final judgment ("folly"/ἀφροσύνη, 98:9b). In the broader context, the same word reappears later in the Divine Warrior passage about the bloody battle and the helplessness of idols (99:6-10). The anti-idol polemic is directed at false teachers. The latter are regarded as idolaters because the author views them as led astray "by the folly of their hearts" (ἐν ἀφροσύνῃ τῆς καρδίας αὐτῶν, 99:8a).[487] Similarly at Qumrân, those who are not enlightened in their hearts with life-giving wisdom are said to walk "in the idols of their heart" (בגלולי לבו, 1QS 2:11) or "in the stubbornness of their heart" (בשרירות לבו, 1QS 2:14, 26; cf. 1QH 4:15).

Yet another word repetition links the opening Woe-oracle in *1 Enoch* 98:9 to the Divine Warrior passage in 99:6-10. The initial characterization of the addressees as "fools" is expanded by the charge that they "do not listen to the wise" (98:9c). In the extended context, those saved on the Day of the Lord are "all who listen to the words of the wise" (99:10a). Thus, the Woe-series opens with characterizations that invite the reader to make connections between the Woe-series and the Divine Warrior passage in the extended context (cf. also "going astray, erring" in 98:15a-b and 99:8-10).

A second correspondence pattern is found in the punishment clause or threat of the expanded Woe-oracle (98:9d-e). As was the case in *1 Enoch* 95:4b and 96:3a-b, the pattern is a variation on *reversal* (good things/evils).[488] Miller, in his study of the correspondence pattern in the prophets, defined one pattern as: "What one did not think would happen does happen."[489] This is precisely the case in *1 Enoch* 98:9d-e. Rival teachers anticipate good things, but instead will be met with evils.

This pattern shows up throughout the Woe-series, either after the messenger formula or within the Woe-oracle itself. Examples include:

1 En   98:10b   and do not hope to be saved, O sinners;
                you will depart and die.
         12b   why do you have good hopes for yourselves?

---

[487] Nickelsburg calls attention to the parallels in 4QpNah 2:8 and 4QPs^a1:18-19, in which those who "lead astray" are interpreters of Torah ("The Epistle of Enoch," 337). See also 1QpHos (on Hos 2:8) and 1QpMic (on Mic 1:5-7).

[488] The verbs in *1 En* 98:9d-e refer to the future. The Greek verbs are not extant. The Ethiopic reads only the first clause (*wa-šannāyt 'i-yerakkebakemu*), omitting the second by homoioteleuton.

[489] Miller, *Sin and Judgment*, 115.

14b   you will have no hope of salvation
99:1c   you will perish, you will have no salvation for good

The rival interpreters of Torah have hopes for good things because they consider themselves observant Jews (99:2c). However, this author regards them as false teachers and states that the Day of the Lord will dash their hopes of salvation. What the opponents least expect will happen to them.

Series 6[490]

1 En   99:11   Woe to you who spread evil for your neighbor;
                    for in Sheol you will be slain.
           12   Woe to you who lay the foundations of sin and deceit,
                    and cause bitterness upon the earth;
                    for because of it they will come to an end.
           13   Woe to those who build their houses not with their own labors,
                    and they make the whole house of the stones and bricks of sin.
                    Woe to you; you will have no peace.
           14   Woe to those who reject the foundation and eternal inheritance
                    of their fathers;
                    and a spirit of error pursues you;
                    You will have no peace.
           15   Woe to you who practice lawlessness and aid iniquity,
                    murdering their neighbor until the day of the great judgment.
           16   For he will destroy your glory and lay affliction on your hearts,
                    and arouse his wrath against you,
                    and destroy all of you with the sword;
                    And all the righteous will remember your unrighteous deeds.

As was the case in Woe-series 3 above, the individual oracles of this series are related through the literary device of shared terms. The first and last Woe-oracles share the words "neighbor" (*biṣ*/no Gk, 99:11a; *biṣ*/πλησίον, 99:15b) and "murder" (*tetqattalu*/no Gk, 99:11b; *yeqattelu*/[φονεύ]οντες, 99:15b). The addressees are characterized as those whose practices are in direct violation of their covenant obligations to love their neighbor and not commit murder. They are described in 99:14 as those who reject the Torah. In reality, the rivals follow interpretations of Torah that differ from the author's ("deceit"/*gʷeḥlut*, 99:12a). The author of this Woe-chain charges his rivals with bloodguilt. Apparently there is a sense in which he can construe the policies advanced by his counterparts as a contributing factor in the death

---

[490] Nickelsburg sorts through the textual corruptions ("Enoch 97-104," 95-96, 108, 119) and comments briefly on *1 En* 99:12, 14 ("The Epistle of Enoch," 339-40).

of the righteous.[491] In combination, the first and last Woe-oracles in the series yield the *Talionsstil*: they "will be murdered" (99:11b) who "murder" (99:15b).

The reference to being murdered *in Sheol* is unusual. A phenomenon associated with the Day of the Lord has encroached into a description of the Sheol experience (cf. *1 En* 103:7-8a). In the broader context of this Woe-chain, the language of murder recurs in a Divine Warrior passage (100:1-6). The motif of the final battle is portrayed as a day of bloodshed in which sinners will smite members of their own family and "they will be murdered" (φονευθήσονται, 100:2e). Further connections between the last oracle of the series and the following Divine Warrior passage are evident from the shared vocabulary: "those who aid iniquity" (ἐπιβοηθοῦντες τῇ ἀδι[κίᾳ, 99:15a; ἐβοήθουν τῇ ἀδικίᾳ, 100:4b), "great judgment" (τῆς κρίσεως τῆς [μεγάλης], 99:15b; κρίσιν μεγάλην, 100:4d), and "arouse" (ἐπεγερεῖ, 99:16b; ἐγερθήσεται, 100:4c). These parallels demonstrate that recompense for sinners is not *really* supplied in Sheol, but only on the Day of the Lord.

The central Woe-oracles of the series (99:12-14) are tied together by the terms "foundation" and "sin" and the imagery of building houses.[492] The addressees are characterized as "you who lay the *foundations of sin* (*la-masfarta xāṭi'at*/no Gk) and deceit" (99:12a) and make the whole house "of sin" (*xāṭi'at*/no Gk, 99:13b). The building image is a metaphor for the production of what the author regards as false interpretations of Torah.[493] This becomes clear when the term "foundation" is reused to define the addressees as those who forsake the Torah: "those who reject the *foundation* (θεμ[ελί]ωσιν/*masfarta*) and eternal inheritance of their fathers" (99:14a).

The correspondence pattern of punishment in the central Woe-oracles is not readily apparent. When the language of building was used literally to characterize the wealthy in *1 Enoch* 94:6-7, the pattern of *reversal* was employed. The same pattern can be found in the extended context of the present Woe-series. The Divine Warrior passage in *1 Enoch* 100:1-6 concludes on the note that the Gentiles will recognize that their wealth cannot save them "when iniquity collapses" (ἐν τῇ πτώσει τῆς ἀδικίας/*ba-mudāqa xāṭi'atomu*, 100:6c). The reversal pattern is: build with sin/sin collapses.

Another connection between the central Woe-oracles and the extended context is supplied by the punishment clause in *1 Enoch* 99:12c. The warning

---

[491] Cf. Isa 59:3, 7; 66:3-4.

[492] We assume that *1 En* 99:13 is in essence a single Woe-oracle, with characterization (vs 13a-b) and punishment clause (vs 13c).

[493] Nickelsburg, "The Epistle of Enoch," 340.

that those who lay foundations of sin and deceit "will come to an end" (*yetwēdde'u*/no Gk) becomes reality on the Day of the Lord when "evil and sin come to an end" (ἐκλείπῃ/*yewēdde'*, 100:5c). The result for the righteous is that the former "bitterness" (99:12b) will give way to a "sweet sleep" (100:5d), a clear pattern of reversal.

Series 7[494]

1 En	100:7	Woe to you, unrighteous, when you afflict the righteous on a day of hard anguish, and burn them in fire; for you will be recompensed according to your deeds.
	8	Woe to you, hard of heart, who lie awake to devise evil; fear will overtake you, and there will be no one to help you.
	9	Woe to you, all you sinners, because of the words of your mouth and the deeds of your hands, for you have strayed from the holy deeds; in the heat of a blazing fire you will burn.

The addressees are characterized as "unrighteous" (ἄδικοι, 100:7a), "hard of heart" (σκληροκάρδιο[ι], 100:8a; cf. 98:11a), and "all you sinners" ([π]ᾶ[σ]ι[ν] τοῖς ἁμαρτωλοῖς, 100:9a). Once again, these individuals are portrayed as acting in defiance of their obligations ("the holy deeds") toward the author's community. The second Woe-oracle pictures them as those "who lie awake to devise evil," an allusion to the oracle in Micah 2:1-5. In the latter passage, "those who devise wickedness and work evil upon their beds" (Mic 2:1) carry out their plans by seizing fields and houses (Mic 2:2). Perhaps something similar is implied in the Enochic description that they "burn them (the righteous) in fire" (100:7b). Have the righteous been burned out of their homes and off their property? Or is the language simply a metaphor for affliction?

In any case, the punishment envisioned for these schemers of evil is not metaphorical. The correspondence pattern is the *Talionsstil*. The general statement "for you will be recompensed according to your deeds" (100:7c) is later defined to mean that, when you burn the righteous, "you will burn in the heat of a blazing fire" (100:9d). The broader context to this Woe-chain returns to this imagery. The theophany in *1 Enoch* 102:1-3 opens with the statement: God "hurls out against you the flood of the fire of your burning."

---

[494] The textual corruptions here are few (Nickelsburg, "Enoch 97-104," 98-99, 120).

There is yet another connection between the Woe-series and the theophany in the extended context. The punishment clause of the second oracle warns that "fear ($\phi \acute{o} \beta o \varsigma$) will overtake you, and there will be no one to help you" (100:8c). In the theophany, the author asks the rhetorical question: when God utters his voice, "will you not be shaken and *frightened*?" ($\phi o \beta o \acute{v} \mu \varepsilon \nu o \iota$, 102:1d). Once again, a Divine Warrior passage in the broader context is linked by word repetition to the punishment clause of a preceding Woe-oracle.

Summary

The characterization of the sin of the addressees falls into one of two general categories; the sins are either "social" or "religious" in nature.[495] The Woe-oracles in series 1-4 most frequently refer to the "social" sins of the wealthy and powerful, while those in series 5-7 shift to the "religious" sins of false interpreters of Torah. In either case, sinners are portrayed as defiant of their responsibilities to the author and his righteous community.

The preponderance of "religious" sins in series 5-7 coincides with the presence of Divine Warrior passages in the extended context. The vocabulary associated with the Day of the Lord was certainly important to Series 1-4, but discrete Divine Warrior passages, as were studied in the first section of this chapter, are associated with Woe-strings 5-7. This raises the question whether there is a relationship between the characterizations of the addressees as false teachers, on the one hand, and sustained motifs from the Divine Warrior Hymn, on the other. There is ample biblical background for stressing that only the intervention of God himself in final judgment will displace the present religious authorities. A prophetic precedent exists for pronouncing Woes on *religious leaders* who act in such self-reliant independence from God that only the Day of the Lord can thwart them.[496] Moreover, the Divine Warrior motifs in Third Isaiah are sometimes joined to a reproach of the normative leadership for speaking lies and abandoning Torah (Isa 57:11; 58:2; 59:3c-d, 4c). Admittedly, such reproaches are distinct from Woe-oracles; yet the sin characterization and the threat of recompense in the reproaches are often identical to what is found in Woe-oracles.

The Enochic Woe-oracles are quite varied in how they display a correspondence pattern between sin and punishment. In a few instances, the

---

[495] Nickelsburg, "The Apocalyptic Message," 310-11.

[496] Cf. Ezek 13; 34; Jer 23; Zech 11:17; and the discussion in Janzen, *Mourning Cry and Woe Oracle*, 76-80.

Woe-oracle is self-contained because it employs a correspondence in the *Talionsstil*. More commonly, individual Woe-oracles are related to other oracles within the series or to passages in the broader context. The correspondence is sometimes marked by word repetition, at other times by ideas such as the victim of the sin executing judgment on the sinner or the unexpected happening to the sinner. These additional patterns help account for some Woe-oracles whose punishment clause is either missing or, when present, appears to lack correspondence to the sin of the addressees. It is common for the threat of punishment, which always alludes to the final judgment, to be related in a linguistic or ideational way to other statements in the series or extended context.

Our analysis of the Enochic Woe-oracles has benefited from the work of Janzen and Miller in the Hebrew prophets. A quite different approach to these oracles has been suggested by Coughenour.[497] Building on the work of Gerstenberger, who sought the origins of the Woe-oracle among the sages, Coughenour argues that the Enochic Woes are a "wisdom element." He describes the function of the Woes in the Epistle of Enoch as similar to the functions of other forms used by wisdom writers; namely, to penetrate the order of the world. More specifically, Coughenour claims their function is educative; the Woes remind the "wise" that the perversion of the social order is the way that leads to death.[498]

The Woe-oracles in the Epistle can be described as a "wisdom element" only if one bears in mind the Enochic conception of wisdom. The Enochic Woes have nothing at all to do with penetrating the order of the world as this was done in traditional wisdom. Enoch's wisdom comes from heaven. He has seen visions through which it is revealed to him that the creation is prepared for God's imminent judgment. He has inscribed this revelation in his books and passed them on to his posterity. From this perspective, Enoch is a messenger who proclaims Woes. The function of the Woe-oracles in the Epistle is not primarily to educate the righteous and wise;[499] rather, they serve to threaten sinners with divine judgment. In this respect, the Enochic Woe-oracles retain the function of their prophetic counterparts. It is best not to describe them as a "wisdom element."

---

[497] "The Woe-oracles in Ethiopic Enoch," *JSJ* 9 (1978) 192-97. See also the reference to his dissertation in n. 1 above.

[498] Ibid., 197.

[499] Of course, the oracles would have this effect. Luke T. Johnson shows that the purpose of polemic between ancient schools was to identify, not rebutt, an opponent and thereby edify one's own school ("The New Testament's Anti-Jewish Slander and the Conventions of Ancient Polemic," *JBL* 108 [1989] 419-41).

6. JUDGMENT IN BEN SIRA'S BOOK OF WISDOM

The theme of judgment occurs in a number of ben Sira's discourses. The judgment of God on the individual is usually in view; a judgment that takes place either during an individual's lifetime or at the moment of death. However, the notion of universal, eschatological judgment is not totally lacking; in fact, motifs from the Divine Warrior Hymn appear in ben Sira's wisdom book. In addition, the genre Disputation Speech and the literary form of the Woe-oracle are used to defend the operation of divine justice and threaten adversaries with judgment.

The literary motifs and forms referred to above display ben Sira's peculiar adaptations and reinterpretations of traditional notions and vocabulary. Analysis of such literary features will provide a basis of comparison to the material just reviewed in *1 Enoch*.

THE DIVINE WARRIOR HYMN

The motifs in this genre are found in two closely related passages, Sirach 35[32]:22b-26 and 36:1-22 [33:1-13a; 36:16b-22]. The material preceding these two passages (34:21-35:22a) ends on the note that God will hear the prayer of the oppressed and judge their cause (35:16-22a; cf. *1 En* 99:3). The idea that prayer triggers the judgment then leads into ben Sira's use of Divine Warrior motifs (35:22b-26), which carry over into his prayer that God judge the nations and deliver Israel from her oppressors (36:1-22). An outline of the Warrior motifs found in these two passages will prove helpful:

TABLE 5
DIVINE WARRIOR MOTIFS IN SIRACH

	Sir 35[32]:22b-26	Sir 36:1-22 [33:1-13a; 36:16b-22]
Combat-Victory over enemies	22b-24	1-12
Salvation of the Nation	25-26	1, 17-18
Victory Shout/ Festive Joy	25b	----
Universal Reign	----	1
Gathering of the Dispersion	----	13, 16
Conversion of the Gentiles	----	5, 22c-d
Fertility/New Creation	----	----
Procession to Temple	----	(13, 16-19)

Sirach 35[32]:22b-26[500]

Sir 35[32]:22b	\<Hb\> 35:18a	Indeed, the Lord will not delay,
c		b and like a warrior, he will not restrain himself
d		c Until he smashes the loins of the cruel,
23a		d and renders vengeance to the nations;
b		e Until he drives out the scepter of arrogance,
c		f and the staff of the wicked he breaks thoroughly;
24a	19a	Until he repays humankind for their actions,
b		b and the deeds of people according to their intrigues;
25a		c Until he prosecutes the case of his people,
b		d and makes them rejoice in his salvation.
26a	20a	Salvation is welcome in time of affliction,
b		b like clouds of rain in the time of drought.

The emphasis in 35[32]:22b-26 falls on the Divine Warrior's combat victory over the enemies of Israel. Ben Sira describes the Lord acting "like a

---

[500] Translation based on Hebrew, ms B, except for verse 26a \<20a\> which is supplied from the Greek. The versification follows the Greek.

warrior" who wins a brutal battle and renders vengeance "to the *nations*." This emphasis is consistent with the early hymnic material[501] and was utilized in the exilic period by Second Isaiah and his disciples.[502] A brief comparison to the biblical prototypes will illustrate how ben Sira adapts the traditional combat motif.

God is "like a warrior" (כגבור, Sir 35:22c).[503] The expression is drawn from Isaiah 42:13 ("The Lord goes forth like a warrior"). The Divine Warrior is the subject of the verbs throughout the Hymn (Sir 35:22d-25b), a fact that suggests the Warrior acts alone.[504] This does not necessarily mean that the people of Israel have no fighting role;[505] however, in post-exilic prophetic texts this appears to be the case (Isa 59:16; 63:5). The possibility should be kept open that ben Sira's view of the Warrior acting alone is similar to that of Third Isaiah.

There is one striking difference from tradition in ben Sira's portrait of the Warrior. He omits any traditional verb to convey the idea that the Warrior "goes forth" or "descends." This is all the more remarkable given the fact that the expression "like a Warrior" is drawn from Isaiah 42:13, a passage in which a traditional verb is present (יהוה כגבור יצא, "The Lord *goes forth* like a warrior").[506] It is possible that ben Sira deliberately avoids the traditional verb because it does not fit his understanding of the eschatological battle.[507]

Related to this important point is ben Sira's muted reference to the storm and fire that often accompany the descent of the Divine Warrior (cf. Isa 66:15-16; *1 En* 1:6; 102:1). In Sirach 35:26 and 36:11a, only a faint remnant of the traditional storm and fire imagery is detectable.

The storm God, or what is left of this ancient image, is redirected in Sirach 35:26 into a comparative proverb that expresses the salvation of the

---

[501] E.g., Judg 5, Exod 15. See Miller, *The Divine Warrior*, 74-128.

[502] See Hanson, *The Dawn of Apocalyptic*, 310-13.

[503] Penar reads an emphatic *kaf* and translates: "And certainly, the Warrior ..." (*Northwest Semitic Philology*, 58). But the parallel in Isa 42:13, which Penar does not cite, speaks against this rendering.

[504] According to von Rad, the traditional theory of Holy War is that "the one who acts is Yahweh alone" (*Holy War*, 44).

[505] Miller agrees with von Rad that the combat victory is primarily a divine one, but stresses the "major and active role" played by the military (*The Divine Warrior*, 159).

[506] Instead of using the traditional verb יצא ("go forth"), ben Sira uses the verb אפק (*hitp.*, "to be restrained"): "Like a Warrior he will not be restrained". In the context of Isa 42:13, the prophet used this verb of himself (Isa 42:14), although it is later applied to God (Isa 64:12a).

[507] We will return to this point below in our treatment of Sir 36:1-22. Skehan's translation of Sir 36:1 ("Come to our aid ...") is misleading (*The Wisdom of Ben Sira*, 413). There is no verb "Come" in the text. We should not supply what ben Sira has been careful to omit! The prayer begins: "Save us ..." (הושיענו).

nation: "Salvation is welcome in the time of affliction, *like clouds of the storm* (כעבי [כע]בי חזיזים) in the time of drought." It is ironic in the extreme that the phrase "like clouds of the storm" (35:26b) links up with "like a Warrior" (35:22c), forming an *inclusio*, because in this Hymn the Warrior has not come in the storm! Rather, the storm imagery is transformed in 35:26 into a metaphor for salvation.

In this same connection, the Warrior does not come forth in fire. When ben Sira mentions fire in his prayer to trigger the judgment ("Let the fugitive be consumed *in fiery wrath*," 36:11a),[508] the reference is metaphorical. There is no hint that God comes with fire, which might also imply that God does not even "come."

Ben Sira's doctrine of opposites accounts for his omission of the Warrior's theophany in storm and fire. Storm and fire are among the elements of creation that God regularly uses to inflict punishment on individuals and nations. The elements of creation do not participate in the eschatological battle.[509] Ben Sira conceives of this battle along entirely different lines.

In accord with tradition, ben Sira does picture the Warrior defeating the enemy nations. Some of the Divine Warrior passages in Third Isaiah offer a variation on the enemy motif, a variation not adopted by ben Sira. In Isaiah 59:15b-20 and 66:14-15, traditional references to enemies have been reapplied to opponents *within* Israel; while in 63:1-6 and 64:1-2, as in Second Isaiah and ancient Warrior tradition, the adversaries are the other nations. Ben Sira's portrayal of the enemy in Sirach 35:22b-26 is totally in line with Isaiah 63:1-6, 64:1-2 and the older tradition.

A few of the terms ben Sira uses for the adversaries in the Warrior Hymn serve to characterize his opponents in other passages.[510] However, these opponents are not envisioned in his use of Divine Warrior motifs. Perhaps this reveals something about the nature of the intra-Jewish opposition. In ben Sira's view, the evils of his rivals are not so pervasive or destructive that he must call for the immediate intervention of God. But the nations, particularly

---

[508] The Greek expression is "ἐν ὀργῇ πυρὸς." The word πῦρ is used as an attributive genitive.

[509] The only passage that gives creation a traditional role in the judgment occurs in the context of a speech by ben Sira's opponents (Sir 16:18-19). We take up this passage in our investigation of the Disputation Speeches below.

[510] Examples are זדון ("arrogance", Sir 35:23b; cf. 32:18); אדם ("mankind," 35:24b; cf. 3:24); and רשע ("wicked", 35:23c; cf. 41:7-8). The latter term is also used by ben Sira for those who will be punished by elements of creation (39:30; 40:10).

those rulers who oppress Israel, are so formidable that they can only be thwarted by a display of God's might and sovereignty.[511]

Ben Sira calls the nations "cruel" (אכזרי, Sir 35:22d) and describes Israel's experience of their rule as a "time of affliction" (בְּעֵת] מצוקה], 35:26a). The assumption may be that the nations have exceeded their mandate as God's instrument of punishment and Israel is now suffering unjustly under their yoke. God's people have a controversy (רִיב, 35:25a) against the nations that ben Sira expects God to prosecute in Israel's favor.

The salvation of Israel is expressed by the term "help" (יְשׁוּעָה, Sir 35:25b).[512] The victory shout associated with divine help is offered by the people who "rejoice" (שׂמח, pi., 35:25b). The nature of the deliverance that will evoke this joy is further expounded in ben Sira's prayer, to which we now turn.

Sirach 36:1-22 [33:1-13a; 36:16b-22]

The prayer ben Sira offers to trigger the judgment upon the nations consists of four stanzas (36:1-5, 6-12, 13-19, 20-22).[513] The initial two stanzas, like the preceding unit, are weighted on the motif of God's combat victory. The prayer will be analyzed in light of the tendencies uncovered above.[514]

---

[511] The terms for the nations are גוים (Sir 35:23a; 36:2) and עם נכר (36:3). It is gratuitous to claim that the reference is to the Seleucids, as does Di Lella (*The Wisdom of Ben Sira*, 421-22) and Martin Hengel (see his two articles, "The political and social history of Palestine from Alexander to Antiochus III [333-187 B.C.E.]" and "The interpenetration of Judaism and Hellenism in the pre-Maccabean period;" *The Cambridge History of Judaism, vol. 2: The Hellenistic Age*, [ed. W. D. Davies and Louis Finkelstein; Cambridge: Cambridge University, 1989] 35-78, esp. 78; and 167-228, esp. 225). What precludes a reference to the Ptolemies at about 200 BCE?

[512] The same word is probably also used in Sir 35:26a, though the Hebrew text is too damaged to read. The Greek ἔλεος translates the Hebrew in both places.

[513] Middendorp raises the issues against authenticity (*Die Stellung*, 125-32). With most scholars, we regard the prayer as original to ben Sira. For a defense of authenticity, see Marböck, "Das Gebet um die Rettung Zions Sir 36,1-22 [G:33,1-13a; 36,16b-22] im Zusammenhang der Geschichtsschau Ben Siras," *Memoria Jerusalem* (ed. J. B. Bauer; Jerusalem/Graz: Akademische Druck- und Verlagsanstalt, 1977) 93-116.

[514] Translation based on ms B with 36:10b-11 supplied by the Greek (Skehan and Di Lella, *Wisdom of Ben Sira*, 415-16). Notice that because the Greek versification is followed after correcting for the dislocation (i.e., 36[33]:1-13a; 36[36]:16b-22) there are no verses numbered 14 and 15 in Sirach 36. The Hebrew versification of ms B begins to vary in verse 6.

Sir 36[33]:1		Rescue us, God of all,
2		and raise your terror over all nations.
3a		Raise your hand over the people of the foreign land,
b		and they shall see your mighty deeds.
4a		As you have shown yourself holy to their eyes through us,
b		so to our eyes be glorifed through them.
5a		And they shall know as we know,
b		that there is no god except you.
6 <Hb>	6a	Renew a sign and repeat an omen,
7	b	make glorious your hand and strengthen your arm and right hand.
8	7a	Let anger be stirred up and wrath poured out,
9	b	and humble the enemy and drive away the foe.
10a	8a	Hasten the end and appoint the designated time,
b	b	and your mighty deeds will be proclaimed.[515]
11a	--	Let fiery wrath consume the one escaping to safety,
b	--	and the oppressors of your people meet destruction.
12a	10a	Remove the head of the rulers of the enemy,[516]
b	b	who says, 'There is none except me.'
13	11a	Gather all the tribes of Jacob,
16	b	and they will possess (the land) as in days of old.
17a	12a	Have compassion upon the people called by your name,
b	b	Israel, whom you named first-born.
18a	13a	Have compassion upon the city of your holiness,
b	b	Jerusalem, the place of your throne.
19a	14a	Fill Zion with your majesty,
b	b	and from your glory (fill) your temple.
20a	15a	Give testimony to your ancient deeds,
b	b	and carry out the vision spoken in your name.
21a	16a	Give rewards to those waiting for you,
b	b	and let your prophets be trustworthy.
22a	17a	Hear the prayer of your servants,
b	b	when your favor (rests) upon your people.
c	c	And let all the ends of the earth know
d	d	that you are the eternal God.

The God to whom ben Sira prays for victory is called "God of all" (אלהי הכל, 36:1). This designation is used elsewhere in Sirach to refer to God as embracing the opposites of creation.[517] Ben Sira makes it clear, however, that

---

[515] Ms B: "For who will say to you: 'What are you doing?'"

[516] Reading B^mg אויב ("enemy") rather than מואב ("Moab").

[517] See Chap. 4, p. 152.

the doctrine of opposites is not in view here. Not only does his prayer lack any reference to the role of creation in the eschatological battle, but the title "God of all" is immediately redefined in 36:2 to express God's universal kingship. The parallel colon picks up the word "all" and applies it to the nations: "raise your terror over *all the nations* (כל הגוים)." Ben Sira's interpretation of eschatological combat has eliminated a role for the created elements. The expression "God of all" is adapted in the present prayer to the motif of universal sovereignty.

In addition to the title "God of all," other terms from the doctrine of opposites undergo redefinition in the context of the eschatological battle. The "mighty deeds" (גבורת) that the nations "see" (ראה, Sir 36:3b) are not related to the "mighty works" one may "see" in creation. Ben Sira does indeed use this vocabulary in his doctrine of opposites (Sir 42:21-22). Here, however, the גבורת seen by the nations are not created elements, but the works of the גבור (Sir 35:22b), the Divine Warrior (cf. Isa 42:13d). References to God's "hand" and "arm" (Sir 36:3a, 7b) are traditional images for depicting combat victory (Exod 15:6; Ps 98:1; Isa 62:8); they imply nothing about the means used to achieve this victory.

Other redefinitions occur in connection with the expression "mighty deeds" in 36:10b.[518] Ben Sira asks God to "hasten the end" and "appoint the designated time" (vs 10a) when these "mighty (= war-like) deeds" will take place and be acknowledged (vs 10b). The verbs "hasten" (חוש) and "appoint" (פקד) are also significant in ben Sira's doctrine of opposites (40:10[519]; 39:30d). But, in the present context the terms are used solely with reference to the eschatological battle among the nations.[520]

The tendency illustrated above is especially clear in ben Sira's request that the nations come to know God as Israel knows God (Sir 36:5, cf. 36:22c-d). A basic omission results from ben Sira's adaptation of this theme. In Third Isaiah, God "makes known" (ידע, *hif.*) his name and the nations "tremble" (רגז) when God "comes down" (ירד) in "fire" (Isa 64:1-2 [63:19c-64:1 Hb]). In ben Sira's prayer, however, the nations are "in dread" (פחד, 36:1b; cf. Exod 15:16) and "know" (ידע, 36:5a) God apart from any explicit reference to descent or the element of fire.

---

[518] We read the Greek in this colon ("And *your mighty deeds* [τὰ μεγαλεῖά σου] will be proclaimed"), rather than the Hebrew of ms B ("For who will say to you, 'What are you doing?'"). In Sir 36:3b, the Greek translation of גבורתיך was τὴν δυναστείαν σου.

[519] The word תמוש in Sir 40:10 (ms B) should be emended to תחוש (Skehan and Di Lella, *The Wisdom of Ben Sira*, 466).

[520] Box and Oesterley note that the terms the "end" and the "appointed time" are used "almost in a technical sense" in Dan 11:27, 35 ("Sirach," *APOT*, 1.440).

If Israel's enemies meet "destruction" (ἀπώλεια, Sir 36:11b), a common fate in Divine Warrior passages, how does ben Sira envision it happening? How does the Warrior fight without going before the armies of Israel or using the elements of creation? Apparently, ben Sira assumes that God will put the nations at war against one another for the purpose of liberating Israel (cf. 36:4b: "to our eyes be glorified through them"). Only in this respect are there some created opposites involved in the final battle, namely, those associated with warfare: the "avenging sword" (39:30b) and "plague and bloodshed ... plunder and ruin" (40:9).

The third stanza of ben Sira's prayer (Sir 36:13, 16-19) reads like a Hymn to Zion,[521] with images that are intelligible in the context of the Warrior Hymn. When God acts to "Show mercy" (רחם, 36:17a, 18a) the result effects both the people and the holy city.

The traditional motif of universal kingship is expressed through images of the gathering of the dispersion and the inheritance of the land (Sir 36:13, 16). Yet, nothing is said of the new experience of the people on the land through the motif of fertility and renewal as in Isaiah 65:17-25. Rather, the people who receive God's eschatological mercy (36:17) are immediately related to city and temple which experience the same mercy (36:18). It is noteworthy that terms used elsewhere to describe the beauty of the works of creation are applied to the temple in Sirach 36:19 (הוד/כבוד).[522] It is the temple, not the creation, that is renewed after combat victory. The creation, functioning as it does according to the doctrine of opposites, is already glorious and beautiful.

The major motifs of this third stanza, therefore, are not fertility and new creation but universal kingship and procession to Jerusalem and the temple mount. In exilic and post-exilic biblical texts, the ancient procession motif is applied to the exiles who return to Zion for worship (Isa 51:9-11). However, ben Sira, unlike Second Isaiah, does not relate the return and procession of exiles to images of cosmic combat and renewal. As the works of creation did not participate in the combat, so they are not involved in the renewal.

There is a mythic allusion of another sort in ben Sira's depiction of the ingathering and the temple. The word pairs Jacob/Israel and Jerusalem/Zion were used earlier in the poem of Wisdom's descent (Sir 24:8-11). Even more to the point, the description of Jerusalem as "your resting place" (מכון שבתיך/τόπον καταπαύματός σου, Sir 36:18b) recalls Wisdom's search for "a resting place" (ἀνάπαυσις, Sir 24:7a) and her subsequent claim that Jerusalem

---

521 Cf. Isa 54:1-8; 60:1-22; 62:1-8; 66:10-11; Tob 13; 11QPsᵃ XXII, 1-15 (Apostrophe to Zion).

522 For example, in Sir 42:15-43:33 the "glory" (כבוד) that fills all of God's created works (42:16b) is interpreted as the "splendor" (הוד, ms M) displayed in the doctrine of opposites (42:25b).

was the city where God "gave (me) rest" (κατέπαυσεν, 24:11). Thus, the traditional motif of the mountain/temple where God dwells (cf. Exod 15:17) is, for ben Sira, the locus of Wisdom. While he has not explicitly mentioned Wisdom in Sirach 36:13, 16-19, the reference to Jerusalem as God's "resting place" is a subtle reminder of her presence.

The underlying implication of the third stanza of this prayer is that God confirm, secure and enhance the status of those persons presently in positions of leadership in the city and temple. Ben Sira shows a strong desire for continuity before and after the eschatological battle. The exiles return to Zion and recognize the legitimacy of the status quo. Indeed, the combat victory brings an added prestige to the present institutions of cult and state. Zion is vindicated as the locus of Wisdom.

In the fourth and concluding stanza of his prayer (Sir 36:20-22), ben Sira shows that his reinterpretation of the eschatological battle has been the result of scripture study. He appeals to visions and the prophets as the basis for his prayer (36:20b, 21b). The reference is to the prophetic books that ben Sira studied in his school (39:1b), and, judging from the many allusions within the prayer itself, principally to the book of Isaiah. In addition, ben Sira's panegyric on the prophet Isaiah (Sir 48:22c-25) in his Hymn to the Fathers includes statements that this prophet was "faithful in his vision" (πιστὸς ἐν ὁράσει αὐτοῦ, 48:22d) and "he saw the last things" (אחרית חזה/εἶδεν τὰ ἔσχατα, 48:24a). The vocabulary of visions and faithfulness in connection with the prophets is also present in 36:20-21. God is asked to fulfil "the visions" (חזון, 36:20b) spoken in his name, one result of which is that his prophets "may be faithful" (יאמינו/ἐμπιστευθήτωσαν, 36:21b).

Summary

Ben Sira has interpreted the prophetic vision, that is, the Warrior motifs from Second and Third Isaiah, in a very tendentious manner. He has not simply adopted motifs unchanged. Ben Sira has been selective in choosing motifs and careful in reinterpreting them so that they fit with his theology. The Divine Warrior does fight against the nations, recompense them for their evil deeds against Israel, save Israel and gather the dispersion to a renewed temple; but noteworthy because of their absence among these themes are several traditional images: the descent of the Warrior, the role of fire and storm in the combat, and the renewal of creation after victory. Ben Sira's retelling of the prophetic vision of the future has resulted in a radical reshap-

ing. In short, he offers an interpretation that is consistent with his own doctrine of opposites.[523]

THE DISPUTATION SPEECH

Ben Sira is an advocate of the traditional doctrine of retribution; namely,
that one receives rewards and punishments in this lifetime.[524] Rewards and
punishments bear a direct relationship to one's obedience or disobedience to
the Law, as interpreted by ben Sira. Ben Sira disputes those, whether his students or his opponents, who reason that divine justice in the present life is
either unfair or altogether lacking. In many instances, his replies are grounded
in his understanding of the doctrine of opposites. Allusions to meteorological
or other elements of the creation, so carefully avoided in the Divine Warrior
passages, now appear in the Disputation Speeches with reference to the doctrine of opposites.

Four discourses in Sirach contain elements of the genre Disputation
Speech. In some cases, the structure outlined earlier, 1) introduction, 2) citation, 3) reply and 4) conclusion, is reflected in the order of the cola in a particular poem. Most often, however, the pattern is subject to various refractions
and recombinations in the interests of the larger aims of the discourse.

Sirach 5:1-8

This discourse contains several citations introduced by the verbs "do not
say" (אל תאמר, vss 1b, 3a, 4a) and "say" (אמרת, vs 6a). The author's reply
consists of a motive clause introduced by the demonstrative particle "for"
(כי).[525] Our translation highlights the subunits that contain the "Do not say/say
… for …" structure.[526]

---

[523] Ben Sira knew of other interpretations of the future quite different from his own and
was critical of them. See Sir 34:7 (Chap. 2, p. 82) and Sir 15:11-20 (below, p. 229, n.
545).

[524] Skehan and Di Lella, *The Wisdom of Ben Sira*, 83-87. In the original Hebrew text
of ben Sira, there are no references to the afterlife (*pace* Penar, *Northwest Semitic Philology, passim*).

[525] The only exception to this structure is the initial "Do not say" formula (Sir 5:1b).
On the function of כי, see James Muilenburg, "The Linguistic and Rhetorical Usages of the
Particle כי in the Old Testament," *HUCA* 32 (1961) 135-60.

[526] The translation is based on ms A, with the following exceptions: disregard the doublets in ms A after Sir 5:2 and 5:4; emend כחו in 5:3a to כחי; read the Greek in 5:3b; from
ms C adopt "Lord" in 5:3b, "and upon" in 5:6d, and "time" in 5:7d.

Sir 5:1 Do not rely on your wealth;
            do not say: "There is power in my hand."
      2   Do not rely on your strength;
            to walk after the desires of your soul.

      3   *Do not say*: "Who can endure my strength?"
            for the Lord will surely avenge.

      4   *Do not say*: "I have sinned, yet did anything happen to me?"
            for the Lord is slow to anger.

      5   Regarding forgiveness, do not be careless
            to add sin upon sin;
      6   *And say*: "His mercies are great;
            he will forgive my many sins."
          For mercy and anger are with him,
            and upon the wicked will rest his wrath.
      7   Do not delay in turning back to him;
            do not put it off from day to day.
          For suddenly his wrath comes forth,
            and in the time of vengeance you will be snatched away.

      8   Do not trust in deceitful riches,
            for they will not help on the day of wrath.

Verses 1, 3 and 4 are good examples of the ancient debate form "Do not say ...".[527] Verses 5-7 show an adaptation of this short form toward the longer Disputation Speech:

1)	Introduction:	instruction on forgiveness	5:5
2)	Citation:	*And say ...*	5:6a-b
3)	Author's reply:	*For ...*	5:6c-d
4)	Conclusion:	turn back, his wrath comes suddenly	5:7

The short (5:1b, 3-4) and expanded (5:5-7) forms have been grouped in this discourse to address the temptations that face the wealthy and powerful person. In the initial two citations (5:1b, 3a), this person expresses the willingness to do whatever he pleases (cf. *1 En* 97:9). In the third citation (5:4a), the wealthy and powerful sinner takes consolation in the fact that he was not

---

[527] James L. Crenshaw, "The Problem of Theodicy in Sirach: On Human Bondage," *JBL* (1975) 48-49. Crenshaw also lists Sir 5:6 among his examples of the ancient debate form, apparently on the basis of the Greek translation μὴ εἴπῃς in 5:6a. But the Hebrew of mss A and C reads ואמרת and this need not be emended (see A. A. Di Lella, *The Hebrew Text of Sirach* [The Hague: Mouton & Co., 1966] 114).

punished (cf. *1 En* 103:5-6). The speech cited in Sirach 5:6 displays an alternate but equally erroneous attitude. The sinner presumes he can be forgiven his many sins because of God's manifold mercies.[528]

Each motive clause that contains ben Sira's reply refers to the reality of coming judgment either in this lifetime or at the moment of death. The first reply is an emphatic statement, the Lord "will surely avenge" (ἐκδικῶν ἐκδικήσει, 5:3b).[529] The remaining answers employ several synonyms for God's anger, as ben Sira develops the ways in which this anger operates in relation to sinners. If judgment is not immediate (5:4a), it is because the Lord is "slow to anger" (ארך אפים, 5:4b = "long of nostrils").[530] If one presumes on the abundant quality of God's mercy (5:6a-b), one should learn that "wrath" (אף, 5:6c) is a co-attribute with mercy, and "his wrath" (רגזו, 5:6d) will rest upon the wicked. For ben Sira, the certainty of divine wrath makes repentance urgent. In the motive clause that concludes the longer Disputation form, ben Sira warns that "*suddenly* his [God's] wrath will go forth" (פתאום יצא זעמו, 5:7c; cf. *1 En* 94:7d; 95:6b; 96:6b; 97:10c; 98:16) and "in the time of vengeance" (ובעת נקם, 5:7d; cf. 5:3b) wealthy and powerful sinners "will be snatched away" (ספה, nif., 5:7d).[531] Finally, the couplet that ends the entire discourse provides a parting instruction and one last synonym for God's anger: wealth will be of no help "on the day of wrath" (ביום עברה, 5:8b).

Among the above expressions, the phrase "*the time* of vengeance" (5:7d, ms C) is unattested in the Hebrew Bible[532] and alludes to the notion of the "*proper time*" in ben Sira's doctrine of opposites (Sir 39:16b, 33b, 34b; cf. 39:30d).[533] Riches are part of the dynamic of opposites (Sir 11:14), and as suddenly as riches are given (11:21c-d) they can be taken away (cf. Sir 40:13-14). When wealth is gained by injustice or leads to a lifestyle of sin, its pos-

---

[528] A related attitude on the part of the sinner is refuted in the instruction and citation in Sir 7:8-9 (assuming we read vs 9 with the Greek and Syriac):

> 7:8   Do not plot to repeat a sin;
> for you will not remain unpunished for each one.
> 9   *Say not*, "He will observe my many gifts;
> the Most High will accept my offerings."

[529] This likely translates the Hebrew: נקם יקם.

[530] The expression comes from the Hebrew Bible (e.g., Exod 34:6; Num 14:18).

[531] This verb alludes to the Sodom and Gomorrah story (Gen 18:23f; 19:15, 17; cf. Sir 16:8).

[532] The point is noted by Di Lella, who seems to imply that he prefers the reading "day of vengeance" (ms A) because of its presence in the Hebrew Bible (Skehan and Di Lella, *The Wisdom of Ben Sira*, 183). But there is a close analogy to ben Sira's expression in the War Rule from Qumrân which speaks of "vengeance in God's appointed time" (נקם במועד אל, 1QM 3:7; cf. 15:6).

[533] See Chap. 4, p. 142.

sessors should expect retribution at any moment. The created elements stand ever ready to execute God's command; if not during one's lifetime, then at the moment of death. The "time of vengeance" (5:7d) can be equated with the "day of wrath" (5:8b), understood as the day of death. Ben Sira brings these concepts together in 18:24: "Think of *wrath* in the *days of the end (= death)*, and the *time of vengeance* when he will hide his face." Ben Sira teaches that sinners who escape God's judgment in life will meet their end with affliction.

Sirach 11:14-28[534]

This passage begins with a terse statement of the doctrine of opposites (Sir 11:14). In the four stanzas that comprise the unit, ben Sira applies this doctrine to the ways the judgment of God functions within the scope of human existence.[535]

Sir	11:14a	Good and evil, life and death,
	b	poverty and wealth, is from the Lord.
	17a	The gift of the Lord remains with the righteous,
	b	his favor succeeds for ever.
	18a	There is a person who is rich through depriving himself,
	b	and this is his allotted reward:
	19a	At the time he says, 'I have found rest,
	b	and I now I will consume my goods.'
	c	He does not know what the extent of his days will be,
	d	and he leaves them to others and dies.
	20a	My son, be steadfast in your duty and attend to it,
	b	and grow old in your work.
	21a	Do not marvel at those who do evil,
	b	but trust in the Lord and wait for his light.
	c	For it is easy in the eyes of the Lord,
	d	suddenly, in a moment, to make a poor man rich.

---

[534] We agree with Skehan's reconstruction of the text. Sir 11:15-16 is a gloss to the original text and Sir 11:25 and 11:26 have been transposed in the Greek. Thus, the versification in this passage is Sir 11:14, 17-24, 26, 25, 27-28 (Skehan and Di Lella, *The Wisdom of Ben Sira*, 235-37).

[535] Ms A is in a broken state and several plausible restorations have been suggested from the Greek (see Box and Oesterley, "Sirach," *APOT* 1.354-56). It is best, however, to simply translate the Greek in vss 17a, 18b, 20a ("attend"), 21b ("trust in the Lord"), 24 (the entire quoted speech), and 26 (lacking in ms A). Ms A does contain the secondary vss 15-16, as well as doublets in vss 25b and 26. Segal suggested that vss 25 and 26 were transposed (noted by Skehan and Di Lella, *The Wisdom of Ben Sira*, 237).

22a   The blessing of God is the lot of the righteous,
  b   and at the appointed time his hope bears fruit.
23a   Do not say: 'What shall I get for having done his will,
  b   and what now will be left for me?'
24a   Do not say: 'I am self-sufficient,
  b   and what will harm me from now on?'
26a   For it is easy for the Lord on the day of death,
  b   to repay a person according to his deeds.

25a   The good day makes one forget evil,
  b   and the evil day makes one forget goodness.
27a   A time of evil makes one forget comfort,
  b   the last end of a person will tell about him.
28a   Do not pronounce a man happy before death,
  b   for a man is known by his end.

Stanzas one (11:14, 17-19) and three (11:22-24, 26) are parallel by virtue of the fact that both contain citations and replies. Stanzas two (11:20-21) and four (11:25, 27-28) are additional instructions that expand upon the author's reply in the preceding stanza. The literary construction can be illustrated as follows:

TABLE 6
THE TWO DISPUTATION SPEECHES IN SIRACH 11:14-28

	Stanza			
	One	Two	Three	Four
1) Introduction:				
on the צדיק	11:14, 17		11:22	
2) Citation:				
he says ([אמר])	11:18-19b			
Do not say (אל תאמר)			11:23, 24	
3) Author's reply:				
ומת	11:19c-d			
ἐν ἡμέρᾳ τελευτῆς			11:26	
4) Expanded instruction:		11:20-21		11:25, 27-28

The citation in the first stanza (11:14, 17-19) is from the man who has become rich by depriving himself. This man has his "reward" (שׂכר/ ἡ μερὶς τοῦ μισθοῦ, 11:18b) "at the time" (ובעת, 11:19a) that he decides to enjoy the good things he has hoarded. At some point in life, he says that "now" (עתה,

11:19b) he will feast. Ben Sira's reply draws attention to another time that this rich man does not know, namely, the limit to his days (חקו, 11:19c). At this time, the rich man leaves his possessions to others and dies (11:19d). In ben Sira's view, God created good and bad things; and while the wicked may enjoy the good for a time, it will turn out evil for them in the end, if not before (Sir 39:25-27; 40:10). In anticipation of this reply, ben Sira's initial instruction to the righteous person was about prosperity that would "last" (לעד, 11:17b).

The expanded instruction in stanza two (11:20-21) emphasizes that the righteous person should be dutiful and patient. Rather than marvel at the deeds of sinners, ben Sira's students should trust the Lord "and wait for his light" (וקוה לא[ו]רו, 11:21b). "Light" is a metaphor for the enduring good things that the righteous will receive as a reward at the appropriate time in life. The final line of stanza two, 11:21d, employs an adverbial phrase to stress how quickly the Lord can act to reverse the fortunes of the patient poor (ב[פת]ע פתאם), "in an instant, suddenly" cf. Isa 30:13; Sir 5:7).

Stanza three (11:22-24, 26) introduces the second Disputation Speech with the assurance that God's blessing is "the lot" (גרל) of the righteous person and *at the appropriate time* his hope will bear fruit" (ובעת תקותו תפרח, 11:22). The citations in 11:23 and 11:24 use the ancient debate formula "Do not say ...". As was the case in stanza one, the content of the speech of sinners centers on the present ("now") as the crucial time (cf. 11:19a-b):

Sir 11:23   "What shall I get for having done his will,[536]
              and what *now* will be left for me?"
              (ומה עתה יעזב לי)

11:24   "I am self-sufficient,
          what will harm me from *now* on?"[537]

The citations call into question God's ability to reward the righteous (cf. *1 En* 102:6-7) and assert that security comes from one's own resources and strength. In contrast to the sinner's view of the present, the doctrine of opposites requires that another time be kept in view, the time of recompense for wealthy sinners. Ben Sira calls attention to this time in his reply when he states that the Lord will repay the sinner "on the day of death" (11:26, Gk). The expanded instruction in stanza four ends on the identical note (11:28). If the wealthy sinner escapes judgment in life, then he is sure to experience a dishonorable death.

---

[536] The text is damaged in 11:23a. For the restoration and translation, see Penar, *Northwest Semitic Philology*, 37-38.

[537] The text of Sir 11:24 in ms A is broken. The Greek reads ἀπὸ τοῦ νῦν in both Sir 11:23b and 11:24b, suggesting that the Hebrew עתה is also present in 11:24b.

Sirach 15:11-16:23

This long discourse opens and closes with citations typical of the Disputation Speech (15:11-12; 16:17a):[538]

Sir 15:11a   Do not say, "From God is my transgression,"
      b   for what he hates, he does not do.
    12a   Lest you say, "He caused me to stumble,"
      b   for there is no necessity for men of violence.
    13a   Evil and abomination the Lord hates,
      b   and he will not let it happen to those who fear him.
    14a   God created humankind from the beginning,
      b   and he gave him into the hand of his inclination.
    15a   If you will, you can keep the commandments,
      b   and to act faithfully is to do his will.
    16a   Poured out before you are fire and water,
      b   on that which you choose stretch out your hands.
    17a   Before a person are life and death,
      b   that which he chooses will be given to him.
    18a   Sufficient is the wisdom of the Lord,
      b   he is strong in power and sees all.
    19a   The eyes of God see his works,
      b   and he knows all the doings of men.
    20a   He did not command a man to sin,
      b   and he did not cause men of deceit to dream.[539]

    16:1a   Do not desire the appearance of vain youths,
      b   and do not rejoice in the children of wickedness.
    2a   Even if they increase, do not rejoice in them,
      b   if there is no fear of the Lord with them.
    3a   Do not trust in their life,
      b   and not rely on their end,
      c   for better is one who does what is acceptable than a thousand,
      d   and one who dies childless than the one who has many
          children of wickedness.
    4a   From one who fears the Lord a city will become inhabited,

---

[538] Translation based on mss A, B. The passage contains a number of glosses and doublets (Skehan and Di Lella, *The Wisdom of Ben Sira*, 269-70). Sir 16:15-16 have long been regarded as secondary (Schechter and Taylor, *The Wisdom of Ben Sira*, xxxiii).

[539] There is a textual problem in Sir 15:20b. Di Lella proposes a plausible emendation of the Hebrew of ms A, but we agree with those commentators who accept the reading of ms A as the *lectio difficilior* (see Di Lella, *The Hebrew Text of Sirach*, 131-33). The use of חלם (*hif.*) with the meaning "cause to dream" occurs only one time in the Hebrew Bible (Jer 29:8). The bicolon in 15:20c-d is secondary.

b   and by a faithless clan it is laid in ruins.

5a   Many things like these my eye has seen,
b   and numerous things like these my ear has heard.
6a   Against the assembly of the wicked fire will burn,
b   and against a godless people wrath will be kindled.
7a   He did not forgive the primeval giants,
b   the rebels of old, because of their might.
8a   And he did not have pity with the neighbors of Lot,
b   with those behaving arrogantly, on account of their
       haughtiness.[540]
9a   And he did not have pity with the people banned to destruction,
b   who were driven out, on account of their iniquity;
10a   nor the six hundred thousand foot soldiers
b   who were taken away because of the arrogance of their heart.
11a   Even if there was one stiff-necked person,
b   it was a marvel if he remained unpunished;
c   for mercy and wrath are with him,
d   who forgives and pardons, but his wrath glows against the
       wicked.
12a   As great as his mercy, so is his punishment,
b   he will judge each person according to his deeds.
13a   He will not let the evildoer escape with stolen goods,
b   and he will not let the longing of the righteous go lacking
       forever.
14a   Everyone who does what is righteous has his reward,
b   and each person, according to his works, appears before him.

17a   Do not say, "From God, I am hidden;
b   and on high, who will remember me?
c   Among numerous people, I am not known;
d   and what am I among the whole (number) of spirits?
18a   Behold, the heavens, and the heaven of heavens,
b   and the abyss and the earth,
c   at his visitation they tremble.[541]
19a   Also, the roots of the mountains and the foundations of the earth,
b   shake exceedingly when he looks at them.
20a   Surely, he will not set his heart upon me;
b   and my ways, who will understand?

---

[540] For the rendering of Sir 16:6-8, see Penar, *Northwest Semitic Philology*, 45-47. Penar's translates לנסיכי קדם (16:17a), "primeval princes," and בגבורתם (16:17b), "in their boldness," and seems to understand the couplet as referring to the rulers of Sodom and Gomorrah (note the connection he makes to 16:8). Against this interpretation, each couplet in 16:6-10 refers to a separate story, and the Greek translator understood 16:7a as a reference to the giants ("περὶ τῶν ἀρχαίων γιγάντων").

[541] With Skehan, emend וכרגשו (ms A) to ירגזו (*The Wisdom of Ben Sira*, 270).

21a   If I have sinned, no eye will see me;
  b   and if I tell lies in total secrecy, who will know?
22a   Who will inform him of any righteous deed;
  b   and what hope is there that I be righteous (in my) duty?"[542]
23a   Those without sense conceive these things,
  b   and a foolish man will think this.

The first word in the citation at each end of the discourse is identical
(מאל, "From God," Sir 15:11a; 16:17a), suggesting that the reader look for
some relationship.   The material that intervenes between citations is instruction that pertains to the subject at issue in the disputes.   Viewed in these terms,
the overall literary pattern is chiastic:[543]

TABLE 7
THE TWO DISPUTATION SPEECHES IN SIRACH 15:11-16:23

Citation and Reply		
Do not say, "From God ..."	15:11a	16:17-22
with motive clause: *for ...*	11b	
with summary statement		16:23
Lest you say, ...	15:12a	
with motive clause: *for ...*	12b	
Instruction		
On human responsibility	15:13-20	
On the many vs one		16:1-14

---

[542] The expression at the end of Sir 16:22b (אצוק חוק, ms A) is unintelligible. If we
emend אצוק to אצדק (Schechter and Taylor, *The Wisdom of Ben Sira*, xxxiv) and take חוק
not as "death" (with Greek) but "duty" (cf. Sir 11:20a, "hold fast to your duty"), the gram-
matical awkwardness of the result is somewhat offset by the nice parallelism with 16:22a.
For the thought, see Sir 11:21.

[543] Thus the strophes of Sir 15:11-16:23 are more than "only loosely related" (Di Lella,
The Wisdom of Ben Sira, 271).

The unit begins abruptly with a pair of ancient debate formulas.[544] The citations represent the sinner's attempt to blame God for sinful deeds.[545] Ben Sira's replies focus on qualities of God that preclude any culpability on God's part.

The instruction in Sirach 15:13-20 is a fundamental assertion of human responsibility (cf. *1 En* 98:4-8). God created humankind and gave him "into the hand of his inclination" (ביד יצרו, 15:14b), leaving him free "to choose" (חפץ, 15:15a, 16b, 17b). One should choose to keep the commandments, but if one chooses wickedness then one can expect death (15:17a). God sees a person's choice and judges accordingly (15:18-19). In sum, God does not issue commands nor send dreams that lead to transgression (15:20).

In the second half of the discourse, Sirach 16:1-23, ben Sira begins with instruction. The instruction is presented in two stanzas. Sirach 16:1-4 introduces the subject of the many versus the one and establishes the principle of the importance of the one (one righteous child, 16:1-3; one wise citizen, 16:4). In the second stanza, Sirach 16:5-14, ben Sira takes up the subject of God's judgment upon the many and argues that corporate judgment in no way overlooks the deeds of one person. God rewards each individual according to his deeds.

Within the second stanza, Sirach 16:6-10 is especially important for the Disputation that will come later. In these verses, ben Sira employs a number of stories from Jewish tradition to serve as examples of the exactitude of God's corporate judgment. The list of those punished includes: Korah, Dathan, Abiram and company (16:6), the giants of old (16:7), the inhabitants of Sodom

---

[544] Cf. the similar pairings in Sir 5:3-4 (with motive clause) and Sir 11:23, 24 (without motive clause). In Sir 15:11-12, the two formulas are not identical (אל תאמר, 15:11a; פן תאמר, 15:12a).

[545] A specific sin may be at issue in the expression "from God is my transgression" (מאל פשעי/διὰ κύριον ἀπέστην, 15:11a). In 2 Chr 21:8, 10, the verb פשע (LXX ἀπέστη) refers to a political and military revolt (cf. Josephus, *Ant.* XX, 102). Because of the collocation with "men of violence" (15:12b), the possibility exists that ben Sira is referring to a military revolt (cf. Sir 10:8: "Dominion is transferred from one people to another because of the violence of the arrogant"). The verb "to stumble" (תקל, *hif.*/ἐπλάνησεν, 15:12a) would then denote military defeat. The tradition preserved in Dan 11:14 uses similar language to depict a Jewish revolt against Egypt: "and the men of violence among your own people ... but they shall stumble" (ובני פריצי עמך ... ונכשלו). Jonathan Goldstein describes the event in Dan 11:14 as "an abortive revolt under Ptolemy IV" (*1 Maccabees* [AB 41; Garden City, NY: Doubleday, 1976] 130). Perhaps ben Sira refers to an abortive revolt in 15:11-12. Finally, if the revolt in Dan 11:14 was conducted "to fulfill the vision," that in Sir 15:11-12 was based on the "dream" of those whom ben Sira labels "men of deceit" (15:20b; cf. 34:7: "For dreams have caused many to stumble [ἐπλάνησεν], and those who based their hopes on them have perished").

and Gomorrah (16:8), the native Canaanites (16:9) and the Israelites in the period of the wilderness wanderings (16:10). Ben Sira explicitly states the means of punishment with his first example only—the fire. But the stories are well-known, and he is probably inviting the reader to supply the other means— whether it be the flood, plagues or the avenging sword. The stories provide case studies in the precision of God's use of the elements of creation to punish the many.

Two observations are in order concerning this litany of God's judgment on the many. First, ben Sira does not use the stories of Sodom and Gomorrah (fire) and the giants (warfare/flood) as types of a final conflagration. Rather, these two stories take their place among others as example stories. This is a subtle indication that ben Sira's view of the judgment does not include a catastrophe of cosmic proportions.

Second, the statement that God "did not forgive the primeval giants" (לא נשא לנסיכי קדם, Sir 16:7a) is intriguing. In the Disputation context of Sirach 5:1-8, ben Sira quoted the sinner as presuming that God in his great mercy "will forgive" (סלח, 5:6b) his many sins. Although the verb in Sirach 5:6b is not reused in 16:7a, the two verbs are synonyms and appear together in the present instruction (16:11d). Along with the idea of presuming on forgiveness, there are a number of other parallels between the two contexts that suggest ben Sira is alluding to 5:6 in 16:7.[546] Ben Sira, then, once again offers instruction about the relationship of forgiveness and judgment, but in this instance the instruction is based on the example of the giants of old. The Hebrew Bible contains no story about petitions of forgiveness being offered for the giants. However, there is such a story in *1 Enoch*.[547] The rebel Watchers ask Enoch to write a petition "that they might have forgiveness" (*1 En* 13:4). This petition, which was subsequently rejected by God, concerned the Watchers and their sons, the giants (14:6-7; cf. 15:3). Ben Sira's appreciation for some Enochic lore (Sir 44:16; 49:14) includes the story of God's rejection of Enoch's petition of forgiveness for the giants (cf. Sir 17:32).[548]

---

[546] Among the parallels: "wrath goes forth" (Sir 16:6b; 5:7c), "mercy and anger are with him" (16:11c; 5:6c), "(as) great is his mercy" (16:12a; 5:6a).

[547] Probably also in 4QEnGiants[a], but the text is too fragmentary to reach a firm conclusion (Milik, *The Books of Enoch*, 298-317).

[548] In view of this fact, Skehan's exegetical note on Sir 16:7a is off the mark. He suggests that ben Sira used the expression "giants of old" (נסיכי פדם) rather than the exact biblical term (נפלים) in "conscious avoidance of the mythological overtones to the Genesis narrative so familiar from the Enoch literature and (later) Jubilees" (*The Wisdom of Ben Sira*, 270). Far from avoiding these overtones, ben Sira uses the myth about Enoch's petition for the Watchers and their halfbreed sons, and its rejection by God, as an example story for his contemporaries.

Ben Sira ends his recital of example stories on the thought that not one person is unjustly treated in the corporate sweep of God's judgment (Sir 16:11-14). It would be shocking to learn of even "one" (אחד, 16:11a) stiff-necked person who went unpunished in the wilderness experience of Israel. God judges "an individual" (איש, 16:12b; אדם, 16:14b) according to his deeds, whether the evil-doer (16:13a) or the just person (16:13b-14). Recompense may not be immediate, but it is certain. The "longing" (תאות, 16:13b)[549] of the righteous man will not go lacking forever. In the background is the notion of the appropriate time, an essential part of the doctrine of opposites.

On the basis of the preceding instruction, the citation in Sirach 16:17-22 stands condemned on its own merits. For this reason, ben Sira offers only a curt reply in 16:23. In the discussion of the citation below, the reasons for its untenability will be noted.

The initial bicolon (Sir 16:17a-b) expresses the confidence of the sinner that he is hidden from God and God will not remember him (cf. *1 En* 98:6-7). This confidence is based on a twofold application of the idea of the one and the many to the theme of judgment. First, the sinner imagines that he (the one) passes unnoticed among the vast number of people (the many) who live upon the earth (16:17c-d). Ben Sira thwarted this line of reasoning with the example stories (16:6-10) and conclusions (16:11-14) of the preceding instruction.

The second application of the idea of the one and the many to the judgment is found in Sirach 16:18-19. The language that creation "trembles" (רגז, cj.) and "shakes" (רעש) comes from descriptions of theophany.[550] It is imperative to keep in mind that this account of cosmic catastrophe is present *in the speech of a sinner.*[551] The sinner reasons that if God's appearance for judgment results in cosmic upheaval, then the elements of creation will not discriminate between the one and the many. All persons will be annihilated, no one will be singled out.

Once again, the example stories of the preceding instruction (16:6-10) have blocked this argument. God used the elements of creation in very precise ways to bring his judgment upon the many, and in doing so, not one person was left unpunished. Moreover, ben Sira, in his doctrine of opposites, teaches the fundamental truth that the creation continues to be used by God as a discriminating tool. In the Hymn to the Creator, Sirach 42:15-43:33, ben Sira pictures an earth that God "makes tremble" (חיל, *hif.*, 43:16a) and whose

---

[549] Skehan suggests the emendation תקות ("hope") on the basis of the Greek (*The Wisdom of Ben Sira*, 270). While plausible, it is not necessary.

[550] See especially Isa 13:13 and Joel 2:10, where the verbs are used in parallel.

[551] This point was urged by Baumgartner, "Die Literarischen Gattungen," 176.

mountains "shake" (נוף, *hif.*, 43:17a) when the destructive storms execute his judgment.[552] This is far from cosmic catastrophe. In 43:16-17, Ben Sira may even be intentionally avoiding the vocabulary he attributes to the sinner in 16:18-19.

The difference between the opponent and ben Sira on this issue can be illustrated through a consideration of the abyss. The sinner states that the abyss trembles with the rest of creation when God appears in final judgment (Sir 16:18b). In the Hymn to the Creator referred to above, ben Sira represents God as searching out the abyss (42:18) and bidding its creatures to carry out his will (43:23-26). Thus, God uses the abyss in precise ways as an instrument to punish the wicked.

In sum, ben Sira's instruction functions as a preemptive response to what the sinner says about the one and the many in relation to God's judgment. The sinner does not pass unnoticed among many people and the elements of creation can single him out for judgment within the mass of humanity.

In the remainder of the citation, Sirach 16:20-22, the sinner concludes that there is no one, including God, to observe his ways (16:20; cf. *1 En* 98:7), whether he sins (16:21) or whether he performs a righteous deed (16:22). He clearly prefers the present advantages of sinning, since he calls into question the "hope" of reward for doing right (cf. *1 En* 102:6-9). This thought was blocked by the instruction in 16:13b. In addition, the language and imagery attributed to the sinner in 16:21 echo the Disputation and instruction that began this discourse. The terms "sin/lie" (חטא/כזב, 16:21) were used in the climax to ben Sira's instruction on human responsibility ("he did not command a man *to sin*, nor did he cause *men of deceit* to dream," 15:20). The expression "no eye will see me" (16:21a) alludes to the same instructional passage ("*The eyes of God see* his work[s]", 15:19a). The reader cannot fail to appreciate the irony of a sinner who concludes he bears no responsibility for his deeds with the same vocabulary that ben Sira used earlier to teach that he does.

Because ben Sira's reply to the long citation in 16:17-22 was contained in the preceding pieces of instruction, he offers only a short response in which he discredits the cited party as senseless and foolish (16:23). It is interesting that a citation introduced with a verb of speech ("Do not say ..." 16:17) is here summarized with verbs of thought (בין, "conceive," 16:23a/חשב, "think," 16:23b). The reply treats the citation as imagined speech and, as such, the citation itself could have been introduced by a verb of thought. This is precisely what happens in the remaining passage to be considered.

---

[552] See Chap. 4, pp. 147-49.

Sirach 23:16-21

The examination of the Disputation Speech concludes with a brief consideration of its application to the adulterer. The passage displays the standard structure:

1) Introduction: Numerical proverb identifies   23:16-18a
                   the addressee
2) Citation: *says in his soul* (cf. *1 En* 98:7)   23:18b-eα
                   (λέγων ἐν τῇ ψυχῇ αὐτοῦ)
3) Reply   23:18eβ-20
4) Conclusion   23:21

The flexibility of the introduction is indicated by its appearance here in the form of a numerical proverb. The final and climactic number of the proverb, the third type of person who incurs wrath (23:16b), is the adulterous man to whom all bread is sweet (23:17) and who violates his marriage bed (23:18a).

The citation reproduces the thought process of a man who commits this sin:

Sir 23:18b   *says in his soul*: "Who sees me?
        c   Darkness surrounds me and the walls hide me;
      d/eα   no one sees me; why should I be afraid / of my sins?"[553]

The adulterer supposes that he is unseen because he is hidden when he commits his sinful act (cf. *1 En* 98:6; 104:7). The notion of hiddenness expressed here differs from that in Sirach 16:17a ("From God, I am hidden"). In Sirach 16:17-22, the sinner argued that he was hidden among the sheer number of people and by a creation that was incapable of isolating him for punishment. In Sirach 23:18c, the adulterer states that creation is itself designed (darkness) and can be made (walls) to hide him. The adulterer is enlisting the created elements as accomplices in his sinful act of adultery.

Although the basis for the sinner's argument that he is hidden varies in the two citations of Sirach 16:17-22 and 23:18b-eα, in both passages he concludes that he is free to sin with impunity since he goes unseen:

---

[553] We accept Skehan's suggestion that the Greek translator has mistakenly placed the whole of Sir 23:18e in the citation. If we end the speech with 23:18eα and emend the Greek slightly in 23:18eβ, the author's reply begins with a balanced couplet in 18eβ-19a (Skehan and Di Lella, *The Wisdom of Ben Sira*, 321).

Sir   16:21a   "If I sin, no eye will see me."
      23:18d-eα   "No one sees me; why should I be afraid of my sins?"

The author's reply in Sirach 23:18eβ-20 is based on the nature of God as it relates to this issue of seeing. God's eyes are unlike human eyes (23:18eβ-19a) and possess an illuminating power all their own, such that sunlight is superfluous (23:19b-c). God's eyes behold all the ways of men and penetrate into hidden corners (23:19d-e). Thus, the adulterer is wrong to suppose that darkness and walls hide his sinful act. The constitutive features of creation and man-made objects offer an illusory cover for sin. Not only does God see the sinful deed take place, but God knows it beforehand and long after it ceases to be (23:20). It follows that the adulterer should be afraid of his sins.

The concluding couplet in Sirach 23:21 is an expression of ben Sira's confidence that the adulterer will be recompensed in his lifetime. In a public forum, he will be punished (ἐκδικέω, *fut. pass.* 23:21a). At a time he does not suspect, he will be caught (πιάζω, *fut. pass.* 23:21b). God's judgment is not immediate, but operates according to its own timetable. The day will come when the adulterer recognizes that it was futile for him to think he could hide his deeds from God.

Summary

Ben Sira uses the ancient debate formula, "Do not say ..." to refute the misplaced security of the wealthy and powerful (5:1-3; 11:23-24), as well as other sinners who have various incorrect notions about their sin (5:4; 15:11-12; 16:17). The debate formulas are not isolated literary features, they occur in combination with larger Disputation Speeches (5:5-7) or are themselves integral parts to the structure of these Speeches (11:14-28; 15:11-16:23).

Incorrect notions about sin cited by ben Sira include the ideas that one may sin and escape punishment (5:4), presume on God's forgiveness (5:6; cf. 16:7), blame God (15:11-12), hide from God among the mass of people (16:17), hide from God when creation disintegrates at his visitation (16:18-19) and hide from God under cover of creation (23:18). Related to these mistaken views of sinners is the suggestion that the righteous will not be rewarded (16:22).

Ben Sira's replies appeal to the nature of God (slow to anger, possesses co-attributes of mercy and anger, has eyes that see everything, commands no one to sin, knows all things before and after they happen) and to the doctrine of opposites (the appropriate time of vengeance, the suddenness of judgment, the precision of the created instruments of wrath). Similarly, God's nature and the doctrine of opposites insure that the hope of the righteous will be fulfilled.

Example stories from Scripture and tradition are an important source for the instructional material that informs ben Sira's replies. He also claims that his replies and conclusions are validated by contemporary human experience. One is judged in this lifetime (the adulterer is caught and punished) or on the day of death.

THE WOE-ORACLE

The study of the judgment theme concludes with an analysis of how ben Sira uses the Woe-oracle. Janzen's distinction between the *hôy*-formula and the *hôy*-pericope will again prove helpful. In the case of Sirach, the pericope is the didactic poem in which the oracle is found. Janzen identified three characteristic features of the prophetic *hôy*-pericope: the self-reliant independence of the addressees, the Day of the Lord context, and the *Talionsstil* or reversal pattern of punishment. The extent to which these features are present in Sirach will be noted below.

Ben Sira's use of the *hôy*-formula has long been viewed as his counterpart to the *'ašrê*-formula.[554] While the two forms do not appear together in any of ben Sira's discourses,[555] the use of one implies its opposite number. Ben Sira extends the blessing to those who follow the way of Wisdom/Torah,[556] and, as will become apparent, issues Woes upon those who forsake this way for some other. The theological framework behind these opposing formulas is the doctrine of opposites. For ben Sira, the Creator has constituted humanity in terms of two opposing ways: "the Lord makes people unlike; in different paths he has them walk ... some he blesses ... others he curses ..." (Sir 33:11-12). Still, as ben Sira argued in the Disputation Speeches, each person is held responsible for the path he chooses to walk and will be recompensed accordingly. The Woe-oracle presupposes sinners are accountable before God and indicts them for disobedience.

---

[554] Baumgartner ("Die literarischen Gattungen," 188) suggests that the Woe-oracle assumes the place originally occupied by the curse (cf. Jer 17:5, 7 and Sir 28:13, 19) in relation to the blessing.

[555] As, for example, in Qoh 10:16-17; Luke 6:20-26.

[556] Sir 14:1-2, 20; 25:7-10; 26:1; 31:8; 34:17; 48:11; 50:28.

Sirach 2:12-14

Early in the book of Sirach, the reader meets a Woe-series, a literary phenomenon typical in the prophets:[557]

Sir	2:12a	Woe to cowardly hearts and drooping hands,
	b	to the sinner who walks on two paths!
	13a	Woe to the fainthearted, because he does not trust;
	b	for this reason, he will not be sheltered!
	14a	Woe to you who have utterly lost endurance!
	b	and what will you do when the Lord visits?

The Woe-oracles characterize the addressees as persons who have given up the disciplined pursuit of wisdom. This sketch can be supplemented from the broader context because ben Sira sets the characterization of the addressees in direct contrast to previous exhortations to his students. In the three couplets of Sirach 2:7-9, ben Sira exhorts "you who fear the Lord" to succeed where the others will be described as failing:

Exhortations to students		*Woe addressees*	
2:7a-b	wait ... do not turn aside	2:12b	walk two paths
2:8a	trust him	2:13a	do not trust
2:9a	hope for good things	2:14a	have utterly lost endurance

The two stanzas, Sirach 2:7-9 and 2:12-14, may therefore be treated together. The comments below focus on each of the contrasting characterizations, along with the punishment or threat associated with each.

First, the addressees turn aside from one path for another or walk two paths. The image of the two ways is a prominent wisdom theme. Ben Sira employs the Woe-oracle to indict those who have strayed from the true path of Wisdom (cf. *1 En* 100:9; 1QS 2:11-12); namely, those who have abandoned or compromised his wisdom instruction. The reference fits those who turn aside to a rival Jewish wisdom tradition; there is no indication in the text, for exam-

---

[557] Translation from the Greek. This Woe-string is part of a didactic poem (Sir 2:1-18) that deals with the theme of the "test" (πειρασμός, 2:1b), a theme familiar to us from our treatment of personified Wisdom's tests or trials in Chap. 2 (see esp. Sir 4:11-19, pp. 57-59 above). The disciplined person will pass the test and possess Wisdom. The undisciplined person will fail the test. The "test" is also referred to in the present context by the expressions "in time of disaster" (ἐν καιρῷ ἐπαγωγῆς, 2:2b), "in payment of humiliation" (ἐν ἀλλάγμασιν ταπεινώσεως, 2:4b, cf. 2:5b), and "in time of affliction" (ἐν καιρῷ θλίψεως, 2:11b).

ple, that the false path has reference to the Greek way of life.⁵⁵⁸ Consistent with the walking metaphor, ben Sira issues the threat that those who turn aside "will fall" (2:7b). The correspondence pattern lies in the two related metaphors, although the element of threat is not explicit in 2:12 (which lacks a punishment clause; cf. *1 En* 99:13).

Second, the addressees are characterized as lacking faith in time of testing. The corresponding punishment is that they "will not be sheltered" (σκεπασθήσεται, 2:13b). In contrast, in Sirach 14:27, those who pursue Wisdom until they find her, "take shelter/refuge" (σκεπασθήσεται/וחוסה) with her. This language alludes to the doctrine of opposites (cf. Sir 2:13; 14:27 and 34:19; 43:3). Shelter denotes protection from the created instruments of God's wrath. Those who remain faithful have such protection, therefore their reward is secure (Sir 2:8b).

The third characteristic of the addressees concerns the matter of hope and endurance. Those who fail under trial do not persevere in the hope of good things, namely, "lasting joy" and "mercy" (cf. *1 En* 104:4: "Take courage, and do not abandon your hope, for you will have great joy ..."). Example stories from the past illustrate the truth that God does not disappoint the hopes of those who fear him, he helps in time of trouble (2:10-11). Conversely, when ben Sira puts the rhetorical question to those who do not endure, "what will you do when the Lord visits?" (τί ποιήσετε ὅταν ἐπισκέπτηται κύριος),⁵⁵⁹ he implies that those who give up the hope for good things can expect to be visited with "evil" things. The verb "visits" refers to the activity of God in the doctrine of opposites.

Sirach 41:8-9

This passage is the only other example of the Woe-oracle in Sirach. The bicolon that characterizes the addressees begins with the second person plural pronoun ("Woe *to you*," 41:8). The verbs in 41:9 are also in the second per-

---

⁵⁵⁸ Di Lella identifies the two paths as "the traditional path of the ancestral faith and the new path of Hellenistic culture and life-style" (Skehan and Di Lella, *The Wisdom of Ben Sira*, 152).

⁵⁵⁹ The word "visits" translates Hebrew פקד, a technical term for the judgment of God. The judgment in view may be either non-eschatological or eschatological. The non-eschatological sense is present in Sir 35:21c-22a: "Nor will it [the prayer of the lowly] withdraw until the Most High *visits* (יפקוד/ἐπισκέψηται), judges justly and affirms the right." The eschatological sense appears in the citation of an opponent in Sir 16:18: the tripartite creation "trembles *at his visitation*" (בפקדו/ἐν τῇ ἐπισκοπῇ αὐτοῦ).

son plural and, therefore, the parallel couplets in 41:9a-b and 41:9c-d should be interpreted as the element of threat.[560]

Sir 41:8a   Woe to you, evil men,
      b   who forsake the Law of the Most High.
      9a   If you are fruitful, it is for injury;
      b   and if you procreate, it is for grief.
      c   If you stumble, it is for eternal joy;
      d   and if you die, it is for a curse.

The Woe-pericope within which this oracle stands is the stanza, 41:5-13. In this stanza, ben Sira labels his adversaries as "sinners" (רעים, 41:5a; cf. 2:12b), the "wicked" (ר[שע, 41:5b, cf. 41:7a) and the "evildoer" (ע[ל, 41:6a). The latter term is picked up in the formula in 41:8a. The addressees are further characterized in the oracle as those who "forsake" (עזב, 41:8b) the Law of the Most High. Ben Sira had earlier charged the opponents of wisdom with analogous expressions; they "drag off" the Law (משך, Sir 32:17b) after their own needs and "hate" the Law (שנא, 33:2a). Likewise, the verb "forsake" refers to the apostasy of fellow Jews, and the Torah which they have forsaken is the Torah as interpreted by ben Sira.[561] The element of threat begins in Sirach 41:9a-b with a reference to children. The children of the adversaries were the focus in 41:5-7. The children were depicted as "reprobate descendants" (נין נמאס, 41:5a) and "foolish offspring" (ונכד אויל, 41:5b). They endure "reproach" (חרפה, 41:6b) and "disgrace" (בוז, 41:7b) on account of their evil fathers. The latter two terms belong to the technical vocabulary for the results of judgment, along with "shame" (בשת).[562] In ben Sira's doctrine of opposites, these terms represent phenomena created for sinners (Sir 5:14c-d; cf. *1 En* 97:6; 98:3, 10).

---

[560] Our translation is based on ms M, with lacunae restored from ms B and Bm (Yadin, *The Ben Sira Scroll*, 41). Penar recognized that 41:9 is part of the oracle, but his suggestion that אסון ("Misfortune") and אנחה ("Sighing") "seem to refer here to Sheol," thus the capital letters, should not be adopted (*Northwest Semitic Philology*, 69).

[561] The verb "forsake" is used in third Isaiah for a rival Jewish group that interprets cultic requirements differently from the author (Isa 58:2; 65:11; see Hanson, *The Dawn of Apocalyptic*, 106-07, 154). The term is also used in this sense in the Qumrân literature; fellow Jews are described as forsaking God, the covenant of God, the commandments of God, the wisdom/truth of God (CD 1:3; 3:11; 8:19; 1QH 9:18; 1QpHab 8:1). In some texts (Dan 11:30; Jub 23:16; 1 Macc 1:15, 52) the expression "forsaking the covenant" is a description of the hellenizers (Nickelsburg, *Resurrection*, 20, n. 53).

[562] Another term in this technical vocabulary is "contempt" (דראון, Isa 66:24; Dan 12:2).

In the conditional clauses of Sirach 41:9a-b, ben Sira returns to the children to illustrate how good things can turn out evil for the wicked (cf. Sir 39:27). Children, who should be the strength and joy of their fathers, instead bring "injury" (אסון, [ms Bm] 41:9a)[563] and "grief" (אנחה, 41:9b). The threat of "injury" or physical harm recalls the punishment clause in the Woe-oracle of Sirach 2:13 (the addressees "will have no shelter"). In 41:9a, the created element that carries out the threat is the children! The addressees are hurt as a consequence of the actions of their own children.

If good things can turn out evil for the wicked, then it follows that evil things can turn out good for the righteous. This is the point of Sirach 41:9c-d. On the one hand, when the wicked "stumble" (כשל, 41:9c) or experience judgment in their lifetime, the righteous have lasting joy. The language of stumbling recalls the threat of the "fall" in the broader context of the earlier Woe-chain (Sir 2:7b). On the other hand, should evildoers escape judgment in their lifetime, they will certainly "die" (מות, 41:9d) and become a curse, that is, experience judgment through a dishonorable death (cf. Sir 11:28).

Summary

In ben Sira's Woe-oracles, the addressees are characterized with typical rhetoric as "sinners" and "evil men." Their sin is defined as leaving the true path of wisdom and forsaking the Torah, related concepts in ben Sira's thought (cf. Sir 15:1). The punishment clauses and threats in 2:12-14 and 41:8-9 do not employ the Day of the Lord context and the *Talionsstil* that Janzen identified as standard features in the prophets. The Day of the Lord context was reserved for ben Sira's prayer for judgment on oppressive Gentile rulers. In the Woe-oracles, the addressees are Jews who follow a different wisdom tradition, and the threat of punishment is the "evils" that come from created instruments of wrath (no shelter) or from the good things that God turns to evil (children). The correspondence pattern between sin and judgment resembles that of reversal, but only because reversal is essential to the doctrine of opposites.

COMPARATIVE ANALYSIS OF THE
JUDGMENT THEME IN *1 ENOCH* AND SIRACH

The groundwork has been laid for a discussion of the similarities and differences in the ways *1 Enoch* and Sirach express and conceptualize the theme

---

[563] Ben Sira teaches his students how to avoid "injury" or "harm" (Sir 31:22d; 38:18a).

of judgment. Literary structures and motifs common in the Hebrew Bible have been utilized: the Divine Warrior Hymn, the Disputation Speech and the Woe-oracle. The authors have shown a great deal of literary creativity in how they write about the judgment. In each book, the older forms and motifs are adapted to fit a peculiar concept of the operations of God's judgment.

The Divine Warrior and Eschatological Judgment

The authors of *1 Enoch* offer a full complement of Divine Warrior motifs in passages spread throughout the corpus. Not a single traditional Hymnic element is missing. However, in the opening description of the theophany, the presence and reaction of the Watchers is substituted for that of humankind (*1 En* 1:5). The Watchers fear and quake, a response typical of sinful humanity. They also hide and sing, ironic references to their imprisonment and final destruction. Of course, the imprisonment itself was already an act of judgment that coincided with the war of destruction among the giants and the flood (*1 En* 10:1-15). The story of the flood supplies a typology for the final judgment in *1 Enoch* 10:16-11:2 and 91:5-9 (cf. 81:8).

Ben Sira's use of Divine Warrior motifs in connection with "the end" is limited to two adjoining passages. In contrast to the authors of *1 Enoch*, ben Sira omitted three typical features of the Warrior Hymn: the descent of the Warrior, cosmic upheaval and cosmic renewal. It is significant that the Divine Warrior does not "come down" and that there is no dissolution and revitalization of creation. The doctrine of opposites precludes the necessity for these motifs which were so prominent in *1 Enoch*. Moreover, ben Sira does not use the story of the flood as a type of eschatological judgment. Rather, the tradition of God's judgment on the giants (Sir 16:7) takes its place as one example story among others (16:6-10).

All of this suggests fundamentally different views of eschatology in *1 Enoch* and Sirach. Indeed, in the context of a Disputation Speech, ben Sira puts the language and imagery found in Enochic Warrior contexts into the citation of a *contemporary opponent*:

TABLE 8
VOCABULARY OF COSMIC UPHEAVEL
IN SIRACH 16:18-19 AND ENOCHIC THEOPHANIES

	Sirach	*1 Enoch*
heavens (and all the luminaries)	16:18a	102:2a
heaven of heavens	18a	1:4c
abyss	18b	(cf. 101:4-9)
earth (all the ends of, all)	18b	1:5c, 7a; 102:2b
visitation	18c	25:3
tremble	18c	102:2b
roots of the mountains	16:19a	(cf. 1:6a; 91:8)
foundations of the earth	19a	----
shake	19b	1:5c, 6a; 102:2

The opponent argues that the disintegration of the cosmos in a final theophany (the Enochic eschatology) cannot single him out for judgment. This argument may illustrate that students who have been instructed elsewhere on eschatology have brought their objections to ben Sira. Ben Sira has contact with students who have been taught the catastrophic consequences of final judgment and who have reasoned that it is inconsistent with judgment on the individual. Ben Sira's response, given in his preceding instruction, is to call the catastrophic notion itself into question. He teaches in his doctrine of opposites that God judges through a precise use of creation's elements, not through a cosmic upheaval in the end-time.

Ben Sira's own version of eschatology does retain the combat motif from the Warrior Hymn and, in this respect, a point of similarity exists with *1 Enoch*. In both books, salvation and destruction take place in the end-time by means of a graphically depicted battle of Holy War (*1 En* 100:1-3; Sir 35:22d-23; 36:12). However, in *1 Enoch*, this battle is a precursor to the descent of the Warrior and his angels (100:4), who decide its outcome. For ben Sira, the battle itself will be decisive because God will employ the nations against one another in mutual destruction.

In both *1 Enoch* and Sirach, the vocabulary of salvation (*1 En* 1:1; 5:6f; 99:10; Sir 35:25b; 36:1) and destruction (*1 En* 1:9; 5:5b; 10:16; 91:8; 99:9; Sir 36:11b) expresses the result of the battle. There is some difference, however, in the recipients of salvation and destruction. In *1 Enoch*, the Warrior saves an oppressed group within Israel and destroys this group's Israelite adversaries along with the wicked among the nations. In Sirach, the nation as a whole is saved and the Gentile oppressors are destroyed. In spite of this difference (and there are antecedents in the Warrior Hymn to either scenario), both ben Sira and the Enochic authors envision Gentiles among the saved; the motif of universal kingship is held in common (*1 En* 10:21; 91:9; 100:6; Sir 36:5, 22c-d).

Yet another difference lies in the conceptualization of salvation and destruction. The ideas have a cosmic and mythic dimension in *1 Enoch*. The saved inherit a renewed earth and live long, peaceful lives. The defeated are gathered for judgment and confined to an accursed valley forever. In Sirach, those saved and those destroyed experience deliverance and defeat solely on the historical level. References to salvation and destruction in Sirach also describe the recompense an individual receives within his lifetime (Sir 2:11; 5:7c-d), over against the nation's end-time. In this case, and only in this case, the elements of creation are involved in delivering recompense. In *1 Enoch*, the fate of the individual righteous or sinful person is inseparably tied to the cosmic and mythic events of the end-time.

Disputations on the Judgment

The Disputation Speech is a form that the author of the Epistle of Enoch and ben Sira use to engage adversaries who question the reality of God's judgment. For the author of the Epistle, it is always eschatological judgment that is at issue. In contrast, ben Sira views eschatological judgment only in terms of Gentile oppressors and he employs no Disputation Speeches on this topic. For ben Sira, the Disputation Speeches revolve around the issue of the validity of judgment within the parameters of individual human existence or at the time of death.

The citations of the opponents in *1 Enoch* and Sirach, introduced by the debate formula ("Do not say ...") are similar in content. In both traditions, adversaries are brought forward to state a number of common erroneous ideas:

	1 Enoch	Sirach
1. The righteous life is not rewarded	What have they gained from their deeds? ... What advantage do they have over us? (103:6c, 7b)	Who will inform him of any righteous deed? What hope is there that I be righteous in my duty? (16:22; cf. 11:23)

2.	Sinners escape judgment in their lifetime	Blessed are the sinners ... judgment was not executed on them in their life (103:6)	I have sinned, yet, did anything happen to me? (5:4)
3.	No one sees or knows their sins	They do not know nor are [my] unrighteous deeds seen in heaven (98:7; cf. 104:7)	If I have sinned, no eye will see me If I tell lies ... who will know? (16:21; cf. 23:18)
4.	Wealth enables one to do whatever one desires	We have become very wealthy ... And all that we wish let us do (97:8-9)	Do not rely on your wealth; do not say: There is power in my hand Do not rely on your strength; to walk after the desires of your soul ... (5:1-3; cf. 11:19)

The replies that the author of the Epistle and ben Sira offer to this challenge are derived from radically different sources. The author of the Epistle uses the vision traditions of Enoch's cosmic journeys to answer every disputant. He agrees with the charge that *in this lifetime* the righteous receive no reward and sinners escape punishment. He counters these facts with what he knows about the separate existence of the righteous and wicked in Sheol, the promised resurrection, and the preparedness of the cosmos for future judgment.

Ben Sira too is dependent on source material when answering the citations of adversaries. Example stories from scripture, even esoteric tradition about the giants (Sir 16:7), support what he has also observed for himself, namely, that God sees and knows everything and uses the elements of creation in precise ways to judge every person according to his deeds. In contrast to the author of the Epistle, ben Sira does not agree that the righteous have no reward and sinners escape judgment within their lifetimes. The appropriate time will always come—no exceptions—when wealthy, powerful and adulterous sinners get what they deserve, and, likewise, the faithful righteous receive their reward.

The contrast stated above can be illustrated by a shared vocabulary that has radically different nuances. For example, in the Disputation Speeches, sinners are warned that they will be recompensed "quickly/suddenly:"

1 En 97:10   For your wealth will not remain,
(cf. 98:16)   but will *quickly* ($\tau\alpha\chi\grave{v}$) ascend from you.

Sir 5:7c-d   For *suddenly* (פתאום/$\dot{\varepsilon}\xi\dot{\alpha}\pi\iota\nu\alpha$) his wrath comes forth,
                   and in the time of vengeance you will be snatched away.

Sir 11:21c-d   For it is easy in the eyes of the Lord
                   suddenly, in a moment (ב[פת]ע פתאם/$\delta\iota\grave{\alpha}\ \tau\acute{\alpha}\chi o\nu\varsigma\ \dot{\varepsilon}\xi\dot{\alpha}\pi\iota\nu\alpha$),
                   to make a poor man rich.

With this adverb, the author of the Epistle means that cosmic catastrophe and final, universal judgment are imminent; in this sense, the term is also used frequently in Woe-oracles (*1 En* 94:6c, 7d; 95:6b; cf. 96:1b). Ben Sira employs the word against the background of creation's opposites ("poverty and wealth is from the Lord," Sir 11:14b). The Creator will issue a command at the appropriate time (note the parallelism in Sir 5:7c-d) to distribute these opposites as each person deserves.

Another term common to the Disputation contexts in both books is "light" with reference to the righteous. In *1 Enoch* 102:8, sinners mock the hope of the righteous and claim "they will not see the light" (cf. 96:3). In the Epistle, this word, along with the verb "shine" (104:2) is a metaphor for resurrection (*1 En* 104:2). Because the righteous will not see the light, sinners plot to continue their life of sin (102:9). In Sirach 11:21a-b, ben Sira exhorts the righteous, who are tempted to marvel at wealthy evil-doers, to "trust in the Lord and wait for his light." In ben Sira's thought, light is a metaphor for the good things of life that the righteous will receive at the appropriate time (cf. 11:22a-b).

The authorial viewpoints expressed in the Disputation Speeches in *1 Enoch* and Sirach should be construed as opposite formulations to the same types of arguments. The same faulty reasoning about God's judgment gets two different answers. The only shared views in the respective replies are that human beings are responsible for their deeds (*1 En* 98:4-5; Sir 15:13-20), will be recompensed according to them (cf. *1 En* 100:7c; Sir 16:12b), and God sees (or in the case of *1 Enoch*, the angels see and record) all human deeds (*1 En* 98:6-8; Sir 15:19; 23:19). From these common traditions, the two books diverge. In *1 Enoch*, God's justice is dispensed in a post-mortem judgment and is universal and cosmic in scope; in Sirach, judgment is given within an individual's lifetime or at death and involves the precise use of selected opposites in the creation.

The Application of the Woe-oracle

The Woe-oracle, like motifs from the Warrior Hymn, is more prevalent in *1 Enoch* than in Sirach. The seven Woe-chains in the Epistle of Enoch begin with a concentration against the wealthy and powerful (series 1-4) and shift to false teachers and their practices (series 5-7). Sirach offers no examples of Woe-oracles against the wealthy and powerful.[564] The Woe-string in Sirach 2:12-14 is directed at those who fail the test and compromise the way of wisdom. The single Woe-oracle in Sirach 41:8 expresses the same thought with reference to the Torah. Thus, the Woe-oracles in Sirach may be compared to the Enochic Woe-series 5-7.

The targets of the Oracles in both traditions are often addressed in the second person ("Woe to you ..."), suggesting some degree of personal contact with the adversaries. Beyond this, the characterizations of the addressees in the Woe-formulas and Woe-pericopes are remarkably similar. The following table juxtaposes the terms employed for the targets of the Woe-oracles:[565]

TABLE 9
VOCABULARY CHARACTERIZING THE ADDRESSEES
IN THE WOE CONTEXTS OF *1 ENOCH* AND SIRACH

	1 Enoch		Sirach
		reprobate	41:5a
fools	98:9	foolish[a]	41:5b
stiff-necked	98:11		
hard of heart[b]	98:11;	cowardly hearts	2:12a
	100:8a	fainthearted	2:13a

[a]The adjective is אויל. For the synonym נבל in a Woe-oracle, see Ezek 13:3.

[b]For ben Sira's portrayal of the hard heart versus the wise heart in 3:26-29, see above, Chap. 2, pp. 74, 77-78.

---

[564] We return to this point in the Conclusion.

[565] Some of the terms were mentioned in Chap. 2 (p. 95) as stereotypical rhetoric used of rival sages.

TABLE 9—*Continued*

	1 Enoch		Sirach
spread/devise evil	99:11; 100:8b	evil men	41:8a, 6a
practice lawlessness^c unrighteous	99:15 100:7	wicked	41:5b, 7a
sinners	100:9	'sinner(s)	2:12b
love deeds of iniquity	98:12		41:5a
lay foundations of sin	99:12		
change/pervert/reject (the Torah)	99:2,14	forsake the Torah	41:8b
lead astray/strayed	98:15; 100:9	turn aside/walk two paths	2:7b/ 2:12b

^cIn the LXX, the Greek terms "lawless" (ἀνομία) and "unrighteous"
(ἀδικία) can translate the Hebrew "wicked" (רשע[ה]), among other
possibilities.

Clearly both authors use traditional rhetoric for their adversaries.
However, the old rhetoric takes on a special cast. Ben Sira and the author of
the Epistle apply the stereotypical language to persons who do not interpret
Torah and practice wisdom as they do. This is intra-Jewish polemic; and
raises the issue of whether the two traditions are rivals. The possibility is
enhanced by a fact stated above, namely, the author of the Epistle of Enoch
and ben Sira give opposite answers to those who have no regard at all for the
reality of God's judgment.

As might be expected, therefore, the threat of punishment in the Woe-
oracle is differently conceived. In the Epistle of Enoch, Woe-strings 5-7 use
the *Talionsstil*, and conceptual and stylistic patterns of correspondence. These
patterns often only become fully intelligible through linkage to a Divine Warrior passage in the extended context. The threat of punishment is always
related to the eschatological judgment. For his part, ben Sira uses the doctrine
of opposites as a threat of punishment. To his mind, this threat is no less
severe than that of universal, catastrophic judgment. Ben Sira uses the technical terms often associated with the latter (reproach, disgrace, curse; 41:6b, 7b,
9d). These opposites will be experienced in the lifetime of the wicked person
or at the time of his death.

In sum, the authors of *1 Enoch* and ben Sira may describe the activity of the Divine Warrior, dispute contrary views of the judgment, and pronounce Woes on anyone who leaves the path of wisdom, but they do so in peculiar ways and with different ideas of the judgment in mind. The common literary forms are adapted to fit their respective concepts. Finally, the authors demonstrate a critical awareness of the conception of judgment present in the other tradition. Ben Sira dismisses the notion that eschatological judgment is accompanied by cosmic catastrophe. The author of the Epistle of Enoch disagrees with the idea that judgment is certain in this lifetime or at the moment of death. Such critical awareness lends further support to the suggestion that one tradition regards the other among its rivals.

CONCLUSION

Our study began with the suggestion that if the labels "apocalyptic" and "wisdom" literature were set aside for *1 Enoch* and Sirach, a wealth of comparative material might emerge from the two books. This was indeed the case. As a result, *1 Enoch* and Sirach have been brought much closer together on the literary and conceptual spectrum.

The same major themes—revelation, creation and judgment—are expressed with similar literary forms. Elements of the prophetic commissioning form are applied to the two revealer figures, Enoch and personified Wisdom.[566] Hymns of Praise to the Creator are utilized in both books. Divine Warrior motifs, Disputation Speeches and Woe-oracles are adapted to expound the judgment. Even when the literary forms are different, they can serve similar functions. For example, while the authors of *1 Enoch* use the device of a blessing-revelation Testament and ben Sira the motifs of the Love Story, the intention in both cases is to present revelation in the framework of wisdom brought from heaven by a revealer figure.

In addition to common themes and forms, a few common traditions emerge from both books. These traditions include a composite picture of the Tree of Wisdom and, from the side of ben Sira, allusions to extra-biblical stories about Enoch, the accountability of angels and the judgment of the giants. There are many other general similarities but it would not be feasible to suggest a specific common tradition behind each one. In some instances, the authors may be independently demonstrating similar perspectives. For example, in both books the creation is prepared for judgment and every aspect of its tripartite structure is designed to teach the importance of obeying God.

The common themes, literary forms, oral traditions and broad perspectives are understandable against the background of common times. The

---

[566] The wisdom writers and teachers regard themselves as heirs of the prophets, a fact that also explains the use of prophetic forms in the two books (Hengel, *Judaism and Hellenism*, 1.134-36).

249

authors are contemporary. Their interests, writing style and patterns of thought are given, at least in part, from their environment and concrete social setting. Much of the comparative material in *1 Enoch* and Sirach has been cut from the same cloth.

Of course, the differences are real and profound. The two traditions go their separate ways on the common ground summarized above. In *1 Enoch*, the content of the extended reaches of the cosmos is revealed by Enoch. Ben Sira shows no interest in speculative creation material; in fact, he warns against it. The divergent concepts of the judgment are directly related to how each author views the creation. For ben Sira, the doctrine of created opposites guarantees that temporal judgment will take place at the appointed time. For the authors of *1 Enoch*, the created places of eschatological significance insure that God will visit the earth in a catastrophic way.

Such differences are the stuff of conflict. In the comparative sections of Parts I-III, the evidence for polemics was stated. It is not conclusive, but it is enough to make a case that each tradition views the other among its rivals. Much of the polemic that occurs, including the charge of idolatry, is standard rhetoric for opposing teachers and traditions. However, ben Sira uses specific vocabulary that indicates his rivals teach esoteric wisdom. His vocabulary brings Enochic tradition to mind. Ben Sira warns his students not to study "things too marvelous," "secret things," "what is beyond you" and "what is too great for you" (Sir 3:21-23). He criticizes the parabolic interpretations of "dream-visions" (Sir 34[31]:1-8). This is the language that the authors of *1 Enoch* use to characterize their wisdom ("beyond their thought," *1 En* 82:2; "great wisdom," 32:3; "dreams ... and visions," 13:8; "mystery," 103:2a; 104:10a, 12a). Moreover, the author of the Epistle of Enoch is aware of opponents who claim his wisdom is "evil" (94:5)—the very charge ben Sira leveled against esoteric wisdom (Sir 3:21b, 24b, 28c).

At the very least, these correspondences assume the openness and accessibility of wisdom traditions. Students must have moved freely among wisdom teachers. Ben Sira can warn his students that a matter too great "has been shown you" (Sir 3:23b). As a former student, he himself sought out the instruction of wisdom teachers (Sir 33:16-17; 51:13) and advises his students to do the same (6:34-36; 51:23). Similarly, the authors of *1 Enoch* continually expand on Enoch's commission and fulfillment scenes to re-present him as carrying out the command to "make known/show/teach/write/testify/ reveal/tell." In reality, it was the authors and bearers of Enochic wisdom who were involved in this activity.

The students who moved among the teachers of the period inevitably heard both esoteric and exoteric wisdom material. It is striking, for example that ben Sira must enter a dispute with students who have learned elsewhere, and in his view incorrectly, about the role of creation in the judgment (Sir 16:18-19). Of course, the esoteric, speculative wisdom of Enoch claims to be parabolic interpretations of scripture (*1 En* 1:2a, 3b). This is also how ben Sira describes his own wisdom activity (Sir 3:29; 39:3). Authors in both traditions get behind scripture to bring out a hidden meaning or mystery.

How then may one describe the product of this prophetic, sapiential, interpretive, mystical activity? Recently, it has become commonplace to characterize wisdom in "apocalyptic" texts as mantic wisdom.[567] VanderKam finds the designation fitting for Enochic wisdom because of the divinatory associations of the Mesopotamian prototype for Enoch, king Enmeduranki. He recognizes that the techniques taught by Enmeduranki (observing oil on water, use of a liver tablet, use of a cedar-rod) and the kinds of techniques found in Mesopotamian omen literature, are not present in Jewish apocalyptic literature. For example, these divinatory techniques are not practiced or taught by Enoch in *1 Enoch*; in fact, the methods are attributed to the fallen angels and their validity is denied (*1 En* 7:1; 8:3; 9:8; 16:3). Still, on a general level, VanderKam sees an influence of omen literature on Jewish apocalyptic literature, and *1 Enoch* in particular. In both traditions, God communicates through opaque signs that must be interpreted by the seer. The signs are often proto-scientific in nature (astronomical) and their interpretations predictive.[568]

The associations drawn by VanderKam are plausible, but our study raises a number of questions about the appropriateness of labeling Enochic wisdom "mantic." The basic conceptual pattern of wisdom present in *1 Enoch* appears also in Sirach. Moreover, on the level of the interpretive enterprise, the task is the same in both books—to find hidden meanings in scripture. Does it follow that ben Sira's wisdom should also be described as "mantic?" If the Enochic authors and ben Sira have more in common with one another than the former does with Mesopotamian concepts and literature, then why use the term "mantic"? Is not a qualifier needed for "wisdom" that applies equally well to both *1 Enoch* and Sirach? The adjective "revealed" wisdom seems the better choice.

A further distinction could be drawn between revealed esoteric wisdom and revealed exoteric wisdom; but even this would not be a hard and fast dis-

---

[567] H. P. Müller argued that the practices of the diviner in Mesopotamia provide the origins of apocalyptic literature ("Mantische Weisheit und Apokalyptik," *Congress Volume, Uppsala 1971* [VTSup 22; Leiden: Brill, 1972] 268-93). J. J. Collins has Müller's work in mind when he writes: "Both *1 Enoch* and Daniel have been aptly described as 'mantic wisdom'" ("The Sage in the Apocalyptic and Pseudepigraphic Literature," *The Sage in Israel and the Ancient Near East* [ed. Gammie and Perdue; Winona Lake: Eisenbrauns, 1990] 351).

[568] VanderKam, *Enoch and the Growth*, 62, 69-71.

tinction. Ben Sira not only appreciates some Enochic lore, he attributes significance to a knowledge of creation's hidden parts (personified Wisdom tours the cosmos) and to eschatological mysteries (he reinterprets the Isaianic end-time).[569] The Enochic authors appeal to exoteric wisdom when they draw lessons from observable reality: the works of God in heaven, earth and sea (*1 En* 2:1-5:4; 101:1-9).

Given the necessary caveats, however, the esoteric/exoteric distinction is helpful. Enoch reveals speculative creation material, personified Wisdom does not.

Another approach to a possible relationship between the authors of *1 Enoch* and ben Sira can be gained through their respective portrayals of the rich and poor. What sociological picture or pictures of the rich and poor emerge from the two books? The author of the Epistle of Enoch uses three prophetic forms against the wealthy: Divine Warrior motifs (95:3; 96:2), the Disputation Speech (97:8-10; 102:9; 103:6) and the Woe-oracle (94:6-8; 96:4-8). Ben Sira uses only the Disputation Speech. What should one make of the lack of a Woe-chain against the wealthy in Sirach?

Two preliminary observations help to put this matter in perspective. First, the Woe-oracle is relatively rare in Sirach. Therefore, its absence with reference to the rich may have no significance whatsoever. Second, ben Sira, through the Disputation Speech, does engage and warn the rich who have become self-reliant and presumptuous (Sir 5:1-8; 11:18-19, 23-24). Ben Sira also writes about wealth gained through deceitful means and the temptation to exploit the poor (cf. Sir 13:3-7). While he recognizes that this happens in society, he does not appear to condemn it categorically.

In contrast, the Enochic Woe-strings 1-4 do this very thing. The author of the Epistle uses this prophetic form to indict the wealthy and mighty elite and consign them to eternal punishment because they persecute the righteous poor.

Tcherikover summarized these two different perspectives on the wealthy:[570]

> Ben Sira speaks of the negative attitude—an attitude of contempt and mock-ery—of the rich to the humble; Enoch speaks of persecution. Ben Sira counsels the humble man not to seek the society of the rich man; but Enoch advocates actual warfare. Ben Sira is still ready to believe that there is wealth that is free from crime; but in Enoch's eyes the wealthy and the

---

[569] Cf. M. Bockmuehl, *Revelation and Mystery in Ancient Judaism and Pauline Christianity* (WUNT 2.36; Mohr/Siebeck: Tübingen, 1990) 67.

[570] Tcherikover, *Hellenistic Civilization and the Jews*, 259.

criminal are identical. Ben Sira is apprehensive lest wealth lead the individual to religious transgression; whereas Enoch regards the rich as heathens
who are fated to be destroyed by the sword. Ben Sira seeks ways of compromise; while Enoch only perceives the antagonisms.

Largely on the basis of his perception of the two contrasting outlooks on
the rich, Tcherikover argued that the Epistle of Enoch is a Pharisaic document
that reflects a class struggle between the Pharisees and the wealthy and powerful Sadducees. The struggle took place sometime late in the reign of John
Hyrcanus (134-04 BCE) or during the rule of Alexander Janneus (103-76
BCE). Tcherikover did acknowledge that the social position of the Sadducees
resembles the Tobiads of a previous century or more[571] (the wealthy type
whom ben Sira addresses), but in his view the class hatred present in the
Epistle of Enoch and missing in Sirach excludes the possibility that representatives of the Tobiad-type are behind the Enochic Woe-oracles.

In the Introduction to this study, it was pointed out that some scholars
place the Epistle of Enoch before 167 BCE.[572] If this is the case, the wealthy
sinners cannot represent a group in Hasmonean times. If the Epistle is contemporary with Sirach, how may one account for the different outlooks toward
the wealthy in the two texts?

Nickelsburg suggested two important factors to bear in mind.[573] First, the
different *Sitz im Leben* of Sirach and the Epistle of Enoch must be given sufficient consideration. Ben Sira is instructing rich youth, the author of the
Epistle is not. The author of the Epistle is indicting the wealthy who persecute
his community, ben Sira is not. Second, one must not immediately assume
that the Epistle describes objective facts; rather, allowance must be made for
the subjective experiences and perceptions of the author. For Nickelsburg, a
proper recognition of these two factors leaves the valid question: "Could *the
poor* of ben Sira's time ... have written *1 Enoch* 92-105?"[574]

There is one additional, relevant factor that follows from our study of the
judgment theme. Ben Sira's criticism of the wealthy appears to be less severe
than that in *1 Enoch* because, given his theology, he cannot threaten rich sinners with eternal punishment. Even if ben Sira had used the Woe-oracle

---

[571] Ibid., 261.

[572] See above, p. 7, n. 15.

[573] "Social Aspects of Palestinian Jewish Apocalypticism," *Apocalypticism in the
Mediterranean World and the Near East* (ed. D. Hellholm; Tübingen: Mohr/Siebeck, 1983)
651.

[574] Ibid. Cf. idem, *Jewish Literature*, 149 ("Whether a group of the poor living in ben
Sira's time could have perceived the actions of the wealthy as 'Enoch' does and might have
cursed the rich among themselves as he does is a question that we cannot answer on the

against the wealthy, the threat of punishment would have related to his doctrine of opposites (as it does in the extant oracles). Indeed, this is precisely the threat that appears in his Disputations against the self-reliant and presumptuous wealthy. As far as ben Sira is concerned, this is as serious a threat as he can muster. If the author of the Epistle uses a Woe-chain to threaten the rich that they "will perish quickly in judgment" (*1 En* 94:7d), then ben Sira warns the wealthy that "suddenly his wrath flames forth, at the time of vengeance you will be snatched away." The latter is an allusion to the Sodom and Gomorrah story, an example of the precise use of created instruments of wrath (cf. Sir 16:8). Since both authors threaten rich sinners with as much ammunition as they have at their disposal, given their theological arsenal, surely they view these sinners in much the same terms.

It is true that the Epistle of Enoch says nothing about the *pious* wealthy (cf. Sir 13:24, "wealth is good if it be without sin"), but one must be cautious about making too much of this. From the perspective of the Enochic community, a community that believes it is being persecuted by wealthy sinners, there is no interest or purpose in identifying the pious wealthy.

In sum, the sin of the wealthy and powerful in Enochic Woe-strings 1-4 and in ben Sira's Disputation Speeches conforms to what Tcherikover attributed to the hellenistic age as a whole ("lust for profit and pursuit of power").[575] There is no basis in the respective books for making a distinction between wealthy Tobiad-types and wealthy Sadducees. Rather, when one takes account of the unique authorial viewpoints and the disparate concepts of judgment present in each book, the hypothesis becomes feasible that the authors are referring to the same wealthy class at about the same time in history.

As for poverty, ben Sira understands it as a time of testing. He exhorts the poor not to envy the rich, but to trust in the Lord and wait for his light. "For it is easy as the Lord sees it, suddenly, in a moment, to make the poor man rich" (Sir 11:21). Again, he encourages the poor on the basis of his doctrine of opposites ("suddenly" refers to the appropriate time). Obviously, if the Enochic poor knew this message, they were not satisfied with it. Indeed, there is no way of knowing how reassuring it was to any poor community of ben Sira's time. He seems to be telling the poor to accept their lot in life.

From what is known of the abusive practices of wealthy Jewish tax-farmers in the Ptolemaic period,[576] it is not unreasonable to assume that the righteous poor in ben Sira's time could have written *1 Enoch* 92-105. Moreover, when full weight is accorded the factors discussed above, there is nothing in the Epistle or in Sirach to definitively exclude this possibility.

---

basis of present evidence").

[575] *Hellenistic Civilization and the Jews*, 142.

The results gained from our comparative analysis suggest an unfinished agenda. There are other Jewish apocalyptic texts which have incorporated sapiential forms and instructions and, conversely, there may be Jewish wisdom texts other than Sirach that have been affected by elements of the apocalyptic worldview.[577] A holistic comparison of such texts, not usually grouped in the same genre of literature, holds out the promise of new discoveries. Further comparative efforts may also benefit our interpretation of certain early Christian texts, such as Q, in which the apocalyptic and sapiential components seem inextricably bound together.

---

[577] See John J. Collins, "Wisdom, Apocalypticism, and Generic Compatibility," *In Search of Wisdom: Essays in Memory of John G. Gammie* (ed. Leo G. Perdue, Bernard Brandon Scott, and William Johnston Wiseman; Louisville: Westminster/John Knox, 1993) 165-85.

EXCURSUS

1 ENOCH 81:1-4: THE SEVENTH VISION OF THE SECOND JOURNEY

An argument can be made that *1 Enoch* 81:1-4 is the seventh vision of Enoch and belongs with chapters 20-32. If this is the case, then the closing scene in 81:5-82:3 also belongs with chapters 20-32 since it is inseparably tied to 81:1-4.[578]

Enoch's Second Journey begins with an onomasticon of seven angels (*1 En* 20). Each angel has a special sphere of responsibility and each later explains the significance of his domain when Enoch arrives on his cosmic tour. A literary pattern is established with the first four angels. Uriel interprets the place of punishment for the stars and rebel angels (*1 En* 20:2; 21:1-10; cf. 18:6-19:2); Raphael, the hollow mountain that contains the souls of human beings who have died (*1 En* 20:3; 22:1-14); Raguel, the fire of the luminaries of heaven (*1 En* 20:4; 23:1-24:1); and Michael, the Tree of Life on the Mountain of God (*1 En* 20:5; 24:2-25:7).[579] If the angelic names in scenes five (*1 En* 27:2) and six (*1 En* 32:6) are emended on the basis of the onomasticon,[580] then the literary pattern continues: Sariel interprets the Valley

---

[578] Among other things, by references to the righteous dead (see below). In Chap. I, *1 En* 81:5-82:3 is analyzed as an adaptation of the testamentary closing scene; a scene that concludes the Second Journey Report, as well as the Book of the Watchers as a whole.

[579] Charles stated that he would expect the name Gabriel in *1 En* 24:6 (*APOT* 2.204). But we show in Chap. III above that the interpretation of the mountain throne of God offered by the angel (*1 En* 25:3-6) utilizes the motifs of Holy War. Therefore, it is quite appropriate that the angel in this scene is Michael.

[580] The two emendations are suggested by George W. E. Nickelsburg in his unpublished translation of *1 Enoch*. For the supporting arguments, see his forthcoming commentary.

of Hinnom (*1 En* 20:6; 26-27);[581] and Gabriel, the Tree of Wisdom in Paradise (*1 En* 20:7; 28-32).[582]

In *1 Enoch* 32, the literary pattern comes to an abrupt end. There is no vision tradition for the sphere of the seventh angel, Remiel, who appears in the angelic list as the one "whom God put in charge of them that rise" (*1 En* 20:8). *1 Enoch* 81:1-4 fills the lacuna and completes the pattern. The second journey report then closes with Enoch's descent to earth and a testament scene in *1 Enoch* 81:5-82:3.[583]

With respect to both form and content, *1 Enoch* 81:1-4 has more in common with chapters 20-32 than with the Astronomical Book in which it is imbedded.[584] The vision form typical of chapters 20-32 consists of four basic elements, as outlined by Wacker.[585] The remnants are still detectable here:

---

[581] In *1 En* 27:2, the majority of Ethiopic manuscripts read Uriel; a few read Raphael. The Greek is missing.

The name Sariel occurs in *1 En* 9:1; 10:1 and 20:6. 4QEn[b] I iii 7 preserves the name [ל]שריא in 9:1, but some Greek and Ethiopic manuscripts use the name Uriel in 9:1 and 10:1. Milik attributes the substitution to the fact that Uriel was regarded as the Guardian of Tartarus (*The Books of Enoch*, 170-74). The same tendency could be at work in *1 En* 27:2.

[582] In *1 En* 32:6, the Ethiopic and Greek versions read Raphael. However, the scene is set in Paradise, which according to the onomasticon is clearly the sphere of the angel Gabriel. Charles is correct to suggest Gabriel here (*APOT* 2.207).

[583] The possibility of a lost ending was already suggested by Charles: "But since only four of the seven archangels mentioned in xx are dealt with in xxi-xxxvi, it is possible that a considerable passage was early lost" (*APOT*, 2.168). However, if we supply the names Sariel in *1 En* 27:2 and Gabriel in *1 En* 32:6, then the lost ending is not as "considerable" as Charles suggested. It involves only the Remiel material and some kind of conclusion.

[584] *Contra* Rau (*Kosmologie*, 307-09). Rau argues that *1 En* 81:1-4 has clear connections to *1 En* 72:1-80:8 (only *1 En* 81:5-82:3 has been interpolated into the Astronomical Book). However, the connections Rau makes between *1 En* 81:1-4 and the Astronomical Book are very tenuous and should be rejected. Rau himself calls attention to several parallels between *1 En* 81:1-4 and the Book of the Watchers, but does not access these properly because of his overriding concern to establish links to *1 En* 72:1-80:8.

[585]   i.   Preliminary indication of the Scene, usually with the formula: "and from there I was carried to another place"

    ii.   Description of what is seen or shown, signaled by a verb of seeing

    iii.   Dialogue between the seer and an *angelus interpres*. The dialogue may have two or four members:

        Type I a) A question or exclamation by the seer about what is seen

              b) An explanatory answer by the *angelus interpres*

        Type II a) An exclamation of surprise by the seer

              b) An inquiry by the *angelus interpres*

              c) An answer by the seer

              d) An explanation by the angel

    iv.   Blessing by the seer (not in all examples)

(Marie-Theres Wacker, *Weltordnung*, 101). Wacker points out that element b) in the dialogue of Types I and II, is characterized by the formula "then he answered and said to me," and is connected with the name of the angel and the apposition "one of the watchers

i.	Scene	[missing]
ii.	Description: Verb of seeing	[incorporated below]
iii.	Dialogue [=monologue]	
	a) angelic command	81:1
	b) Enoch's response	81:2
iv.	Blessing	
	a) the Lord	81:3
	b) the righteous dead	81:4

From the standpoint of literary form, the passage begins abruptly and it is apparent that the first element, the preliminary indication of the scene, is missing.[586] The remaining elements of the form have been altered. The description of what is seen, with a verb of seeing, is incorporated into the address of the angel ("Look, Enoch ...") and the element of dialogue with the angel appears here as a monologue because the angel issues a command that Enoch obeys. Finally, the blessing element has been expanded to include a blessing on the righteous dead as well as on God. Even with these differences from the typical vision form, 81:1-4 has more in common with the visions of chapters 21-32 than with the literary structures in the Astronomical Book.

A consideration of the content of the vision will establish the plausibility of the hypothesis that it belongs after chapter 32. The content may be approached through the figure of the angel. If *1 Enoch* 81:1-4 is the last stop on Enoch's cosmic tour, then the anonymous angel of the passage must be Remiel, "whom God has put in charge of them that rise" (*1 En* 20:8). Is it conceivable that Remiel is the angel who commands Enoch to look at the heavenly tablets? What possible connection is there between tablets and resurrection? Finally, if resurrection is the sphere of Remiel, what related motifs might be present in the passage?

---

and holy ones, who was with me" (ibid). In addition, Martha Himmelfarb has called attention to the stereotypical use of the demonstrative pronouns "this" and "these" in the angelic interpretations (*Tours of Hell*, 54-58).

[586] Nickelsburg suggests to me that material may have dropped out by homoioteleuton. Chapter 33 has to do with the "number" and "names" of the stars of heaven which are written down. This offers an enticing parallel to chapter 81, which is about the recorded number and names of the righteous (who will rise and shine like the luminaries of heaven!). As we argue in Chap. 5, the author of the Disputation Speeches in *1 En* 102:4-104:8 uses the Remiel tradition in 81:1-4 to give hope to the righteous.

Answers to these questions will begin to emerge through a study of the settings and themes associated with the figure of Remiel elsewhere in Jewish literature. It has long been recognized that an angel appears in Jewish tradition with a variety of names that look suspiciously like the name Remiel.[587] The names include Jeremiel (4 Ezra 4:36; Syr: Ramael), Ramiel (*2 Apoc Bar* 55:3; 63:6; *Sib Or* 2.214-19), Eremiel (*Apoc Zephaniah* 6:15) and Jerahmiel (*Zohar*).[588] It may be possible to posit the presence of a single figure behind these names without demonstrating an etymological relationship among the names themselves.[589] The key is whether this angelic figure with the Remiel-type name has a consistent role throughout the literature. This does appear to be the case.

In an attempt to answer the questions raised above regarding the presence of Remiel in *1 Enoch* 81:1-4, the role of this angel in 4 Ezra, *2 Apoc Baruch* and the *Apoc Zephaniah* will be investigated.[590] While these three texts are all later than the Book of the Watchers, they draw upon traditions that pre-date their own composition. This is readily apparent in 4 Ezra.

The reference to Jeremiel in 4 Ezra occurs early in the book. In his first vision, Ezra sees the desolation of Zion (3:1-3). He responds with anguish and complains about God's justice (3:4-36). When the angel Uriel is sent to Ezra, Ezra disputes with the angel on the subject of theodicy (4:1-25). When one of Uriel's responses finally turns toward the subject of eschatology (4:26-32), Ezra wants to know when the end will come (4:33). At this point in the dispute, the author either quotes from or alludes to a preexisting source that mentions the archangel Jeremiel. The source material is used in the reply of Uriel to Ezra and is best restricted to 4:35-36a:[591]

---

[587] See George W. E. Nickelsburg, "Jeremiel," *ABD* 3.722-23.

[588] Nickelsburg called my attention to other passages which, while they do not explicitly mention the angel, nonetheless contain the themes that reflect his domain. See the themes of prayer for vindication, blood of the martyrs, endurance, and number of the righteous dead in Rev 6:9-11 and *1 En* 47:1-4 (the latter passage also includes a reference to books opened at the judgment).

[589] Michael Stone states that the angel Jeremiel/Eremiel is not the same angel as Remiel/Ramiel because the former name apparently reflects an original ירחמיאל (*Fourth Ezra* [Hermeneia; Philadelphia: Fortress, 1990] 97). But even if the names are etymologically distinct, this does not necessarily rule out the possibility of a single figure behind the names.

[590] The reference to Ramiel in *Sib Or* 2.215 is disputed because it only appears in the φ family of manuscripts. See J. J. Collins, "Sibylline Oracles: A New Translation and Introduction," *OTP* 1.350. A consideration of Jerahmiel in the Zohar would take us too far afield.

[591] Stone, *Fourth Ezra*, 96-97.

Did not the souls of the righteous in their chambers ask about these matters, saying, 'How long are we to remain here? And when will come the harvest of our reward?' And Jeremiel the archangel answered them and said, 'When the number of those like yourselves is completed ...'

In this traditional piece, Jeremiel is portrayed as presiding over the righteous dead in their chambers or treasuries. In particular, this angel keeps an exact count of the souls of the righteous dead until their number is complete, thus marking the end of the age. The point of apppealing to the source is to establish that God has a purpose and a timetable that cannot be rushed, though the righteous dead are growing impatient. The end will come when God determines and only then will the righteous dead receive their reward and no longer have to remain in their chambers.[592]

In the ensuing context of 4 Ezra 4, Ezra asks whether the end has been delayed because of the ungodliness of the people (4:38-39). The angel Uriel assures Ezra that this is not the case. As a woman in labor hastens to give birth when her nine months are completed, so the chambers of Sheol, which are like a womb, hasten to give back those things that have been committed to them (4:40-43). Once again the point is made that the righteous dead will depart from Sheol at the end of the age.

Later in the book, when the author returns to the theme of the chambers giving back their souls, he explicitly mentions that at this time God's *patience* with sinners will be withdrawn and only judgment will remain (7:32-34; cf. 7:74, 134; *1 En* 81:3). It was this very patience or restraint on God's part that gave rise to the earlier questions of Ezra and, from the standpoint of tradition, the even earlier questions of the souls of the righteous dead in the Jeremiel source material. That is, the questions "How long ...? When ...?" (4 Ezra 4:33, 35) are necessitated by God's patience with sinners.

The second text that mentions an angel of the Remiel-type is *2 Apoc Baruch*. In Baruch's final vision (chaps 53-54), he sees a cloud that rains a sequence of twelve waters, black and bright, plus a final shower of each kind of water. Baruch prays that the interpretation be revealed to him. In answer to his prayer, God sends the angel Ramiel in chapter 55. This angel offers a lengthy interpretation of the vision, covering chapters 56-74.

The angel Ramiel explains that the cloud symbolizes the age of the world from the creation until the consummation. The black and bright waters

---

[592] There is no mention of a book in which Jeremiel numbers the souls of the righteous dead until the end of the age. It is possible, however, that Jeremiel records the names in the Book of Life. A similar allusion may also be present in Ezra's address to the people in 4 Ezra 14:36: "For after death the judgment will come, when we shall live again; and then the names of the righteous will become manifest ...".

represent alternating periods of falsehood and truth in the history of Israel, which reach a culmination near the end of the age (thus, the significance of the final shower). Apparently Ramiel is qualified to offer this extensive interpretation because he plays an important role in God's judgment throughout history and knows the identity of the wicked and the righteous in the period from creation to consummation.

This assumption receives an indirect confirmation in Baruch's response to Ramiel in *2 Apoc Baruch* 75. Baruch praises God for the "compassion"[593] shown in the past to "those who are under thy right hand" (75:6a-b). The reference is to the souls of the righteous dead throughout history who were symbolized by the bright waters. These souls are described as residing in a special chamber under God's throne (cf. "Sheol," 23:5; "treasuries," 30:2; "under the altar," Rev 6:9). Baruch goes on to characterize the souls of the righteous dead as those called to be among the number God has set (75:6d; cf. 30:2). He then describes how the knowledge of one's purpose in life, or the lack thereof, will be a source of joy or grief at the resurrection (75:7-8). It is striking that Baruch should mention God's compassion, the special chamber of the righteous dead, their predetermined number, and the resurrection in response to an interpretation offered by Ramiel. This makes sense if the angel who separates all of humanity into the wicked and the righteous has a special role in overseeing the number of the righteous dead until the judgment. This role may be intimated in earlier descriptions of the judgment: the books of sin and of righteous deeds will be opened (24:1), God will be praised for his patience (24:2), and the souls of the righteous will come out of their treasuries (30:2).

A third text in which the angelic figure is named is the *Apoc Zephaniah*. This fragmentary text apparently contained a number of Zephaniah's cosmic journeys. In *Apoc Zephaniah* 6-7, the seer discovers that he has journeyed to Hades, where he encounters two angels:[594] an accusing angel and "the great angel, Eremiel, who is over the abyss and Hades, the one in which all of the souls are imprisoned from the end of the Flood, which came upon the earth, until this day" (6:15).[595]

---

[593] This might suggest that the name Ramiel is related to an original ירחמיאל, "may God have compassion" (*pace* Stone, *Fourth Ezra*, 97).

[594] Cf. *T. Abr.* 12-13 (Rec A). On the two angelic scribes, and the background in Jewish tradition, see George W. E. Nickelsburg, "Eschatology in the Testament of Abraham: A Study of the Judgment Scenes in the Two Recensions," *Studies on the Testament of Abraham* (ed. Nickelsburg; Missoula, MT: Scholars, 1976) 36-39.

[595] Translation by O. S. Wintermute, "Apocalypse of Zephaniah: A New Translation and Introduction," *OTP* 1, 513.

The accusing angel has a manuscript in his hand on which are written all the sins Zephaniah committed in his lifetime (7:1-7). Zephaniah appeals to God to show mercy and wipe out this manuscript (7:8). A great angel (anonymous, but probably Eremiel) responds that Zephaniah has triumphed over the accuser and "you have come up from Hades and the abyss" (7:9). This angel then brings another manuscript and begins to read (7:10-11).

Unfortunately, the next two pages of the *Apoc Zephaniah* are missing. Presumably, this second manuscript read by the angel is a book of Zephaniah's good deeds or the Book of Life in which his name is written. In any case, the entire process of triumphing over the accuser in Hades and coming up from there is one that is overseen by Eremiel and involves manuscripts or books.

The passages surveyed above indicate what would be characteristic of the context in *1 Enoch* 81:1-4 if the angel was Remiel. The angel is associated with the themes of books, numbering the souls of the righteous dead, God's compassion and patience, and the resurrection. A review of the vision in *1 Enoch* 81:1-4 will show that the same themes are present here.

In *1 Enoch* 81:1, Enoch hears the threefold command: look at the "heavenly tablets" (*daf̣daf̣a samāy*),[596] read what is written on them, and learn every single fact; a command that he carries out point for point in 81:2a-c. The remainder of 81:2 defines the content of the tablets in terms of the special interest of this vision. Enoch reads "the book" (*maṣḥaf*) in which are written "all the deeds of men and all the sons of flesh that will be upon the earth until the generations of eternity" (81:2d-f). Still later in the vision, when Enoch blesses the man who dies righteous, he refers to the absence of a "book of iniquity" (*maṣḥafa 'ammaḍā*) against the righteous man (81:4). It would seem, then, that the object of this vision is brought increasingly into focus: heavenly tablets = book of all human deeds = book of iniquity.[597]

After Enoch has read about the wicked deeds of humankind until eternity, he responds by blessing God (81:3). This is curious to say the least. One line in the blessing may offer the rationale: "I glorified the Lord because of his *patience (te'geštu)*." Enoch praises God because God has exercised restraint

---

[596] The heavenly tablets were originally the "tablets of destiny" known from ancient Babylonian texts (Geo Widengren, *The Ascension of the Apostle and the Heavenly Book* [Uppsala: A. B. Lundequistska, 1950] 7-39). VanderKam sees Enoch as the Jewish counterpart to Enmeduranki, and the two seventh antediluvian leaders, founders of a guild of diviners, are both associated with a celestial tablet (*Enoch and the Growth*, 152). He acknowledges, however, that there are Jewish parallels, both biblical and extra-biblical, to the concept of heavenly tablets of destiny.

[597] The identification of the heavenly tablets and the book of deeds/iniquity is a conflation of two originally separate motifs. The tablets give divine authority to what the seer reads in the book. See Rau, *Kosmologie*, 307-09.

in withholding the judgment and has allowed the creation to continue in spite of the iniquitious deeds of men. It goes without saying, however, that God's patience will not last forever.

Enoch not only responds to the vision by blessing God for his patience, he also pronounces a blessing on "the man who dies righteous and good" (81:4). Why the additional makarism? And why does the blessing shift from God to the righteous man who has died? This man is characterized as having no book of iniquity against him and thus no guilt. It is reasonable to conclude that when God's patience has reached its limit, and the book of iniquity is opened, sinners will be punished. In contrast, the righteous dead are blessed because they have no such book against them and therefore receive their reward. But what is this reward?

Remiel was described in *1 Enoch* 20:8 as the one "whom God has put in charge of them that rise." The connection to *1 Enoch* 81:1-4 is now obvious: the righteous dead concerning whom no book of iniquity has been written will rise from their chambers. Remiel has oversight of the books that guarantee the resurrection of the righteous.[598]

The righteous man is singled out for emphasis in 81:4 because his death resulted from the deeds of all the sons of flesh referred to in 81:3. That the works of sinners contributed to the death of the righteous finds support from *1 Enoch* 81:5-10.

In 81:5, after Enoch is returned to his home, part of his commission is to "show all your sons that all flesh is not righteous before the Lord, for he has created them." The reference to "all flesh" (*kʷellu za-šegā*) recalls the expression "all the children of flesh" (*kʷellu weluda šegā*) from the end of 81:2. Moreover, this language occurred early in *1 Enoch*, at the conclusion of the theophany of judgment ("Behold, he comes ... to convict all flesh" *1 En* 1:9). The expression "all flesh" is drawn from the flood story in Genesis ("*all flesh* had corrupted their way upon the earth," Gen 6:12). In *1 Enoch* 81:5, this flood language is conflated with Psalm 143:2 ("every living thing [*all flesh, 1 En* 81:5] is not justified before you."[599] In short, the angels commission Enoch to inform his sons about persons subject to judgment and eternal

---

[598] Resurrection is not necessarily bodily in nature. Elsewhere in *1 Enoch*, the spirits of the righteous rise from Sheol or are exalted to heaven. Indeed, we know from the journey traditions that the souls of the righteous have been separated in the hollow mountain of Sheol (*1 En* 22:9), presumably because they will one day rise from there. This future resurrection is explicitly denied to sinners: "nor will they rise from here" (*1 En* 22:13). The notion that the righteous will rise is also present in *1 En* 91:10; 92:3-5; 102-104. See Nickelsburg, *Resurrection*, 123.

[599] E. Käsemann (*Commentary on Romans* [Grand Rapids: Eerdmans, 1980] 88) points out that this same substitution is made by the Apostle Paul in Rom 3:20 and Gal 2:16.

punishment because of their destructive deeds. This emphasis is intelligible against the background of the visions in *1 Enoch* 20-32 which dealt with the coming judgment of the wicked.

Any remaining doubt about the character of the deeds of "all flesh," in particular, whether such deeds contribute to the death of the righteous, is removed by the exhortation that Enoch hears from the angels in *1 Enoch* 81:7-9. In addition, the fate of apostates here is described in flood language ("will sink", 81:8b), as was the case in 81:5. But beyond this, 81:9 explicitly states that the righteous will die because of the works of men and the deeds of the impious. However, Enoch and his descendents are to derive strength from the fact that the pious transmit his revelation and thereby are guaranteed salvation. In conjunction with 81:1-4, the implication is that the blessing of future resurrection is promised to those persecuted or martyred by sinners.

The thematic parallels between *1 Enoch* 20:8 and 81:1-4 and the three Jewish texts surveyed earlier are numerous and close. An angel with a Remiel-type name is present in all of the texts. The angel appears in contexts in which the souls of the righteous dead are confined in their chamber in the period of God's restraint before the judgment (*1 En* 81:3-4; *4 Ezra* 4:35). While the angel remains especially concerned for the righteous, his oversight of human souls extends to the wicked as well; either in the whole period of world history (*1 En* 81:2d-f; *2 Apoc Bar* 56-74) or the time since the flood (*Apoc Zephaniah* 6:15). In connection with these two classes of people, the angel meets his responsibilities by keeping a tally of the righteous dead (*4 Ezra* 4:36; *2 Apoc Bar* 75:6) and a book of iniquity against sinners (*1 En* 81:4). In *Apoc Zephaniah* 7, a separate, accusing angel has possession of the manuscript of sins. Nonetheless, Eremiel is able to insure that this manuscript is wiped out and that the seer comes up from Hades. The connection of the angel to the idea of a resurrection of righteous souls from Sheol is made not only in the *Apoc Zephaniah*, but also in *1 En* 20:8; *4 Ezra* 4:35-36, 42; *2 Apoc Bar* 75:7-8.

The consistent role of the angel in early Jewish literature supports the claim that Remiel (*1 En* 20:8) is the unnamed angel in *1 Enoch* 81:1-4. It follows that the vision of the heavenly tablets, with its application to the book of inquity and to the blessedness of the righteous dead, is the seventh vision of the Second Journey of Enoch and was originally located after *1 Enoch* 32.

BIBLIOGRAPHY

Anderson, B. W. *Creation versus Chaos: The Reinterpretation of Mythical Symbolism in the Bible.* New York: Association, 1967.

Anderson, B. W., ed. *Creation in the Old Testament.* Issues in Religion and Theology 6. Philadelphia: Fortress, 1984.

Aune, D. E. *Prophecy in Early Christianity and the Ancient Mediterranean World.* Grand Rapids: Eerdmans, 1983.

Baillet, M., J. T. Milik and R. de Vaux. *Les 'petites grottes' de Qumrân.* DJD 3. Oxford: Clarendon, 1962.

Baltzer, K. *The Covenant Formulary.* Philadelphia: Fortress, 1971.

Barthélemy, D., and O. Rickenbacher. *Konkordanz zum hebräischen Sirach.* Göttingen: Vandenhoeck & Ruprecht, 1973.

Bauer, W., *A Greek-English Lexicon of the New Testament and Other Early Christian Literature.* Second ed. revised and augmented by F. W. Gingrich and F. W. Danker. Chicago: University of Chicago, 1979.

Baumgartner, W. "Die literarischen Gattungen in der Weisheit des Jesus Sirach." *ZAW* 34 (1914) 161-98.

_____. "The Wisdom Literature," *The Old Testament and Modern Study*, ed. H. H. Rowley. Oxford: Clarendon, 1951 [repr. 1961], pp. 210-37.

Behm, J. "ἀνάθεμα," *TDNT* 1 (1964) 354-55.

Biblia Sacra iuxta latinam vulgatam versionem. 12: Sapientia Salomonis, Liber Hiesu filii Sirach. Rome: Typis Polyglottis Vaticanis, 1964.

Bickerman, E. *The Jews in the Greek Age.* Cambridge, MA: Harvard University, 1988.

Black, M. *The Book of Enoch or 1 Enoch: A New English Edition with Commentary and Textual Notes.* SVTP 7. Leiden: Brill, 1985.

Blass, F., and A. Debrunner. *A Greek Grammar of the New Testament and Other Early Christian Literature*, trans. by R. W. Funk. Chicago: University of Chicago, 1961.

Boccaccini, G. "Jewish Apocalyptic Tradition: The Contribution of Italian Scholarship," *Mysteries and Revelations*, ed. J. J. Collins and J. H. Charlesworth, 1991, pp. 33-50.

Bockmuehl, M. N. A. *Revelation and Mystery in Ancient Judaism and Pauline Christianity.* WUNT 2.36. Tübingen: J.C.B. Mohr (Paul Siebeck), 1990.

Bonner, C. *The Last Chapters of Enoch in Greek.* Studies and Documents 8. London: Christophers, 1937.

Box, G. H. and W. O. E. Oesterley, "Sirach," *APOT*, ed. R. H. Charles, 1913, 1.268-517.

Braun, H. "πλανάω κτλ," *TDNT* 6 (1968) 228-53.

Brown, F., S. R. Driver and C. A. Briggs. *A Hebrew and English Lexicon of the Old Testament.* Corrected edition. Oxford: Clarendon, 1907, 1977.

Bryce, G. E. *A Legacy of Wisdom: The Egyptian Contribution to the Wisdom of Israel.* Lewisburg: Bucknell University, 1979.

Charles, R. H. *The Ethiopic Version of the Book of Enoch:Edited from twenty-three mss. together with the fragmentary Greek and Latin versions.* Oxford: Clarendon, 1906.

_____. *The Greek Versions of the Testaments of the Twelve Patriarchs: Edited from nine MMS together with the Variants of the Armenian and Slavonic Versions and some Hebrew Fragments.* Reprint. Oxford: Clarendon, 1908.

_____. *The Apocrypha and Pseudepigrapha of the Old Testament.* 2 vols. Oxford: Clarendon, 1913.

Charlesworth, J. H. *The Old Testament Pseudepigrapha.* 2 vols. New York: Doubleday, 1983, 1985.

Clifford, R. J. "The Use of *Hôy* in the Prophets." *CBQ* 28 (1966) 458-64.

Collins, J. J. "Apocalyptic Eschatology as the Transcendence of Death." *CBQ* 36 (1974) 21-43.

_____. "Jewish Apocalyptic against its Hellenistic Near Eastern Environment." *BASOR* 220 (1975) 27-36.

_____. "Cosmos and Salvation: Jewish Wisdom and Apocalyptic in the Hellenistic Age." *HR* 17 (1977) 121-42.

_____. "Methodological Issues in the Study of 1 Enoch: Reflections on the articles of P. D. Hanson and G. W. Nickelsburg." *SBLSP* (1978) 315-22.

_____. "Introduction: Towards the Morphology of a Genre." *Semeia* 14 (1979) 1-20.

_____. "The Jewish Apocalypses." *Semeia* 14 (1979) 21-59.

_____. "The Apocalyptic Technique: Setting and Function in the Book of the Watchers." *CBQ* 44 (1982) 91-111.

_____. "Sibylline Oracles: A New Translation and Introduction," *The Old Testament Pseudepigrapha*, ed. J. H. Charlesworth, 1983, 1.317-472.

_____. *The Apocalyptic Imagination: An Introduction to the Jewish Matrix of Christianity*. New York: Crossroad, 1987.

_____. "The Sage in the Apocalyptic and Pseudepigraphic Literature," *The Sage in Israel and the Ancient Near East*, ed. J. G. Gammie and L. G. Perdue, 1990, pp. 343-54.

_____. "Genre, Ideology and Social Movements in Jewish Apocalypticism," *Mysteries and Revelations*, ed. J. J. Collins and J. H. Charlesworth, 1991, pp. 11-32.

_____. "Apocalypses and Apocalypticism: Early Jewish Apocalypticism," *ABD*, 1992, 1.282-88.

_____. "Wisdom, Apocalypticism, and Generic Compatibility," *In Search of Wisdom*, ed. L. G. Perdue, B. B. Scott and W. J. Wiseman, 1993, 165-85.

Collins, J. J. and J. H. Charlesworth, eds. *Mysteries and Revelations: Apocalyptic Studies since the Uppsala Colloquium*. JSPS 9. Sheffield: JSOT Press, 1991.

Conzelmann, H. "The Mother of Wisdom," *The Future of Our Religious Past: Essays in Honour of Rudolf Bultmann*, ed. J. M. Robinson, trans. by C. E. Carlston and R. P. Scharlemann. London: SCM, 1971, pp. 230-43.

Coughenour, R. A. *Enoch and Wisdom: A Study of Wisdom Elements in Ethiopic Enoch*. Diss., Case Western Reserve University, Cleveland, Ohio, 1972.

_____. "The Woe-Oracles in Ethiopic Enoch." *JSJ* 9 (1978) 192-97.

_____. "The Wisdom Stance of Enoch's Redactor." *JSJ* 13 (1982) 47-55.

Crenshaw, J. L. "Wisdom," *Old Testament Form Criticism*, ed. John H. Hayes, 1974, pp. 225-64.

_____. "The Problem of Theodicy in Sirach: On Human Bondage." *JBL* 94 (1975) 47-64. Reprinted in *Theodicy in the Old Testament*, ed. J. L. Crenshaw, 1983, pp. 119-40.

_____. "Prolegomenon," *Studies in Ancient Israelite Wisdom*, ed. J. L. Crenshaw, 1976, pp. 1-60.

_____. "Wisdom and Authority: Sapiential Rhetoric and Its Warrants," *Congress Volume: Vienna, 1980*. VTSup 32. Leiden: Brill, 1981. Pp. 10-29.

_____. *Old Testament Wisdom: An Introduction*. Atlanta: John Knox, 1981.

_____. "Education in Ancient Israel." *JBL* 104 (1985) 601-15.

Crenshaw, J. L., ed. *Studies in Ancient Israelite Wisdom*. The Library of Biblical Studies, ed. H. M. Orlinsky. New York: Ktav, 1976.

_____, ed. *Theodicy in the Old Testament*. Issues in Religion and Theology 4. Philadelphia: Fortress, 1983.

Cross, F. M. *Canaanite Myth and Hebrew Epic: Essays in the History of the Religion of Israel*. Cambridge: Harvard University, 1973.

Davidson, M. J. *Angels at Qumran: A Comparative Study of 1 Enoch 1-36, 72-108 and Sectarian Writings from Qumran*. JSPSup 11. Sheffield: JSOT, 1992.

Davies, P. R. "Calendrical Change and Qumran Origins: An Assessment of VanderKam's Theory." *CBQ* 45 (1983) 80-89.

Davies, W. D., and L. Finkelstein, eds. *The Cambridge History of Judaism. Volume Two: The Hellenistic Age*. Cambridge: Cambridge University, 1989.

Denis, A-M. *Concordance Grecque des Pseudépigraphes D'Ancien Testament*. Louvain: Université Catholique Institut Orientaliste, 1987.

Deutsch, C. "The Sirach 51 Acrostic: Confession and Exhortation." *ZAW* 94 (1982) 400-09.

Dexinger, F. *Henochs Zehnwochenapokalypse und offene Probleme der Apokalyptikforschung*. SPB 29. Leiden: Brill, 1977.

Di Lella, A. A. "The Recently Identified Leaves of Sirach in Hebrew." *Bib* 45 (1964) 153-67.

_____. *The Hebrew Text of Sirach: A Text-Critical and Historical Study*. The Hague: Mouton, 1966.

_____. "The Newly Discovered Sixth Manuscript of Ben Sira from the Cairo Geniza." *Bib* 69 (1988) 226-38.

_____. "The Meaning of Wisdom in Ben Sira," *In Search of Wisdom*, ed. L. G. Perdue, B. B. Scott and W. J. Wiseman, 1993, pp. 133-48.

Dillmann, A. *Lexicon Linguae Aethiopicae cum Indice Latino*. Reproductio phototypica editionis 1865. Osnabrück: Biblio, 1970.

Fournier-Bidoz, A. "L'Arbre et la demeure: Siracide xxiv 10-17." *VT* 34 (1984) 1-10.

Gammie, J. G. "Spatial and Ethical Dualism in Jewish Wisdom and Apocalyptic Literature." *JBL* 93 (1974) 356-85.

_____. "The Sage in Sirach," *The Sage in Israel and the Ancient Near East*, ed. J. G. Gammie and L. G. Perdue, 1990, pp. 355-72.

_____. "From Prudentialism to Apocalypticism: The Houses of the Sages amid the Varying Forms of Wisdom," *The Sage in Israel and the Ancient Near East*, ed. J. G. Gammie and L. G. Perdue, 1990, pp. 479-97.

Gammie, J. G., W. A. Brueggemann, W. L. Humphreys and J. M. Ward, eds. *Israelite Wisdom: Theological and Literary Essays in Honor of Samuel Terrien*. Missoula, MT: Scholars, 1978.

Gammie, J. G. and L. G. Perdue, eds. *The Sage in Israel and the Ancient Near East*. Winona Lake, IN: Eisenbrauns, 1990.

Gerstenberger, E. "The Woe-oracles of the Prophets." *JBL* 81 (1962) 249-63.

_____. *Psalms: Part I, with an Introduction to Cultic Poetry*. FOTL 14. Grand Rapids: Eerdmans, 1988.

Gese, H. "Wisdom literature in the Persian period," *The Cambridge History of Judaism*, vol. 1, ed. W. D. Davies and L. Finkelstein. Cambridge: Cambridge University, 1984, pp. 189-218.

Gilbert, M. "L'éloge de la Sagesse (Siracide 24)." *RTL* 5 (1974) 326-48.

Gilbert, M., ed. *La Sagesse de l'Ancien Testament*. BETL 51. Gembloux: Leuven University, 1979.

Goldstein, J. A. "Review of *The Psalms Scroll of Qumrân Cave 11* (11QPsᵃ) by J. A. Sanders." *JNES* 27 (1967) 302-09.

_____. "The Tales of the Tobiads," *Christianity, Judaism, and Other Graeco-Roman Cults: Studies for Morton Smith at Sixty*, ed. J. Neusner. Leiden: Brill, 1975, pp. 85-123.

_____. *I Maccabees*. AB 41. Garden City: Doubleday, 1976.

Greenfield, J. C. and M. E. Stone. "Remarks on the Aramaic Testament of Levi from the Geniza," *RB* 86 (1979) 214-30.

Gruenwald, I. "Jewish Apocalyptic Literature." *ANRW* II.19.1 (1979) 89-118.

Hanson, P. D. "Apocalypse, Genre," "Apocalypticism." *IDBSup* (1976) 27-34.

_____. "Rebellion in Heaven, Azazel, and Euhemeristic Heroes in 1 Enoch 6-11." *JBL* 96 (1977) 195-233.

_____. *The Dawn of Apocalyptic: The Historical and Sociological Roots of Jewish Apocalyptic Eschatology.* Rev. ed. Philadelphia: Fortress, 1979.

Harrington, D. J. "The Wisdom of the Scribe According to Ben Sira," *Ideal Figures in Ancient Judaism*, ed. J. J. Collins and G. W. E. Nickelsburg. SBLSCS 12. Chico, CA: Scholars, 1980, pp. 181-88.

Hartman, L. *Prophecy Interpreted: The Formation of Some Jewish Apocalyptic Texts and of the Eschatological Discourse Mark 13 par.* Lund: Gleerup, 1966.

_____. "'Comfort of the Scriptures'—an Early Jewish Interpretation of Noah's Salvation, I En. 10:16-11:2." *SEÅ* 41-42 (1976-77) 87-96.

_____. *Asking for a Meaning: A Study of 1 Enoch 1-5.* ConBNT 12. Lund: Gleerup, 1979.

Hatch, E. and H. A. Redpath. *A Concordance to the Septuagint and the Other Greek Versions of the Old Testament (Including the Apocryphal Books).* 2 Vols. Grand Rapids: Baker, 1987 reprint (orig. 1897).

Hauck, F. "παραβολή," *TDNT* 5 (1967) 744-61.

Hayes, J. H., ed. *Old Testament Form Criticism.* San Antonio: Trinity University, 1974.

Hellholm, D., ed. *Apocalypticism in the Mediterranean World and the Near East: Proceedings of the International Colloquium on Apocalypticism, Uppsala, August 12-17, 1979.* Tübingen: Mohr(Siebeck), 1983.

Hengel, M. *Judaism and Hellenism. Studies in their Encounter in Palestine during the Early Hellenistic Period*, trans. by J. Bowden. 2 vols. in 1. Philadelphia: Fortress, 1974.

Herr, M. D. "The Calendar," *The Jewish People in the First Century.* CRINT 1.2. Ed. S. Safrai and M. Stern. Philadelphia: Fortress, 1976, pp. 834-64.

Hillers, D. *Treaty-Curses and the Old Testament Prophets.* BibOr 16. Rome: Pontifical Biblical Institute, 1964.

Himmelfarb, M. *Tours of Hell. An Apocalyptic Form in Jewish and Christian Literature.* Philadelphia: University of Pennsylvania, 1983.

_____. "Heavenly Ascent and the Relationship of the Apocalypses and *Hekhalot* Literature." *HUCA* 59 (1988) 73-100.

_____. *Ascent to Heaven in Jewish & Christian Apocalypses.* New York: Oxford University, 1993.

Historical Dictionary of the Hebrew Language. The Book of Ben Sira: Text, Concordance and an Analysis of the Vocabulary. Jerusalem: Academy of the Hebrew Language and the Shrine of the Book, 1973.

Holladay, W. L. *A Concise Hebrew and Aramaic Lexicon of the Old Testament.* Grand Rapids: Eerdmans, 1971.

_____. *Jeremiah 1.* Hermeneia. Philadelphia: Fortress, 1986.

Hollander H. W. and M. de Jonge. *The Testaments of the Twelve Patriarchs. A Commentary.* SVTP 8. Leiden: Brill, 1985.

Horsley, R. A. "Wisdom Justified by All Her Children: Examining Allegedly Disparate Traditions in Q." *SBLSP* 1994 (733-51).

Houston, M. V. *The Identification of Torah as Wisdom: A Traditio-Critical Analysis of Dt. 4:1-8 and 30:11-20.* Diss., University of Iowa, 1987.

Jansen, H. L. *Die Henochgestalt.* Oslo: Dybwad, 1939.

Janzen, W. *Mourning Cry and Woe Oracle.* BZAW 125. Berlin: de Gruyter, 1972.

Jastrow, M., compiler. *A Dictionary of the Targumin, the Talmud Babli and Yerushalmi, and the Midrashic Literature.* 2 vols. Brooklyn: P. Shalom, 1967 (orig. 1926).

Jepsen, A. "חזה" *TDOT* 4 (1980) 280-90.

Johnson, L. T. "The New Testament's Anti-Jewish Slander and the Conventions of Ancient Polemic." *JBL* 108 (1989) 419-41.

Jonge, M. de *The Testaments of the Twelve Patriarchs: A Study of their Text, Composition and Origin.* 2nd ed. Assen: Van Gorcum, 1975.

Jonge, M. de, ed. *Studies on the Testaments of the Twelve Patriarchs: Text and Interpretation.* SVTP 3. Leiden: Brill, 1975.

_____, in cooperation with H. W. Hollander, H. J. de Jonge, Th. Korteweg. *The Testaments of the Twelve Patriarchs: A Critical Edition of the Greek Text.* PVTG 1.2. Leiden: Brill, 1978.

Josephus. *Josephus*, vols. I-X. Edited with an English translation by H. St. John Thackeray, R. Marcus, A. Wikgren, and L. H. Feldman. LCL. Cambridge, MA: Harvard University, 1926-65.

Käsemann, E. *Commentary on Romans*. Grand Rapids: Eerdmans, 1980.

Kearns, C. "Ecclesiasticus or the Wisdom of Jesus the Son of Sirach," *A New Catholic Commentary on Holy Scripture*. London: Nelson, 1969, pp. 541-62.

Kenik, H. A. *Design for Kingship: The Deuteronomistic Narrative Technique in 1 Kings 3:4-15*. SBLDS 69. Chico, CA: Scholars, 1983.

Kloppenborg, J. S. *The Formation of Q: Trajectories in Ancient Wisdom Collections*. Philadelphia: Fortress, 1987.

Knibb, M. *The Ethiopic Book of Enoch: A New Edition in the Light of the Aramaic Dead Sea Fragments*. 2 vols. Oxford: Clarendon, 1978.

Koch, K. *The Growth of the Biblical Tradition: The Form-Critical Method*. Trans. from the 2nd German ed. by S. M. Cupitt. New York: Charles Scribner's Sons, 1969.

_____. *The Rediscovery of Apocalyptic*. SBT 2.22. Naperville, IL: Allenson, 1972.

Kolenkow, A. B. "The Genre Testament and Forecasts of the Future in the Hellenistic Jewish Milieu." *JSJ* 6 (1975) 57-71.

_____. "The Genre Testament and the Testament of Abraham," *Studies in the Testament of Abraham*, ed. G. W. E. Nickelsburg, Jr. SBLSCS 6. Missoula: Scholars, 1976, pp. 139-52.

Kraft, R. A. and G. W. E. Nickelsburg, eds. *Early Judaism and Its Modern Interpreters*. Philadelphia: Fortress, 1986.

Kraus, H.-J. *Psalms 60-150: A Commentary*. Trans. by H. C. Oswald. Minneapolis: Augsburg, 1989.

Kuhn, K. G. *Konkordanz zu den Qumrantexten*. Göttingen: Vandenhoeck & Ruprecht, 1960.

Kuhn, T. S. *The Structure of Scientific Revolutions*. 2nd ed. Chicago: University of Chicago, 1970.

Kuntz, J. K. "The Canonical Wisdom Psalms of Ancient Israel: Their Rhetorical, Thematic and Formal Dimensions," *Rhetorical Criticism: Essays in Honor of James Muilenburg*, ed. J. J. Jackson and M. Kessler. Pittsburgh: Pickwick, 1974, pp. 186-222.

_____. "The Retribution Motif in Psalmic Wisdom." *ZAW* 89 (1977) 223-33.

Lambdin, T. O. *Introduction to Classical Ethiopic (Ge'ez)*. Harvard Semitic Studies 24. Cambridge, MA: The President and Fellows of Harvard College, 1978.

Landes, G. M. "Jonah: A *MĀŠĀL*?" *Israelite Wisdom: Theological and Literary Essays in Honor of Samuel Terrien*, ed. J. G. Gammie, W. A. Brueggemann, W. L. Humphreys, and J. M. Ward, 1978, pp. 137-58.

Lemaire, A. "The Sage in School and Temple," *The Sage in Israel and the Ancient Near East*, ed. J. G. Gammie and L. G. Perdue, 1990, pp. 165-81.

Lewis, N. *The Interpretation of Dreams and Portents*. Toronto & Sarasota: Hakkert, 1976.

Liddell, H. G. and R. Scott. *A Greek-English Lexicon*. Abridged. Oxford: Clarendon, 1984.

Lisowsky, G. *Kondordanz zum hebräischen Alten Testament*. 2nd ed. Stuttgart: Württenbergische Bibelanstalt, 1958.

Lohse, E., ed. *Die Texte aus Qumran: hebräisch und deutsch*. München: Kösel, 1971.

McKane, W. *Prophets and Wise Men*. SBT 44. London: SCM, 1965.

_____. *Proverbs*. The Old Testament Library. Philadelphia: Westminster, 1970.

Mack, B. L. *Wisdom and the Hebrew Epic: Ben Sira's Hymn in Praise of the Fathers*. Chicago Studies in the History of Judaism. Chicago: University of Chicago, 1985.

Maier, G. *Mensch und freier Wille, Nach den jüdischen Religionsparteien zwischen Ben Sira und Paulus*. WUNT 12. Tübingen: Mohr [Siebeck], 1971.

Marböck, J. *Weisheit im Wandel: Untersuchungen zur Weisheitstheologie bei Ben Sira*. BBB 37. Bonn: Peter Hanstein, 1971.

_____. "Das Gebet um die Rettung Zions Sir 36,1-22 (G:33,1-13a; 36,16b-22) im Zusammenhang der Geschichtsschau Ben Siras," *Memoria Jerusalem*, ed. J. B. Bauer. Jerusalem/Graz: Akademische Druck- und Verlagsanstalt, 1977, pp. 93-116.

_____. "Sir., 38,24-39,11: Der schriftgelehrte Weise. Ein Beitrag zu Gestalt und Werk Ben Siras," *La Sagesse de l'Ancien Testament*, ed. M. Gilbert. Gembloux: Leuven University, 1978, pp. 293-316.

_____. "Henoch-Adam-der Thronwagen: Zu frühjüdischen pseudepigraphischen Traditionen bei *Ben Sira*." *BZ* N.F. 25 (1981) 103-11.

March, W. E. "Prophecy," *Old Testament Form Criticism*, ed. John H. Hayes, 1974, pp. 141-177.

Martinez, F. G. *Qumran and Apocalyptic: Studies on the Aramaic Texts from Qumran.* STDJ 9. Leiden: E. J. Brill, 1992.

Martinez, F. G. and E. J. C. Tigchelaar. "The *Books of Enoch* (*1 Enoch*) and the Aramaic Fragments from Qumran." *RQ* 14 (1989) 131-46.

_____. "*1 Enoch* and the figure of Enoch: A Bibliography of Studies 1970-1988." *RQ* 14 (1989) 149-74.

Middendorp. T. *Die Stellung Jesu ben Siras zwischen Judentum und Hellenismus.* Leiden: Brill, 1973.

Milik, J. T., with M. Black. *The Books of Enoch. Aramaic Fragments of Qumrân Cave 4.* Oxford: Clarendon, 1976.

Miller, P. D., Jr. *The Divine Warrior in Early Israel.* HSM 5. Cambridge, MA: Harvard University, 1973.

_____. *Sin and Judgment in the Prophets: A Stylistic and Theological Analysis.* SBLMS 27. Chico, CA: Scholars, 1982.

Miller, P. D., Jr., P. D. Hanson and S. D. McBride, eds. *Ancient Israelite Religion: Essays in Honor of Frank Moore Cross.* Philadelphia: Fortress, 1987.

Morgan, D. F. *Wisdom in the Old Testament Traditions.* Atlanta: John Knox, 1981.

Muilenburg, J. "Form Criticism and Beyond." *JBL* 88 (1969) 1-18.

_____. "The Linguistic and Rhetorical Usages of the Particple כי in the Old Testament," *HUCA* 32 (1961) 135-60.

Müller, H.-P. "Mantische Weisheit und Apokalyptik," *Congress Volume: Uppsala 1971.* VTSup 22. Leiden: Brill, 1972, pp. 268-93.

Munck, J. *Paul and the Salvation of Mankind.* Atlanta: John Knox, 1959.

Muraoka, T. "Sir. 51,13-30: An Erotic Hymn to Wisdom?" *JSJ* 10 (1979) 166-78.

Murphy, F. J. "Sapiential Elements in the Syriac Apocalypse of Baruch." *JQR* 76 (1986) 311-27.

Murphy, R. E. *Wisdom Literature: Job, Proverbs, Ruth, Canticles, Ecclesiastes, and Esther.* FOTL 13. Grand Rapids: Eerdmans, 1981.

_____. "Religious Dimensions of Israelite Wisdom," *Ancient Israelite Religion*, ed. P. D. Miller, Jr., P. D. Hanson, and S. D. McBride, 1987, pp. 449-58.

_____. *The Tree of Life: An Exploration of Biblical Wisdom Literature.* The Anchor Bible Reference Library. New York: Doubleday, 1990.

Murphy-O'Connor, J. "An Essene Missionary Document? CD 2:14-6:1." *RB* 77 (1970) 201-09.

Nel, P. J. *The Structure and Ethos of the Wisdom Admonitions in Proverbs.* BZAW 158. New York: de Gruyter, 1982.

Nelson, M. D. *The Syriac Version of the Wisdom of Ben Sira Compared to the Greek and Hebrew Materials.* SBLDS 107. Atlanta: Scholars, 1988.

Neugebauer, O. "The 'Astronomical' Chapters of the Ethiopic Book of Enoch (72 to 82)," *The Book of Enoch or 1 Enoch: A New English Edition with Commentary and Textual Notes,* M. Black, 1985, pp. 386-419.

Newsom, C. "The Development of 1 Enoch 6-19: Cosmology and Judgment." *CBQ* 42 (1980) 310-29.

_____. *Songs of the Sabbath Sacrifice: A Critical Edition.* Atlanta: Scholars, 1985.

Nickelsburg, G. W. E. *Resurrection, Immortality, and Eternal Life in Intertestamental Judaism.* HTS 26. Cambridge, MA: Harvard University, 1972.

_____. "Eschatology in the Testament of Abraham: A Study of the Judgment Scene in the Two Recensions," *Studies on the Testament of Abraham,* ed. G. W. E Nickelsburg, Jr. Missoula, MT: Scholars, 1976, pp. 23-64.

_____. "Enoch 97-104: A Study of the Greek and Ethiopic Texts," *Armenian and Biblical Studies,* ed. M. E. Stone. Jerusalem: St. James, 1976, pp. 90-156.

_____. "Apocalyptic and Myth in 1 Enoch 6-11." *JBL* 96 (1977) 383-405.

_____. "The Apocalyptic Message of *1 Enoch* 92-105." *CBQ* 39 (1977) 309-28.

_____. "Reflections upon Reflections: A Response to John Collins' 'Methodological Issues in the Study of 1 Enoch.'" *SBLSP* (1978) 311-14.

_____. "Riches, the Rich, and God's Judgment in 1 Enoch 92-105 and the Gospel According to Luke." *NTS* 25 (1979) 324-44.

_____. "Enoch, Levi, and Peter: Recipients of Revelation in Upper Galilee." *JBL* 100 (1981) 575-600.

_____. "The Books of Enoch in Recent Research." *RelSRev* 7 (1981) 210-17.

_____. *Jewish Literature Between the Bible and the Mishnah: A Historical and Literary Introduction.* Philadelphia: Fortress, 1981.

_____. "The Epistle of Enoch and the Qumran Literature." *JJS* 33 (1982) 333-48.

_____. "Social Aspects of Palestinian Jewish Apocalypticism," *Apocalypticism*, ed. D. Hellholm, 1983, pp. 641-54.

_____. "*1 Enoch* and Qumran Origins: The State of the Question and Some Prospects for Answers." *SBLSP* (1986) 341-60.

_____. "Revealed Wisdom as a Criterion for Inclusion and Exclusion: From Jewish Sectarianism to Early Christianity," *"To See Ourselves As Others See Us"*: *Christians, Jews, "Others" in Late Antiquity*, ed. J. Neusner and E. S. Frerichs. Missoula, MT: Scholars, 1986, pp. 73-91.

_____. "Tobit and Enoch: Distant Cousins with a Recognizable Resemblance." *SBLSP* (1988) 54-68.

_____. "The Apocalyptic Construction of Reality in *1 Enoch*," *Mysteries and Revelations*, ed. J. J. Collins and J. H. Charlesworth, 1991, pp. 51-64.

_____. "Eschatology (Early Jewish)," *ABD*, 1992, 2.579-94.

_____. "Jeremiel," *ABD*, 1992, 3.722-23.

_____. "The Qumranic Transformation of a Cosmological and Eschatological Tradition (1QH 4:29-40)," *The Madrid Qumran Congress: Proceedings of the International Congress on the Dead Sea Scrolls Madrid 18-21 March, 1991*, vol 2, ed. J. T. Barrera and L. V. Montaner. STDJ 11.2. Leiden: E. J. Brill, 1992, pp. 649-59.

_____. "Wisdom and Apocalypticism in Early Judaism: Some Points for Discussion." *SBLSP* (1994) 715-32.

Noth, M., and D. W. Thomas, eds. *Wisdom in Israel and in the Ancient Near East. Presented to Professor Harold Henry Rowley*. VTSup 3. Leiden: Brill, 1955.

Osburn, C. D. "*1 Enoch* 80:2-8 (67:5-7) and Jude 12-13." *CBQ* 47 (1985) 296-303.

Osten-Sacken, P. von der *Die Apokalyptik in ihrem Verhaltnis zu Prophetie und Weisheit*. Theologische Existenz Heute 157. Munich: Kaiser, 1969.

Penar, T. *Northwest Semitic Philology and the Hebrew Fragments of Ben Sira*. BibOr 28. Rome: Biblical Institute, 1975.

Perdue, L. G. *Wisdom and Cult*. SBLDS 30. Missoula, MT: Scholars, 1977.

_____. "Cosmology and the Social Order in the Wisdom Tradition," *The Sage in Israel and the Ancient Near East*, ed. J. G. Gammie and L. G. Perdue, 1990, pp. 457-78.

Perdue, L. G., B. B. Scott and W. J. Wiseman, eds. *In Search of Wisdom: Essays in Memory of John G. Gammie*. Louisville: Westminster/John Knox, 1993.

Pfeiffer, R. H. *History of New Testament Times: With an Introduction to the Apocrypha.* New York: Harper & Row, 1949.

Plöger, O. *Theocracy and Eschatology.* Trans. by S. Rudman. Richmond: John Knox, 1968.

Polk, T. "Paradigms, Parables, and *Mĕšālim*: On Reading the *Māšāl* in Scripture." *CBQ* 45 (1983) 564-83.

Pope, M. H. *Job.* AB 15. Garden City, NY: Doubleday, 1965.

_____. *Song of Songs.* AB 7C. Garden City, NY: Doubleday, 1977.

Pritchard, J. B. *Ancient Near Eastern Texts Relating to the Old Testament.* 2nd ed. corrected and enlarged. Princeton: Princeton University, 1955.

Rad, G. von *Holy War in Ancient Israel.* Trans. and ed. M. J. Dawn. Grand Rapids: Eerdmans, 1991 [orig. 1958].

_____. *Old Testament Theology.* 2 vols. Trans. by D. M. G. Stalker. New York: Harper & Row, 1962, 1965.

_____. *Wisdom in Israel.* Nashville and New York: Abingdon, 1972.

Rahlfs, A., ed. *Septuaginta.* 2 vols. in 1. Stuttgart: Württembergische Bibelanstalt, 1935.

Rau, E. *Kosmologie, Eschatologie und die Lehrautorität Henochs: Traditions- und formgeschichtliche Untersuchungen zum äth. Henochbuch und zu verwandten Schriften.* Diss., Universität Hamburg, 1974.

Rickenbacher, O. *Weisheits Perikopen bei Ben Sira.* OBO 1. Göttingen: Vandenhoeck & Ruprecht, 1973.

Ringgren, H. "בין," *TDOT* 2 (1975) 99-107.

Rosenthal, F. *A Grammar of Biblical Aramaic.* Porta linguarum orientalium n.s. 5. Wiesbaden: Harrassowitz, 1974.

Rowland, C. *The Open Heaven: A Study of Apocalyptic in Judaism and Early Christianity.* New York: Crossroad, 1982.

Rüger, H. P. *Text und Textform im hebräischen Sirach.* BZAW 112. Berlin: de Gruyter, 1970.

Saldarini, A. J. "Scribes," *ABD*, 1992, 5.1012-16.

Sanders, J. A. *The Psalms Scroll of Qumrân Cave 11* (11QPs[a]). DJD 4. Oxford: Clarendon, 1965.

_____. *The Dead Sea Psalms Scroll.* Ithaca, N.Y.: Cornell University, 1967.

_____. "The Sirach 51 Acrostic," *Hommages à André Dupont-Sommer*. Paris: Adrien-Maisonneuve, 1971, pp. 429-38.

_____. "The Qumran Psalms Scroll (11QPs[a]) Reviewed," *On Language, Culture and Religion: In Honor of Eugene A. Nida*, ed. M. Black and W. W. Smalley. The Hague: Mouton, 1974, pp. 88-95.

Sanders, J. T. *Ben Sira and Demotic Wisdom*. SBLMS 28. Chico, CA: Scholars, 1983.

Schechter, S. and C. Taylor. *The Wisdom of Ben Sira. Portions of the Book Ecclesiasticus.* Amsterdam: APA-Philo, 1899, reprint 1979.

Schökel, L. Alonso. "The Vision of Man in Sirach 16:24-17:14," *Israelite Wisdom: Theological and Literary Essays in Honor of Samuel Terrien*, ed. J. G. Gammie, W. A. Brueggemann, W. L. Humphreys and J. M. Ward, 1978, pp. 235-45.

Schürer, E. *The History of the Jewish People in the Age of Jesus Christ (175 B.C.-A.D. 135)*. Vols. 1 and 2 rev. and ed. G. Vermes, F. Millar and M. Black. Vol. 3, pts. 1 and 2, rev. and ed. G. Vermes, F. Millar and M. Goodman. Edinburgh: T. & T. Clark, 1973-87.

Scott, R. B. Y. "Wise and Foolish, Righteous and Wicked," *Studies in the Religion of Ancient Israel*. VTSup 23. Leiden: Brill, 1972, pp. 146-66.

Sheppard, G. T. *Wisdom as a Hermeneutical Construct: A Study in the Sapientializing of the Old Testament*. BZAW 151. New York: de Gruyter, 1980.

Skehan, P. W. "The Acrostic Poem in Sirach 51:13-30." *HTR* 64 (1971) 387-400.

_____. *Studies in Israelite Poetry and Wisdom*. CBQMS 1. Washington, DC: CBA, 1971.

_____. "Ecclesiasticus," *IDBSup* (1976) 250-51.

Skehan, P. W., and A. A. Di Lella. *The Wisdom of Ben Sira*. AB 39. New York: Doubleday, 1987.

Smend, R. *Die Weisheit des Jesus Sirach, hebräisch und deutsch*. Berlin: Reimer, 1906.

Smith, J. Z. "Wisdom and Apocalyptic," *Religious Syncretism in Antiquity*, ed. B. Pearson. Missoula, MT: Scholars, 1975, pp. 131-56.

Smith, M. "On the History of ΑΠΟΚΑΛΥΠΤΩ and ΑΠΟΚΑΛΥΨΙΣ," *Apocalypticism*, ed. D. Hellholm, 1983, pp. 9-20.

Sparks, H. F. D. *The Apocryphal Old Testament*. Oxford: Clarendon, 1984.

Stadelmann, H. *Ben Sira als Schriftgelehrter*. WUNT 2.6. Tübingen: Mohr (Siebeck), 1980.

Stone, M. E. "Paradise in IV Ezra iv.8 and vii.36, viii.52." *JJS* 17 (1966) 85-88.

_____. "Lists of Revealed Things in the Apocalyptic Literature," *Magnalia Dei: The Mighty Acts of God. Essays on the Bible and Archaeology in Memory of G. Ernest Wright*, ed. F. M. Cross, W. E. Lemke and P. D. Miller. Garden City, NY: Doubleday, 1976, pp. 414-52.

_____. "The Book of Enoch and Judaism in the Third Century B.C.E." *CBQ* 40 (1978) 479-92.

_____. *Scriptures, Sects, and Visions: A Profile of Judaism from Ezra to the Jewish Revolts*. Philadelphia: Fortress, 1980.

_____. "Ideal Figures and Social Context: Priest and Sage in the Early Second Temple Age," *Ancient Israelite Religion*, ed. P. D. Miller, Jr., P. D. Hanson, and S. D. McBride, 1987, pp. 575-86.

_____. "Enoch, Aramaic Levi and Sectarian Origins." *JSJ* 19 (1988) 159-70.

_____. *Fourth Ezra*. Hermeneia. Minneapolis: Fortress, 1990.

Stone, M. E., ed. *Jewish Writings of the Second Temple Period: Apocrypha, Pseudepigrapha, Qumran Sectarian Writings, Philo, Josephus*. CRINT 2.2. Philadelphia: Fortress, 1984.

Strugnell, J. "Notes and Queries on 'The Ben Sira Scroll from Masada.'" *Eretz-Israel* 9 (1969) 109-19.

Suter, D. W. "Fallen Angel, Fallen Priest. The Problem of Family Purity in 1 Enoch 6-16." *HUCA* 50 (1979) 115-35.

_____. "MĀŠĀL in the Similitudes of Enoch." *JBL* 100 (1981) 193-212.

Tcherikover, V. *Hellenistic Civilization and the Jews*, trans. by S. Applebaum. New York: Atheneum, 1959, 1982.

VanderKam, J. C. "The Theophany of Enoch i, 3b-7,9." *VT* 23 (1973) 129-50.

_____. "The Origin, Character and Early History of the 364-Day Calendar: A Reassessment of Jaubert's Hypotheses." *CBQ* 41 (1979) 390-411.

_____. "The 364-Day Calendar in the Enochic Literature." *SBLSP* (1983) 157-65.

_____. "1 Enoch 77,3 and a Babylonian Map of the World." *RQ* 11 (1983) 271-78.

_____. "Studies in the Apocalypse of Weeks (*1 Enoch* 93:1-10; 91:11-17." *CBQ* 46 (1984) 511-23.

_____. *Enoch and the Growth of an Apocalyptic Tradition.* CBQMS 16. Washington, DC: CBA, 1984.

Vattioni, F. *Ecclesiastico: Testo ebraico con apparato critico e versioni greca, latina e siriaca.* Pubblicazioni del Seminario di Semitistica, Testi 1. Naples: Istituto Orientale di Napoli, 1968.

Vermes, G. *The Dead Sea Scrolls in English.* 2nd ed. New York: Penguin, 1975.

Wacker, M.-T. *Weltordnung und Gericht: Studien zu 1 Henoch 22.* Würzburg: Echter, 1982.

Wagner, S. "דרש," *TDOT* 3 (1978) 293-307.

Westermann, C. *Basic Forms of Prophetic Speech.* Trans. by H. C. White. Philadelphia: Westminster, 1967.

_____. *Isaiah 40-66: A Commentary.* Old Testament Library. Trans. by D. M. G. Stalker. Philadelphia: Westminster, 1969.

_____. *The Structure of the Book of Job: A Form-Critical Analysis.* Philadelphia: Fortress, 1981.

Whybray, R. N. *Wisdom in Proverbs: The Concept of Wisdom in Proverbs 1-9.* SBT 45. Naperville, IL: Allenson, 1965.

_____. *The Intellectual Tradition in the Old Testament.* BZAW 135. Berlin/New York: de Gruyter, 1974.

Widengren, G. *The Ascension of the Apostle and the Heavenly Book.* Uppsala: Almqvist & Wiksells, 1950.

Wilckens U., and F. Fohrer, "σοφία κτλ," *TDNT* 7 (1971) 465-528.

Williams, J. G. "The Alas-Oracles of the Eighth Century Prophets." *HUCA* 38 (1967) 75-91.

Winter, P. "Ben Sira (33[36],7-15) and the Teaching of 'Two Ways.'" *VT* 5 (1955) 315-18.

Wintermute, O. S. "Apocalypse of Zephaniah: A New Translation and Introduction," *The Old Testament Pseudepigrapha*, ed. J. H. Charlesworth, 1983, 1.497-515.

Wright, B. G. *No Small Difference: Sirach's Relationship to Its Hebrew Parent Text.* SBLSCS 26. Missoula, MT: Scholars, 1989.

Yadin, Y. *The Ben Sira Scroll from Masada: with Introduction, Emendations and Commentary.* Jerusalem: Israel Exploration Society, 1965.

Yarbro Collins, A. "Introduction: Early Christian Apocalypticism." *Semeia* 36 (1986) 1-11.

Ziegler, J. *Sapientia Iesu Filii Sirach.* Septuaginta 12/2. Göttingen: Vandenhoeck & Ruprecht, 1965.

Zimmerli, W. *Ezekiel 1.* Trans. by R. E. Clements. Hermeneia. Philadelphia: Fortress, 1979.

_____. *Ezekiel 2.* Trans. by J. D. Martin. Hermeneia. Philadelphia: Fortress, 1983.

Zuntz, G. "Notes on the Greek Enoch." *JBL* 61 (1942) 193-204.

INDEX OF NAMES

INDEX OF PASSAGES